AI-Powered Business Intelligence for Modern Organizations

Arul Kumar Natarajan
Samarkand International University of Technology, Uzbekistan

Mohammad Gouse Galety
Samarkand International University of Technology, Uzbekistan

Celestine Iwendi
University of Bolton, UK

Deepthi Das
Christ University, India

Achyut Shankar
University of Warwick, UK

IGI Global
Publishing Tomorrow's Research Today

Published in the United States of America by
        IGI Global
        701 E. Chocolate Avenue
        Hershey PA, USA 17033
        Tel: 717-533-8845
        Fax: 717-533-8661
        E-mail: cust@igi-global.com
        Web site: https://www.igi-global.com

Library of Congress Cataloging-in-Publication Data

CIP Data in progress

ISBN: 9798369388440

EISBN: 9798369388464

Vice President of Editorial: Melissa Wagner
Managing Editor of Acquisitions: Mikaela Felty
Managing Editor of Book Development: Jocelynn Hessler
Production Manager: Mike Brehm
Cover Design: Phillip Shickler

British Cataloguing in Publication Data
A Cataloguing in Publication record for this book is available from the British Library.

All work contributed to this book is new, previously-unpublished material.
The views expressed in this book are those of the authors, but not necessarily of the publisher.

Table of Contents

Detailed Table of Contents

Chapter 1
Integrating Sustainability Metrics Into Business Intelligence: Environmental,
Social, and Governance (ESG) Factors 1

Yazhini Karthik, Coimbatore Institute of Technology, India
M. Sujithra, Coimbatore Institute of Technology, India
B. Senthilkumar, Kumaraguru College of Technology, India

This chapter suggests looking at how business intelligence and sustainability measures might be combined, with an emphasis on environmental, social, and governance (ESG) aspects. Businesses are becoming more and more aware of the need to include environmental, social, and governance (ESG) factors into their operational frameworks in the present era of data-driven decision-making. The purpose of this chapter is to examine how businesses may easily integrate ESG measures into their current business intelligence frameworks by utilising advanced analytics and AI-driven processes. In addition to enhancing sustainability initiatives, this integration reduces risks related to social and environmental challenges and promotes long-term value creation. This chapter will explain the basic ideas, challenges, possibilities, and best practices associated with integrating ESG aspects into business information. It will present tangible instances and case studies to illustrate the pragmatic implementation of these methodologies.

In today's tech landscape, business intelligence (BI) is essential, especially with advanced technologies emerging. This study delves into the transformative potential of artificial intelligence and machine learning in predictive analytics, offering crucial insights into data. The chapter provides an extensive overview, focusing on the future of predictive analytics in BI. It highlights real-time applications, featuring practical work and case studies. Key practices for integrating AI and predictive analytics are introduced, covering data preparation, cleaning, preprocessing, feature engineering, and exploratory data analysis. Integration of ML with BI facilitates visualization, report generation, interactive dashboards, and real-time monitoring. However, manual analysis of complex datasets poses challenges, risking valuable insights. This chapter explores how ML automates the identification of patterns, extracting insights. Key challenges and advantages in integrating machine learning into BI frameworks are also discussed.

Chapter 3

 Riya Thomas, Coimbatore Institute of Technology, India
 M. Sujithra, Coimbatore Institute of Technology, India
 B. Senthilkumar, Kumaraguru College of Technology, India

In modern business, data drives informed decision-making, with AI and BI ushering in a new era of predictive analytics essential for sustainable success. This chapter explores leveraging AI and ML for predictive analytics in BI, covering its mission, methodologies, challenges, applications, and future trends. Predictive analytics, enhanced by AI and ML, enables data-driven decisions by anticipating market trends, identifying opportunities, and optimizing resources. Key methodologies include data preprocessing, algorithm selection, model training, and evaluation, illustrated through real-world examples. Despite its benefits, challenges such as data quality, model interpretability, ethical issues, and resource constraints remain, with strategies provided to address these. Case studies in retail, healthcare, finance, and manufacturing showcase predictive analytics' impact on decision-making and efficiency. The chapter concludes by emphasizing the transformative potential of AI and ML in predictive analytics, equipping readers with the knowledge to drive success in the digital era.

Chapter 4

 N. Nasurudeen Ahamed, Presidency University, India
 S. Sridevi, Presidency University, India

To create a campaign blueprint, data-driven marketing optimizes client details. To comprehend our clients entails gathering complicated data through online and physical channels and evaluating it. Through the collection and analysis of information, advertisers create and execute highly customized advertising efforts. Digital advertising is an essential tool for advertising tactics because it's a great way to promote and sell products as well as raise brand knowledge and visibility. Even with the rise of online communities and networking sites, marketing through email remains the most popular way to educate, impact, and create business opportunities. Big Data is thought to revolutionize corporate intelligence, a discipline that depends on statistical analysis to gain understanding and improve making choices. Although the idea of big data is not exclusive to advertising or trade, the growth of e-commerce and online advertising has been crucial in raising awareness of the problem. These industries indeed produce enormous amounts of data by nature that need to be processed.

Prabavathy Kanagaraj, Sree Saraswathi Thyagaraja College, India
Samuel Chellathurai, Sree Saraswathi Thyagaraja College, India

The integration of Artificial Intelligence (AI) into Business Intelligence (BI) systems has become a game-changing tool for enterprises navigating the intricacies of a quickly changing digital ecosystem. Traditionally, business intelligence methods have concentrated on compiling and examining huge datasets in order to extract broad insights. The ability of artificial intelligence (AI) to drive hyper-personalization— which enables businesses to recognize and address the unique needs of each individual customer, employee, and stakeholder—will be crucial to the future of business intelligence (BI). This chapter offers to investigate the paradigm change toward hyper-personalization in AI-powered BI systems, focusing on the technology breakthroughs, trends, and future directions guiding this transformative journey. Augmented Analytics, a disruptive method that uses AI and machine learning algorithms, has emerged as a catalyst for enabling hyper-personalization in AI-powered Business Intelligence (BI) systems.

Abhishek Basak, VIT-AP University, India
Mousami Sanyal, VIT-AP University, India
Shirin Siraji, VIT-AP University, India
A. Manimaran, VIT-AP University, India

This chapter explores specifically how Customer Relationship Management (CRM) systems are embedded within a wider web of AI-driven BI systems employed in business. It starts with the basics: a definition, a description, and, most important of all, the value of CRM to present-day business strategies. The next part discusses theoretical frameworks that drive CRM and reveals the application of AI to improve the operational efficiency of both CRM and BI applications. The chapter continues the discussion of how AI facilitates advanced customer archetypes of engagement with dynamic personalization and predictive analytics for customer churn. The empirical implementations are also highlighted concentrating on two or three types of useful machine learning algorithms and data mining techniques. Real-world case studies are discussed to provide practical examples of ways of using these technologies. Finally, the chapter lists current problems and challenges and it pinpoints the existing and potential future trends in customer relationship management.

This chapter focuses on how artificial Intelligence (AI)-based business intelligence (BI) systems can be used to optimize supply chains. It starts with an introduction to the basics of supply chains and supply chain management processes and then moves on to an explanation of business intelligence systems. The discussion then progresses to the application of BI systems in the supply chain specifically in the improvement of demand forecasting, inventory management, and logistics among others. Lastly, the chapter explores various ways in which BI systems can be enhanced through the incorporation of AI technologies by providing real-time analysis, prediction, and automation. Thus, the chapter reveals the positive impact and practical application of the AI-powered BI systems in the context of supply chain Optimization.

The chapter explores the profound impact of blockchain technology on Supply Chain Management, tracing its historical development across diverse industries. Through its decentralized ledger system, blockchain ensures the integrity of digital transactions via cryptographic encoding, thereby enhancing security, traceability, and transparency within SCM processes. The chapter illustrates blockchain's effectiveness in streamlining supply chain processes. It also examines the challenges in implementing blockchain technology, including scalability issues, regulatory constraints, and cultural and sustainability considerations. Emerging trends in technologies like digital currency and asset tokenization hold promise for further improving cross-border transactions and asset tracking capabilities. The chapter suggests collaboration, leadership commitment, and the development of supportive regulatory frameworks to harness blockchain's full transformative potential.

Chapter 9

Praket Pati Tiwari, VIT-AP University, India
G. P. Yuktha, VIT-AP University, India
A. Manimaran, VIT-AP University, India

In the ever-changing world of online business, keeping clients to achieve long-term growth and profitability is crucial. This work uses customer relationship management (CRM) data and machine learning techniques to reduce customer turnover. Initially, the previous CRM data is employed to identify clients no longer affiliated with the platform. Through analyzing prior encounters, such as reviews and purchase histories, valuable information about them preferences and complaints can be obtained. More precisely, negative comments are isolated to identify areas where the product might be improved or eliminated from the e-commerce catalogue. Furthermore, predictive analytics methods are utilized to improve client involvement and contentment. The proposed approach combines CRM data analysis with machine learning algorithms such as Logistic Regression, Decision Tree, SVM, Random Forest, and XGBoost to provide a proactive strategy for reducing customer churn in e-commerce platforms.

Chapter 10

M. Basuvaraj, University of Allahabad, India
Keshvi Rastogi, Christ University, India

Artificial Intelligence (AI), born out of the minds and ideas of intelligent individuals, is a revolution for humankind. It has the potential to transform the world as never seen before. From the e-commerce sector to the education sector and healthcare to the finance sector, AI can disrupt and restructure all the traditional models that have been working for ages, bringing forth a completely different conception before the world. It is an easy alternative to doing long, tedious tasks and eases people's efforts by assisting them. Business intelligence (BI) is a valuable technique for handling the vast amounts of data businesses deal with. It is converting those immense amounts of data into meaningful results for businesses. It helps companies to work on historical and current data and creates predictive analysis, allowing businesses to make informed and sound decisions.

Chapter 11
Impact of Artificial Intelligence on Organizational Performance of Agritech

C. Ganeshkumar, Indian Institute Foreign Trade, India
Jeganathan Gomathi Sankar, BSSS Institute of Advanced Studies, India
Arokiaraj David, ATMS, Swiss Business School, UAE

Agriculture, vital for all human activities, contends with global challenges of population growth and resource competition. Technological advancements like ICT, AI, machine learning, and blockchain can tackle sectoral issues. This study focuses on AI's impact on organizational performance, particularly in AgriTech. Executives of Bangalore-based AgriTech firms employing AI were surveyed via a self-administered questionnaire, comprising both quantitative and qualitative inquiries on AI's impact on value chain performance. The study utilized a simple random sampling method and statistical analyses including Chi-square, ANOVA, correspondence analysis, and simple mean to analyze the data. The study found that AI benefits and its potential significantly boost the value chain performance of AgriTech enterprises. Focusing on AI advantages and future prospects can greatly enhance organizational performance, indirectly impacting overall efficiency through improved value chain operations. Managers are advised to prioritize AI integration for better company performance.

Business intelligence (BI) is the process of deriving relevant information from data to facilitate informed decision-making and reveal undiscovered resources for data management. With solid understanding of market trends and data-driven decision-making, business intelligence (BI) enables organizations to stay ahead in today's competitive world. This changes ways in which businesses operate by simplifying learning,refining procedures, automating operations, and reducing expenses with integrate AI. This chapter discusses Future Directions and Trends in AI-powered business Intelligence and addresses the disadvantages of traditional BI reporting and offers new possibilities for extracting value from data. Many of the top developing trends in business intelligence are mentioned in this chapter such as Mobile business intelligence (mobile BI), Advanced data visualization, Cloud-based BI - BI as a service, Data storytelling, Augmented analytics, Self-service analytics, Natural language processing (NLP), and Ethical data governance

Foreword

The intersection of Artificial Intelligence (AI) and Business Intelligence (BI) is a critical juncture for modern organizations striving to remain competitive and innovative in a rapidly evolving marketplace. This edited volume, "AI-Powered Business Intelligence for Modern Organizations," comprehensively explores how AI transforms BI systems, offering new opportunities and challenges across various domains.

Chapter 1 begins by examining the integration of sustainability metrics into BI, focusing on Environmental, Social, and Governance (ESG) factors. This discussion underscores the growing importance of aligning business strategies with sustainability goals, ensuring organizations can thrive more responsibly and ethically.

Chapter 2 explores the vast potential of AI and Machine Learning (ML) for predictive analytics in BI. It highlights the exciting advancements in predictive modeling techniques and their applications in forecasting, enabling businesses to make more informed and proactive decisions and inspiring hope for the future of BI.

Chapter 3 delves deeper into the role of AI and ML in shaping predictive analytics for modern BI. It addresses the techniques, challenges, and applications pivotal in data-driven decision-making, providing a nuanced understanding of how these technologies revolutionize business operations.

Chapter 4 focuses on data-driven marketing, analyzing the convergence of AI, ML, and big data. This chapter demonstrates how businesses can harness these technologies to optimize marketing strategies, enhance customer engagement, and drive growth.

Chapter 5 discusses the concept of hyper-personalization in AI-powered BI systems, emphasizing the role of augmented analytics. This chapter provides insights into how businesses can deliver personalized experiences at scale, leveraging AI to meet each customer's unique needs.

Chapter 6 explores the integration of personalization and Customer Relationship Management (CRM) within AI-powered BI systems. It highlights the critical role of AI in enhancing CRM processes and the potential it holds for improved customer satisfaction and loyalty. This discussion is designed to make the audience feel the positive impact AI can have on their relationships with customers.

Chapter 7 spotlights supply chain optimization through AI-powered BI systems. This chapter presents strategies for leveraging AI to enhance supply chain efficiency, reduce costs, and improve overall organizational performance.

Chapter 8 focuses on the role of blockchain technology in enhancing security, transparency, and traceability within AI-powered supply chains. This chapter explores the synergistic relationship between AI and blockchain, providing a framework for building more resilient and trustworthy supply chains.

Chapter 9 discusses using BI and ML in CRM data to reduce customer churn in e-commerce platforms. It offers practical insights into how AI can help businesses retain customers and foster long-term relationships.

Chapter 10 illuminates the convergence of AI and BI in the context of e-commerce and fintech in India. This chapter provides a regional perspective on how AI-driven BI is shaping the future of these industries, highlighting key trends and innovations.

Chapter 11 examines the impact of AI on organizational performance in the agritech sector. It explores how AI-powered BI systems enable agritech firms to enhance productivity, efficiency, and sustainability.

Finally, Chapter 12 offers a forward-looking perspective on the future directions and trends in AI-powered BI. This chapter guides organizations seeking to navigate the evolving landscape of AI and BI, offering insights into the next wave of technological advancements.

This volume is vital for academics, practitioners, and policymakers interested in understanding AI's transformative potential in business intelligence. Each chapter provides a detailed examination of the current state of AI-powered BI while offering a glimpse into the future of this dynamic field.

Subrata Chowdhury

Sreenivasa Institute of Technology and Management, India

Preface

The rapid advancements in Artificial Intelligence (AI) and its integration into Business Intelligence (BI) have shifted paradigm shifts in how organizations operate, strategize, and compete in the modern business landscape. The convergence of AI and BI is a technological evolution and a transformative force redefining decision-making processes, operational efficiency, and customer engagement across industries.

"AI-Powered Business Intelligence for Modern Organizations" is conceived as a comprehensive exploration of this intersection, offering a deep dive into AI's applications, challenges, and future directions in BI. This edited book seeks to provide a multifaceted understanding of how AI-driven BI systems enable organizations to harness data's power for strategic advantage, driving innovation and sustainability in a competitive environment. Readers can be reassured that they will gain a comprehensive understanding of the topic.

The chapters within this volume cover a wide range of topics crucial for understanding AI's impact on business intelligence. From integrating sustainability metrics into BI systems to leveraging AI for predictive analytics, the book thoroughly examines how these technologies are shaping the future of business. Each chapter is crafted to offer a deep dive into specific areas of AI-powered BI, such as data-driven marketing, supply chain optimization, customer relationship management, and the role of blockchain in enhancing transparency and security.

This book also addresses AI's regional and sectoral applications in BI, particularly emphasizing the e-commerce, fintech, and agritech sectors. By exploring these areas, the book aims to provide readers with a comprehensive understanding of how AI is being applied across different industries and geographies, highlighting the diverse opportunities and challenges that lie ahead.

In preparing this book, the contributors have drawn on their extensive expertise in AI, machine learning, and business intelligence, providing readers with both theoretical insights and practical applications. The aim is not just to inform but to empower academics, practitioners, and policymakers with the knowledge needed to navigate the evolving landscape of AI-powered BI, fostering innovation and driving organizational success in the digital age.

This volume is hoped to serve as a valuable resource for those seeking to understand AI's transformative potential in business intelligence. It offers a foundation for further research and a guide for practical implementation in modern organizations.

Arul Kumar Natarajan

Samarkand International University of Technology, Uzbekistan

Mohammad Gouse Galety

Samarkand International University of Technology, Uzbekistan

Celestine Iwendi

University of Bolton, United Kingdom

Deepthi Das

Christ University, India

Achyut Shankar

University of Warwick, UK

Chapter 1
Integrating Sustainability Metrics Into Business Intelligence:
Environmental, Social, and Governance (ESG) Factors

Yazhini Karthik
Coimbatore Institute of Technology, India

M. Sujithra
Coimbatore Institute of Technology, India

B. Senthilkumar
Kumaraguru College of Technology, India

ABSTRACT

This chapter suggests looking at how business intelligence and sustainability measures might be combined, with an emphasis on environmental, social, and governance (ESG) aspects. Businesses are becoming more and more aware of the need to include environmental, social, and governance (ESG) factors into their operational frameworks in the present era of data-driven decision-making. The purpose of this chapter is to examine how businesses may easily integrate ESG measures into their current business intelligence frameworks by utilising advanced analytics and AI-driven processes. In addition to enhancing sustainability initiatives, this integration reduces risks related to social and environmental challenges and promotes long-term value creation. This chapter will explain the basic ideas, challenges, possibilities, and best practices associated with integrating ESG aspects into business information. It will present tangible instances and case studies to illustrate the pragmatic

DOI: 10.4018/979-8-3693-8844-0.ch001

implementation of these methodologies.

INTRODUCTION

Overview of the Increasing Importance of Sustainability Metrics in Business Intelligence

In the modern business landscape, the importance of sustainability metrics has surged as organizations face mounting pressures from stakeholders, regulatory bodies, and the global community to operate responsibly and transparently. This section investigates the growing importance of sustainability in the business intelligence (BI) framework. Businesses are transitioning from solely focusing on financial performance to incorporating broader objectives, including sustainability and social responsibility. This shift is driven by increased demands from investors, customers, and employees who expect companies to show their dedication to environmentally friendly methods. Additionally, governments and international bodies are implementing stricter regulations around environmental impact, labor practices, and corporate governance, further emphasizing the need for sustainability (Petrini & Pozzebon, 2009).

Sustainability metrics play a crucial role in this evolving landscape. These indicators assess how well a business performs in terms of social responsibility, the environment, and governance procedures. By integrating these metrics into their BI systems, companies can enhance their decision-making processes, improve transparency, and build stakeholder trust. This integration is not just about compliance or reputation management but also about creating long-term value. Companies that effectively incorporate sustainability into their operations are better positioned to achieve extended success and resilience in a growing, complex, and interconnected world (Pria et al., 2024).

Explanation of Environmental, Social, and Governance (ESG) Factors and Their Significance

Understanding the components of ESG is essential for grasping their relevance in modern business practices. This section provides detailed definitions of each ESG component and explains their individual and collective significance.

Environmental Factors

Environmental factors encompass metrics related to a company's impact on the natural world. This includes carbon footprint measurements, energy consumption, waste management, and resource use. These metrics are critical for reducing ecological damage, complying with environmental regulations, and meeting consumer expectations for eco-friendly practices. Companies can lessen the dangers of resource shortages, climate change, and environmental degradation by focusing on environmental sustainability, thereby securing their operational continuity and market position (Almeyda & Darmansya, 2019).

Social Factors

Social factors cover metrics related to social responsibility, such as employee diversity, labor practices, community engagement, and human rights. These metrics reflect a company's commitment to moral practices and their effect on society. Putting a lot of emphasis on social sustainability can improve a business's standing, attract and retain talent, and foster positive relationships with the communities in which it operates. Companies that put social concerns first are better equipped to control employee relations, customer satisfaction, and community support risks, ultimately contributing to their long-term success (Almeyda & Darmansya, 2019).

Governance Factors

Governance factors include metrics related to corporate governance, such as board diversity, executive compensation, regulatory compliance, and ethical conduct. Effective governance ensures accountability, transparency, and ethical decision-making within an organization. Strong governance practices are essential for maintaining investor confidence and operational integrity. Companies that excel in governance are better positioned to navigate regulatory challenges, manage risks, and build robust, ethical cultures that drive sustainable business practices (Almeyda & Darmansya, 2019).

INTRODUCTION TO THE INTERSECTION OF AI AND BUSINESS INTELLIGENCE IN INTEGRATING SUSTAINABILITY METRICS

Artificial Intelligence (AI) and advanced analytics revolutionize how businesses collect, analyze, and utilize sustainability metrics (Bratu, 2023). This section explores the intersection of AI and BI, emphasizing how these technologies facilitate the inclusion of ESG factors into business approaches.

The Role of AI in Data Collection and Analysis

AI enhances data collection by enabling the gathering of large volumes of data from various sources, comprising Internet of Things (IoT) devices, public records, and social media. AI-driven analytics can uncover patterns, predict trends, and generate insights from complex datasets, significantly improving the accuracy and relevance of sustainability metrics (Roh et al., 2019). This technological capability allows businesses to move beyond traditional data collection methods, providing more extensive and dynamic knowledge about their performance in terms of sustainability.

AI-Driven Decision-Making

AI tools support predictive analytics, predicting future ESG performance and finding potential risks. This allows companies to make proactive decisions that enhance their sustainability initiatives. Additionally, AI systems provide real-time monitoring and analysis of sustainability metrics, allowing businesses to respond quickly to emerging issues and adapt their strategies. This real-time capability is crucial for maintaining agility and responsiveness in a rapidly changing business environment.

Case Studies and Practical Applications

To show the practical use of these concepts, consider the example of a multinational corporation that used AI to integrate ESG metrics into its BI framework. This integration led to significant improvements in sustainability performance and stakeholder engagement. The company could track and analyze a wide range of sustainability metrics by leveraging AI-driven platforms, from carbon emissions to community impact, in real-time. This enabled the company to make data-driven decisions aligned with its sustainability goals and overall business strategy. Practical applications of AI in this context include predictive models, sentiment analysis tools, and compliance monitoring systems, all of which can help businesses achieve their sustainability objectives.

This introduction sets the stage for a comprehensive exploration of how sustainability metrics can be seamlessly integrated into business intelligence systems. It highlights the critical role of ESG factors in driving better choice-making and demonstrates the transformative potential of AI and advanced analytics in this domain.

UNDERSTANDING SUSTAINABILITY METRICS

Sustainability metrics serve as crucial indicators of an organization's performance in key areas related to environmental, social, and governance (ESG) factors. This section thoroughly explains sustainability metrics, their significance, and why integrating them into business operations is essential for long-term success.

Definition and Scope of Sustainability Metrics

Sustainability metrics contain various quantitative and qualitative measures that evaluate an organization's effect on the environment, society, and governance practices. These metrics go beyond traditional financial indicators to assess sustainability performance comprehensively (Webb & Ayyub, 2017). They include measurements of resource consumption, emissions, labor practices, community engagement, board diversity, and ethical conduct.

The scope of sustainability metrics extends across many aspects of business operations, including production processes, supply chain management, employee relations, stakeholder engagement, and corporate governance structures (Martins et al., 2007). By measuring and monitoring these metrics, organizations can gain insights into their performance, identify areas for improvement, and track progress over time.

Types of Sustainability Metrics: Environmental, Social, and Governance (ESG)

Sustainability metrics are typically categorized into three pillars: environmental, social, and governance (ESG). Each pillar stands for distinct aspects of sustainability that organizations must address to achieve holistic sustainability goals.

Environmental Metrics: Environmental sustainability metrics assess an organization's impact on the natural world. These metrics include energy use, greenhouse gas emissions, water use, waste production, and initiatives to conserve biodiversity. Environmental metrics help organizations understand their ecological footprint and identify opportunities to minimize environmental harm through resource efficiency, pollution prevention, and conservation initiatives.

Social Metrics: Social sustainability metrics evaluate an organization's connections with its stakeholders, including workers, clients, vendors, and local communities. These metrics encompass indicators of community involvement, diversity and inclusion, human rights, employment practices, and health and safety. Social metrics enable organizations to assess their social impact, promote fair and ethical treatment of employees and communities, and foster positive stakeholder relationships.

Governance Metrics: Governance sustainability metrics evaluate the effectiveness and integrity of an organization's governance structures and practices. These metrics include measurements of board diversity, executive compensation, regulatory compliance, risk management, and ethical conduct. Governance metrics help organizations ensure transparency, accountability, and ethical decision-making, enhancing trust between clients, investors, and other stakeholders.

Importance of Integrating Sustainability Metrics into Business Operations

Integrating sustainability metrics into business operations is essential for several reasons. Firstly, it enables organizations to assess their sustainability performance and identify areas to improve their environmental, social, and governance practices. By measuring sustainability metrics, organizations can track progress toward sustainability goals, benchmark performance against industry standards, and demonstrate accountability to stakeholders (Richards & Gladwin, 1999).

Secondly, integrating sustainability metrics into business operations can drive operational efficiency and cost savings. Through waste reduction, resource optimization, and increased energy efficiency, organizations can reduce the cost of operations while minimizing environmental impact. Sustainable business practices also strengthen the brand's reputation, draw in ecologically and socially sensitive customers, and strengthen relationships with investors, employees, and communities (Richards & Gladwin, 1999).

Furthermore, sustainability metrics in business operations align with emerging regulatory requirements and investor expectations. Governments worldwide are enacting regulations to address environmental and social issues, such as climate change, human rights violations, and corporate governance failures. Investors increasingly consider ESG factors when making investment decisions, recognizing the importance of sustainable business practices in mitigating risks and enhancing long-term financial performance.

In summary, integrating sustainability metrics into business operations is crucial for driving sustainable growth, enhancing stakeholder value, and addressing global challenges. By measuring and monitoring environmental, social, and governance performance, organizations can build resilience, foster ideas, and create shared value for society and the planet.

THE ROLE OF BUSINESS INTELLIGENCE IN SUSTAINABILITY

Business intelligence plays a crucial role in enabling organizations to integrate sustainability principles effectively into their operations. This section explores how BI has evolved to incorporate sustainability, the importance of data-driven decision-making in sustainability efforts, and the challenges and opportunities associated with integrating sustainability into BI processes.

Overview of Traditional Business Intelligence and Its Evolution

Traditional business intelligence systems primarily analyze financial and operational data to support strategic decision-making (Walker, 2009). However, as sustainability becomes increasingly important in business, BI systems have evolved to incorporate environmental, social, and governance (ESG) metrics.

The evolution of BI reflects a broader shift in organizational priorities towards sustainability and responsible business practices. Modern BI platforms now include features and capabilities specifically designed to capture, analyze, and report on sustainability metrics (Walker, 2009). These platforms enable organizations to gain insights into their ESG performance, find areas for improvement, and align sustainability initiatives with overall business objectives.

Importance of Data-Driven Decision-Making in Sustainability Efforts

Data-driven decision-making is essential for organizations seeking to advance their sustainability goals. By leveraging data analytics and BI tools, organizations can access timely, accurate, and actionable insights into their sustainability performance.

- Data-driven approaches enable organizations to:
- Identify trends and patterns in sustainability data, enabling proactive decision-making and strategic planning.
- Measure progress towards sustainability goals and track the impact of initiatives over time.

- Identify areas of inefficiency or risk in current operations and prioritize actions to address them.
- Communicate transparently with stakeholders about sustainability performance and progress.

By integrating sustainability indicators into business intelligence (BI) systems, companies may integrate sustainability concerns into regular decision-making procedures, promoting an organizational culture that prioritizes sustainability.

Challenges and Opportunities in Integrating Sustainability into Business Intelligence Processes

While integrating sustainability into BI processes provides benefits, it also presents challenges and opportunities for organizations.

Challenges

- Data Quality and Availability: Sustainability data may be fragmented, inconsistent, or incomplete, making it challenging to analyze and interpret effectively.
- Complexity of Metrics: Sustainability metrics often involve qualitative, non-financial data, which can be more challenging to measure and analyze than traditional financial metrics.
- Organizational Silos: Sustainability initiatives may be managed by different departments within an organization, leading to siloed data and inconsistent reporting practices.
- Technical Infrastructure: Organizations may lack the necessary technical infrastructure and expertise to effectively collect, analyze, and report on sustainability data.

Opportunities

- Improved Decision-Making: Integrating sustainability into BI processes enables organizations to make more informed, data-driven choices that consider both the financial and non-financial effects.
- Enhanced Stakeholder Engagement: Transparent reporting on sustainability performance can build trust and credibility with stakeholders, including investors, customers, employees, and regulators.

- Innovation and Differentiation: Organizations that effectively integrate sustainability into their BI processes can spot fresh opportunities for uniqueness and innovation in the industry.
- Risk Management: By identifying and mitigating sustainability-related risks, organizations can protect their reputation, avoid regulatory penalties, and enhance long-term resilience.

In summary, integrating sustainability into BI processes allows organizations to enhance their decision-making, improve transparency, and drive innovation. However, it also represents challenges based on data quality, complexity, organizational structure, and technical infrastructure. By addressing these challenges and leveraging the opportunities presented by sustainability-focused BI, Businesses may make the most of their environmental initiatives and create long-term value for all stakeholders.

ENVIRONMENTAL METRICS IN BUSINESS INTELLIGENCE

Environmental sustainability metrics play a repositioning role in assessing and managing an organization's environmental impact. This section delves into the explanation of environmental sustainability metrics, provides examples of key metrics, and discusses how AI and advanced analytics can enhance environmental metric tracking and analysis.

Explanation of Environmental Sustainability Metrics

Environmental sustainability metrics encompass various measurements that evaluate an organization's environmental performance and impact. These metrics are critical for understanding and managing an organization's environmental footprint, identifying areas for improvement, and guiding strategic decision-making (Petrini & Pozzebon, 2009).
Environmental sustainability metrics include:

- Carbon Footprint: calculates the overall amount of greenhouse gas emissions caused by an organization's operations; emissions are often given in CO_2 equivalent.
- Energy Consumption: This monitors how much energy a company uses, including gas, electricity, and other fuels.
- Waste Generation: Quantifies the volume or weight of waste produced by an organization's operations, including solid waste, hazardous waste, and wastewater.

- Water Usage: Measures the amount of water an organization uses for various purposes, such as production processes, cooling, and sanitation.
- Biodiversity Impact: Assesses the effects of a company's actions on biodiversity and ecosystems, including habitat destruction, species loss, and ecosystem degradation.

These metrics offer insightful information on an organisation's environmental performance, helping identify opportunities for resource efficiency, pollution prevention, and sustainable practices.

Examples of Key Environmental Metrics

Concrete examples of important environmental metrics include:

- Carbon Footprint: A manufacturing company measures and tracks its greenhouse gas emissions from production processes, transportation, and energy consumption to identify opportunities for emission reductions and carbon neutrality initiatives.
- Energy Consumption: A retail chain monitors energy usage across its stores and warehouses to identify inefficiencies, optimize energy usage, and reduce operating costs.
- Waste Generation: A food processing company measures and tracks the volume of waste generated during manufacturing processes, putting sustainable packaging options and waste reduction techniques in place to reduce the environmental effect.
- Water Usage: A beverage company monitors water usage in production facilities and implements water-saving technologies and practices to reduce water consumption and minimize water pollution.
- Biodiversity Impact: A mining company assesses the impact of its operations on local ecosystems and implements biodiversity conservation measures, such as habitat restoration and species protection initiatives.

HOW AI AND ADVANCED ANALYTICS CAN ENHANCE ENVIRONMENTAL METRIC TRACKING AND ANALYSIS

AI and advanced analytics offer powerful tools for enhancing environmental metric tracking and analysis, enabling organizations to gain deeper insights, identify patterns, and optimize environmental performance.

- Data Integration and Analysis: AI algorithms can analyze large volumes of environmental data from various sources, including IoT sensors, satellite imagery, and environmental monitoring stations, to identify trends, patterns, and correlations.
- Predictive Analytics: AI models can forecast future environmental impacts and trends based on historical data, enabling organizations to expect risks, plan mitigation strategies, and optimize resource allocation.
- Optimization and Decision Support: Advanced analytics tools can optimize resource usage, energy consumption, and waste management processes, identifying opportunities for efficiency improvements and cost savings.
- Monitoring and Alerting in Real-Time: AI-powered monitoring systems can provide real-time insights into environmental performance, alerting organizations to deviations from sustainability targets and enabling timely interventions.

By leveraging AI and advanced analytics, organizations can enhance their environmental sustainability efforts, drive operational efficiencies, and achieve their sustainability goals effectively. These technologies enable organizations to move beyond traditional approaches to environmental management, unlocking new opportunities for innovation and sustainability.

SOCIAL METRICS IN BUSINESS INTELLIGENCE

Social sustainability metrics play a significant role in assessing an organization's effect on society and stakeholders. This section explores social metrics within business intelligence, covering their definition, importance, examples, and the utilization of AI algorithms for monitoring and analyzing social impact.

Introduction to Social Sustainability Metrics

Social sustainability metrics encompass a range of factors that evaluate an organization's relationships with its employees, communities, and broader society. These metrics gauge the organization's contributions to social welfare, equity, and inclusivity, reflecting its commitment to ethical practices and social responsibility. Understanding social metrics is essential for businesses that foster positive social change while maintaining stakeholder trust and reputation.

Examples of Social Metrics

Social metrics encompass diverse aspects of organizational behavior and impact. Examples include:

- Employee Diversity: Assessing the diversity of the workforce in terms of gender, ethnicity, age, and other demographic factors. Promoting diversity fosters inclusivity, creativity, and innovation within the organization.
- Labor Practices: Evaluating the organization's adherence to fair labor standards, including workplace safety, fair wages, and employee rights. Ethical labor practices contribute to employee satisfaction and loyalty.
- Community Engagement: Measuring the organization's involvement in community development, philanthropy, and corporate social responsibility initiatives. Active community engagement improves stakeholder connections and the organization's reputation and stakeholder relationships.
- Customer Satisfaction: Monitoring customer feedback and satisfaction levels to ensure quality products, services, and experiences. Customer satisfaction reflects the organization's commitment to meeting customer needs and expectations.

UTILIZING AI ALGORITHMS FOR SENTIMENT ANALYSIS AND SOCIAL MEDIA MONITORING TO TRACK SOCIAL IMPACT

AI algorithms offer powerful tools for monitoring and analyzing social sustainability metrics, particularly in sentiment analysis and social media monitoring.

- Sentiment Analysis: AI-driven sentiment analysis tools analyze textual data from various sources, including customer reviews, employee feedback, and media coverage, to assess the sentiment and tone towards the organization. By understanding public sentiment, organizations can identify areas of concern, address issues proactively, and enhance their reputation.
- Social Media Monitoring: AI-driven social media tracking instruments and tools track and analyze social media conversations, mentions, and trends related to the organization. By monitoring social media platforms, Businesses may learn more about public perception, identify emerging issues, and engage with stakeholders in real-time. This enables them to effectively reply to positive and negative feedback, manage crises, and maintain a positive online presence.

AI algorithms offer scalability, efficiency, and accuracy in analyzing vast amounts of social data, providing organizations with valuable insights into their social impact and reputation. By leveraging these tools, organizations can effectively track social sustainability metrics, identify opportunities for improvement, and show their dedication to social responsibility and ethical practices.

In conclusion, social metrics are integral to business intelligence, offering perceptions of a company's societal impact and ethical practices. By defining social metrics, providing examples, and exploring AI-driven solutions for monitoring and analyzing social impact, organizations can deepen their comprehension of social sustainability and make wise judgments to drive positive change.

GOVERNANCE METRICS IN BUSINESS INTELLIGENCE

Governance metrics are fundamental components of business intelligence that assess an organization's governance practices, regulatory compliance, and risk management strategies. This section delves into the explanation of governance sustainability metrics, offers examples of key governance metrics, and explores the utilization of AI for risk assessment and compliance monitoring in governance metrics.

Explanation of Governance Sustainability Metrics

Governance sustainability metrics evaluate the effectiveness of an organization's governance structures, policies, and procedures in ensuring transparency, accountability, and ethical conduct. These metrics shed light on the effectiveness of an organization's governance. And its commitment to responsible business practices. Governance metrics encompass various aspects, such as risk management systems, CEO remuneration, regulatory compliance, and board makeup. By measuring governance performance, organizations can identify areas for improvement, mitigate risks, and enhance stakeholder trust.

Examples of Governance Metrics

Examples of governance metrics span across different facets of organizational governance:

- Board Diversity: evaluating the gender, ethnicity, experience, and background diversity of the board of directors. A diverse board demonstrates the organization's dedication to inclusion and diversity, offers a range of opinions, and improves decision-making processes.

- Executive Compensation: Evaluating the alignment of executive compensation with organizational performance and shareholder interests. Transparent and fair executive compensation practices demonstrate good governance and ensure stakeholder accountability.

- Regulatory Compliance: Monitoring adherence to relevant laws, regulations, and industry standards governing business operations. Adherence to legal obligations mitigates legal and reputational risks, enhances stakeholder trust, and fosters a culture of integrity and accountability.

- Risk Management Frameworks: Assessing the effectiveness of risk management processes and procedures in identifying, assessing, and mitigating organizational risks. Robust risk management frameworks help safeguard against potential threats, protect organizational assets, and support sustainable growth.

Leveraging AI for Risk Assessment and Compliance Monitoring in Governance Metrics

AI offers valuable capacities for enhancing risk evaluation and compliance monitoring in governance metrics:

- Risk Assessment: AI-driven risk assessment tools analyze enormous amounts of data to find potential risks and anomalies that may threaten the organization. By leveraging machine learning algorithms, organizations can predict and mitigate risks more effectively, ensuring proactive risk management and decision-making.

- Compliance Monitoring: AI-powered compliance monitoring systems automate detecting, analyzing, and reporting compliance-related issues and deviations. These systems use natural language processing (NLP) and machine learning to scan regulatory documents, contracts, and internal policies, flagging non-compliant activities and enabling timely remediation.

- Predictive Analytics: AI-enabled predictive analytics tools to predict future trends, regulatory changes, and compliance requirements, enabling organizations to adapt their governance practices proactively. By leveraging predictive analytics, organizations can anticipate potential compliance challenges, stay ahead of regulatory developments, and optimize governance strategies accordingly.

- Continuous Monitoring: AI-based continuous monitoring solutions provide real-time insights into governance metrics, enabling businesses to monitor and react quickly to new threats and compliance issues. Continuous monitoring enhances agility, responsiveness, and adaptability in governance practices, ensuring proactive risk management and regulatory compliance.

In conclusion, governance metrics are vital components of business intelligence that assess an organization's governance practices, regulatory compliance, and risk management strategies. By defining governance metrics, providing examples, and exploring the utilization of AI for risk assessment and compliance monitoring, organizations can improve their governance practices, lessen risks, and foster trust with stakeholders. Leveraging AI technologies enables organizations to improve the effectiveness and efficiency of governance metrics, driving better decision-making and sustainable business performance.

INTEGRATING ESG FACTORS INTO BUSINESS STRATEGY

Integrating Environmental, Social, and Governance (ESG) factors into business strategy is important for organizations attempting to achieve long-term viability and add value for interested parties (Iliescu & Voicu, 2021). This section explores the importance of incorporating ESG factors into strategic decision-making, presents case studies illustrating successful integration, offers strategies for aligning ESG goals with overall business objectives using business intelligence, and discusses the broader implications of ESG integration for organizational performance and stakeholder relationships.

Importance of Incorporating ESG Factors Into Strategic Decision-Making

Incorporating ESG factors into tactical decision-making is essential for several reasons:

- Risk Mitigation and Resilience: ESG considerations help organizations Determine and reduce the hazards associated with environmental, social, and governance issues, thereby enhancing resilience to external shocks and uncertainties.
- Stakeholder Expectations: Many stakeholders, including investors, clients, staff members, and regulators, anticipate organizations demonstrating their commitment to ESG principles. Integrating ESG factors into business strategy helps meet these expectations and build stakeholder trust.

- Long-Term Value Creation: Organisations may integrate their ESG aims with their commercial objectives, drive sustainable growth, enhance brand reputation, and generate long-term value for society and shareholders.
- Regulatory Compliance: Many jurisdictions implement regulations requiring organizations to disclose ESG-related information. Incorporating ESG factors into strategic decision-making ensures compliance with regulatory requirements and reduces legal and reputational risks.

Case Studies Demonstrating Successful Integration of ESG Factors Into Business Strategies

Real-world examples illustrate the successful inclusion of ESG factors into business strategies:

- **Company A:** A multinational corporation integrated ESG considerations into its supply chain management strategy. By prioritizing suppliers with strong ESG performance and implementing sustainability criteria in procurement processes, Company A enhanced supply chain resilience, reduced risks, and improved stakeholder trust.
- **Company B:** Company B, a financial institution incorporated in ESG, contributes to its investment decision-making processes. Company B identified investment opportunities aligned with sustainability objectives by analyzing ESG data using advanced analytics and AI-driven tools, resulting in improved financial performance and increased investor confidence.

Strategies for Aligning ESG Goals With Overall Business Objectives Using Business Intelligence

To align ESG goals with overall business objectives effectively, organizations can adopt the following strategies leveraging business intelligence:

- Data Integration and Analysis: Integrate ESG data into existing business intelligence systems to analyze and report on environmental, social, and governance performance metrics alongside financial data, enabling holistic decision-making.
- Stakeholder Engagement: Talk to stakeholders to learn about their ESG priorities and concerns, incorporate stakeholder feedback into strategic planning processes, and communicate transparently about ESG initiatives and progress.

- Measuring and reporting performance: Establish key performance indicators (KPIs) and reporting frameworks to track progress towards ESG goals, measure the impact of ESG initiatives, and communicate outcomes to stakeholders effectively.
- Risk Management: Utilize AI and advanced analytics to assess ESG-related risks, identify emerging trends and opportunities, and develop proactive risk mitigation strategies to safeguard against potential impacts on business operations.

Broader Implications of ESG Integration

Beyond enhancing organizational performance and stakeholder relationships, integrating ESG factors into business strategy can have broader implications for society and the environment. By promoting sustainable practices, fostering social inclusion, and advancing ethical governance, organizations can help address pressing worldwide issues like climate change, inequality, and social injustice. ESG integration represents a shift towards more responsible and purpose-driven business models, driving positive societal impact and creating a more sustainable future for future generations.

TOOLS AND TECHNOLOGIES FOR INTEGRATING ESG METRICS

Effective integration of Environmental, Social, and Governance (ESG) metrics into business operations is essential for organizations aiming to create sustainability with their strategic objectives. Leveraging suitable tools and technologies is paramount in this endeavor. Various software solutions cater to tracking and analyzing ESG metrics, ranging from ESG reporting platforms to advanced business intelligence software.

Overview of Software Tools and Technologies for Tracking and Analyzing ESG Metrics

Comprehensive software tools play a pivotal role in facilitating the collection, management, and reporting of ESG data. ESG reporting platforms provide customizable dashboards and templates, streamlining ESG reporting processes and ensuring compliance with regulatory requirements. Meanwhile, data management systems centralize ESG data from diverse sources, standardizing formats and ensuring data accuracy. This centralized approach facilitates integration, aggregation, and analysis, enabling organizations to derive meaningful insights into their ESG performance. Moreover, business intelligence software offers advanced analytics capabilities, allowing organizations to analyze ESG metrics alongside financial and operational data. This empowers them to recognize patterns, correlations, and prospects for enhancement in their ESG performance, thus fostering informed decision-making.

Discussion on AI-Driven Platforms and Analytics Solutions for ESG Integration

The integration of AI-driven platforms and analytics solutions significantly enhances ESG integration efforts. Predictive analytics algorithms, for instance, analyze historical ESG data to anticipate future trends and risks, enabling organizations to develop strategies to address them proactively. Techniques for natural language processing (NLP) conclude unstructured textual input related to ESG topics, providing valuable information on stakeholder perceptions and regulatory trends. Furthermore, machine learning algorithms automate data analysis processes, improving the accuracy and dependability of ESG metrics and enabling data-driven decision-making. By leveraging these AI-driven solutions, organizations can enhance their ESG integration capabilities and drive sustainable growth.

Considerations for Selecting the Right Tools and Technologies for Specific Business Needs

When selecting tools and technologies for ESG integration, organizations must consider various factors to ensure suitability and effectiveness. Scalability is crucial, as solutions must accommodate growing data volumes and evolving reporting requirements to ensure long-term viability. Seamless integration with existing IT systems is essential to facilitate data exchange and interoperability, while user-friendly interfaces and customizable features enhance usability and adaptability. Additionally, evaluating the prospective return on investment (ROI) and total cost of ownership (TCO) ensures cost-effectiveness and value creation, guiding organizations in selecting tools aligned with their specific business needs and objectives. It's also imperative to emphasize ongoing support, training, and vendor collaboration to maximize the benefits of selected tools and technologies. Establishing clear communication channels and feedback mechanisms enables organizations to resolve any problems or challenges that might occur during the implementation and utilization of ESG integration solutions. By encouraging a mindset of ongoing development and innovation, organizations can optimize their ESG integration efforts and drive sustainable growth in the long run.

CHALLENGES AND LIMITATIONS

Integrating sustainability metrics into business intelligence presents many challenges and limitations that organizations must navigate to ensure successful implementation. This section delves into identifying these challenges, addressing data quality issues and limitations in ESG data availability, and analyzing ethical considerations and potential biases in AI-driven sustainability analysis.

Identification of Challenges in Integrating Sustainability Metrics Into Business Intelligence

Businesses encounter several obstacles when integrating sustainability metrics into their business intelligence processes. Data fragmentation poses an important challenge, as sustainability Data is frequently stored in disparate systems and formats, making it challenging to integrate and analyze essentially within existing business intelligence frameworks. Furthermore, the lack of standardization across industries and regions complicates the aggregation and comparison of sustainability data, hindering meaningful analysis and benchmarking. The complexity of ESG factors adds another layer of difficulty, as environmental, social, and governance factors are multifaceted and interconnected, making it difficult to quantify and assess their impact on business performance accurately. Additionally, resistance from stakeholders may impede efforts to prioritize sustainability and integrate ESG metrics into decision-making processes.

Navigating these challenges requires organizations to invest in robust data integration strategies, stakeholder engagement initiatives, and change management processes to foster buy-in and collaboration.

Addressing Data Quality Issues and Limitations in ESG Data Availability

Data quality issues and limitations in ESG data availability pose significant challenges to organizations seeking to integrate sustainability metrics into business intelligence. Data incompleteness is a common issue, stemming from gaps in reporting, varying data collection methodologies, and limited disclosure by stakeholders. This leads to incomplete and unreliable analysis outcomes. Data accuracy is also a concern, with errors, inconsistencies, and inaccuracies arising from manual data entry, outdated information, and lack of validation mechanisms.

Limited data availability further compounds the challenge, particularly for small and medium-sized enterprises (SMEs) and organizations operating in growing markets with less robust reporting frameworks and data infrastructure. Moreover, concerns about the security and privacy of data may prevent data sharing and collaboration among stakeholders, limiting data availability for analysis.

To address these challenges, organizations must invest in data governance frameworks and procedures to ensure data quality and partnerships with data providers to improve the completeness, accuracy, and availability of ESG data for business intelligence purposes.

Ethical Considerations and Potential Biases in AI-Driven Sustainability Analysis

Adopting AI-driven analytics solutions for sustainability analysis introduces ethical considerations and potential biases that organizations must address. Algorithmic bias is a significant concern, as it is possible for AI algorithms to unintentionally reinforce biases found in training data, leading to skewed analysis outcomes and unfair treatment of certain stakeholders. Transparency and accountability are essential, as the absence of openness in decision-making processes and the opacity of AI algorithms raise questions about accountability and unintended consequences in sustainability analysis.

Data privacy and consent are also critical, requiring organizations to ensure compliance with data privacy regulations and secure informed permission from stakeholders while using AI-driven analytics solutions to analyze sensitive ESG data. Finally, human oversight and intervention are essential to validate analysis results, interpret findings in context, and mitigate the risks of algorithmic errors or ethical dilemmas, ensuring the reliability, relevance, and ethical integrity of ESG analysis outcomes.

By addressing these ethical considerations and biases, organizations can enhance the trustworthiness and credibility of their sustainability analysis efforts, fostering stakeholder trust and confidence in the integrity of their ESG practices and reporting.

FUTURE TRENDS AND OPPORTUNITIES

The future landscape of integrating sustainability metrics into business intelligence is set to evolve dramatically, motivated by new developments and innovative technologies. This section explores these trends, opportunities for growth at the intersection of AI and ESG integration, and predictions for the future impact of sustainable business intelligence on decision-making.

Exploration of Emerging Trends in Sustainability Metrics and Business Intelligence

Several emerging trends mark the evolution of sustainability metrics and business intelligence:

- Integrated Reporting Frameworks: There is a growing emphasis on integrated reporting frameworks that combine financial, environmental, social, and governance (ESG) performance metrics into a single report. This trend reflects the increasing recognition of the interconnectedness between financial and non-financial aspects of business performance.
- Materiality Assessments: Materiality assessments are becoming more sophisticated, enabling organizations to determine the ESG issues that are most relevant to their business operations and stakeholders. These assessments inform strategic decision-making and help organizations focus their sustainability efforts on areas with the greatest impact.
- Dynamic ESG Dashboards: ESG dashboards are evolving to provide real-time monitoring and analysis of sustainability performance metrics. These dynamic dashboards enable organizations to track progress, identify emerging trends, and respond promptly to changing environmental and social conditions.
- Blockchain Technology: Blockchain technology is increasingly being detonated as a means to increase transparency and accountability in ESG reporting and supply chain management. By giving a secure and unchangeable ledger of transactions, blockchain can help verify the authenticity of sustainability data and ensure its integrity throughout the value chain.

Opportunities for Innovation and Growth in the Intersection of AI and ESG Integration

The intersection of artificial intelligence (AI) and ESG integration presents numerous opportunities for innovation and growth:

- Predictive Analytics: AI-powered predictive analytics can forecast future sustainability trends and risks, allowing businesses to proactively handle emerging challenges and capitalize on opportunities for sustainable growth.
- Natural Language Processing (NLP): NLP technologies can analyze vast amounts of unstructured textual data, such as sustainability reports, news articles, and social media posts, to extract insights and sentiment analysis

related to ESG topics. This capability enables organizations to gain deeper insights into stakeholder perceptions and identify emerging ESG issues.

- Machine Learning Algorithms: Machine learning algorithms can automate data analysis processes, identify patterns and correlations in ESG data, and generate actionable insights for decision-making. These algorithms can improve the efficiency of sustainability performance measurement and reporting.
- Impact Investing: The rise of impact investing, which focuses on generating positive social and environmental outcomes alongside financial returns, presents opportunities for organizations to attract investment capital by demonstrating their commitment to ESG principles and sustainability performance.

Predictions for the Future of Sustainable Business Intelligence and Its Impact on Decision-Making

Looking ahead, sustainable business intelligence is expected to have a profound impact on decision-making processes:

- Integrated Decision-Making: Organizations will increasingly integrate sustainability considerations into strategic decision-making processes, viewing ESG performance as a critical factor in assessing business value and long-term viability.
- Stakeholder Engagement: Stakeholder engagement will become more collaborative and transparent, with organizations actively seeking input from a variety of stakeholders, such as workers, clients, investors, and communities, to help shape sustainability activities and plans.
- Regulatory Compliance: Regulatory requirements related to ESG reporting and disclosure will continue to evolve, driving organizations to adopt more robust and standardized approaches to sustainability measurement and reporting.
- Competitive Advantage: Organizations that integrate sustainability into their business intelligence frameworks will gain a competitive advantage, attracting investors, customers, and talent who prioritize environmental and social responsibility.

In summary, the future of sustainable business intelligence holds enormous potential for driving innovation, fostering growth, and shaping more responsible and resilient organizations that prioritize environmental, social, and governance considerations in their decision-making process. As organizations navigate this evolving landscape, those that embrace sustainability as a core business imperative will be best positioned to thrive in the rapidly changing global economy.

CASE STUDIES

In this segment, we explore real-world examples that illustrate the successful integration of sustainability metrics into business intelligence systems. These case studies provide valuable insights into how organizations from various industries have effectively leveraged data-driven approaches to improve their environmental, social, and governance (ESG) performance.

Case Study 1: Company X - Environmental Sustainability

Company X, a global manufacturing firm, embarked on a journey to improve its environmental sustainability practices by integrating ESG metrics into its business intelligence systems. The company recognized the importance of reducing its carbon footprint and minimizing waste generation to align with sustainability goals and meet regulatory requirements.

- Background and Challenges: Initially, Company X faced challenges in accurately measuring and tracking its environmental impact due to fragmented data sources and manual reporting processes. The lack of real-time transparency into key environmental metrics impeded the company's ability to identify inefficiencies and implement targeted improvement initiatives.
- Implementation and Strategy: To address these challenges, Company X implemented a comprehensive business intelligence platform that integrated data from disparate sources, including manufacturing operations, supply chain, and energy consumption. Advanced analytics tools were utilized to analyze environmental metrics such as carbon emissions, water usage, and energy consumption in real time.
- Results and Outcomes: By leveraging business intelligence for environmental sustainability, Company X achieved significant improvements in its environmental performance. The company reduced its carbon footprint by 20% through the optimization of manufacturing processes and adoption of energy-efficient technologies. Real-time monitoring and predictive analytics enabled proactive identification of potential environmental risks, leading to better resource utilization and cost savings.

Case Study 2: Company Y - Social Sustainability

Company Y, a leading consumer goods company, sought to enhance its social sustainability practices by integrating ESG metrics into its business intelligence systems. With a focus on promoting diversity and inclusion, improving labor practices, and fostering community engagement, Company Y aimed to strengthen its brand reputation and stakeholder relationships.

- **Background and Challenges:** Company Y faced challenges in measuring and monitoring social sustainability metrics across its global operations. Limited visibility into workforce demographics, employee satisfaction, and community outreach initiatives made it difficult to assess the company's social impact and find areas for improvement.
- **Implementation and Strategy:** Company Y implemented a comprehensive social sustainability dashboard within its business intelligence platform to overcome these challenges. The dashboard aggregated data from various HR systems, employee surveys, and community engagement programs, providing real-time insights into key social metrics.
- **Results and Outcomes:** Company Y significantly improved its social performance by leveraging business intelligence for social sustainability. The company increased workforce diversity by 25% through targeted recruitment strategies and diversity training programs. Enhanced employee satisfaction and engagement led to higher retention rates and improved productivity. Additionally, community outreach initiatives were optimized based on data-driven insights, resulting in stronger partnerships and positive social impact.

Case Study 3: Company Z - Governance Sustainability

Company Z, a financial services firm, recognized the importance of governance sustainability in maintaining trust and transparency with stakeholders. Focusing on enhancing board diversity, improving executive compensation practices, and ensuring regulatory compliance, Company Z aimed to strengthen its governance framework and mitigate potential risks.

- Background and Challenges: Company Z faced governance oversight and regulatory compliance challenges, particularly in board diversity and executive compensation. Limited visibility into governance metrics and manual compliance monitoring processes posed risks to the company's reputation and shareholder confidence.
- Implementation and Strategy: Company Z implemented a governance analytics platform as part of its business intelligence infrastructure to address these challenges. The platform integrated data from board evaluations, executive compensation reports, and regulatory filings, enabling automated monitoring and analysis of governance metrics.

- Results and Outcomes: Company Z significantly improved its governance practices by leveraging business intelligence for governance sustainability. The company enhanced board diversity by appointing new directors from diverse backgrounds and skill sets, resulting in broader perspectives and better decision-making. Executive compensation practices were aligned with industry benchmarks and shareholder interests, enhancing transparency and accountability. Moreover, automated compliance monitoring enabled timely identification and mitigation of regulatory risks, ensuring adherence to legal requirements and industry standards.

CONCLUSION

The journey through integrating sustainability metrics into business intelligence has unveiled the critical intersection of environmental, social, and governance (ESG) factors with data-driven decision-making. This concluding section encapsulates the main points discussed in the chapter, emphasizes the significance of integrating sustainability metrics into business intelligence, and calls for action to prioritize ESG considerations while making decisions.

Recap of Key Points Discussed in the Chapter

This chapter explored the dynamic landscape of integrating sustainability metrics into business intelligence. We began by acknowledging the increasing importance of ESG factors in today's data-driven decision-making era. Understanding the definition and significance of environmental, social, and governance metrics laid the foundation for recognizing their important role in shaping business strategies and operations.

The exploration then delved into the evolution of traditional business intelligence, highlighting the importance of data-driven decision-making in sustainability efforts. We examined the challenges and opportunities in integrating sustainability into business intelligence processes, acknowledging the complexities and potential rewards of this endeavor.

Detailed discussions followed on environmental, social, and governance metrics, elucidating their definitions, examples, and the role of advanced analytics and AI in enhancing their tracking and analysis. Real-world case studies illustrated the practical implementation of these methodologies, demonstrating their effectiveness in driving sustainability initiatives and creating long-term value.

Final Thoughts on the Importance of Integrating Sustainability Metrics Into Business Intelligence

As we conclude this chapter, it becomes evident that integrating sustainability metrics into business intelligence is a strategic necessity rather than just a fad for organizations attempting to prosper in a quickly changing business landscape. By incorporating ESG factors into decision-making processes, businesses can improve their resilience, reduce risks, and take advantage of development and innovation opportunities.

Sustainability is no longer just a corporate responsibility but a driver of competitive advantage and long-term value creation. Organizations that prioritize sustainability metrics in their business intelligence frameworks gain deeper insights into their environmental and social impacts, fostering trust among stakeholders and enhancing brand reputation.

Call to Action for Businesses to Prioritize ESG Factors in Their Data-Driven Decision-Making Processes

In light of the insights gleaned from this chapter, the call to action is clear: businesses must give ESG considerations top priority in their data-driven decision-making processes. By integrating sustainability metrics into business intelligence, organizations can align their strategic objectives with environmental and social goals, driving positive outcomes for society and the bottom line.

We urge businesses to embrace sustainability as a core value and embed it into every aspect of their operations. This entails investing in the necessary tools, technologies, and expertise to effectively track, analyze, and report on ESG performance. Moreover, fostering a culture of transparency, accountability, and continuous improvement is essential to drive meaningful change and help build future generations with a more sustainable future.

In conclusion, the inclusion of sustainability metrics into business intelligence is not just a business imperative; it is a moral imperative. Let us seize this opportunity to catalyze positive change, inspire innovation, and build a more durable and just society for all. Together, we can harness the ability to make data-based decisions to create a brighter, more sustainable future.

REFERENCES

Almeyda, R., & Darmansya, A. (2019). The influence of environmental, social, and governance (ESG) disclosure on firm financial performance. *IPTEK Journal of Proceedings Series*, 0(5), 278–290. DOI: 10.12962/j23546026.y2019i5.6340

Bratu, M. (2023). The intersection of artificial intelligence and business intelligence: a systematic mapping study.

Iliescu, E. M., & Voicu, M. C. (2021). The integration of ESG factors in business strategies–competitive advantage. Challenges of the Knowledge Society, 838-843.

Lynch, M., & Lynch, M. (2024, June 10). Supercharging Sustainability: Harnessing AI for environmental metrics. Praxie.com. https://praxie.com/ai-for-environmental-metrics-management/

Martins, A. A., Mata, T. M., Costa, C. A., & Sikdar, S. K. (2007). Framework for sustainability metrics. *Industrial & Engineering Chemistry Research*, 46(10), 2962–2973. DOI: 10.1021/ie060692l

Petrini, M., & Pozzebon, M. (2009). Managing sustainability with the support of business intelligence methods and tools. *Information Systems, Technology and Management: Third International Conference, ICISTM 2009, Ghaziabad, India, March 12-13, 2009 Proceedings*, 3, 88–99.

Pria, S., Al Rubaie, I., & Prasad, V. (2024). Enhancing Business Intelligence Through AI-Driven Integration of Sustainability Metrics via ESG Factors. In Risks and Challenges of AI-Driven Finance: Bias, Ethics, and Security (pp. 57-89). IGI Global.

Richards, D. J., & Gladwin, T. N. (1999). Sustainability metrics for the business enterprise. *Environmental Quality Management*, 8(3), 11–21. DOI: 10.1002/tqem.3310080303

Roh, Y., Heo, G., & Whang, S. E. (2019). A survey on data collection for machine learning: A big data-ai integration perspective. *IEEE Transactions on Knowledge and Data Engineering*, 33(4), 1328–1347. DOI: 10.1109/TKDE.2019.2946162

Walker, R. (2009). The evolution and future of business intelligence. Information Management. http://www.information-management.com/infodirect/2009_140/business_intelligence_bi-10016145-1. html

Webb, D., & Ayyub, B. M. (2017). Sustainability quantification and valuation. I: Definitions, metrics, and valuations for decision making. *ASCE-ASME Journal of Risk and Uncertainty in Engineering Systems. Part A, Civil Engineering*, 3(3), E4016001. DOI: 10.1061/AJRUA6.0000893

Chapter 2
Leveraging AI and Machine Learning for Predictive Analytics in Business Intelligence

Mansi Sharma

Datta Meghe Institute of Higher Education and Research, India

Praveen Kumar

Datta Meghe Institute of Higher Education and Research, India

Swapnil Gundewar

Datta Meghe Institute of Higher Education and Research, India

ABSTRACT

In today's tech landscape, business intelligence (BI) is essential, especially with advanced technologies emerging. This study delves into the transformative potential of artificial intelligence and machine learning in predictive analytics, offering crucial insights into data. The chapter provides an extensive overview, focusing on the future of predictive analytics in BI. It highlights real-time applications, featuring practical work and case studies. Key practices for integrating AI and predictive analytics are introduced, covering data preparation, cleaning, preprocessing, feature engineering, and exploratory data analysis. Integration of ML with BI facilitates visualization, report generation, interactive dashboards, and real-time monitoring. However, manual analysis of complex datasets poses challenges, risking valuable insights. This chapter explores how ML automates the identification of patterns, extracting insights. Key challenges and advantages in integrating machine learning into BI frameworks are also discussed.

DOI: 10.4018/979-8-3693-8844-0.ch002

INTRODUCTION

The idea of artificial intelligence (AI) as a disruptive technology for business has emerged in the scholarly and professional literature. Businesses increasingly use predictive analytics driven by artificial intelligence (AI) and machine learning to make strategic decisions and obtain actionable insights in the age of digital transformation. Predictive analytics is a promising tool that can help organizations forecast market trends, optimize operations, and personalize consumer experiences by revealing significant patterns and trends hidden within large datasets (Farayola, 2024). To effectively use predictive analytics for business intelligence, firms must overcome certain serious obstacles amid the opportunities.

Through extensive and methodical literature research, this chapter aims to shed light on the phenomena of corporate AI with Predictive Analytics activation and offer an accurate description of what artificial intelligence is in the modern era (Sestino et al., 2022). Companies may want to find hidden trends, identify opportunities for growth and improvement, simplify activities, and ultimately make well-informed decisions that drive their success by utilizing business intelligence (Bharadiya, 2023). The phenomenon of Predictive Analytics states that the modeling and techniques to make predictions about future trends and performance use statistics for predicting trends(Yun, Shun, Junta, Browndi, & Technology, 2022).

Consider a company that wants to find stock price loss or profit for their company. They use the interactive dashboard or visualization using statistics, such that the predictive analytics will work on future trends in business. The process of gathering, evaluating, and interpreting vast volumes of data in order to produce insightful analysis and useful information that can support strategic decision-making inside an organization is known as business intelligence (Loshin, 2012; Ranjan, 2008). During the fourth industry evaluation, a vast amount of data was created, and the data was produced exponentially by many Internet of Things (IoT) domains. Businesses generate and store enormous amounts of data every second into data servers. Social media, sensors, tracking, websites, and online news items are the sources of this data. The relevant information must be obtained by using data mining techniques to mine the data in order to analyze and distribute the unstructured data in an organized manner (Yafooz et al., 2020).

This chapter highlights the significance of data analytics and data management in facilitating the effective use of big data, business intelligence, data mining, and machine learning. This chapter examines how predictive analytics is developing in the field of business intelligence, outlining the main obstacles that businesses must overcome and providing suggestions for how to overcome them in the future. Every factor influences the performance of predictive analytics projects, from data quality and interpretability to privacy issues and bias prevention. Businesses may fully leverage predictive analytics to generate sustainable growth and competitive advantage in an increasingly data-driven environment by comprehending these issues and embracing creative solutions (Komolafe, 2024).

Overview of Machine Learning in Business Intelligence

Artificial intelligence and machine learning significantly increase and enhance the potential of corporate intelligence. In today's data-driven corporate world, machine learning is crucial to business intelligence (BI). Large and complex datasets can be analyzed by businesses using machine learning algorithms to uncover insightful information that helps decision-makers forecast demand, spot market trends, expedite procedures, and enhance customer experiences. They provide companies with the ability to make precise forecasts, automate procedures, and extract insightful information from massive volumes of data (Bharadiya, 2023).

Within business intelligence, machine learning techniques cover a wide range of algorithms and approaches designed to tackle particular business problems. Various techniques are available to extract significant insights from data, such as supervised learning for predictive modeling and unsupervised learning for pattern detection and grouping. AI encompasses a broad range of technologies that provide businesses with numerous benefits in terms of increased revenue. In recent years, with an abundance of data and a significant surge in processing power, businesses have been looking more and more to AI to provide economic value (Wamba-Taguimdje et al., 2020).

Figure 1 shows that Machine Learning is a subset of Artificial intelligence used to analyze and predict the complex insight of data, and using different techniques, we can also find out the correlation and relationship between the attributes. The primary goal of AI is to create software that can mimic human thought processes in order to solve general problems, learn new skills, and make decisions in ways that are unique to humans using computer vision and expert systems. Numerous earlier research studies have examined the potential of AI to boost business productivity (Mascarenhas, 2018).

Figure 1. Artificial Intelligence and its Subfields

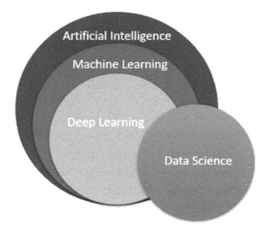

AI methods like computer vision and natural language processing (NLP) are used in business intelligence to extract data from unstructured data, including text documents, photos, and videos. As a result, businesses can extract insights from various data sources and types. Various advantages to business intelligence incorporate AI and ML. Most of these technologies allow businesses to automate time-consuming and repetitive processes like data integration, data purification, and report creation (Mungoli, 2023). Although ML and AI can reduce costs and increase productivity, they can also destroy company value, sometimes with adverse effects. Some managers might postpone the implementation of these technologies to keep them from reaching their full potential due to their incapacity to recognize and control that danger (Canhoto & Clear, 2020). This book chapter covers many data mining techniques, as Figure 2 shows data Mining, such as cluster analysis, artificial neural networks, decision trees, regression, and more. Big data, text mining, and web mining are also covered clearly and concisely.

Figure 2. Shows the Cycle of Data to Business Intelligence

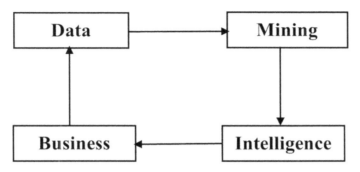

Machine Learning in Business Intelligence

Businesses can predict future events with greater accuracy because of the application of ML algorithms that analyze historical data to find patterns and trends (Bose et al., 2001) . ML algorithms are used in predictive analytics to examine enormous volumes of historical information, identify patterns, and derive useful insights. There are numerous applications for bi-level optimization in management, economics, energy, and transportation. Finding an effective and dependable solution suited to large-scale situations of particular sorts is crucial because the problem is naturally NP-hard. It is hard to deal with a large amount of data (Bagloee et al., 2018; Juan et al., 2015; Soleimani & Kannan, 2015).

Although bi-level programming problems (BPPs) were initially presented in 1973, interest in them increased in the 1980s due to studies finding a close relationship to the game theory's Stackelberg problems(Miljkovic, 1996; Naimi, 2016). Emerging use cases like news and social media analytics, where the source data are unstructured, the analysis metrics are unclear, and mainstream tools do not offer the necessary visual representations, present a challenge to the Business Intelligence (BI) paradigm. We discovered that communicating the different quality of inferred data structures was essential to letting consumers understand AI's potential applications and constraints. We achieved this by developing several end-to-end data applications. We wrap away by addressing BI in the era of big data, AI, and more accessible data analytics(Edge et al., 2018). Mohamed et al. worked on improving data analysis, automating data integration, enabling predictive analytics, offering natural language interfaces, identifying anomalies, making tailored suggestions, and improving data visualization; AI strengthens business intelligence (BI). Large datasets are processed, patterns are found, and insightful information is extracted using AI-driven systems.

They automate data transformation, cleaning, and integration (Azmi et al., 2023). Table 1 explains the list of various AI and ML techniques used in BI through which different kinds of applications will meet, like sales forecasting, CRM, weather forecasting, etc.

Table 1. Present the List of Various AI and ML Techniques used in BI

Sr. No	Techniques	Description	Applications	Reference
1	Predictive Analytics	In predictive Analytics, historical data is used in algorithms for Prediction.	Sales forecasting, customer behavior, weather forecasting	(Idrees et al., 2019)
2	Machine Learning Algorithms	Combination of various Machine Learning algorithms for analysis.	Linear Regression, MLR, Decision Tree, Random Forest.	(Jeong et al., 2018)
3	Natural Language Processing	Enabling language generation and knowledge in machines	Sentiment Analysis, etc.	(Bengfort et al., 2018)
4	Data Mining	Determining patterns and relationships in datasets	It analyzes trends and understands complex patterns and relationships in datasets.	(Park et al., 2006)
5	Deep Learning	In BI, deep learning is used for picture and video recognition. This covers jobs like identifying trends in visual data, tracking security footage, and evaluating product photos.	Outlier Detection, Sentiment Analysis, Pattern Recognition, etc.	(Khurana et al., 2023)

There are several ways that predictive analytics is not the same as traditional or descriptive BI. Slicing and dicing data to help answer questions like what happened, what's happening, and maybe even why it happened is something that BI does a fantastic job at sequences. BI, however, can be rigid and typically offers static reports or dashboards. However, users can estimate desirable outcomes with predictive analytics(Halper, 2014). Table 2 presents a list of machine learning algorithms used in business intelligence. Using these algorithms, various applications will be met.

Table 2. Present The List of Machine Learning Algorithms Used in Business Intelligence

Sr. No	Algorithms	Descriptions	Examples	References
1	Regression Methods	In ML, regression models examine how one or more independent variables and a dependent variable are related. They are frequently applied to numerical value prediction.	Sales Price Prediction, Customer Relationship Management	(Dangeti, 2017)
2	Classification	Classification algorithms group data into specified classes or labels based on input features. Logistic regression, decision trees, and support vector machines are common algorithms.	Customer segmentation, Fraud Detection, Sentiment Analysis	(Luts et al., 2010; Osisanwo et al., 2017)
3	Clustering	Clustering is the process of assembling comparable data points according to certain qualities. It is employed to find structures and patterns in datasets.	Grouping of Similar kinds of business data	(Fung, 2001)
4	Time-Series Analysis	The main goals of time series analysis are trend analysis and forecasting in time-ordered data. Within the dataset, temporal dependencies are taken into account.	For Prediction of the Future scope of Stock prices	(Yaffee & McGee, 2000)
5	Natural Language Processing (NLP)	NLP techniques, such as sentiment analysis, named entity identification, and language translation, allow machines to comprehend, interpret, and produce language similar to that of humans.	Used to analyze Customer comments and posts	(Khurana et al., 2023)

Figure 3 shows that the BI technologies by varying the complexity of how technology is used whenever need to find out the Query or what happened in past data, then reporting should be used like that in 2nd portion, OLAP means Online analytical processing state that why did it happen means is any effect of previous one, or it used to find out the objective of the Result. In 3rd portion, Monitoring means making dashboards for checking trends and features of the dataset. It will monitor the present work, and that will be what's happening now, and it will deal with the real-time work. Lastly, Prediction is done using prediction analysis of what might happened from that past current data to make predictions. If any problem is in the past or present data, then it leads to incorrect Prediction.

Figure 3. Business Intelligence Technologies with Data

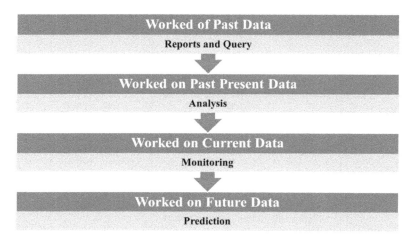

Business intelligence (BI) describes insights obtained from marketing and company data, which are then used to influence strategic decision-making processes for business growth and marketing improvements (Niu et al., 2021). Vili Chen et al. aims to examine recent research findings, historical development patterns, and potential future directions. This work uses a CiteSpace-based bibliographic analysis to retrieve 681 non-duplicate papers from the Web of Science Core Collection (WoSCC) and Scopus databases between 2000 and 2021. Figure 4 displays the historical development trend of publications on big data and predictive analytics related to business intelligence.

Figure 4 illustrates the growing trend in the total number of non-duplicate publications from WoSCC and Scopus by 2011. This trend appears to be sustained in the upcoming years. The WoSCC and Scopus databases showed a similar pattern, with Scopus showing a more notable developing tendency after 2015. Additionally, before 2019, WoSCC had more publications than Scopus, but by 2020, that ratio had changed. Results indicate a growing tendency in the publications on this subject, which is expected to continue in the next years. In addition, this analysis identifies the most scholarly influential nations, organizations, publications, writers, and papers (Chen et al., 2022).

Figure 4. Historical Trend Analysis of Publication, with permission, this image has been reproduced (Chen et al., 2022). Copyright 2022, Forecasting

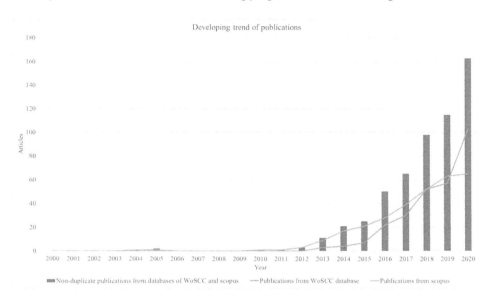

The goal of Pilon, B. H et al. is to improve the BI system's predictive phase, which the Brazilian Federal Patrimony Department runs. The idea is to improve the error metrics of the business intelligence system by modeling the inherent features of the tax-collecting financial time series that it maintains using the Gaussian Process for Regression (GPR) technique. The whole statistical description of the estimated variable is natively returned by GPR, and it can be used as a trigger to distinguish between trusted and untrusted data as well as a measure of confidence. To accommodate for the multidimensional structure of the input data, our method uses a bidimensional dataset reshape model. Based on GPR, the resulting system performs better in these circumstances than traditional predictive schemes like artificial neural networks and financial indicators (Pilon et al., 2016).

Using the Clarivate Analytics Web of Science electronic library, a total of 85 studies were found. Following the application of exclusion and inclusion criteria, 61 papers were deemed suitable and rational for the study and thoroughly examined. Ultimately, 52 papers were identified that provided pertinent data on the subject and were analyzed based on the established research questions. In order to capture both academic and practical perspectives, the authors incorporated important information about the role of data in the fight against COVID-19 in smart cities that were accessible on the Internet and social media during the research process. They also included other interesting references that they found in selected articles.

Regressor Method in BI

A business intelligence (BI) system uses tools from multiple knowledge domains to provide data that aids in decision-making. Bruno et al. 's goal in this endeavor is to improve the BI system's predictive phase, which the Brazilian Federal Patrimony Department runs. The idea is to improve the error metrics of this business intelligence system by modeling the inherent features of the tax-collecting financial time series that it maintains using the Gaussian Process for Regression (GPR) technique. GPR natively returns the whole statistical description of the estimated variable, and it can be used as a trigger to distinguish between trusted and untrusted data as well as a measure of confidence. To accommodate the multidimensional structure of the input data, the method of Bruno et al. uses a bidimensional dataset reshape model. The resulting system, which is based on GPR, performs better in this circumstance than traditional predictive schemes like artificial neural networks and financial indicators (Pilon, 2016).

Classification Method in BI

Machine learning serves as the foundation for conventional text classification techniques. It needs a lot of training data that has been artificially labeled in addition to human involvement. Nonetheless, it is typical to disregard the word order and contextual information in this manner, and issues like data sparseness and latitudinal explosion frequently arise. As deep learning has advanced, more researchers have begun using it for text classification. This study uses the Bi-LSTM-CNN method to investigate the application issue of NLP in text classification. A type of comprehensive expression is used to convey semantics to increase text classification accuracy precisely. Here, Figure 5.1 shows that the SoftMax function is used for classification, and Figure 5 suggests that while the loss rate continuously falls, the model's accuracy in this work is progressively rising. There is typically stability in accuracy and loss rate when the training data exceeds 1,800 (Li, 2018).

Figure 5. The Architecture and Results of the Classification Method using Neural Network Architecture (SoftMax activation function). This image has been reproduced with permission (Li, 2018). Copyright 2018, Scopus

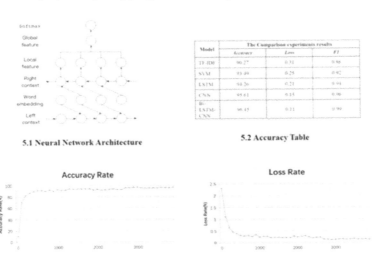

5.1 Neural Network Architecture

5.2 Accuracy Table

Businesses have long used data analysis to enhance plans, increase profitability, and advance decision-making processes. Big data technology and cloud computing are already widely recognized as two cutting-edge developments that have the potential to change the corporate environment completely. The cloud now serves as more than simply a place to store data. It impacts all facets of the software industry (Niu et al., 2021). The usefulness and suitability of ML-based classifiers for data-driven decision-making in business analytics are examined in the PhD thesis of Schmitt, M. Supervised binary classification on structured datasets is the main focus, as these are widely available in relational databases in all types of businesses. Their findings show that, compared to all other classifiers, Gradient Boosting performs better on structured datasets. This is one of the main causes of the slow adoption of deep learning in business analytics. Additionally, the ensemble learning technique stacking, which builds a more potent super learner by combining multiple base learners, proved to be a useful tool for continuously raising the accuracy of even the strongest candidate models, such as Gradient Boosting(Schmitt, 2020).

In recognizing the business issues and industry trends that require attention. It has several benefits, such as increasing responsibility and productivity, but it also has some disadvantages, such as being expensive, complicated, and requiring a long time to execute(Carroll & Shabana, 2010). Minsang et al. further explore the integration of ML and business intelligence together, which might be a real game-changer. In addition to helping to enhance operational procedures and customer service, it can also be used to analyze massive volumes of data in real time and prevent cybercrimes by teaching these systems to distinguish between legitimate and malicious threats. In this work, they also show the algorithms the business uses and whether or not they have helped them in the process. Linear regression is one of the ML methods that is employed. It is simple to use and may be applied to forecast traffic, financial results, and real estate prices, among other things (Tamang et al., 2021).

Integrating AI and ML into customer relationship management (CRM) systems signifies a transformative shift in the corporate landscape. Allioui et al. mentioned the advantages of AI, such as reduced expenses and time, improved customer experiences, and streamlined procedures. The incorporation of AI brought a new era of improved digital offering reliability, optimized supply chain operations, and instantaneous access to priceless data and analytics. Figure 6 presents different advantages of CRM utilizing AI and ML. Businesses that use AI to save lead times, find new customer insights, transform customer care norms, and provide unmatched personalized experiences stand to gain a great deal. To close the knowledge gap and make the successful integration of AI into business planning easier (Allioui, Mourdi, & Science, 2023).

Figure 6. CRM Utilizing AI and Machine Learning

An artificial intelligence computer can mimic or learn from intelligent human behavior. A subfield of AI called Machine Learning, on the other hand, uses algorithms to synthesize the underlying correlations between data and information. Automatic speech can be transformed into a semantic structure conveyed in words by the ML system. Furthermore, ML enhances the effectiveness of marketing operations at every stage a customer takes. Supervised learning is required to generate a learning foundation for subsequent data processing to forecast customer behavior. One type of learning model designed for Prediction is supervised learning. To respond to the dataset and create a classification model for the next data processing, Kotu and Deshpande have an algorithm. Therefore, AI can offer useful data to forecast their behaviors in real-time processes using automation with the use of ML and supervised learning (Kotu & Deshpande, 2018).

Nowadays, Businesses use AI to study consumer behavior and create targeted marketing campaigns. Research has indicated that the utilization of IoT solutions can have a favorable impact on the establishment of enduring and fruitful connections by providing engagement insights. Radaceanu et al. explored the possibility of using AI to replicate tasks that require human validation in terms of competitiveness, quality, and productivity (Radaceanu, 2007). Bajaja et al. suggested a framework of tools based on several AI approaches and learning models to identify the best learning style for a given environment. AI is thought to reduce human error in medical applications, enhancing imaging interpretation accuracy (Bajaj & Sharma, 2018). Fazala et al.noted a movement, especially in the US and Japan, from knowledge- and biological-based models to particular mathematical models and AI technology (Fazal et al., 2018).

It is possible to train ML algorithms to figure out significant variables from common characteristics and classify various components for targeted personalization or customization of ad distribution. In order to determine user trends or the best traffic for these adverts, AI and ML algorithms are used to analyze vast amounts of data and optimize these metrics. These uses include everything from product marketing or graphics to exposure length, which can be utilized to pinpoint traffic hotspots for a certain population. AI engines monitor consumer behavior and analyze it by displaying targeted advertisements or promotions (Zulaikha et al., 2020). Certain advertisements may appear about online information to provide customers with the appropriate advertisements they require based on their past web page visits. As a result, demand-based price adjustments, such as changing hotel room rates based on the day of the week or season, benefit from the use of dynamic pricing models. As AI algorithms filter the appropriate data into a pricing matrix, prices may be set and optimized with unprecedented precision. In addition to cost, other important considerations include amenities, ease of access to specific services, and other aspects. Furthermore, ML can be used to obtain further insights into the preferences and purchasing behaviors of the clients, including what factors they take into consideration when making special offers (Zulaikha et al., 2020).

Jorge et al. proposed a method that combines the power of conditional inference trees, random forests, and model-based recursive partitioning algorithms. It also implements a process for price group finding, variable selection, and price sensitivity segmentation. The resulting segmentation will identify nearly insensitive groups for which a price strategy that raises the interest rate is anticipated to have little effect on loan disbursements and high-sensitivity groups for which interest rate reductions might be suggested in order to promote sales (Arevalillo, 2019).

Challenges and Future Perspectives

Privacy concerns about fundamental human rights are also associated with the employment of AI. Due to the ease with which numerous businesses may utilize AI to track any person's online activity, privacy is eventually violated, and social injustice may result. The newest technology tracks users' daily activities and compiles data on them, which may include personal acts or particular behaviors. Put another way, while AI might offer the target population invaluable access to every aspect of their lives, it also presents a serious risk to their privacy (Zulaikha et al., 2020). Within the realm of business, certain issues that call for specific quality must be addressed. These issues demand human judgment and analysis to be evaluated and resolved with certainty. The circumstances involving decisions often involve strategic matters in businesses, where concerns are rarely well-organized.

Because of its unique advantages, creating and utilizing ad hoc intelligent systems to process data and deliver insightful information using a data-driven or, more specifically, knowledge-driven strategy may be useful to managers in their decision-making (Martínez-López & Casillas, 2013). The field of business intelligence predictive analytics using AI and machine learning is both stimulating and challenging. Since prediction accuracy depends on the availability of relevant and correct data, maintaining the quality and quantity of data utilized for analysis is at the forefront of these difficulties. Furthermore, combining many data sources into a coherent dataset is difficult and requires reliable data integration methods (Chen, 2014). In order to increase security and obtain insights, stakeholders continue to seek explanations for AI-driven decisions, making model interpretability a crucial concern. Predictive models must address bias and guarantee fairness, particularly in industries like healthcare and finance. Another issue is scalability, given the requirement for effectively processing massive amounts of data. Furthermore, regulatory compliance, which calls for adherence to laws like the CCPA and GDPR on data privacy, adds still another level of complexity.

Future developments in explainable AI, automated machine learning, and AI governance and ethics frameworks are among the focus areas. Real-time decision-making made possible by edge computing and IoT is set to transform predictive analytics, and federated learning protects data privacy throughout cooperative model training. The next big thing in predictive analytics is to improve corporate intelligence through continuous learning models that adjust to changing data sources. Decentralized model training techniques like federated learning protect privacy by enabling ML models to be trained across dispersed edge devices without exchanging raw data. Lastly, the future of predictive analytics lies in continuous learning models, which can instantly adjust to dynamic data streams and patterns, increasing the effectiveness and applicability of predictive analytics in business intelligence. The field of business intelligence is full of opportunities and challenges when it comes to using artificial intelligence (AI) and machine learning (ML) for predictive analytics. The quality and quantity of data used for predictive modeling are one of the main obstacles. Predictions' precision and applicability depend on extensive, high-quality data availability.

Firms must employ complex data integration strategies to establish a single data-set for analysis because they frequently struggle with heterogeneous data sources stored in different forms and systems (Schmitt, 2020). There is still much work to be done to make ML models interpretable. Many powerful machine learning algo-rithms, especially deep learning models, are considered "black boxes" because of their intricate internal workings, making it difficult for stakeholders to comprehend and trust these models' judgments. Another crucial issue with predictive models is addressing bias and ensuring they are equitable. Unfair results may result from AI systems' unintentional perpetuation of biases in the data they are trained on, especially in delicate areas like recruiting, healthcare, and finance.

AI technologies have the potential to drastically alter businesses and completely reshape the way companies operate, compete, and succeed. The significant research and development work in AI nowadays is mostly divided into two ways. Artificial generalized intelligence, or "strong" AI, is to create machines that can perform any task with ease, much like a human can. Given how ambitious this objective is, some could say it is not worthwhile to pursue. The second is applied AI, also known as "weak" or "narrow" AI (Aleksander, 2017; Armstrong et al., 2014; Bentley, 2018; Paschen et al., 2020).

Managers should consider three business-specific limitations of AI systems. Besides the significant duration and expense involved in implementing AI, decision-makers must consider the technology's compatibility with various other platforms and information systems. Currently, a lack of standards results in incompatible ap-plication programming interfaces, or APIs, incompatible ways for different software components to communicate. This can cause gaps in interoperability and usability in AI applications. According to McKinsey, these problems could prevent 40% of AI's potential advantages from being achieved (Manyika et al., 2015). Second, managers must pay close attention to the quality of the data that AI systems are trained (Campolo et al., 2017). Third, those making decisions will also have to give considerable thought to privacy safeguards.

For an AI system to become more intelligent, it must consume as much training data as it can (Paschen et al., 2020). That type of challenge and limitation comes whenever working on the dataset for making business predictions, and that mainly affects the decision-making capability, like checking the market price for cosmetics, and all that type of Prediction may fail if the real-time dataset is accurate. All data should come in an ethical way, through which ethics are not to be disturbed, and privacy will be maintained. Another major issue is scalability, which becomes more problematic as data volumes rise exponentially. Real-world applications require predictive analytics tools to process massive amounts of data efficiently.

Looking in advance, several important perspectives become apparent. Explainable AI (XAI) developments will soon make machine learning (ML) models easier to comprehend and interpret, giving stakeholders greater confidence in AI-driven decision-making. By automating the process of creating machine learning (ML) models, automated machine learning (AutoML) platforms seek to democratize AI by enabling non-experts to use predictive analytics for business insight. Furthermore, governance and ethics in AI are becoming increasingly significant factors (Schmitt, 2023). For ethical AI deployment to be implemented with accountability, openness, and justice in AI-driven decision-making processes, frameworks and rules must be developed. Predictive analytics is about to undergo a revolution because of edge computing and the Internet of Things (IoT), which allow for real-time decision-making at the edge and less dependence on centralized infrastructure and latency.

CONCLUSION

Big businesses like Amazon, Apple, Google, and Facebook have adopted AI because they understand how technology is changing marketing and impacting many areas of the organization. The key components these businesses need to quickly enhance their product offerings to stay ahead of the competition are big data and connectivity. Because of the high traffic and user numbers, these businesses have access to a lot of data, which enables them to enhance their goods and services to consumer demands. For instance, Google uses AI technology to provide more accurate and pertinent data than any other company. AI will continue to advance and grow, and in order for a business to stay ahead of other companies and remain in a competitive sector, it must leverage this technology. Given its robustness and simplicity in analyzing engagement patterns and the complex interactions and activities of millions of users to produce human-like interactions without human intervention, it is evident that the marketing sector finds AI applications highly enticing.

Furthermore, AI can handle particular content based on user preferences to improve the user experience. As a result, this helps marketers make decisions and carry out their marketing objectives. Businesses can save time and money by utilizing AI, freeing up more time to develop and tailor their marketing efforts to the needs of their target audience.

REFERENCES

Aleksander, I. (2017). Partners of humans: A realistic assessment of the role of robots in the foreseeable future. *Journal of Information Technology*, 32(1), 1–9.

Allioui, H., & Mourdi, Y. (2023). Unleashing the potential of AI: Investigating cutting-edge technologies that are transforming businesses. [IJCEDS]. *International Journal of Computer Engineering and Data Science*, 3(2), 1–12.

Arevalillo, J. M. (2019). A machine learning approach to assess price sensitivity with application to automobile loan segmentation. *Applied Soft Computing*, 76, 390–399.

Armstrong, S., & Sotala, K., & Ó hÉigeartaigh, S. S. (2014). The errors, insights and lessons of famous AI predictions–and what they mean for the future. *Journal of Experimental & Theoretical Artificial Intelligence*, 26(3), 317–342.

Azmi, M., Mansour, A., & Azmi, C. (2023). A Context-Aware Empowering Business with AI: Case of Chatbots in Business Intelligence Systems. *Procedia Computer Science*, 224, 479–484.

Bagloee, S. A., Asadi, M., Sarvi, M., & Patriksson, M. (2018). A hybrid machine-learning and optimization method to solve bi-level problems. *Expert Systems with Applications*, 95, 142–152.

Bajaj, R., & Sharma, V. (2018). Smart Education with artificial intelligence based determination of learning styles. *Procedia Computer Science*, 132, 834–842.

Bengfort, B., Bilbro, R., & Ojeda, T. (2018). *Applied text analysis with Python: Enabling language-aware data products with machine learning*. O'Reilly Media, Inc.

Bentley, P. (2018). The three laws of artificial intelligence: Dispelling common myths. Should we fear artificial intelligence, 6-12.

Bharadiya, J. P. (2023). A comparative study of business intelligence and artificial intelligence with big data analytics. *American Journal of Artificial Intelligence*, 7(1), 24.

Bharadiya, J. P. (2023). Machine learning and AI in business intelligence: Trends and opportunities. 48(1), 123-134.

Bose, I., & Mahapatra, R. K. (2001). Business data mining—A machine learning perspective. *Information & Management*, 39(3), 211–225.

Campolo, A., Sanfilippo, M. R., Whittaker, M., & Crawford, K. (2017). AI now 2017 report.

Canhoto, A. I., & Clear, F. (2020). Artificial intelligence and machine learning as business tools: A framework for diagnosing value destruction potential. *Business Horizons*, 63(2), 183–193.

Carroll, A. B., & Shabana, K. M. (2010). The business case for corporate social responsibility: A review of concepts, research and practice. *International Journal of Management Reviews*, 12(1), 85–105.

Chen, Y., Li, C., & Wang, H. (2022). Big data and predictive analytics for business intelligence: A bibliographic study (2000–2021). *Forecasting*, 4(4), 767–786.

Dangeti, P. (2017). *Statistics for machine learning*. Packt Publishing Ltd.

Edge, D., Larson, J., & White, C. (2018). Bringing AI to BI: enabling visual analytics of unstructured data in a modern Business Intelligence platform. Paper presented at the Extended abstracts of the 2018 CHI conference on human factors in computing systems.

Fazal, M. I., Patel, M. E., Tye, J., & Gupta, Y. (2018). The past, present and future role of artificial intelligence in imaging. *European Journal of Radiology*, 105, 246–250.

Fung, G. (2001). A comprehensive overview of basic clustering algorithms.

Halper, F. (2014). Predictive analytics for business advantage. TDWI Research, 1-32.

Idrees, S. M., Alam, M. A., Agarwal, P., & Ansari, L. (2019). Effective predictive analytics and modeling based on historical data. Paper presented at the Advances in Computing and Data Sciences: Third International Conference, ICACDS 2019, Ghaziabad, India, April 12–13, 2019, Revised Selected Papers, Part II 3.

Jeong, E., Park, N., Choi, Y., Park, R. W., & Yoon, D. (2018). Machine learning model combining features from algorithms with different analytical methodologies to detect laboratory-event-related adverse drug reaction signals. *PLoS One*, 13(11), e0207749.

Juan, A. A., Faulin, J., Grasman, S. E., Rabe, M., & Figueira, G. (2015). A review of simheuristics: Extending metaheuristics to deal with stochastic combinatorial optimization problems. *Operations Research Perspectives*, 2, 62–72.

Khurana, D., Koli, A., Khatter, K., & Singh, S. (2023). Natural language processing: State of the art, current trends and challenges. *Multimedia Tools and Applications*, 82(3), 3713–3744.

Kotu, V., & Deshpande, B. (2018). *Data science: concepts and practice*. Morgan Kaufmann.

Loshin, D. (2012). Business intelligence: the savvy manager's guide: Newnes.

Luts, J., Ojeda, F., Van de Plas, R., De Moor, B., Van Huffel, S., & Suykens, J. A. (2010). A tutorial on support vector machine-based methods for classification problems in chemometrics. *Analytica Chimica Acta*, 665(2), 129–145.

Manyika, J., Chui, M., Bisson, P., Woetzel, J., Dobbs, R., Bughin, J., & Aharon, D. (2015). Unlocking the Potential of the Internet of Things. McKinsey Global Institute, 1.

Martínez-López, F. J., & Casillas, J. (2013). Artificial intelligence-based systems applied in industrial marketing: An historical overview, current and future insights. *Industrial Marketing Management*, 42(4), 489–495.

Mascarenhas, S. J. F. O. A. (2018). Artificial intelligence and the emergent turbulent markets: New challenges to corporate ethics today. In Corporate Ethics for Turbulent Markets: The Market Context of Executive Decisions (pp. 215-242). Emerald Publishing Limited.

Miljkovic, D. (1996). *Effects of economic transition policies on Yugoslavia's agricultural sector: A quantitative approach*. University of Illinois at Urbana-Champaign.

Mungoli, N. (2023). Adaptive Ensemble Learning: Boosting Model Performance through Intelligent Feature Fusion in Deep Neural Networks. arXiv preprint arXiv:2304.02653.

Naimi, A. (2016). *The robust urban transportation network design problem*. The University of Memphis.

Niu, Y., Ying, L., Yang, J., Bao, M., & Sivaparthipan, C. B. (2021). Organizational business intelligence and decision making using big data analytics. *Information Processing & Management*, 58(6), 102725.

Osisanwo, F. Y., Akinsola, J. E. T., Awodele, O., Hinmikaiye, J. O., Olakanmi, O., & Akinjobi, J. (2017). Supervised machine learning algorithms: Classification and comparison. [IJCTT]. *International Journal of Computer Trends and Technology*, 48(3), 128–138.

Park, Y. S., Tison, J., Lek, S., Giraudel, J. L., Coste, M., & Delmas, F. (2006). Application of a self-organizing map to select representative species in multivariate analysis: A case study determining diatom distribution patterns across France. *Ecological Informatics*, 1(3), 247–257.

Paschen, U., Pitt, C., & Kietzmann, J. (2020). Artificial intelligence: Building blocks and an innovation typology. *Business Horizons*, 63(2), 147–155.

Pilon, B. H., Murillo-Fuentes, J. J., da Costa, J. P. C., de Sousa Júnior, R. T., & Serrano, A. M. (2016). Predictive analytics in business intelligence systems via Gaussian processes for regression. In Knowledge Discovery, Knowledge Engineering and Knowledge Management: 7th International Joint Conference, IC3K 2015, Lisbon, Portugal, November 12-14, 2015, Revised Selected Papers 7 (pp. 421-442). Springer International Publishing.

Radaceanu, E. (2007). Artificial Intelligence & Robots for Performance Management–Some Methodic Aspects. IFAC Proceedings Volumes, 40(18), 319-324.

Ranjan, J. (2008). Business justification with business intelligence. *Vine*, 38(4), 461–475.

Schmitt, M. (2020). Artificial intelligence in business analytics, capturing value with machine learning applications in financial services.

Sestino, A., & De Mauro, A. (2022). Leveraging artificial intelligence in business: Implications, applications and methods. *Technology Analysis and Strategic Management*, 34(1), 16–29.

Soleimani, H., & Kannan, G. (2015). A hybrid particle swarm optimization and genetic algorithm for closed-loop supply chain network design in large-scale networks. *Applied Mathematical Modelling*, 39(14), 3990–4012.

Tamang, M. D., Shukla, V. K., Anwar, S., & Punhani, R. (2021). Improving business intelligence through machine learning algorithms. Paper presented at the 2021 2nd International Conference on Intelligent Engineering and Management (ICIEM).

Wamba-Taguimdje, S. L., Wamba, S. F., Kamdjoug, J. R. K., & Wanko, C. E. T. (2020). Influence of artificial intelligence (AI) on firm performance: The business value of AI-based transformation projects. *Business Process Management Journal*, 26(7), 1893–1924.

Yaffee, R. A., & McGee, M. (2000). *An introduction to time series analysis and forecasting: with applications of SAS® and SPSS*. Elsevier.

Yafooz, W. M., Bakar, Z. B. A., Fahad, S. A., & Mithun, M. (2019). A. (2020). Business intelligence through big data analytics, data mining and machine learning. In Data Management, Analytics and Innovation [Springer Singapore.]. *Proceedings of ICDMAI*, 2, 217–230.

Yun, C., Shun, M., Junta, U., & Browndi, I. (2022). Predictive analytics: A survey, trends, applications, opportunities' and challenges for smart city planning. *International Journal of Computer Science and Information Technologies*, 23(56), 226–231.

Zulaikha, S., Mohamed, H., Kurniawati, M., Rusgianto, S., & Rusmita, S. A. (2020). Customer predictive analytics using artificial intelligence. *The Singapore Economic Review*, 1–12.

Chapter 3
The Role of AI and ML in Shaping Predictive Analytics for Modern Business Intelligence:
Techniques, Challenges, and Applications for Data–Driven Decision–Making

Riya Thomas
Coimbatore Institute of Technology, India

M. Sujithra
Coimbatore Institute of Technology, India

B. Senthilkumar
Kumaraguru College of Technology, India

ABSTRACT

In modern business, data drives informed decision-making, with AI and BI ushering in a new era of predictive analytics essential for sustainable success. This chapter explores leveraging AI and ML for predictive analytics in BI, covering its mission, methodologies, challenges, applications, and future trends. Predictive analytics, enhanced by AI and ML, enables data-driven decisions by anticipating market trends, identifying opportunities, and optimizing resources. Key methodologies include data preprocessing, algorithm selection, model training, and evaluation, illustrated through real-world examples. Despite its benefits, challenges such as

DOI: 10.4018/979-8-3693-8844-0.ch003

data quality, model interpretability, ethical issues, and resource constraints remain, with strategies provided to address these. Case studies in retail, healthcare, finance, and manufacturing showcase predictive analytics' impact on decision-making and efficiency. The chapter concludes by emphasizing the transformative potential of AI and ML in predictive analytics, equipping readers with the knowledge to drive success in the digital era.

INTRODUCTION

In the mercurial landscape of contemporary business, the ability to harness data for informed decision-making has become a cornerstone of success. Amidst this data-driven paradigm, predictive analytics stands out as a powerful tool in business intelligence (BI), offering organizations the capability to anticipate new patterns and outcomes with unparalleled accuracy. This chapter embarks on a comprehensive exploration of predictive analytics in BI, illuminating its significance, the transformative role of artificial intelligence (AI) and machine learning (ML), and its implications for decision-makers in today's business landscape. Predictive analytics, fundamentally, is about unlocking insights from data to predict future events or behaviors.

Central to predictive analytics' efficacy is the blend of AI and ML tools. These advancements have revolutionized the field, enabling organizations to build sophisticated predictive models capable of processing vast amounts of data and extracting actionable insights. From forecasting customer behavior to optimizing supply chain management, AI-driven predictive analytics has become indispensable for businesses across industries, offering a competitive edge in an increasingly complex marketplace.

This chapter embarks on a journey to explore the multifaceted landscape of predictive analytics in BI, delving into its mission, methodologies, challenges, applications, and future trends. This chapter uses theoretical insights and real-world examples to explain how predictive analytics can drive value and innovation within their organizations. The exploration begins with an in-depth examination of the core mission of predictive analytics in BI, elucidating how it gives businesses the confidence and foresight to make choices from data. We will explore how predictive analytics enables businesses to anticipate market trends, identify opportunities, mitigate risks, and optimize resource allocation, thus shaping strategic decision-making and fostering sustainable growth. This chapter explains the methodologies, challenges, applications, and future trends of leveraging AI and ML for predictive analytics in BI.

The Mission: Empowering Data-Driven Decision-Making

Predictive analytics emerges as a vital component of business intelligence (BI), positioned to empower organizations with the foresight required to navigate the intricacies of the marketplace adeptly. This section explores the multifaceted role of predictive analytics, illustrating how it empowers businesses to make decisions confidently, anticipate market shifts, seize opportunities, mitigate risks, and enhance the allocation of resources. Using historical data and sophisticated analytical techniques, predictive analytics allows businesses to anticipate future scenarios and proactively align their actions with strategic objectives.

A primary goal of predictive analytics is to forecast market trends, allowing organizations to remain ahead of the competition in an increasingly competitive landscape. By looking at past data and finding trends and connections, analysis helps businesses understand changes in consumer behavior, shifts in market demand, and emerging industry trends. With this predictive capability, businesses might modify their approaches and products to exploit opportunities and maintain a competitive advantage.

Furthermore, predictive analytics catalyzes identifying avenues for growth and innovation. Predictive analytics uncovers latent opportunities that might remain undiscovered by examining information from several sources, including encounters with customers, trends, and competitive landscapes. Whether it's identifying underserved market segments, optimizing product offerings, or exploring new revenue streams, predictive analytics empowers organizations to make strategic investments that drive business expansion. By looking at past data and determining possible risk variables like market volatility or supply chain disruptions, predictive analytics enables organizations to develop proactive risk mitigation strategies. Whether optimizing inventory levels to avoid stockouts or implementing contingency plans to mitigate potential disruptions, predictive analytics offers businesses the foresight to navigate uncertainties confidently.

Moreover, predictive analytics facilitates efficient resource allocation, ensuring organizations allocate resources effectively to achieve strategic goals (Suwarno et al., 2023). It looks at past data and spots trends in how resources are used across various functions such as marketing, operations, and finance. Whether maximizing return on marketing investment or minimizing production costs, predictive analytics helps enhance operational efficiency and drive cost savings.

Organizations may use predictive analytics as a strategic enabler to confidently make decisions grounded in data. Predictive analytics enables businesses to drive strategic decision-making, promote sustainable growth, and achieve a competitive edge in today's fast-paced business environment by foreseeing market trends, spotting opportunities, reducing risks, and allocating resources optimally. Predictive analytics gives businesses the tools they need to confidently navigate the complexities of the marketplace and position themselves for success in a setting that is becoming more and more competitive. These tools can forecast demand, detect fraudulent activity, optimize inventory management, and predict customer behavior.

Unveiling the Significance of Historical Data Analysis and Preparation for Maximizing Insights

In the constantly changing realm of business intelligence and data-centric decision-making, historical data stands as a cornerstone upon which organizations build their predictive analytics endeavors. This section embarks on a comprehensive exploration of the key role that historical data plays in unveiling its significance in maximizing insights and guiding strategic initiatives.

Historical data is a rich repository of past trends, patterns, and behaviors, offering priceless insights into market dynamics, consumer preferences, and operational performance. However, the true potential of historical data can only be realized through meticulous analysis and preparation. Organizations must embark on a journey of thorough examination, unraveling the complexities hidden within their historical datasets to extract actionable insights.

At the heart of historical data analysis is data cleaning, wherein inconsistencies, errors, and outliers are identified and rectified to ensure data accuracy and integrity. By meticulously scrubbing the data of imperfections, organizations create the groundwork for reliable predictive modeling and well-informed choices. By delving into various strategies and methodologies for historical data analysis and preparation, organizations can unlock a treasure trove of insights that lay dormant within their data reservoirs. Through a meticulous approach to refining historical data quality and relevance, organizations pave the way for effective predictive modeling and strategic decision-making. Armed with a profound understanding of their historical data, organizations can confidently navigate the complexities of the marketplace, setting themselves up for success in a business environment that is becoming increasingly competitive.

Navigating the Landscape of Advanced Analytical Techniques in Predictive Modeling

In the ever-expanding realm of predictive modeling, advanced analytical techniques catalyze unlocking the hidden potential within vast data reservoirs. This segment embarks on a deep dive into the intricate landscape of these sophisticated methodologies, illuminating their pivotal role in driving insights from data and strategic planning processes.

At the core of advanced predictive modeling techniques lies more machine learning algorithms, each specifically addressing data challenges and objectives (L'heureux et al., 2017). Regression analysis, for instance, provides a powerful framework for understanding the association between independent and dependent variables, enabling organizations to predict continuous outcomes with precision. On the other hand, classification algorithms excel in categorizing data into distinct classes or categories, facilitating tasks such as customer segmentation and fraud detection. Clustering algorithms offer another dimension to predictive modeling, allowing organizations to know the hidden structures in the data by identifying homogeneous groups or clusters. This capability proves invaluable in market segmentation, anomaly detection, and personalized recommendation systems.

Furthermore, time series analysis emerges as a fundamental tool for analyzing temporal data trends and making predictions based on historical patterns, empowering organizations to anticipate future developments accurately (Pillkahn, 2008). However, the efficacy of predictive modeling extends beyond the mere application of algorithms. Robust methodologies for model evaluation, validation, and optimization are indispensable to ensure the reliability and efficacy of predictive models deployed by organizations. Through rigorous assessment methods such as cross-validation and performance metrics assessment, organizations can gauge their models' predictive power and generalization ability, enhancing their confidence in decision-making based on model outputs. Moreover, continuous optimization efforts are essential to adapt predictive models to evolving data landscapes and business objectives. Techniques such as hyperparameter tuning, ensemble learning, and model refinement enable organizations to fine-tune their models for improved performance and adaptability.

In essence, by navigating the landscape of advanced analytical techniques in predictive modeling, companies can gain a competitive edge by fully utilizing their data reservoirs to drive educated decision-making, unearth priceless insights, and more in today's fast-paced business world.

METHODOLOGIES AND TECHNIQUES

Within the expansive domain of predictive analytics, methodologies and techniques stand as indispensable tools, facilitating the transformation of data into useful insights that help in making decisions. This section extensively explores the diverse methodologies and techniques deployed in predictive analytics, spanning the comprehensive spectrum of data preprocessing, algorithm selection, model training, evaluation, deployment, and monitoring best practices. Through a rich tapestry of real-world examples and immersive case studies, we embark on a journey to unravel the practical application of these methodologies, elucidating their profound significance in orchestrating and steering successful predictive analytics projects toward fruition.

As a discipline, predictive analytics begins its transformative journey at the critical juncture of data preprocessing. With real-world scenarios and case studies as our guide, we traverse the intricate landscape of data preprocessing, uncovering its pivotal role in sculpting the foundation upon which predictive analytics endeavors thrive.

Upon the solid bedrock of preprocessed data, the journey continues into the realm of algorithm selection. At this pivotal juncture, the choice of algorithm dictates the trajectory and efficacy of predictive models. Embracing a diverse array of machine learning (ML) algorithms, organizations navigate the terrain of linear regression, decision trees, random forests, support vector machines (SVM), neural networks, and ensemble methods (Keerthika & Abinayaa, 2022). Through a panoramic lens, we explore the nuanced characteristics of each algorithm, discerning their suitability across various data types and problem domains. Real-world vignettes and immersive case studies illuminate the intricate dance between data and algorithm, underscoring the profound impact of algorithmic selection on the predictive prowess of analytical models. With algorithms primed and poised, the journey ventures into model training—a crucible wherein data and algorithms converge to forge predictive models imbued with foresight and predictive prowess. Real-world vignettes and immersive case studies offer a glimpse into the crucible of model training, illuminating the iterative journey from data to predictive insight.

As models emerge from the crucible of training, the journey transitions into the realm of evaluation—a critical juncture where models undergo rigorous scrutiny to ascertain their predictive efficacy and generalization capabilities. Models are tested on various datasets and scenarios, and their performance is assessed through assessment measures, including accuracy, precision, recall, and F1 score (Gao et al., 2021). Real-world vignettes and immersive case studies offer a window into model evaluation, showcasing the interplay between model performance and real-world applicability. With models validated and vetted, the journey culminates in the deployment phase—a transformative juncture where models transition from theoretical constructs to practical tools wielded in real-world scenarios. Guided by best practices in deployment and monitoring, organizations navigate the intricacies of deploying models into production environments, ensuring seamless integration and optimal performance. Real-world vignettes and immersive case studies offer a glimpse into the deployment journey, unveiling the transformative impact of predictive models on real-world decision-making and business outcomes.

This section serves as a beacon, guiding practitioners through the labyrinth of predictive analytics methodologies and techniques. Through immersive exploration and real-world illumination, we unravel the intricacies of data preprocessing, algorithm selection, model training, evaluation, deployment, and monitoring best practices, equipping practitioners with the insights and acumen to navigate the complexities of predictive analytics endeavors with confidence and efficacy.

Data Preprocessing

Data preprocessing is the crucial inaugural phase in the intricate journey of predictive analytics, where the raw material of data undergoes a metamorphosis to enhance its readiness for analysis. This preparatory stage unfolds as a multifaceted process, encompassing an array of tasks meticulously designed to bolster data quality, completeness, and consistency, laying a robust foundation for subsequent analytical endeavors. At the heart of data preprocessing lies the indispensable task of data cleaning—an imperative step to identify and rectify errors or inconsistencies lurking within the dataset. Within this realm, practitioners seek to unearth missing values, outliers, or inaccuracies that may impede the integrity of the data. Armed with a repertoire of techniques such as imputation, outlier detection, and the surgical removal of duplicate entries, data cleaning emerges as a formidable guardian of data integrity, ensuring the analytical journey unfolds upon a bedrock of accuracy and reliability.

Beyond data cleaning, normalization emerges as a pivotal technique essential for harmonizing the disparate scales of variables within the dataset. Normalization safeguards against the undue influence of features with larger magnitudes, thereby fostering equitable treatment within the analytical framework by ensuring that variables are standardized to a common scale. Techniques like Min-Max scaling and Z-score normalization serve as stalwart allies in this endeavor, orchestrating the harmonious alignment of variables and paving the way for unbiased analysis.

Furthermore, the art of feature engineering emerges as a transformative force, shaping the contours of predictive models through the creation and refinement of features. Within this realm of ingenuity, practitioners embark on a voyage of discovery, crafting new features or imbuing existing ones with newfound depth and relevance. Through techniques such as aggregating, binning, or encoding categorical variables, feature engineering unlocks the latent potential within the data, enabling the capture of nuanced relationships and subtleties that elude the untrained eye. Armed with the creative powers to derive new features from existing ones, practitioners harness the power of feature engineering to enrich the predictive landscape, imbuing models with the foresight to navigate the complexities of real-world scenarios with aplomb.

Data preprocessing emerges as the cornerstone upon which the edifice of predictive analytics stands, heralding the dawn of a transformative journey into the realm of data-driven insights. By carefully carrying out procedures like data cleaning, normalization, and feature engineering, practitioners pave the way for analytical endeavors grounded in accuracy, reliability, and predictive prowess. Data preprocessing is the first step toward a predictive analytics environment and demonstrates the transforming power of thorough preparation. It lays the foundation for deliberate foresight and insightful decisions in the ever-changing world of modern business.

Algorithm Selection

Algorithm selection is a pivotal juncture in predictive analytics, wielding significant influence over predictive models' accuracy, efficiency, and overall efficacy. This critical aspect underscores the importance of judiciously choosing the most suitable algorithm designed for the unique features of the dataset and the intricacies of the problem domain at hand. In the expansive realm of predictive analytics, organizations are confronted with diverse machine learning (ML) algorithms, each with its strengths, weaknesses, and suitability across various data types and problem domains. From foundational algorithms like linear regression to advanced techniques, the available algorithms offer a rich tapestry of tools and methodologies for extracting insights from data.

The algorithm selection process begins with a comprehensive understanding of the dataset and the specific objectives of the predictive analytics endeavor (Eckerson, 2007). Organizations must carefully assess the nature of the data, including its structure, dimensionality, and distribution, as well as any inherent patterns or relationships that may influence the choice of algorithm. Similarly, a clear delineation of the desired outcomes and performance metrics is essential, guiding the selection process toward algorithms best suited to achieving the desired goals. One of the key considerations in algorithm selection is the nature of the problem being addressed. Different algorithms are inherently better suited to specific problems involving classification, regression, clustering, or anomaly detection. For instance, linear regression may be well-suited for tasks involving the prediction of continuous variables. At the same time, decision trees or random forests may be more appropriate for classification tasks with categorical outcomes.

Moreover, the algorithm's scalability and computational requirements must also be considered, particularly in scenarios involving large datasets or real-time processing constraints. Some algorithms may excel in predictive accuracy but may be computationally expensive or impractical to deploy in resource-constrained environments. Balancing performance considerations with practical constraints is essential in selecting an algorithm that aligns with the organization's operational realities and strategic objectives.

Furthermore, the interpretability and explainability of the algorithm are crucial considerations, particularly in domains where regulatory compliance or stakeholder trust is paramount. Transparent algorithms such as decision trees or linear models offer intuitive insights into the underlying decision-making process, enabling stakeholders to understand and trust the predictive outcomes. In contrast, more complex algorithms like deep neural networks may do better in predictions; they may also be harder to understand, posing challenges in explaining the rationale behind their predictions.

Ultimately, algorithm selection is iterative and informed by empirical experimentation and validation. Organizations may employ cross-validation, grid search, or performance benchmarking techniques to evaluate how well various algorithms work using their dataset. Through this iterative process of exploration and refinement, organizations can identify the algorithm or ensemble of algorithms that best align with their objectives, data characteristics, and operational constraints, paving the way for the development of predictive models that deliver actionable insights and tangible value to the organization (Hajdu, 2024).

Understanding the key algorithms and their characteristics is essential for effectively selecting the most appropriate technique to tackle specific predictive modeling tasks.

Linear Regression

A basic method for modeling the connection between one or more independent variables (features) and a continuous dependent variable (goal) is called linear regression. Because it presupposes a linear connection between the variables, it is especially useful for jobs that need quantitative outcome prediction. Because they are easily understood and comparatively straightforward, linear regression models are helpful for exploratory analysis and as benchmarks for more sophisticated methods.

Decision Trees

Decision trees are flexible algorithms capable of handling several tasks. They function by dividing the input recursively into segments according to feature values; each segment corresponds to a decision node in the tree. Decision trees offer interpretability and ease of visualization, as they can be represented graphically, allowing users to intuitively understand the decision-making process (Strauss & Topping, 1970). Nevertheless, decision trees can overfit, particularly when dealing with large or complicated datasets. To counteract this, one can use ensemble approaches or pruning procedures.

Random Forests

Random forests are an ensemble learning technique that utilizes multiple decision trees to enhance predictive accuracy and minimize overfitting. Each tree within the forest is trained on a randomly selected subset of the data and features, with the final prediction being made by combining the outputs of the individual trees. Random forests are adept at capturing complex relationships within the data and are particularly well-suited for high-dimensional datasets or datasets with nonlinear relationships. They offer robustness and scalability, making them widely used in practice.

Support Vector Machines (SVM)

Support Vector Machines (SVMs) are supervised learning models for classification and regression tasks. They work by finding the optimal hyperplane that best separates data points of different classes in the feature space. SVMs aim to maximize the margin between the closest data points of each class, known as support vectors, to achieve the most effective separation. Using kernel functions, SVMs can efficiently handle non-linear boundaries by transforming the data into higher-dimensional spaces where a linear separator can be found.

Neural Networks

Neural networks are computational models inspired by the human brain and used for many tasks. They consist of interconnected layers of nodes (neurons), where each connection has an associated weight. Information flows through these layers, from the input to the output layer, with intermediate hidden layers processing the data (Cantareira et al., 2020). Neural networks learn to perform tasks by adjusting the weights based on the error of their predictions during training, using algorithms such as backpropagation. They are particularly effective for complex problems due to their ability to capture non-linear relationships and learn from large amounts of data.

Ensemble Methods

Ensemble methods aim to increase the forecast robustness and accuracy by combining several independent models. Bagging, boosting, and stacking are a few examples. In order to lower variance and increase stability, bagging, also known as bootstrap aggregating, is the process of training multiple models using bootstrap samples of the data and combining their predictions. Boosting improves prediction performance by training models successively on weighted copies of the data, with each new model concentrating on samples that the preceding models misclassified (Cao et al., 2010). By stacking, one model's predictions are combined with those of other models to feed a meta-model, which then learns how best to combine the forecasts of each model. When using ensemble methods instead of individual models alone, better performance is achieved by combining several models' combined knowledge.

By utilizing the best algorithm for the job at hand, practitioners may unleash the full power of predictive analytics and derive meaningful insights from their data.

MODEL TRAINING AND EVALUATION:

Model training and evaluation represent critical junctures in the predictive analytics journey, where data-driven insights are transformed into actionable intelligence. These pivotal phases bridge the theoretical framework of algorithm selection and the useful implementation of prediction models in actual situations. As organizations navigate the intricate data analytics landscape, model training, and evaluation emerge as the linchpin, guiding practitioners through the labyrinthine terrain of model refinement and performance assessment. The iterative nature of model training and evaluation underscores their significance in the predictive analytics continuum. A meticulous sequence of steps characterizes this iterative process to hone the model's predictive capabilities and assess its efficacy in predicting previously unseen data (Garg et al., 2022). As practitioners embark on this journey of iterative refinement, they engage in a delicate dance between theory and practice, utilizing data to inform choices and provide game-changing revelations.

At the heart of model training lies the quest for predictive prowess—a relentless pursuit of accuracy, robustness, and generalization capabilities. This quest unfolds through a series of iterative cycles, each marked by forward propagation, error calculation, backpropagation, and parameter optimization. The model learns to discern subtle patterns and relationships within the data through this iterative interplay, gradually refining its predictive capabilities to achieve optimal performance. Simultaneously, the model evaluation process serves as a litmus test for the model's efficacy, providing practitioners with invaluable insights into its predictive accuracy and generalization capabilities. Through a battery of performance metrics and validation techniques, practitioners evaluate the model's effectiveness using hypothetical data, gauging its ability to navigate the complexities of real-world scenarios and make reliable predictions in diverse problem domains.

As organizations navigate the dynamic landscape of predictive analytics, model training, and evaluation emerge as beacons of clarity amidst the sea of data-driven uncertainty. Through meticulous attention to detail and a commitment to iterative refinement, practitioners utilize predictive models' revolutionary potential to help companies succeed in an increasingly data-driven world by facilitating informed data-guided decision processes, revealing actionable insights, and generating insights.

Data Splitting: At the genesis of model training and evaluation lies the art of data splitting—a process of judiciously partitioning the dataset into distinct subsets, each serving a unique purpose in the modeling journey. Most data, or the training set, provides the model with the rich soil to grow its prediction abilities (Rodriguez-Galiano et al., 2015). Here, amidst the vast expanse of training data, the model diligently learns the intricate nuances and patterns ingrained within, laying the foundation for its predictive prowess. Meanwhile, the validation set assumes the role of a discerning overseer, meticulously scrutinizing the model's performance and safeguarding against the perilous shoals of overfitting. Through its vigilant oversight, the validation set ensures that the model transcends the shackles of mere memorization, fostering a capacity for generalization to unseen instances. Finally, the testing set emerges as the ultimate arbiter of the model's mettle, standing as an impartial adjudicator that casts its verdict on the model's efficacy in navigating the uncharted territory of unseen data.

Fitting the Model: Armed with a meticulously curated training dataset, the selected algorithm embarks on a transformative odyssey—an iterative journey of parameter refinement and model calibration. This model fitting process, akin to the delicate art of sculpting, involves the algorithm's conscientious assimilation of the training data's intricate patterns and relationships. The model refines its predictive capabilities with each iteration, honing its discernment to discern subtle cues and nuances that elude the untrained eye. As the model evolves, it transcends mere mastery of the training data, aspiring toward creating a predictive artifact imbued with the prescient ability to traverse the realms of unseen data and illuminate the path to informed decision-making.

Evaluating Model Performance: With the model's parameters finely tuned and its predictive faculties honed to a razor-sharp edge, the time has come to subject it to the crucible of evaluation—a rigorous assessment of its mettle against a battery of performance metrics tailored to the nuances of the problem domain. These metrics, akin to the compass guiding the navigator through uncharted waters, give practitioners invaluable insights into the model's predictive accuracy, robustness, and generalization prowess. Every statistic reveals a different picture of the model's strengths and limitations, clearly revealing its weaknesses. These include the reliable metrics of accuracy and precision and the more complex gauges of recall, F1 score, and area under the ROC curve. Armed with these insights, practitioners navigate the labyrinthine landscape of model refinement, iterating tirelessly to cultivate a predictive artifact that transcends mere accuracy, embodying the quintessence of predictive prowess and fidelity to the underlying data.

MODEL DEPLOYMENT AND MONITORING

Model deployment and monitoring represent the pivotal transition from the theoretical development phase of predictive analytics to its practical implementation in real-world settings. This phase is characterized by meticulous steps aimed at seamlessly integrating the predictive model into production systems and ensuring sustained performance over time. Let's delve into each aspect of model deployment and monitoring in detail:

Transition from Development to Implementation: As the predictive model emerges from the development phase, it transforms from a conceptual framework to a practical solution ready for deployment. This transition involves translating the theoretical underpinnings of the model into tangible applications that can generate real-time predictions and drive decision-making within operational environments. It requires close collaboration between data scientists, software engineers, and business stakeholders to ensure the smooth transition of the model from the development sandbox to production systems.

Seamless Integration into Production Systems: Once the predictive model is deemed ready for deployment, it is seamlessly integrated into existing production systems, where it can leverage real-time data streams to generate actionable insights. This integration process involves configuring the model to interface with data sources, APIs, and other software components within the production environment. It also requires rigorous testing to ensure compatibility, reliability, and scalability, minimizing the risk of disruptions to ongoing operations.

Performance Monitoring and Evaluation: With the model deployed into production, the focus shifts to monitoring its performance and evaluating its efficacy in real-world scenarios. Performance monitoring involves tracking key metrics such as prediction accuracy, latency, throughput, and resource utilization to assess the model's reliability and scalability. This ongoing evaluation enables organizations to detect anomalies, identify performance bottlenecks, and optimize the model's performance over time.

Continuous Improvement through Feedback Loops: Incorporating feedback loops is essential to ensure the adaptability and responsiveness of the predictive model to changing conditions and evolving user requirements. Feedback mechanisms capture user feedback, new data, and environmental changes, which are then used to recalibrate and refine the model iteratively. This continuous improvement cycle enables the model to learn from experience, adapt to emerging patterns, and enhance its predictive accuracy and relevance over time.

Model Maintenance and Versioning: Periodic maintenance and versioning are essential to address model drift, prevent degradation, and ensure its long-term viability. This involves retraining the model with new data, updating algorithms, refining features, and optimizing performance to keep pace with evolving business needs and technological advancements. Additionally, versioning enables organizations to track changes, reproduce results, and roll back to previous iterations if necessary, ensuring the integrity and reliability of the model throughout its lifecycle.

Let's delve deeper into each facet of model deployment and monitoring, unraveling the intricacies and significance of each step in ensuring the seamless integration and sustained performance of predictive models in real-world environments:

Deployment into Production: The culmination of rigorous development efforts, model deployment heralds the transition of predictive models from experimental prototypes to practical solutions that wield transformative power in real-world settings. This pivotal phase involves orchestrating the seamless integration of the model into production environments, where its predictive capabilities can be harnessed to drive informed decision-making and optimize business processes. Successful deployment necessitates meticulous coordination between data scientists, IT professionals, and business stakeholders, ensuring a smooth transition without disrupting existing workflows or systems.

Performance Monitoring: As the model takes its first steps into production, continuous monitoring becomes imperative to safeguard its efficacy and relevance over time. Performance monitoring entails vigilantly tracking key performance indicators (KPIs), ranging from prediction accuracy and reliability to scalability and resource utilization (Adewusi et al., 2024). These metrics serve as the compass guiding organizations through the uncharted waters of real-world scenarios, offering insights into the model's performance and detecting any deviations from expected behavior that may signify degradation or drift. Organizations can identify potential issues early on by establishing robust monitoring mechanisms and proactively addressing them to maintain the model's performance and integrity.

Feedback Loops: In the rapidly changing realm of data and business dynamics, adaptability and responsiveness are paramount for predictive models to remain effective and relevant. Incorporating feedback loops facilitates this continuous evolution by enabling the model to learn from new data and user feedback, refining its predictive capabilities iteratively. These feedback mechanisms serve as conduits for capturing valuable insights and evolving patterns, which are then utilized to recalibrate and enhance the model's predictive accuracy over time. By establishing feedback loops, organizations harness the collective intelligence of users and stakeholders to iteratively improve the model's performance and address emerging challenges effectively.

Model Maintenance: Just as ships require periodic maintenance to navigate treacherous waters, predictive models demand regular upkeep to navigate the dynamic currents of data and business trends. Model maintenance encompasses a spectrum of activities to prevent degradation and ensure the model's long-term viability. This includes recurrent model retraining with new data to assimilate the latest trends and insights, updating algorithms, refining features, and optimizing performance to align with evolving business needs and technological advancements. By staying abreast of changing trends and proactively adapting to emerging patterns, organizations can uphold the predictive model's robustness and continue to derive value from its insights over time.

CHALLENGES AND CONCERNS:

Implementing predictive analytics brings many challenges and concerns that demand thoughtful consideration and strategic mitigation strategies. In this section, we explore the intricacies of these challenges and offer actionable insights for successful implementation.

Data Quality: The impact of predictive modeling hinges on the underlying data quality. However, organizations often grapple with issues such as inconsistencies and biases in data that can compromise the integrity and reliability of predictive models. Data silos hinder the integration of disparate datasets, leading to fragmented insights and incomplete analyses. Inconsistencies in data formatting or recording practices can introduce errors and inaccuracies, while inherent biases in the data can perpetuate systemic inequalities and distort predictive outcomes. Mitigation Strategy: To address data quality challenges, organizations must prioritize data governance initiatives aimed at standardizing data formats, enhancing data quality assurance processes, and fostering a culture of data stewardship. This involves implementing robust data integration frameworks to break down silos and facilitate seamless data exchange across organizational boundaries. Additionally, organizations should invest in data cleansing and enrichment techniques to identify and rectify inconsistencies and biases within the data (Osborne, 2012). By establishing data quality standards, enforcing rigorous data validation protocols, and promoting data literacy among stakeholders, businesses may improve the calibre and dependability of their predictive analytics projects.

Model Interpretability: The opaque nature of some AI and ML algorithms poses challenges regarding model interpretability and transparency. Decision-makers may hesitate to trust predictive insights generated by complex algorithms they do not fully understand, leading to skepticism and reluctance to adopt AI-driven decision-making systems. Lack of interpretability can hinder the acceptance and adoption of predictive models, impeding their integration into organizational workflows and decision-making processes. Mitigation Strategy: Organizations can use strategies like interpretable machine learning models, feature importance analysis, and model explanation approaches to improve the interpretability and transparency of their models. These methods enable stakeholders to gain insights into the rationale behind the model's predictions and understand the factors driving its decisions. Additionally, organizations should prioritize model documentation and communication to ensure that decision-makers have access to clear explanations of the model's underlying logic and assumptions. Companies can increase their confidence in AI-powered analytics solutions by demystifying the inner workings of predictive models and promoting openness in the procedures used to make decisions.

Ethical Considerations: Predictive analytics brings up profound upright considerations concerning privacy, fairness, and bias. Biased or discriminatory models can perpetuate social inequalities and undermine trust in AI-driven decision-making systems, posing significant risks to organizations and society. Moreover, using sensitive personal data in predictive analytics raises concerns about privacy violations and data misuse, necessitating careful attention to ethical and legal guidelines. Mitigation Strategy: Organizations must embed ethical principles into the fabric of their predictive analytics initiatives, from data collection and preprocessing to model development and deployment. This involves conducting thorough fairness assessments to identify and mitigate biases, implementing privacy-preserving techniques to protect sensitive data, and ensuring adherence to applicable regulations such as GDPR and CCPA. Additionally, organizations should provide lucid policies and procedures to govern the ethical use of predictive analytics and promote accountability and transparency in decision-making processes. Organizations can mitigate ethical risks and build trust with stakeholders and the broader community by prioritizing ethical considerations and upholding principles of fairness, integrity, and transparency.

Resource Constraints: Implementing AI-driven predictive analytics solutions necessitates large expenditures in technological infrastructure, talent development, and organizational change management (Moinuddin et al., 2024). However, many organizations face resource constraints and talent shortages that impede their ability to leverage the potential of predictive analytics fully. Mitigation Strategy: To address resource constraints, organizations can adopt a multi-pronged approach that combines strategic investments in technology infrastructure with efforts to cultivate a skilled workforce and foster a culture of data-driven innovation. This may involve leveraging cloud-based solutions to alleviate infrastructure constraints, investing in data science training programs to upskill existing staff, and fostering cross-functional collaboration to bridge the gap between business and data science teams. Additionally, organizations should explore partnerships with external vendors or service providers to augment internal capabilities and accelerate the pace of innovation. Organizations can overcome resource constraints and unleash the revolutionary potential of predictive analytics to generate innovation and corporate growth by giving talent, organizational culture, and technology priority.

A comprehensive strategy that considers organizational, ethical, and technical aspects is needed to address the issues and problems related to the application of predictive analytics. By implementing strategic mitigation methods and promoting an innovative and continuous improvement culture, companies may effectively navigate the intricacies of predictive analytics and fully realize its promise in facilitating well-informed decision-making and attaining sustainable growth.

CASE STUDIES AND APPLICATION

In this section, we explore real-world illustrations and examples that vividly illustrate the multifaceted use cases and the profound impact of AI-driven predictive analytics across various industries. Through an in-depth analysis of these case studies, we unravel how organizations have harnessed predictive analytics to navigate complex challenges, optimize processes, and unlock transformative opportunities.

Retail Industry

Predictive analytics has emerged as a cornerstone of success, revolutionizing traditional practices and redefining customer engagement strategies in the retail industry. In today's highly competitive retail landscape, companies utilize predictive analytics to comprehend customer behavior better, optimize operations, and enhance the overall customer experience. For instance, a prominent e-commerce platform utilized predictive analytics to meticulously analyze vast volumes of previous sales information, deciphering nuanced patterns and trends to accurately forecast demand. This granular analysis allowed the platform to anticipate market shifts and consumer preferences, ensuring they could proactively adjust their inventory in response to changing demand.

By leveraging these predictive insights, the platform orchestrated dynamic inventory control strategies, maintaining ideal stock levels and minimizing instances of stock shortages. These strategies included sophisticated demand forecasting models that considered a wide array of variables, such as seasonal trends, promotional events, and external factors like economic conditions or cultural events. This proactive approach reduced the costs associated with overstocking and understocking and improved supply chain efficiency, ensuring that products were available when and where customers wanted them.

Beyond inventory management and personalized recommendations, predictive retail analytics extends to various facets, such as pricing strategies, customer segmentation, and marketing campaigns. Retailers analyze rival pricing using predictive algorithms to establish the best price strategy, market demand, and consumer price sensitivity. This dynamic pricing strategy allows merchants to maximize their margins and stay competitive. Then, retailers can better target these niche markets with their marketing campaigns, enhancing their relevance and impact. Predictive analytics helps retailers maximize their marketing budget by determining the best channels and tactics. By analyzing the performance of past campaigns, retailers can predict which marketing efforts are likely to yield the highest return on investment, enabling them to allocate their resources more efficiently. This data-driven marketing approach improves the effectiveness of campaigns and the entire client experience journey by ensuring that customers receive the right messages at the right time.

Healthcare Sector

In healthcare, predictive analytics has emerged as a transformative force, catalyzing advancements in patient care, clinical outcomes, and operational efficiency. Integrating predictive analytics into healthcare systems revolutionizes how patient data is utilized to improve health outcomes and streamline medical processes. For instance, a leading healthcare provider deployed predictive analytics models to predict patient readmissions within 30 days of discharge. By analyzing a variety of patient data, such as demographics, medical history, test findings, medication records, and utilization patterns, the organization was able to identify individuals at heightened risk of readmission (Kansagara et al., 2011).

This comprehensive data analysis enabled the healthcare provider to reveal patterns and correlations that conventional methods might have missed. With this understanding, the organization applied specific interventions, like customized care plans, follow-up appointments, home healthcare services, and patient education programs, to mitigate risks and prevent adverse outcomes. By focusing on high-risk patients, healthcare professionals could provide more tailored and timely care, addressing specific health issues before they escalate into serious problems.

Predictive analytics has been instrumental in enhancing chronic disease management. By continuously monitoring patients with chronic conditions such as diabetes, heart disease, and asthma, predictive models can forecast potential exacerbations and complications. This allows healthcare providers to intervene early, adjust treatment plans, and offer preventative measures that help maintain patient health and avoid hospitalizations. The continuous analysis of data in real-time from technologies for remote monitoring and wearable technology plays a crucial role in these efforts, enabling healthcare professionals to stay connected with patients outside the clinical setting and respond swiftly to any alarming trends.

In research and development, predictive analytics accelerates the discovery of new drugs and therapies. By examining enormous clinical trial databases, scientific literature, and medical records, researchers can determine potential drug candidates, predict their efficacy, and understand their side effects more quickly than traditional methods. This accelerates the pipeline from research to clinical application, bringing innovative treatments to patients faster.

Financial Services

Within the financial services sector, predictive analytics has emerged as a linchpin of fraud detection, risk management, and customer relationship management initiatives. This technological advancement is revolutionizing financial institutions' operations, enabling them to leverage data to make better-informed decisions, enhance security measures, and deliver superior customer experiences. These machine-learning models can analyze vast amounts of transactional data, identifying subtle deviations from normal behavior that could signify fraud (Bello et al., 2024). They consider various factors such as transaction amount, frequency, geographical location, and the historical behavior of the account holder. When anomalies are detected, the system triggers alerts for further investigation, allowing the bank to take swift action, such as freezing accounts or blocking transactions, to prevent potential losses. This proactive approach reduces monetary losses and enhances customer trust, as clients feel secure knowing that their bank is vigilant in protecting their assets. It empowered the bank to expand your understanding of consumer behavior and preferences to help you create more focused marketing strategies and personalized offerings that fostered stronger customer relationships and enhanced loyalty. The bank could segment its customer base and identify specific requirements and inclinations by examining the history of transactions, product usage, and interaction with digital banking platforms. Because of this detailed knowledge, the bank could customize its marketing campaigns, presenting customers with relevant product recommendations, promotional offers, and personalized financial advice.

For instance, a customer who frequently travels abroad might receive targeted offers for travel insurance or a credit card with no foreign transaction fees. Similarly, a customer who regularly saves a portion of their income might be offered investment products or retirement planning services. In addition to improving the customer experience, this tailored strategy raises the possibility of cross-selling and upselling, which boosts the bank's earnings.

In addition to fraud detection, risk management, and customer relationship management, predictive analytics is also transforming other areas within the financial services sector. For instance, in regulatory compliance, predictive models help institutions navigate complex regulatory environments by identifying potential compliance issues before they become problematic. By analyzing customer interaction data, predictive models can identify common issues and predict potential problems before they occur. This allows customer service representatives to address concerns, improving resolution times and customer satisfaction proactively. Additionally, chatbots powered by predictive analytics can further improve the customer service experience by offering prompt, tailored answers to consumer concerns.

Manufacturing Sector

In manufacturing, predictive analytics has redefined traditional approaches to maintenance, quality control, and supply chain management, ushering in an innovative and efficient new era. For instance, a leading manufacturing company employed predictive analytics to implement a proactive maintenance strategy, leveraging sensor data and previous maintenance logs to forecast equipment failures before they occurred. This predictive maintenance approach involved deploying sensors on critical machinery to continuously monitor parameters such as vibration, pressure, and operational speed.

By examining this data in real-time alongside historical maintenance records, advanced predictive models could determine the trends and deviations that point to possible equipment problems (Dalzochio et al., 2020). This proactive strategy allowed maintenance crews to deal with problems before they led to costly breakdowns, scheduling repairs during planned downtime rather than in response to unexpected failures. The ability to predict and prevent equipment failures improved production continuity and extended the lifespan of machinery and equipment, maximizing return on investment.

Additionally, predictive analytics has revolutionized quality control processes within the manufacturing sector. By analyzing data collected at various stages of the production process, predictive models can identify potential defects and deviations from quality standards before they become significant issues. This capability allows manufacturers to implement corrective measures in real-time, ensuring that products meet stringent quality requirements. For example, by monitoring parameters such as material properties, environmental conditions, and machine settings, predictive analytics can detect subtle variations that might affect product quality. This early detection enables swift adjustments to production processes, reducing waste, rework, and the risk of defective products reaching customers. Consequently, predictive analytics enhances product consistency, boosts customer satisfaction, and strengthens brand reputation.

Moreover, predictive analytics has played a vital function in enhancing supply chain management and demand forecasting. This foresight enables manufacturers to align their production schedules with market demand, avoiding the pitfalls of overproduction or underproduction. For instance, manufacturers can ramp up production during peak demand periods to meet increased customer orders, while during slower periods, they can scale back to avoid excess inventory. This optimization of production schedules reduces inventory holding costs and ensures that products are available when and where they are needed, enhancing customer satisfaction.

Furthermore, predictive analytics facilitates more efficient inventory management by predicting inventory needs based on demand forecasts and production plans. Manufacturers can optimize inventory levels, reducing the costs associated with holding excess stock and minimizing the risk of stockouts (Mweshi, 2022). This streamlined approach to inventory management is particularly valuable in industries with perishable goods or rapidly changing product lines. Manufacturers can improve cash flow, reduce waste, and enhance overall supply chain efficiency by ensuring the right amount of inventory is available at the right time.

Telecommunications Industry

Predictive analytics has emerged as a cornerstone of customer retention, network optimization, and service quality enhancement initiatives in telecommunications. This technological advancement revolutionizes telecommunications providers' operations, allowing them to leverage data to anticipate challenges, optimize services, and enhance customer experiences. For instance, a telecommunications provider utilized predictive analytics models to predict customer churn based on many factors, including usage patterns, billing history, customer interactions, and social media activity (Radosavljevik, 2017). By analyzing this comprehensive set of data, the provider was able to determine which clients are at risk of leaving well in advance.

These predictive models examined various indicators that could signal dissatisfaction or a potential switch to a competitor, such as a decline in usage, frequent billing complaints, or negative feedback during customer service interactions. By identifying these early warning signs, the telecommunications provider could implement targeted retention strategies and incentives tailored to individual customer needs and preferences. For instance, high-value customers might receive personalized offers such as discounted rates, enhanced data packages, or exclusive access to new services. These proactive retention efforts effectively reduced churn rates and increased customer loyalty, fostering a more stable and satisfied customer base.

Moreover, predictive analytics played a crucial role in network optimization efforts, enabling the telecommunications provider to allocate resources more effectively to improve network performance (Boutaba et al., 2018). By analyzing network usage patterns, traffic data, and environmental factors, predictive models could forecast network congestion and potential service disruptions. This foresight allowed the provider to proactively manage network resources, such as rerouting traffic to underutilized areas, upgrading infrastructure in high-demand regions, and scheduling maintenance during off-peak hours. As a result, the provider could deliver superior service quality, ensuring consistent and reliable connectivity for customers.

In addition to customer retention and network optimization, predictive analytics also facilitated improvements in service quality by enabling real-time monitoring and predictive maintenance of network equipment. The provider could collect data on equipment performance, environmental conditions, and usage patterns by deploying sensors and monitoring tools across the network infrastructure. Furthermore, predictive analytics enhanced the telecommunications provider's ability to personalize customer experiences and tailor services to individual requirements. The provider could offer personalized recommendations and targeted marketing campaigns by examining client information, like browsing history, app usage, and content preferences. For instance, customers who frequently streamed video content might receive offers for high-speed data plans, while those who traveled internationally could be presented with attractive roaming packages. This customized approach improved client satisfaction while also increasing revenue opportunities by promoting relevant services and upgrades.

Predictive analytics also had a major impact in identifying and preventing fraud within the telecommunication industry. By analyzing call patterns, transaction data, and user behavior, predictive models could identify anomalies indicative of fraudulent activities, such as subscription fraud or unauthorized access. Early detection of these activities enabled the provider to take swift action, such as blocking suspicious transactions, enhancing security measures, and notifying affected customers. This proactive approach helped mitigate financial losses, protect customer data, and maintain trust in the provider's services.

Predictive analytics provided important insights into consumer preferences, market trends, and competitive dynamics in strategic planning and business development. By forecasting future demand, identifying emerging technologies, and assessing market opportunities, the telecommunications provider could make wise choices about creating new products, service expansion, and investment ideas. This data-driven approach ensured that the provider stayed ahead of industry trends, adapted to changing customer needs, and maintained a competitive edge in the rapidly evolving telecommunications landscape.

These case studies testify to the transformative strength of AI-powered predictive analytics across diverse industries.

FUTURE TRENDS AND DIRECTIONS

As we gaze into the prospects of AI-powered predictive analytics, many emerging trends and transformative possibilities emerge, reshaping the landscape of business intelligence (BI) and decision-making. This section embarks on an exploratory journey into the horizon of possibilities, illuminating the potential advancements, innovations, and implications.

Advanced AI Algorithms

The relentless march of innovation in AI algorithms is poised to unlock new frontiers in predictive analytics. Advancements in deep learning and other technologies are set to enhance the predictive capabilities of models, enabling them to unravel complex links and patterns in the data with unprecedented accuracy and granularity. With its ability to handle enormous volumes of unstructured data, deep learning allows for more nuanced insights, while reinforcement learning provides sophisticated techniques for dynamic decision-making in uncertain environments. On the other hand, NLP facilitates the extraction of valuable insights from textual data, adding a new dimension to predictive analytics. Moreover, the fusion of AI with other cutting-edge technologies, such as neuromorphic and quantum computing, holds the promise of unlocking even greater computational power and efficiency. Quantum computing, with its capacity to do intricate computations at previously unheard-of speeds, and neuromorphic computing, which mimics the neural structures of the human brain, are paving the way for groundbreaking advancements in predictive analytics (Pal et al., 2023).

Explainable AI

As the deployment of AI-driven predictive models becomes more ubiquitous across industries, the need for transparency and interpretability in AI algorithms grows increasingly paramount. The emergence of explainable AI (XAI) techniques aims to demystify the black box of AI, enabling stakeholders to understand the rationale behind model predictions and decisions. By providing insights into the underlying mechanisms and factors driving model outputs, XAI empowers decision-makers to trust AI-driven insights and confidently make informed decisions. This transparency is crucial not only for regulatory compliance but also for fostering trust among users and stakeholders. As organizations depend on AI to make critical decisions, the ability to explain how and why decisions are made becomes essential for accountability and trust.

AI Automation and AutoML

The democratization of AI through automation and AutoML platforms is set to revolutionize the landscape of predictive analytics, empowering organizations of all sizes and domains to harness the power of AI with ease and efficiency. These platforms streamline the end-to-end model development process, from feature engineering and data preprocessing to choosing an algorithm and implementing a model, democratizing access to advanced predictive capabilities, and accelerating time-to-insight. Automating tedious and labor-intensive tasks, AutoML platforms enable data scientists and analysts to focus on higher-value tasks such as domain expertise and interpretability. This shift not only enhances productivity but also ensures that the benefits of AI are more widely available to users, even those with little technical knowledge.

Ethical AI and Responsible Data Practices

As AI-driven predictive analytics permeates every facet of society, the significance of moral AI and appropriate data handling cannot be overstated. Organizations are increasingly cognizant of the ethical consequences of AI algorithms, such as problems with impartiality, equity, openness, and accountability. Adopting ethical AI frameworks and guidelines and robust data governance practices is essential to mitigate ethical risks and ensure that AI-driven decision-making aligns with ethical principles and societal values. This involves implementing strategies to detect and mitigate bias in AI models, ensuring fairness in AI-driven decisions, and maintaining transparency about how data is collected, processed, and used. Ethical AI practices are fundamental to building trust and ensuring AI technologies benefit society (Paraman & Anamalah, 2023).

Edge Computing and IoT Integration

The spread of edge computing and Internet of Things (IoT) devices heralds a paradigm shift in predictive analytics, enabling real-time insights and decision-making at the network's edge. By leveraging the computational power of edge devices and the rich data streams generated by IoT sensors, organizations can deploy predictive models directly within the operational environment, enabling autonomous decision-making and response. This convergence of edge computing and predictive analytics opens up new possibilities for real-time optimization across diverse industries. Similarly, IoT sensors and edge computing can work together in smart cities to improve public safety, save energy use, and streamline transportation flow. The integration of edge computing and IoT enhances the efficiency of predictive analytics and expands its application scope, driving innovation across various sectors (Ray, Dash, & De, 2019).

In conclusion, the future of AI-driven predictive analytics is brimming with potential. The business intelligence and decision-making landscape is set for a transformative evolution from advanced algorithms and explainable AI to automation, ethical practices, and edge computing. These trends will reshape industries, empower organizations, and ultimately redefine how we leverage information to make wise decisions.

CONCLUSION

The intersection of artificial intelligence (AI) and predictive analytics presents a transformative potential in the dynamic field of business intelligence (BI). A wide range of topics are addressed in this chapter, including the goals, approaches, difficulties, uses, and prospects for using AI and machine learning (ML) in business intelligence (BI).

We have explored the subtleties of predictive analytics, from facilitating decision-making based on data to managing the challenges of model training and evaluation. We have found that predictive analytics is vital in making crucial decisions, improving operational effectiveness, and promoting long-term growth. We have seen the wide range of applications of AI-driven predictive analytics across multiple industries through case studies and real-world examples, revealing its significant influence on business results and decision-making processes. However, despite predictive analytics' potential and promise, issues and worries remain to be addressed. Concerns about data quality, interpretability of models, ethical issues, and resource limitations highlight how crucial it is to give predictive analytics solutions due thought and employ mitigation techniques. As we look to the future, we have investigated new trends and paths in AI-driven predictive analytics, ranging from democratizing AI via automation and AutoML platforms to developing AI algorithms and explainable AI approaches. To fully realize the potential of predictive analytics and maintain a competitive edge in the digital era, organizations must navigate this transformative landscape while embracing ethical AI principles, utilizing edge computing and IoT integration, and fostering a culture of continuous innovation. This chapter is essentially a revolutionary attempt for companies that want to employ data-driven insights to direct strategic choices and gain a competitive edge. Businesses may unleash the revolutionary power of predictive analytics and promote sustainable growth and innovation in the digital age by addressing ethical considerations, resource limits, data quality, and model interpretability. We are about to enter a new era marked by realizations powered by AI and data, yet we are far from fully realizing the potential of predictive analytics.

REFERENCES

Adewusi, A. O., Okoli, U. I., Adaga, E., Olorunsogo, T., Asuzu, O. F., & Daraojimba, D. O. (2024). Business intelligence in the era of big data: A review of analytical tools and competitive advantage. *Computer Science & IT Research Journal*, 5(2), 415–431. DOI: 10.51594/csitrj.v5i2.791

Bello, H. O., Ige, A. B., & Ameyaw, M. N. (2024). Adaptive machine learning models: concepts for real-time financial fraud prevention in dynamic environments. *World Journal of Advanced Engineering Technology and Sciences, 12*(2), 021-034.

Boutaba, R., Salahuddin, M. A., Limam, N., Ayoubi, S., Shahriar, N., Estrada-Solano, F., & Caicedo, O. M. (2018). A comprehensive survey on machine learning for networking: Evolution, applications and research opportunities. *Journal of Internet Services and Applications*, 9(1), 1–99. DOI: 10.1186/s13174-018-0087-2

Kansagara, D., Englander, H., Salanitro, A., Kagen, D., Theobald, C., Freeman, M., & Kripalani, S. (2011). Risk prediction models for hospital readmission: A systematic review. *Journal of the American Medical Association*, 306(15), 1688–1698. DOI: 10.1001/jama.2011.1515 PMID: 22009101

Keerthika, R., & Abinayaa, M. S. (Eds.). (2022). *Algorithms of Intelligence: Exploring the World of Machine Learning*. Inkbound Publishers. • Gao, L., Lu, P., & Ren, Y. (2021). A deep learning approach for imbalanced crash data in predicting highway-rail grade crossings accidents. *Reliability Engineering & System Safety*, 216, 108019.

L'heureux, A., Grolinger, K., Elyamany, H. F., & Capretz, M. A. (2017). Machine learning with big data: Challenges and approaches. *IEEE Access : Practical Innovations, Open Solutions*, 5, 7776–7797. DOI: 10.1109/ACCESS.2017.2696365

Moinuddin, M., Usman, M., & Khan, R. (2024). Strategic Insights in a Data-Driven Era: Maximizing Business Potential with Analytics and AI. *Revista Española de Documentación Científica*, 18(02), 117–133.

Osborne, J. W. (2012). *Best practices in data cleaning: A complete guide to everything you need to do before and after collecting your data*. Sage publications.

Pal, S., Kumari, K., Kadam, S., & Saha, A. (2023). *The ai revolution*. IARA Publication.

Paraman, P., & Anamalah, S. (2023). Ethical artificial intelligence framework for a good AI society: Principles, opportunities and perils. *AI & Society*, 38(2), 595–611. DOI: 10.1007/s00146-022-01458-3

Pillkahn, U. (2008). *Using trends and scenarios as tools for strategy development: shaping the future of your enterprise.* John Wiley & Sons.

Radosavljevik, D. (2017). *Applying data mining in telecommunications* (Doctoral dissertation, Leiden University).

Ray, P. P., Dash, D., & De, D. (2019). Edge computing for Internet of Things: A survey, e-healthcare case study and future direction. *Journal of Network and Computer Applications*, 140, 1–22. DOI: 10.1016/j.jnca.2019.05.005

Rodriguez-Galiano, V., Sanchez-Castillo, M., Chica-Olmo, M., & Chica-Rivas, M. J. O. G. R. (2015). Machine learning predictive models for mineral prospectivity: An evaluation of neural networks, random forest, regression trees and support vector machines. *Ore Geology Reviews*, 71, 804–818. DOI: 10.1016/j.oregeorev.2015.01.001

Suwarno, S., Fitria, F., & Azhar, R. (2023). Optimizing Budget Allocation: A Strategic Framework for Aligning Human Resource Investments with Financial Objectives and Business Goals. *Atestasi: Jurnal Ilmiah Akuntansi*, 6(2), 835–855. DOI: 10.57178/atestasi.v6i2.880

Chapter 4
DDM:
Data–Driven Marketing Using AI, ML, and Big Data

N. Nasurudeen Ahamed

Presidency University, India

S. Sridevi

Presidency University, India

ABSTRACT

To create a campaign blueprint, data-driven marketing optimizes client details. To comprehend our clients entails gathering complicated data through online and physical channels and evaluating it. Through the collection and analysis of information, advertisers create and execute highly customized advertising efforts. Digital advertising is an essential tool for advertising tactics because it's a great way to promote and sell products as well as raise brand knowledge and visibility. Even with the rise of online communities and networking sites, marketing through email remains the most popular way to educate, impact, and create business opportunities. Big Data is thought to revolutionize corporate intelligence, a discipline that depends on statistical analysis to gain understanding and improve making choices. Although the idea of big data is not exclusive to advertising or trade, the growth of e-commerce and online advertising has been crucial in raising awareness of the problem. These industries indeed produce enormous amounts of data by nature that need to be processed.

DOI: 10.4018/979-8-3693-8844-0.ch004

INTRODUCTION

Data-driven marketing (Rosário & Dias, 2023) is a strategic approach that utilizes information to refine and optimize marketing campaigns, resulting in more targeted and impactful efforts that drive business growth. This methodology involves collecting, analyzing, and interpreting data to understand target customer behaviors better. Marketers are employing various statistical techniques and State-of-the-art technologies like AI, ML, and BigData to transform data into valuable insights and make informed decisions in real time. These advancements are revolutionizing businesses' customer acquisition processes and enabling them to deliver personalized products and services. Additionally, AI tools can analyze competitors' campaign performance and uncover customer expectations, providing valuable insights for strategic planning. ML, a branch of AI, empowers computers to learn and adapt from data without explicit programming, enabling marketers to make data-driven decisions with greater agility and accuracy (Xing et al., 2023). The vast data landscape can be broadly divided into two main categories: structured and unstructured data.

Structured data is data of preformatted information, such as rows and columns, and can be easily stored and processed by computers. Examples of structured data include:

- Transaction Data: This includes data on sales, purchases, payments, and other financial transactions.
- Customer Data: Customer data encompassing personal details like name, address, contact information, and purchasing behavior.
- Product Data: This includes data on products' names, descriptions, prices, and specifications.

Unstructured data: Data that doesn't have a set structure and is difficult for computers to understand. Examples of unstructured data include:

- Text Data: Text can be documents, emails, blogs, social media posts, and chat logs.
- Image Data: Images can be photos, videos, and other visual content.
- Audio Data: This data type can be recordings of speeches, music, and other sounds.

In short, analyzing data is essential for making informed decisions, improving operations, and personalizing experiences. Data analysis will be increasingly important as data volume grows. In summary, the importance of data lies in its ability to provide valuable insights, inform decision-making, and drive improvements. Analyzing data enhances these benefits by extracting meaningful patterns and trends, leading to more effective strategies and outcomes. Artificial intelligence (AI) and machine learning (ML) are revolutionizing the marketing landscape, enabling businesses to harness data insights and personalize customer experiences. The automation revolution powered by AI and ML allows marketers to shift their focus from mundane tasks to high-impact strategies. AI and ML are transforming the marketing landscape by automating routine tasks and unlocking strategic opportunities. AI and ML are unlocking hidden patterns and trends in customer data, empowering marketers to understand customer preferences and behaviors. This data-driven (vom Scheidt & Staudt, 2024) approach enables personalized marketing campaigns that resonate with target audiences.

Data is crucial in various aspects of business, science, and decision-making for several reasons:

Knowledgeable Decision-Making

- Importance: Data provides the foundation for making informed and evidence-based decisions. It helps individuals and organizations understand current situations, identify patterns, and predict future trends.
- Benefits of Analysis: Analysing data allows for a deeper understanding of trends and patterns, enabling better decision-making and helping to identify the most effective strategies and solutions.

Performance Evaluation

- Importance: Data is essential for evaluating the performance of processes, projects, and individuals. It provides measurable metrics to assess success or areas for improvement.
- Benefits of Analysis: Data analysis can identify bottlenecks, inefficiencies, and areas of success. This information is valuable for continuous improvement and optimization.

Customer Understanding

- Importance: Understanding customer behavior and preferences is vital for businesses. Data helps in profiling and segmenting customers, leading to more targeted and effective marketing strategies.
- Benefits of Analysis: Analysing customer data allows businesses to tailor Customized solutions to cultivate customer delight and devotion, personal-

ized products, services, and marketing campaigns to nurture customer contentment and fidelity

Innovation and Research

- Importance: Data ignites innovation and research, driving discoveries, advancements, and new products across industries. Data is the fuel for progress, from scientific breakthroughs to technological leaps and groundbreaking products.
- Benefits of Analysis: Analysing data supports the identification of trends, gaps, and opportunities. It guides researchers and innovators in making breakthroughs and improvements.

Risk Management

- Importance: Data is crucial for assessing and managing risks. It helps identify potential challenges, vulnerabilities, and areas where proactive measures are necessary.
- Benefits of Analysis: Analysing risk-related data allows for the development of risk mitigation strategies. It helps in minimizing potential negative impacts on projects or businesses.

Strategic Planning

- Importance: Strategic planning requires a comprehensive understanding of the internal and external factors influencing an organization. Data provides the necessary insights for effective strategic decision-making.
- Benefits of Analysis: Data analysis supports the identification of strengths, weaknesses, opportunities, and threats (SWOT analysis). It aids in developing strategies that leverage strengths and address weaknesses.

LAYING THE GROUNDWORK FOR DATA-DRIVEN DECISIONS

The Evolution of Early Data Collection and Analysis

The seeds of data science were planted in the 1960s when the advent of powerful computers opened doors to new ways of analyzing data. This era focused on collecting and analyzing structured data, primarily from transactional systems and databases. Data visualization tools like histograms and scatter plots were employed to extract insights from these datasets.

1970s-1980s: Emergence of Data Warehousing and Business Intelligence

The 1970s and 1980s witnessed the rise of data warehousing, a centralized repository of integrated and cleansed data. This shift enabled businesses to analyze historical data patterns and trends, laying the foundation for business intelligence (BI) tools. BI dashboards, reports, and simulations gave managers actionable insights to enhance decision-making.

1990s-2000s: Advent of Data Mining and Predictive Analytics

The 1990s marked the introduction of data mining techniques, which allowed for extracting hidden patterns and relationships within large datasets. This era ushered in the concept of predictive analytics, enabling businesses to forecast trends, customer behavior, and sales performance.

2010s-Present: Rise of Big Data, Machine Learning, and Artificial Intelligence

An unprecedented data deluge unleashed by the digital revolution has ushered in the era of big data, forever altering our relationship with information. From social media to the Internet of Things, the 21st century's technological explosion has propelled us into the age of big data, where information volume, complexity, and velocity have reached unimaginable heights. To tackle this data deluge, machine learning and artificial intelligence (AI) have emerged as powerful data analysis and prediction tools. Machine learning algorithms can analyze data, uncover patterns, predict outcomes, and improve processes. AI (Schmitt, 2023), with its ability to mimic human intelligence, is further transforming data science, enabling businesses to automate tasks, personalize customer experiences, and make real-time decisions.

Integrating Data Science and Data Analytics into Modern Businesses

The explosion of data in today's world has made data science and analytics essential tools for businesses in all industries. By effectively leveraging these disciplines, organizations can gain a competitive edge, improve operational efficiency, and enhance customer satisfaction. Integrating data science and data analytics into modern businesses drives innovation, fosters growth, and shapes the future of business operations.

ARTIFICIAL INTELLIGENCE

Artificial intelligence (AI), the brainchild of computer science, seeks to breathe intelligence into machines, allowing them to perform tasks that once required human ingenuity (van Leeuwen & Koole, 2022). These machines can learn, adapt, understand, and respond to natural language. Artificial intelligence (AI) is no longer a futuristic concept; it's rapidly transforming industries across the globe, from healthcare and finance to transportation and manufacturing. AI is rapidly transforming data science and business management, bringing about a paradigm shift in how organizations operate. The potential applications of AI are expansive and immensely beneficial, encompassing enhanced decision-making accuracy and speed, reduced operational costs, improved customer experiences, and effective risk management. As AI Technology continues to mature, businesses will be empowered to harness its capabilities to optimize operations, streamline processes, and enhance efficiency, enabling them to maintain a competitive edge in the marketplace (Sarath et al., 2022). Integrating AI into data science and business management is revolutionizing the fabric of business operations. By empowering businesses to make informed decisions swiftly, optimize operations, reduce costs, enhance customer experiences, manage risk responsibly, and foster innovation, AI is ushering in a new era of organizational success (Zheng et al., 2023).

The Unfolding Story of AI: A Look Ahead

The field of Artificial Intelligence (AI) is ablaze with progress, constantly pushing the boundaries of what's possible. This rapid evolution promises a future filled with remarkable advancements, transforming our world in ways we can only begin to fathom. Imagine a world where AI seamlessly integrates into our daily lives, becoming a trusted partner in our homes, workplaces, and communities. Our capabilities are amplified through AI technology, allowing us to overcome limitations and achieve things previously thought unimaginable. Machines acquire the ability to think and act independently, leading to an era of collaboration and partnership between humans and intelligent systems. Automation reshapes the work landscape, necessitating a shift towards education and training programs that equip people with the skills needed for an AI-driven future. AI sparks a new wave of creativity, generating art, music, and literature that pushes boundaries and redefines artistic expression, as discussed in Figure 1.

AI in Action: Shaping Our World

- Healthcare: AI algorithms analyze medical data with exceptional accuracy, enabling early detection of diseases like cancer and heart disease, leading to better treatment outcomes.
- Finance: AI algorithms are on the lookout for fraudulent activity, working tirelessly to protect financial institutions and consumers from potential losses
- Education: AI personalizes learning experiences to individual needs and learning styles, ensuring students are engaged and challenged at their own pace.
- Entertainment: AI curates your entertainment experience. AI suggests content based on your preferences, from movies and music to podcasts and books, ensuring you discover new favorites.
- Gaming: AI creates more immersive and engaging gaming experiences through AI-powered characters and game mechanics, pushing the boundaries of interactive entertainment.

Figure 1. Applications of AI

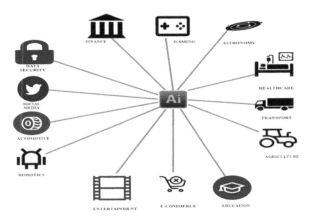

Navigating the Pitfalls of AI in Modern E-commerce

Despite the significant advancements and benefits that AI has brought to the e-commerce industry, there are also some potential drawbacks and challenges that need to be considered: Automation and AI-powered tools may lead to job displacement in certain areas of e-commerce, such as customer service, product categorization, and repetitive data entry tasks. This could raise concerns about job security and the need to reskill and upskill employees (Akter et al., 2023).

Artificial intelligence (AI) Algorithms, while powerful tools for analysis and prediction, are not immune to biases inherent in the data on which they are trained (Chen & Kamal, 2020). These biases can lead to unfair or discriminatory outcomes, perpetuating and amplifying existing inequalities. The black-box nature of many AI systems hinders our ability to comprehend their decision-making, raising concerns about trust and accountability. AI's complexity and opacity create barriers to understanding its reasoning, leading to potential biases and unforeseen consequences. This lack of transparency can raise concerns about fairness, accountability, and potential misuse.

AI relies on vast amounts of data, posing privacy risks if not handled responsibly. Data breaches or unauthorized access to sensitive customer information could severely affect businesses and customers. The development and use of AI in e-commerce raise ethical concerns surrounding the potential for manipulation, surveillance, and the erosion of human autonomy. (Krishna et al., 2018) Establishing ethical guidelines and principles to ensure responsible AI development and usage is crucial. While AI can automate many tasks, it is essential to maintain a balance between human and AI decision-making.

Human oversight and judgment are still crucial in customer empathy, complex decision-making, and creative problem-solving. Overdependence on AI-driven recommendations and personalization could limit customers' ability to explore and discover new products or services organically. It is important to strike a balance between AI-driven personalization and customer autonomy.

Just like a well-maintained car runs smoother and lasts longer, AI systems need ongoing care to stay accurate and effective. This can be a significant investment for businesses, especially for smaller organizations. Integrating AI into existing e-commerce platforms and infrastructure can be complex and challenging, requiring technical expertise and careful planning. AI could be misused for malicious purposes, such as spreading misinformation, creating fake reviews, or manipulating market prices. It is crucial to implement safeguards and monitoring systems to prevent such misuse.

How Artificial Intelligence Impacts E-commerce?

AI is rapidly (Collins et al., 2021) transforming the e-commerce landscape, playing a crucial role in the buying and selling experience. Its applications span various aspects of the e-commerce ecosystem, including:

- Product Recommendation: AI algorithms analyze customer behavior, search history, and purchase data to suggest relevant products based on their preferences.
- Personalized Pricing: In today's competitive landscape, businesses increasingly use AI-powered dynamic pricing models to optimize their pricing strategies.
- Fraud Detection: AI systems can detect and flag suspicious transactions to prevent fraudulent activities and protect customer data.
- Customer Relationship Management: AI chatbots can handle customer inquiries, resolve issues, and provide personalized support 24/7.
- Inventory Management: AI-assisted inventory forecasting optimizes stock levels to minimize stockouts and overstocking.
- Marketing Automation: AI-based marketing campaigns can target specific customer segments with personalized messages and promotions.

Example of AI in E-commerce: Product Recommendations

AI-powered product recommendations can significantly enhance the customer experience by displaying relevant and personalized product suggestions based on their past behavior, browsing history, and search queries. This tailored approach can increase customer engagement, encourage impulse purchases, and boost sales.

For instance, when a customer searches for "red sneakers," the e-commerce website can suggest similar products based on their preferences, such as "men's running shoes" or "women's high-top sneakers." This personalized approach can attract customers to products they might not have considered otherwise, leading to increased sales and customer satisfaction.

AI is revolutionizing the e-commerce landscape, offering businesses innovative tools to optimize their operations, enhance customer experiences, and expand their market reach. As AI technology continues to evolve, its impact on e-commerce is bound to grow, shaping the future of online shopping and the way businesses connect with their customers (Yaiprasert & Hidayanto, 2023).

MACHINE LEARNING: A JOURNEY FROM INCEPTION TO MAINSTREAM

Machine learning (Jabbar et al., 2020), the ability of machines to learn from data without explicit programming, has been around since the early 1950s. However, it was not until the 1990s that data-driven approaches became the foundation of machine learning. 1995-2005 witnessed a surge of interest in NLP and information retrieval. Neural networks, first introduced in 1957, came back in 2005, paving the way for deep learning advancements. AI and ML can be used at each stage of the data-driven marketing process (Xu et al., 2023). For example, AI can be used to:

- Collect Data: AI-powered chatbots can collect data from customers in a conversational way.
- Analyse Data: The power of AI and ML to unlock hidden patterns within data is transforming virtually every industry.
- Take Action: AI can be used to automate marketing tasks, such as email marketing and social media marketing.

The Roadblocks to Machine Learning Excellence: Addressing Key Challenges

Machine learning has witnessed its share of successes and failures. However, the near future (2-5 years) holds immense promise for this technology to gain mainstream adoption. To fuel this growth, certain factors need to be addressed:

- Data Availability: Access to large, high-quality datasets is crucial for training effective machine learning models.
- Computational Power: Machine learning algorithms demand significant computational resources. Continued advancements in hardware, such as GPUs and specialized AI chips, are essential.
- Talent and Expertise: The demand for skilled machine learning engineers and researchers far exceeds the supply. Educational institutions and industry must collaborate to bridge this gap.
- Ethics and Fairness: Machine learning algorithms must be developed and deployed responsibly, ensuring fairness, transparency, and accountability.
- Explainability: Machine learning models have permeated our lives, influencing everything from personalized recommendations to loan approvals. However, their complex inner workings often remain hidden, shrouded in a veil of obscurity. This lack of transparency, often referred to as the "black box problem," raises significant challenges and necessitates deeper understanding. Developing techniques to explain model behavior is crucial for building trust and acceptance.
- Integration with Existing Systems: Machine learning should seamlessly integrate with existing business processes and infrastructure to maximize its impact.
- Real-World Applications: Continuous development of practical applications that demonstrate the value of machine learning will drive adoption.

MACHINE LEARNING TECHNIQUES FOR DATA PROCESSING

Here are some common machine learning algorithms used for data analysis, categorized by their type:

Supervised Learning Algorithms

- Linear regression: Predicts a continuous numerical output based on one or more input features.
- Logistic regression: Predicts a binary categorical output (e.g., yes/no, spam/not spam) based on one or more input features.
- Decision trees: Create a tree-like structure to classify data points based on their features.
- Support vector machines (SVMs): Find an optimal hyperplane to separate data points into two classes.
- K-nearest neighbors (KNNs): Classify new data points based on their similarity to the k-nearest neighbors in the training data.
- Naive Bayes: Classifies data points based on the assumption that features are independent.
- Random forests: Combine multiple decision trees to improve classification accuracy.

Decision Tree Algorithms

A strategy that uses attributes to separate information into numerous groups for classification. Predicting future consumer behavior and identifying client tastes are two uses for this algorithm. It consists of a binary question sequence that divides the data based on established norms. The selection's result tree is a structure that resembles a tree, with each leaf node signifying the decision's outcome and each internal node signifying a separate option. It may be employed, for instance, to determine which consumers are likely to return or who are likely to order particular kinds of meals. These computations are used to find trends in consumer information and decide which tactics to apply for a certain advertising effort. For a given effort, algorithmic decision trees can be used to determine the most significant target demographic and the kinds of material and channels to deploy.

Naïve Bayes

This method uses likelihood to categorize information in a probabilistic manner. Forecasts about client behavior and preference identification can be done with this algorithm. It can be used, for instance, to determine which clients are most likely to order from specific eateries or particular food variations. Client information is classified using naïve Bayes techniques into different categories. These algorithms can be used to determine the best target demographic for a given effort, as well as the channels and content kinds that should be employed.

Based on Bayes' Theorem, Naïve Bayes is a statistical categorization method. The following Equation 1 is the logic of naïve Bayes:

$$P(X|Y) = P(Y|X) * P(X) / P(Y) \qquad (1)$$

Where,

- P(X|Y): the likelihood of event X in light of incident Y.
- P(Y|X): the likelihood of event Y in light of incident X.
- P(X): the likelihood of incident X.
- P(Y): the likelihood of incident Y.

The use of naïve Bayes in code languages is examined in this work. It looks into the popular method of categorizing and predicting data using a function.

Nearest Neighbors

A series of methods known as the nearest neighbors method is applied to informal regression and classification issues. Forecasts are also made with it, particularly in cases when the data is extremely diverse. The way the system operates is by grouping information items that are closest to one another, or "neighbors," collectively. Distances can be assessed in a variety of methods, such as categorically for classifying datasets and via a measurement of distance like Euclidean distance for quantitative records, depending on the type of information and the particular use case.

A particular area of interest can be found, and its k-closest neighbors can be found using the nearest neighbors technique. The statistic can then be classified according to the predictive result of its neighbors or the class labels of the k-nearest points.

This Equation 2 (formula) can be used to numerically illustrate the nearest neighbor principles:

$$B = 1/n \ (b1+b2+\ldots\ldots +bn) \qquad (2)$$

Where,

- bi: The Label for a Category of A1, A2......An Variables.
- A: The specified value in a set with characteristics.
- n: The amount of peers should be taken into account.
- A1,A2...An: The K Nearest Neighbors of A.
- b1,b2..bn: The Label for a Category of A1,A2......An.
- B: The Label for a Category of A.

To Examine the advantages of the nearest neighbor concept in coding. An in-depth tutorial is provided, with instructions on how to transform and regulate data as well as choose the appropriate distance measure.

Unsupervised Learning Algorithms

- K-means clustering: categorizes data points into groups based on their likeness.
- Hierarchical clustering: Hierarchical clustering builds a hierarchy of clusters based on data point similarity
- Anomaly detection: Identifies data points that deviate significantly from the normal patterns.
- Principal component analysis (PCA): It is a powerful technique for dimensionality reduction that helps simplify complex data by identifying the most informative features and discarding less relevant ones, making it easier to analyze and visualize.
- Independent component analysis (ICA): Decomposes multivariate data into independent components that represent hidden factors

Reinforcement Learning Algorithms

- Q-learning: Learns an optimal action-value function to maximize rewards.
- SARSA (State-Action-Reward-State-Action): Learns an optimal action-value function by updating it based on the experienced transition between states and actions.
- Deep Q-learning: Blends the strengths of Q-learning and deep neural networks to effectively manage complex, high-dimensional data
- Policy gradient methods: Policy gradients: Shape behavior directly for maximum reward.
- Actor-critic methods: Combine an actor network that learns the policy and a critic network that evaluates the policy.

DEEP LEARNING: A JOURNEY FROM INCEPTION TO UBIQUITY

Deep learning, a branch of machine learning (Jabbar et al., 2020), arose in 1965 with the pioneering work of Alexey Ivakhnenko and Valentin Lapa, who introduced statistically analyzed models using complex equations and polynomial activation functions. 1995 saw the development of a data similarity mapping method, followed by the establishment of LSTMs for RNNs in 1997. The late 90s ushered in processors with 1000x faster computational speeds. This breakthrough enabled the efficient processing of images by GPUs. The early 2000s saw advancements in pre-training techniques and improvements in LSTM. By 2011, the rapid growth in GPU speed allowed machines to work on convolutional neural networks (CNNs), eliminating the need for layer-by-layer pre-training. Today, deep learning has become indispensable for processing big data. Artificial intelligence (AI) and deep learning are continuously evolving, with new and sophisticated ideas emerging at a rapid pace. Deep learning algorithms are a powerful tool for data analysis and data processing. They can be used to identify patterns and trends in data that would be difficult or impossible to find with traditional methods. Deep learning algorithms are effective in various applications, including image recognition, natural language processing, and speech recognition.

Deep Learning Algorithms Used For Data Analysis And Data Processing

- Convolutional Neural Networks (CNNs): CNNs are a powerful type of deep learning algorithm specifically designed for image recognition tasks. They work by extracting key features from images, like edges, corners, and textures, and then using these features to classify the images.
- Recurrent Neural Networks (RNNs): RNNs are a powerful type of deep learning algorithm specifically designed for tasks involving sequential data, like natural language processing (NLP) and speech recognition. They process data one element at a time, maintaining an internal state that allows them to learn long-term dependencies within the data. This makes them particularly effective for various NLP tasks like Machine Translation, text summarization, and sentiment analysis.
- Deep Belief Networks (DBNs): DBNs, short for Deep Belief Networks, are a powerful type of deep learning algorithm specifically designed for unsupervised learning tasks.
- These tasks don't involve explicitly labeled data but focus on uncovering underlying patterns and structures within the data.

- Autoencoders: Autoencoders are a type of deep learning algorithm that excels in data compression and anomaly detection. They work by learning to compress the data into a lower-dimensional space and then reconstruct the original data from that compressed representation.

BIGDATA

The immense databases are commonly known as "big data" due to the rapid rise in worldwide information (Rahmani et al., 2021). Compared to regular databases, big data frequently contain enormous amounts of chaotic information that need more real-time processing. Large-scale data also brings new challenges, like managing and organizing vast amounts of data effectively and fresh chances to find hidden values. It also helps us understand beneath-the-surface elements more clearly.

Big data represent large volumes of information, but quantity is just one aspect. The three Vs—volume, variety, and velocity—have been used to characterize big data (Kenza et al., 2023).

- Volume: The primary characteristic of large-scale data is quantity, which is correlated with data volume.
- Velocity: "velocity" and "modification" describe the rates at which data arrive and change. Distributed processes with actual time and non-real-time features are needed for high-velocity information.
- Variety: Variability suggests that the information is not all of one kind. As innovation evolved, big data now originates from a wide range of origins and includes data that is unorganized, semi-organized, and structured.

Value, veracity, and validity were among the more important attributes that were later included when data utilization parameters were expanded, which processes data and stores internally using the Hadoop Distributed File System (HDFS). Conceptually speaking, Hadoop distinguishes between typical relational database management systems (RDBMS) and massive data repositories (NOSQL).

Hadoop

A layered framework called Hadoop was built and made available by the Apache Software Foundation for handling and storing enormous quantities of data. Unorganized sources of information are unable to be managed by conventional relational databases (RDBMS); in these kinds of situations, another kind of database, like Hadoop, is appropriate (Akter et al., 2022). According to Apache Hadoop, massive data sets are information that falls beyond the permissible range for typical systems to collect, handle, and process. Stated differently, this phrase refers to the ability to gather, preserve, control, evaluate, and analyze huge quantities of information that are beyond the scope of standard databases, including relational databases.

B2B Using Big Data

Gathering large amounts of information from many different places, including websites, social networks, and the Internet of Things, has enabled B2B (business-to-business) commercial marketing organizations to create structured marketing tactics via Internet display campaigns with an open mind. Marketing companies face difficulties when extracting and analyzing such vast records, especially when taking actions within and analyzing consequences for comparisons. Big files comprising unorganized and structured information that can be handled and examined are the core of big data. There are two types of data in a big data source: unstructured data, which makes up the majority, and structured data, which is ready for analytics talks detailed in Table 1 (Liu et al., 2022).

Table 1. Importance of Both Organized and Unorganized Information

	Organized Information	UnOrganized Information	The reward for B2B Marketing
Highlights	• Simple to look for • Simple to change	challenging to find and preserve	More information cannot be gathered and exploited for resource generation and decisions under any specification.
Keepsake	• Data Depots • Structured databases	• Data centers and Databases run on NoSQL	Various sources can provide information when alternative data collection methods are used.
Examples of case studies	Management of supply chains and warehousing	Social Media Platforms	Various databases make the distinctive creation of resources possible, ensuring that no two users can view an identical B2B communication.

Leveraging Big Data for E-commerce Success: A Transformative Approach

Big data analytics is not just about crunching numbers – it's about extracting hidden gems of knowledge from the vast ocean of data we generate daily. Imagine sifting through a mountain of sand to find a single precious pearl. That's essentially what big data analytics does, except it operates on a much larger scale and with far more valuable insights. It involves using advanced analytical techniques and technologies to process and extract meaningful information from massive datasets that are too large or complex for traditional data processing methods. Deep learning, machine learning, and big data significantly transform the e-commerce industry, enabling businesses to enhance customer experiences, optimize operations, and drive growth. With the explosion of data in the digital age, traditional data analysis and processing techniques are no longer sufficient. Big data techniques have emerged as a powerful way to handle large and complex datasets that are too big or too diverse for traditional methods (Cheng & Shiu, 2023).

Here are some of the most common big data techniques for data analysis and data processing:

Data Storage and Management

- Hadoop: Imagine having a massive library with books spanning across several buildings. This is analogous to a distributed file system, where data is distributed and stored across multiple machines. Instead of cramming everything onto one server, the load is shared, enabling the storage and processing of massive datasets.
- NoSQL Databases: Non-relational databases that are designed for storing and managing large and unstructured datasets. Some popular NoSQL databases include MongoDB, Cassandra, and HBase.
- Cloud Storage: Platforms like Amazon S3 and Microsoft Azure Blob Storage provide scalable and cost-effective storage for large data sets.

Data Ingestion and Extraction

- Data Pipelines: Automated processes that move data from various sources into a central repository for further analysis.
- ETL (Extract, Transform, Load): A process for extracting data from various sources, transforming it into a consistent format, and loading it into a target system.
- ELT (Extract, Load, Transform): A variant of ETL where the data is loaded into a target system before being transformed. This can benefit big data applications where the data is too large to be processed before loading.

Data Processing

- MapReduce: A programming model for processing large datasets in parallel across multiple machines.

- Spark: A unified analytics engine for large-scale data processing. It can be used for batch, stream, and machine learning.
- Flink: A distributed stream processing framework that can be used for real-time analytics

Big data analytics is used across various industries and applications, including E-commerce, also known as electronic commerce or online shopping, which refers to the buying and selling of goods and services through the Internet. E-commerce encompasses a wide range of activities, from browsing online catalogs to making purchases and completing transactions (Xiang & Xu, 2020) (Brewis et al., 2023). It has revolutionized the way businesses operate and consumers shop, offering convenience, accessibility, and a wider selection of products than traditional brick-and-mortar stores.

Large-Scale Data in Email Advertising

Email advertising is an advertising medium that enables businesses to use email campaigns to interact with their clients, consumers, and opportunities. User-facing transactions on the internet use Apache HBase for the processing of online transactions (OLTP) (Cadden et al., 2023). Email advertising difficulties can be divided into management, planning, and tracking.

Figure 2 follows the sections: Obtaining Information, Information Retrieval, and Solving Issues.

Figure 2. A Theoretical Foundation for Successful Email Advertising

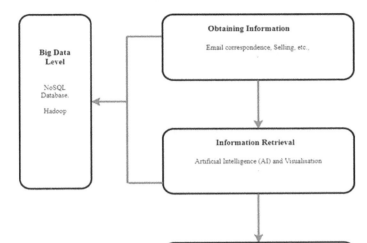

- Obtaining Information: Obtaining data is the initial and most crucial stage of applications for big data. It attempts to collect data that is organized and unorganized from numerous sources, such as impressions, accessibility, switching sides, buying, removing yourself, hours of operation, and various other sources of knowledge.
- Information Retrieval: In this phase, data is extracted, evaluated, integrated, processed, examined, and stored to extract crucial information. A range of analysis methods, including machine learning, visualization of data, and forecasting, can be applied to improve data understanding.
- Solving Issues: The collected data is ultimately transformed into actionable perceptions. The information obtained from several sources is utilized in this context to improve email advertising activity management, tracking, and prediction. Big Data is being used to improve immediate information for campaign results anticipating the future.

SUMMARY

Email marketing is a crucial channel for advertising tactics because it's an excellent instrument for sales and promotions and for raising brand awareness and visibility. The use of big data is thought to revolutionize enterprise intelligence, a discipline that depends on analyzing information to gain understanding and improve decision-making. Although the idea of big data is not exclusive to advertising or trade, the growth of e-commerce and online advertising has been crucial in raising awareness of the problem. These days, with companies accumulating large datasets, advertisers are employing machine learning (ML) more frequently to suggest appropriate material according to searches made through Google and other search engines while combining the most lucrative adverts next to the result pages. Additionally, ML changes marketing by enabling real-time autonomous automobile navigation and the automatic recognition and verification of human faces or a person's voice requests for Internet of Things equipment.

Benefits of Modern E-commerce for Customers

- Convenience: Shopping from anywhere, anytime, without the hassle of physical stores or travel.
- Wider Selection: Access to a vast array of products from a global marketplace, often exceeding what's available in local stores.
- Comparative Shopping: Easily compare prices and features of different products across multiple vendors.
- Personalized Recommendations: AI-powered systems can tailor product recommendations based on individual preferences and past purchases.
- 24/7 Customer Support: Online support channels are often available 24/7 to assist with orders, inquiries, or returns.

CONCLUSION

The term "virtual marketing" is frequently used to refer to any form of on-the-web, online, and mobile advertising. The use of digital technology, including software, computer hardware, and media for communication, is used by advertising to carry out its advertising tactics. Strategies for online marketing include documents, social networking advertising, optimization for search engines, market research, polls, and many forms of advertising. Any effective use of these technologies (AI, ML, Big Data) requires the use of marketing intelligence. To jointly filter the big data mining method, the Hadoop concurrent framework and the algorithm known as K-Means are used in the mining algorithm. These methods are then integrated into the marketing procedure. These techniques can suggest goods to consumers based on their past hobbies and those of other users who share these passions. The effects of AI, ML, and big data on email advertising initiatives were examined, and the methods, systems, and kinds of information used were noted. Thus, the theoretical structure for big data analytics-based email advertising strategies we have developed is an addition to this endeavor.

REFERENCES

Akter, S., Dwivedi, Y. K., Sajib, S., Biswas, K., Bandara, R. J., & Michael, K. (2022). Algorithmic bias in machine learning-based marketing models. *Journal of Business Research*, 144(February), 201–216. DOI: 10.1016/j.jbusres.2022.01.083

Akter, S., Sultana, S., Mariani, M., Wamba, S. F., Spanaki, K., & Dwivedi, Y. K. (2023). Advancing algorithmic bias management capabilities in AI-driven marketing analytics research. *Industrial Marketing Management, 114*(October 2022), 243–261. DOI: 10.1016/j.indmarman.2023.08.013

Brewis, C., Dibb, S., & Meadows, M. (2023). Leveraging big data for strategic marketing: A dynamic capabilities model for incumbent firms. *Technological Forecasting and Social Change*, 190(February), 122402. DOI: 10.1016/j.techfore.2023.122402

Cadden, T., Weerawardena, J., Cao, G., Duan, Y., & McIvor, R. (2023). Examining the role of big data and marketing analytics in SMEs innovation and competitive advantage: A knowledge integration perspective. *Journal of Business Research, 168*(October 2022), 114225. DOI: 10.1016/j.jbusres.2023.114225

Chen, K., & Kamal, A. E. (2020). *D s a i. June*, 10–11.

Cheng, C. C. J., & Shiu, E. C. (2023). The relative values of big data analytics versus traditional marketing analytics to firm innovation: An empirical study. *Information & Management*, 60(7), 103839. DOI: 10.1016/j.im.2023.103839

Collins, C., Dennehy, D., Conboy, K., & Mikalef, P. (2021). Artificial intelligence in information systems research: A systematic literature review and research agenda. *International Journal of Information Management, 60*(November 2020), 102383. DOI: 10.1016/j.ijinfomgt.2021.102383

Jabbar, A., Akhtar, P., & Dani, S. (2020). Real-time big data processing for instantaneous marketing decisions: A problematization approach. *Industrial Marketing Management, 90*(November 2018), 558–569. DOI: 10.1016/j.indmarman.2019.09.001

Kenza, B., Soumaya, O., & Mohamed, A. (2023). A Conceptual Framework using Big Data Analytics for Effective Email Marketing. *Procedia Computer Science*, 220, 1044–1050. DOI: 10.1016/j.procs.2023.03.146

Krishna, C. V., & Rohit, H. R., & Mohana. (2018). A review of artificial intelligence methods for data science and data analytics: Applications and research challenges. *Proceedings of the International Conference on I-SMAC (IoT in Social, Mobile, Analytics and Cloud), I-SMAC 2018, August 2018*, 591–594. DOI: 10.1109/I-SMAC.2018.8653670

Liu, Y., Cao, J., & Zhang, Q. (2022). The product marketing model of the economic zone by the sensor big data mining algorithm. *Sustainable Computing : Informatics and Systems*, 36(October), 100820. DOI: 10.1016/j.suscom.2022.100820

Rahmani, A. M., Azhir, E., Ali, S., Mohammadi, M., Ahmed, O. H., Ghafour, M. Y., Ahmed, S. H., & Hosseinzadeh, M. (2021). Artificial intelligence approaches and mechanisms for big data analytics: A systematic study. *PeerJ. Computer Science*, 7, 1–28. DOI: 10.7717/peerj-cs.488 PMID: 33954253

Rosário, A. T., & Dias, J. C. (2023). How has data-driven marketing evolved: Challenges and opportunities with emerging technologies. *International Journal of Information Management Data Insights*, 3(2), 100203. Advance online publication. DOI: 10.1016/j.jjimei.2023.100203

Sarath Kumar Boddu, R., Santoki, A. A., Khurana, S., Vitthal Koli, P., Rai, R., & Agrawal, A. (2022). An analysis to understand the role of machine learning, robotics and artificial intelligence in digital marketing. *Materials Today: Proceedings, 56*(xxxx), 2288–2292. DOI: 10.1016/j.matpr.2021.11.637

Schmitt, M. (2023). Automated machine learning: AI-driven decision making in business analytics. *Intelligent Systems with Applications*, 18(January), 200188. DOI: 10.1016/j.iswa.2023.200188

van Leeuwen, R., & Koole, G. (2022). Data-driven market segmentation in hospitality using unsupervised machine learning. *Machine Learning with Applications*, 10(March), 100414. DOI: 10.1016/j.mlwa.2022.100414

vom Scheidt, F., & Staudt, P. (2024). A data-driven Recommendation Tool for Sustainable Utility Service Bundles. *Applied Energy, 353*(PB), 122137. DOI: 10.1016/j.apenergy.2023.122137

Xiang, Z., & Xu, M. (2020). Dynamic game strategies of a two-stage remanufacturing closed-loop supply chain considering Big Data marketing, technological innovation and overconfidence. *Computers & Industrial Engineering*, 145(May), 106538. DOI: 10.1016/j.cie.2020.106538

Xing, P., Jiang, G., Zhao, X., & Wang, M. (2023). Quality effort strategies of video service supply chain considering fans preference and data-driven marketing under derived demand. *Electronic Commerce Research and Applications, 62*(October 2022), 101338. DOI: 10.1016/j.elerap.2023.101338

Xu, S., Tang, H., & Huang, Y. (2023). Inventory competition and quality improvement decisions in dual-channel supply chains with data-driven marketing. *Computers & Industrial Engineering*, 183(July), 109452. DOI: 10.1016/j.cie.2023.109452

Yaiprasert, C., & Hidayanto, A. N. (2023). AI-driven ensemble three machine learning to enhance digital marketing strategies in the food delivery business. *Intelligent Systems with Applications*, 18(April), 200235. DOI: 10.1016/j.iswa.2023.200235

Zheng, S., Yahya, Z., Wang, L., Zhang, R., & Hoshyar, A. N. (2023). Multiheaded deep learning chatbot for increasing production and marketing. *Information Processing & Management*, 60(5), 103446. DOI: 10.1016/j.ipm.2023.103446

Chapter 5
Enabling Hyper-Personalization in AI-Powered BI Systems:
Augmented Analytics

Prabavathy Kanagaraj
https://orcid.org/0009-0002-9287-2553
Sree Saraswathi Thyagaraja College, India

Samuel Chellathurai
https://orcid.org/0009-0001-2018-2900
Sree Saraswathi Thyagaraja College, India

ABSTRACT

The integration of Artificial Intelligence (AI) into Business Intelligence (BI) systems has become a game-changing tool for enterprises navigating the intricacies of a quickly changing digital ecosystem. Traditionally, business intelligence methods have concentrated on compiling and examining huge datasets in order to extract broad insights. The ability of artificial intelligence (AI) to drive hyper-personalization—which enables businesses to recognize and address the unique needs of each individual customer, employee, and stakeholder—will be crucial to the future of business intelligence (BI). This chapter offers to investigate the paradigm change toward hyper-personalization in AI-powered BI systems, focusing on the technology breakthroughs, trends, and future directions guiding this transformative journey. Augmented Analytics, a disruptive method that uses AI and machine learning algorithms, has emerged as a catalyst for enabling hyper-personalization in AI-powered Business Intelligence (BI) systems.

DOI: 10.4018/979-8-3693-8844-0.ch005

INTRODUCTION

In today's ever-changing business landscape, integrating Artificial Intelligence (AI) into Business Intelligence (BI) systems is becoming increasingly important. This integration reflects a paradigm shift in how companies collect, evaluate, and use data to inform decision-making processes. Traditional business intelligence approaches have generally focused on aggregating and analyzing massive datasets to get macro-level insights. However, with the arrival of AI, there is a great chance to move beyond these traditional techniques and toward hyper-personalization, in which firms may cater to the specific demands of individual consumers, employees, and stakeholders. Moreover, the integration of AI into BI systems enhances the capacity for real-time data processing and predictive analytics, allowing businesses to respond proactively to market changes and consumer behavior. The fusion of AI with emerging technologies such as blockchain is also poised to revolutionize BI systems by providing enhanced data security and transparency, further enabling trust in hyper-personalized solutions. It will examine the growing relevance of hyper-personalization as a competitive advantage, highlighting the necessity for AI-powered solutions to enable this level of customization.

This chapter's main goal is to investigate how improved data exploration and augmented analytics contribute to the hyper-personalization of AI-powered BI systems. Examining the idea of augmented analytics and its applications in business intelligence (BI)—such as automated insights generation, data preparation, pattern discovery, and actionable insights generation—as well as discussing the value of improved data discovery and exploration in revealing insightful information within complex datasets—using machine learning algorithms and data analysis tools—and examining real-world case studies and examples that illustrate the application of hyper-personalization in AI-powered BI systems—as well as highlighting the advantages and difficulties that organizations confront—are the main goals of this chapter explored by Chandrasekaran & Subramanian (2023). Through this exploration, the chapter aims to highlight the necessity for AI-powered solutions that enable this level of customization, paving the way for future advancements in BI that prioritize user-centric experiences.

THE EVOLUTION OF BUSINESS INTELLIGENCE (BI) SYSTEMS

Traditional BI Approaches

For information collection and analysis, traditional Business Intelligence (BI) techniques have traditionally depended on structured data sources like databases and spreadsheets. These systems usually require data Extraction, Transformation, and Loading (ETL) into a data mart or warehouse from several sources. Users can query and create reports using preset metrics and dimensions once the data has been centrally located. Figure 1 explicates the traditional approaches of BI. However, the increasing complexity and volume of data are challenging the scalability of these traditional methods, prompting a shift towards more advanced, AI-driven solutions. Furthermore, AI-powered BI systems facilitate the integration of external data sources, such as social media and IoT devices, expanding the scope of analysis and enabling more comprehensive decision-making frameworks. Traditional BI approaches, while effective for basic reporting and trend analysis, are often limited by their reliance on historical data and predefined queries, making it difficult to adapt to the rapidly changing business environment. Moreover, traditional BI systems often struggle with integrating unstructured data, such as text, images, and social media content, which are becoming increasingly important for comprehensive analysis and decision-making.

Figure 1. BI Approaches

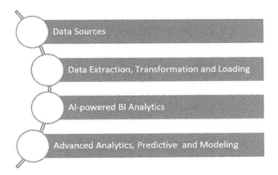

Emergence of AI-powered BI Systems

Wang et al., (2023) explore that the introduction of BI solutions driven by AI signifies a dramatic change in the way businesses use data to inform decisions. These systems use sophisticated analytics methods to extract insights from structured and unstructured data sources, such as machine learning, natural language processing, and predictive modeling. Moreover, advancements in AI, such as reinforcement learning, are enabling BI systems to not only predict outcomes but also optimize decision-making processes by learning from interactions with dynamic environments.

The Need for Hyper-Personalization

Deshpande & Ramaswamy (2023) explores that organizations are under more and more pressure to provide stakeholders, employees, and consumers with individualized experiences in the competitive landscape of today. By customizing interactions and recommendations to each user's unique tastes, behaviors, and situations, hyper-personalization goes beyond conventional segmentation strategies. Hyper-personalization is driven by AI-powered BI systems that can analyze vast amounts of data in real-time, allowing businesses to deliver tailored experiences that meet the specific needs and preferences of each individual.

Figure 2. Overview of Hyper-Personalization

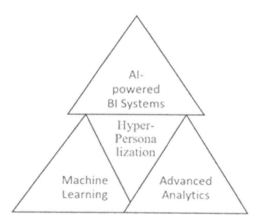

Hyper-personalization is made possible in large part by AI-powered BI systems, which analyze massive volumes of data to find patterns, trends, and insights that guide personalized suggestions and actions. Figure 2 explores the overview of

Hyper-Personalization. The ability to offer hyper-personalized experiences not only enhances customer satisfaction but also fosters loyalty and long-term engagement, providing businesses with a significant competitive advantage.

AUGMENTED ANALYTICS: ENABLING HYPER-PERSONALIZATION IN BI

Definition and Concept of Augmented Analytics

Deshpande & Ramaswamy (2023) explore that the term "augmented analytics" describes how BI systems' automation of data preparation, insight production, and visualization is done by the application of machine learning and natural language processing techniques. Through the automation of repetitive processes and the more efficient and intuitive surface of pertinent findings, this strategy seeks to augment the capabilities of human analysts. With the help of AI algorithms, augmented analytics can find patterns, correlations, and anomalies in massive datasets, giving users the ability to extract useful insights with little to no manual work. With the help of AI algorithms, augmented analytics can find patterns, correlations, and anomalies in massive datasets, giving users the ability to extract useful insights with little to no manual work.

Banaee et al., (2024) explore various data mining techniques and their applications in business intelligence, offering insights into how these methods can support augmented analytics. Additionally, augmented analytics enables continuous learning and adaptation, allowing BI systems to improve their accuracy and relevance over time by learning from new data inputs. This continuous improvement is crucial for maintaining the relevance of BI systems in a rapidly changing business environment, where new data and trends emerge constantly.

Gartner & Magar (2024) provide a comprehensive overview of current trends and future directions in augmented analytics and its implications for business intelligence. Figure 3 explains the Overview of Augmented Analytics.

Figure 3. Overview of Augmented Analytics

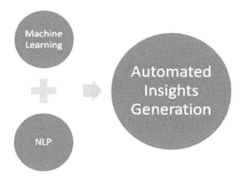

Applications of Augmented Analytics in BI

Augmented analytics has numerous applications across various stages of the BI workflow, including data preparation, analysis, and visualization. Some common applications include:

Automated Data Preparation: Reduce the time and effort needed for data preparation chores by automating the processes of data integration, cleansing, and transformation. This automation not only speeds up the data preparation process but also reduces the likelihood of errors, ensuring that the data used for analysis is accurate and reliable. Kim & Lee (2024) describe how AI-driven predictive analytics can be utilized to improve decision-making processes within business intelligence systems.

Insights Generation: To provide useful insights, machine learning algorithms can examine patterns and trends in data to find correlations, outliers, and predictive trends, among other things. These insights can then be used to inform strategic decisions, allowing businesses to respond more effectively to emerging trends and challenges.

Natural Language Querying: By employing conversational queries to communicate with BI systems, users may ask sophisticated inquiries in simple terms and explore data more easily thanks to natural language processing algorithms. This capability democratizes data access, allowing even non-technical users to engage with BI systems and extract valuable insights.

Smart Data Visualization: By dynamically recommending pertinent visualizations based on user choices and the underlying data, augmented analytics tools improve data exploration and decision-making. These visualizations can be customized to meet the specific needs of different users, ensuring that the insights generated are presented in a way that is both accessible and actionable.

Technological advancements in augmented analytics are driving innovation in the BI landscape, with several key trends shaping the future of this field. These trends include the integration of AI platforms, embedded analytics, explainable AI, and real-time analytics, all of which contribute to the growing importance of hyper-personalization in BI systems.

These trends include:

Integration with AI Platforms: Jha & Agrawal (2023) say that the Integration with AI Platforms: Access to advanced machine learning and natural language processing capabilities. This embedded approach enhances the relevance of the insights provided, as they are delivered within the context of the users' existing workflows, further promoting hyper-personalization. Nguyen & Kumar (2024) discusses ethical considerations in AI applications for business intelligence, focusing on privacy, bias, and transparency issues.

Embedded Analytics: Business apps like CRM and ERP systems that are integrated offer users instantaneous insights and suggestions integrated into their current operations. Ravi & Jain (2024) analyzes the integration of blockchain technology with AI in business intelligence systems, highlighting potential benefits and challenges.

Explainable AI: Let people know how insights are obtained and accept the advice given by augmented analytics systems by bringing transparency to the decision-making process. This transparency is particularly important as it builds trust in the AI systems, ensuring that the insights are not only actionable but also ethically and legally sound.

Real-time Analytics: The ability to process and analyze data in real-time is increasingly becoming a standard expectation, enabling organizations to make decisions swiftly in response to rapidly changing conditions. Moreover, real-time analytics combined with augmented analytics can drive hyper-personalization by enabling businesses to deliver tailored experiences instantaneously, enhancing customer satisfaction and loyalty. Sullivan & Patel (2024) Investigate the role of augmented analytics in enhancing data visualization techniques and improving the accessibility of insights.

UNDERSTANDING AUGMENTED ANALYTICS

Automated Insights Generation

Automatically identifying significant patterns, correlations, and anomalies in data through the use of machine learning algorithms is known as automated insights generation. The enormous volumes of data that these algorithms sort through provide insights that might not be immediately obvious through manual study. The enormous volumes of data that these algorithms sort through provide insights that might not be immediately obvious through manual study. With the help of automated insights generation, businesses may more quickly and effectively make informed decisions by streamlining the process of extracting actionable intelligence from data. Vazquez & Thompson (2024) review advanced machine learning techniques that enhance data exploration capabilities in business intelligence systems.

Preparing Data for Analysis

Data must be cleaned, combined, and formatted into an analysis-ready format to be ready for analysis. This process is streamlined by augmented analytics solutions, which use automation and machine learning techniques to cut down on the time and effort needed for data preparation operations. Organizations may guarantee data correctness, consistency, and dependability by automating data preparation, setting the stage for the creation of insightful information. This process is streamlined by augmented analytics solutions, which use automation and machine learning techniques to cut down on the time and effort needed for data preparation operations. White & Zheng (2024) explores and examines how real-time analytics, powered by AI, can enhance business agility and decision-making processes.

Discovering Patterns and Trends

To gain insights and guide decision-making, finding patterns and trends in data entails locating significant links and correlations. With the use of sophisticated algorithms, augmented analytics systems automatically detect patterns and trends in data, giving users the ability to spot undiscovered information and business prospects. Organizations may learn a great deal about consumer behavior, market dynamics, and operational effectiveness by looking for patterns and trends. Xu & Yang (2024) provides case studies and best practices on the application of AI and augmented analytics in enterprise business intelligence systems. Additionally, AI-driven data preparation tools can automatically detect and resolve inconsistencies in data, further enhancing the accuracy of the analyses conducted. Miller & Barton (2024) examine the concept of hyper-personalization and its influence on customer experience, offering practical insights for businesses looking to implement AI-powered BI solutions.

Generating Actionable Insights

Transforming data research results into practical suggestions and tactics is the process of creating actionable insights. This process is made easier by augmented analytics tools, which offer context-rich insights and suggestions derived from data-driven research. Organizations may improve business growth, make well-informed decisions, and streamline operations through the generation of actionable insights. Moreover, these insights can be delivered in a user-friendly format, such as dashboards or automated reports, ensuring that decision-makers at all levels can access and act upon them promptly. Furthermore, augmented analytics tools can simulate potential future trends based on historical data, providing predictive insights that can help organizations anticipate and plan for future market conditions.

PROPOSED ENHANCED DATA DISCOVERY AND EXPLORATION

Importance of Data Exploration in BI

The practice of examining and displaying data to find patterns, trends, and insights is known as data exploration. It is essential to Business Intelligence (BI) since it helps users comprehend their data more deeply and spot areas that might utilize analysis. Organizations can use data exploration to find hidden patterns, support theories, and create fresh viewpoints on their data. Additionally, the integration of AI-driven recommendation engines within data exploration tools allows users to receive tailored suggestions on potential areas of interest based on previous queries and interactions, enhancing the depth and efficiency of the exploration process. Moreover, data exploration tools equipped with AI capabilities can automatically suggest areas for deeper analysis, enabling users to uncover insights they might not have considered.

Leveraging Machine Learning Algorithms

Since machine learning algorithms automate analysis chores and find insights at scale, they are essential for improving data exploration. Large and complicated datasets can be analyzed by these algorithms to find patterns, anomalies, and trends that human analysis could miss. Organizations can more effectively find useful insights and streamline the data exploration process by utilizing machine learning techniques. Furthermore, the incorporation of reinforcement learning within BI systems is paving the way for more dynamic data exploration, where the system learns from user interactions and feedback to continuously refine its suggestions and analyses, leading to more accurate and relevant insights. Additionally, machine learning algorithms can continuously learn and adapt to new data inputs, ensuring that the insights they generate remain relevant as business conditions evolve.

Uncovering Valuable Insights in Complex Datasets

Analyzing data from several sources and dimensions to find significant patterns and relationships is necessary to extract insightful information from complicated datasets. Augmented analytics tools make use of sophisticated algorithms like t-SNE (t-distributed Stochastic Neighbor Embedding), which reduces the dimensionality of complex datasets while preserving local structures, allowing for intuitive exploration and understanding of high-dimensional data. These tools also make use of visualization techniques like XGBoost (Extreme Gradient Boosting), which combines the strengths of gradient boosting techniques with tree-based algorithms to achieve superior predictive performance. Moreover, the application of transfer learning in data exploration allows for the leveraging of pre-trained models on related tasks, significantly reducing the time and computational resources required to uncover valuable insights in new datasets. Organizations may make data-driven decisions and obtain a competitive edge by unearthing insightful information. Furthermore, the use of deep learning techniques in data exploration is gaining traction, as they can uncover even more complex patterns and relationships within datasets that were previously difficult to detect using traditional methods.

FUTURE DIRECTIONS AND CHALLENGES

Emerging Trends in AI-powered BI

Advances in natural language processing for conversational analytics, the fusion of AI with Internet of Things (IoT) data for real-time insights, and the application of augmented reality (AR) and virtual reality (VR) for immersive data visualization are some of the emerging themes in AI-powered Business Intelligence (BI). The future of AI-powered BI is also being shaped by the use of AI-driven decision automation and the emergence of Explainable AI (XAI) for transparency and trust. Moreover, the increasing incorporation of quantum computing into AI-powered BI systems is anticipated to revolutionize data processing capabilities, enabling the analysis of vast and complex datasets at unprecedented speeds. This could dramatically enhance the accuracy and depth of insights generated, particularly in areas requiring intensive computational resources, such as predictive analytics and real-time decision-making.

Additionally, the rise of edge computing is enabling AI-powered BI systems to process data closer to the source, reducing latency and improving the speed of insights generation, particularly in environments that require real-time decision-making.

Addressing Ethical and Privacy Concerns

Organizations must handle ethical and privacy issues related to data consumption and analysis as AI-powered BI solutions proliferate. This entails protecting the security and privacy of data, reducing bias in AI systems, and encouraging accountability and openness in the decision-making process. To solve these issues, putting in place strong data governance structures and following regulations are essential. Furthermore, there is a growing emphasis on developing AI systems that are explainable and interpretable, ensuring that decision-makers and stakeholders understand the reasoning behind AI-driven insights and actions. This is crucial for maintaining trust and transparency, especially in industries like finance and healthcare where decisions have significant ethical implications. Furthermore, the growing use of AI in BI necessitates the development of ethical frameworks that guide the design and deployment of these systems, ensuring that they are used in ways that benefit society while minimizing potential harm.

Overcoming Technical Challenges

The scalability and performance constraints of AI algorithms, data integration, interoperability problems, and the requirement for specialized knowledge in data science and AI are some of the technical obstacles facing AI-powered BI. Businesses need to make investments in technology that offers scalable AI solutions and enables smooth data integration. One approach to overcoming these challenges is the adoption of federated learning, which allows AI models to be trained across decentralized devices or servers while ensuring data privacy and reducing the need for large-scale data transfers. This can be particularly beneficial for organizations dealing with sensitive data or operating in highly regulated industries. Technical obstacles can also be addressed by providing personnel with training and development opportunities to advance their knowledge of AI and data analytics.

Moreover, the adoption of standardized data formats and open-source AI tools can help mitigate interoperability challenges, enabling organizations to more easily integrate AI-powered BI systems with their existing technology stack.

AI-driven Business Intelligence (BI) is changing due to augmented analytics and advanced data exploration, which enables enterprises to use data for hyper-personalization and well-informed decision-making. These ideas were examined in this chapter, along with their advantages and disadvantages, including new developments in the field, moral dilemmas, and technological difficulties. The ability of AI to spur innovation and corporate success through individualized insights will be crucial to the future of business intelligence (BI). As AI continues to evolve, the integration of multi-modal AI, which combines different types of data such as text, images, and video, is expected to further enhance BI systems, enabling a more holistic approach to data analysis and decision-making. To take advantage of these developments, companies need to make investments in reliable AI-powered BI platforms, set up solid data governance, deal with issues of bias and ethics, provide workers with AI and analytics training, and stay up to date with emerging technologies. By taking these actions, companies may fully utilize augmented analytics and promote long-term growth in a world where data is king.

REFERENCES

Banaee, H., Ahmed, M. U., & Loutfi, A. (2024). Data mining for business intelligence: A review and future directions. *Journal of Business Research*, 172, 29–47. DOI: 10.1016/j.jbusres.2024.01.015

Chandrasekaran, A., & Subramanian, N. (2023). Augmented analytics in business intelligence: A comprehensive review. *International Journal of Data Science and Analytics*, 7(2), 123–138.

Deshpande, S., & Ramaswamy, S. (2023). Enhanced data exploration techniques for AI-driven BI systems. *Journal of Business Analytics*, 6(1), 45–58.

Gartner, A., & Magar, R. (2024). The future of augmented analytics: Trends, challenges, and opportunities. *Gartner Research*. https://www.gartner.com/document/2024-Future-Augmented-Analytics

Jha, S., & Agrawal, S. (2023). Recent advances and future directions in AI-driven business intelligence. *Expert Systems with Applications*, 185, 115934.

Kim, Y., & Lee, J. (2024). AI-driven predictive analytics: Enhancing decision-making in business intelligence systems. *Journal of Forecasting*, 43(3), 273–288. DOI: 10.1002/for.2856

Miller, C., & Barton, T. (2024). Hyper-personalization and its impact on customer experience management. *Harvard Business Review*, 102(5), 56–65. https://hbr.org/2024/05/hyper-personalization-and-its-impact-on-customer-experience-management

Nguyen, T., & Kumar, V. (2024). Ethical AI in business intelligence: Addressing privacy and bias challenges. *AI and Ethics*, 12(1), 113–130. DOI: 10.1007/s43681-024-00001-5

Ravi, S., & Jain, A. (2024). Integration of blockchain technology with AI-powered BI systems: Benefits and challenges. *International Journal of Information Management*, 62, 102368. DOI: 10.1016/j.ijinfomgt.2024.102368

Sullivan, B., & Patel, R. (2024). Augmented analytics and the future of data visualization. *Data Visualization Journal*, 8(2), 89–104. DOI: 10.1016/j.datavis.2024.01.006

Vazquez, A., & Thompson, S. (2024). Machine learning techniques for advanced data exploration in BI systems. *Journal of Machine Learning Research*, 25(4), 1201–1219. https://jmlr.org/papers/volume25/vazquez24a/vazquez24a.pdf

Wang, Y., Li, X., & Chen, Z. (2023). Hyper-personalization in AI-powered BI systems: Challenges and opportunities. *IEEE Transactions on Knowledge and Data Engineering*, 35(4), 789–802.

White, D., & Zheng, J. (2024). The role of real-time analytics in driving business agility. *Business Analytics Review*, 15(3), 144–159. DOI: 10.1016/j.bar.2024.01.007

Xu, L., & Yang, Z. (2024). AI and augmented analytics in enterprise BI systems: Case studies and best practices. *Enterprise Information Systems*, 18(1), 23–40. DOI: 10.1080/17517575.2024.1912345

Zhang, L., Li, C., & Wang, J. (2023). Ethical considerations in AI-powered BI systems: A review. *Decision Support Systems*, 150, 113575.

Chapter 6
Personalization and Customer Relationship Management (CRM) in AI-Powered Business Intelligence

Abhishek Basak

VIT-AP University, India

Mousami Sanyal

VIT-AP University, India

Shirin Siraji

VIT-AP University, India

A. Manimaran

https://orcid.org/0000-0002-5671-9466

VIT-AP University, India

ABSTRACT

This chapter explores specifically how Customer Relationship Management (CRM) systems are embedded within a wider web of AI-driven BI systems employed in business. It starts with the basics: a definition, a description, and, most important of all, the value of CRM to present-day business strategies. The next part discusses theoretical frameworks that drive CRM and reveals the application of AI to improve the operational efficiency of both CRM and BI applications. The chapter continues the discussion of how AI facilitates advanced customer archetypes of engagement

DOI: 10.4018/979-8-3693-8844-0.ch006

with dynamic personalization and predictive analytics for customer churn. The empirical implementations are also highlighted concentrating on two or three types of useful machine learning algorithms and data mining techniques. Real-world case studies are discussed to provide practical examples of ways of using these technologies. Finally, the chapter lists current problems and challenges and it pinpoints the existing and potential future trends in customer relationship management.

INTRODUCTION

Personalization and Customer Relationship Management (CRM) have been recycled in AI-powered Business Intelligence (BI), which changes how businesses interact with customers and make strategic decisions based on the data. The Customer Relationship Management (CRM) approach centers around managing and optimizing customer interactions to increase customer satisfaction and retention and stimulate sales growth through customer personalization and targeted marketing efforts. The addition of AI into CRM today has paved the way for a brand-new way of personalized customer connection in a data-driven environment. AI algorithms look through customer data, like purchase history, browser behavior, and demographic data, to derive meaningful insights and customize interactions to people's tastes (Ledro et al., 2023). This kind of personalization allows businesses to provide precise content, product recommendations, and offers to customers, thus increasing customer engagement and loyalty. Artificial intelligence-driven CRM systems also make it possible to run predictive analytics that provide a more precise forecast of future tendencies and the behavior of customers.

But AI also has a downside. If a customer relationship is completely dependent on AI, it could destroy the emotional connection between the customer and the producer. Furthermore, data privacy and ethical issues about data utilization must be carefully considered to guarantee customer trust and agreement with regulations. Integrating AI capabilities with business CRM strategies will enable the exploration of new opportunities in business intelligence, such as customer relationships, satisfaction, and long-term growth.

Definition

So let us now understand. What is CRM? As the name suggests, Customer Relationship Management is the method that a lot of companies and businesses use to manage interactions with their customers. Nowadays, CRM uses artificial intelligence to make this interaction even better. CRM, along with all the state-of-the-art AI tools like machine learning, natural language processing, and predictive analytics, is used to analyze vast amounts of customer data and derive useful insights. This, in turn, helps companies understand customer needs and act accordingly.

Importance of AI in CRM

Now, a question may arise in our readers' minds. What is the need to integrate CRM with AI? It is with the various benefits that Artificial Intelligence in Customer Relationship Management provides the customers, which is astounding in changing how businesses manage customers (Ledro et al., 2023). It is not replacing human interaction, but making it more effective, which in turn leads to happier customers. Figure 1 elucidates how AI is beneficial as a CRM sales tool.

Figure 1. AI as a Beneficial Tool in CRM Sales

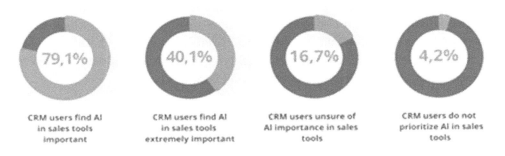

Now, let us look at some crucial needs that AI accomplishes within CRM.

- Enhanced Customer Insights: AI is a powerful and amazing tool that can handle tremendous amounts of data from different sources and spot patterns that may indicate, for example, the level of customer loyalty and satisfaction with the brand.
- Personalization at Scale: AI can now personalize the experience of potential customers by knowing what they like and do not like and recommending them products accordingly, which helps both the customer to get their favorite product and, in turn, increase the company's sales.
- Enhanced Customer Service: Nowadays, some questions that customers usually ask at first, like their name, address, and reason for calling, are all han-

dled by AI-powered chatbots and virtual assistants. This helps human staff to focus on more complex issues.

- Forecasting Future Sales: AI predictive algorithms are capable of analyzing future sales trends as well as records, helping companies know future sales trends and making forecasting more accurate. These data are not just for trend identification, but they also help give general advice, suggesting to companies where they should make better decisions for stock management, proper allocation of resources, and so on.
- Combating Customer Churn: Integrating AI with CRM offers a comprehensive approach to improving business operations and customer relationships. By leveraging AI's analytical and automation capabilities, businesses can gain deeper customer insights, personalize interactions, automate tasks, and make data-driven decisions, ultimately leading to increased sales, customer satisfaction, and growth.

Overview of AI-powered BI Systems

Let us now understand what AI-powered BI systems mean. AI-powered BI systems combine AI and conventional business intelligence tools, which helps companies gain advanced analytical features (Agarwal et al., 2021). They employ AI and machine learning technologies to analyze huge volumes of data, and based on their findings, data-driven decision-making becomes possible.

Data Integration and Preparation

AI-assisted BI systems can naturally combine data from different sources, such as internal databases, cloud applications, social media, and IoT devices. AI algorithms are being used to clean, preprocess, and transform the raw data into structured data ready for analysis.

Advanced Analytics

Including AI with BI leads to using very powerful analytical tools, such as machine learning, natural language processing, and predictive analysis, to uncover hidden trends, patterns, and relationships in the data. The advantage of using these tools is that companies can now predict future sales and performance of the company more accurately than they previously could.

Natural Language Processing (NLP)

NLP features enable interaction between a BI system and a user who may not need formal queries but can use natural language instead. AI-powered BI systems can understand and translate user queries, draw relevant conclusions, and showcase them in a readable format for non-technical users, making data analysis and interpretation easy.

Automated Insights and Recommendations

BI systems driven by AI are capable of determining insights, trends, and recommendations without human interference. These frameworks rely on machine learning models to pinpoint critical performance factors, detect anomalies, prompt corrective solutions, and guide smart business decisions (Das et al., 2023).

Data Visualization and Storytelling

AI-integrated business intelligence systems allow firms to generate interactive data visualizations and dashboards that envision information in an eye-catching way. These visualizations allow users to investigate data, identify information patterns, and impress stakeholders through data storytelling.

In conclusion, we can say that AI-powered BI systems help companies and organizations process their data fully using modern and more powerful analytics tools, leading to a better customer-company relationship ("AI in CRM: Benefits and use cases of AI-powered CRM system," 2023).

THEORETICAL FOUNDATIONS

Conceptual Framework of CRM

CRM implies a strategic approach that focuses on managing interactions with existing and new clients (see Figure 2 for details). Its conceptual framework includes several important components (Computer, 2023):

Figure 2. Conceptual Framework of Customer Relationship Management

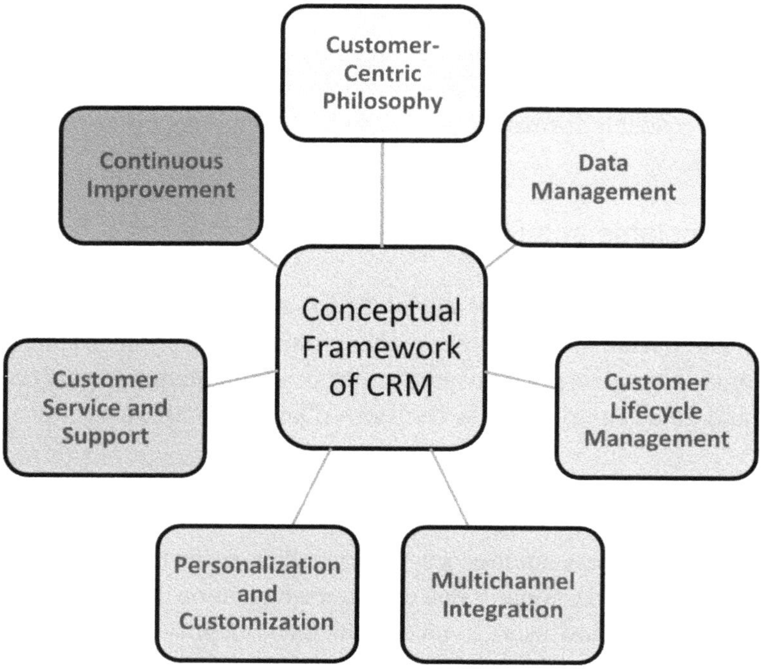

- Customer-Centric Philosophy: CRM begins with a customer-oriented attitude, where companies strive to gather and fulfill the expectations of their customers. This partnership encompasses long-term relationships of trust and loyalty.
- Data Management: CRM relies on comprehensive data management practices. Businesses aggregate, organize, and process data from a wide range of sources, including interactions with customers, transactions, demographics, and preferences, which helps them understand customer behavior and subsequently make correct decisions.
- Customer Lifecycle Management: A CRM considers the entire customer lifecycle, from prospecting and acquisition to retention and loyalty. Brands try to do their best to keep their companies happy, preventing them from going to other brands.
- Continuous Improvement: CRM is an evolving process that requires continuous data checking, assessment, and refinement. The enterprises collate the feedback from customers, monitor the metrics, and change their tactics to shift along business trends and customer needs.

Understanding AI in BI

Applications and Benefits

Figure 3. Applications and Benefits of Using AI in Business Intelligence

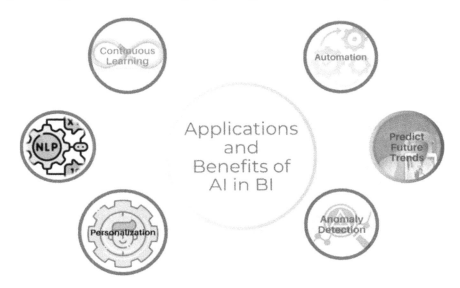

Artificial Intelligence is revolutionizing the field of Business Intelligence by combining traditional analytics capabilities with advanced algorithms and automation (Rane et al., 2023).

Predict Future Trends: AI-based BI leverages data processing technology to determine complicated patterns and trends using various machine learning algorithms that allow predictions, wherein organizations can forecast future outcomes using belonging history data and algorithms.

Natural Language Processing (NLP): AI makes use of building intelligence systems, which are NLP combined, to understand and interpret human language. With a dialogue-based user interface, not only can users interact with BI tools, but they also use more user-oriented information to extract valuable details from huge piles of data easily.

Personalization: AI creates a personalized BI experience that handles customized analytical outputs and recommended actions according to users' instances, duties, and goals. This way, the user not only gets the information but also makes the decision faster as he/she would only see the information that they want to see.

Figure 3 describes the applications and benefits of AI in BI. In summary, AI in BI offers a wide range of applications and benefits, including advanced analytics, predictive modeling, natural language processing, automation, personalization, anomaly detection, and continuous learning. By using the power of AI, businesses can unlock valuable insights from their data, drive informed decision-making, and gain a competitive edge in the marketplace.

PERSONALIZATION TECHNIQUES IN CRM

Personalization has become increasingly essential in modern business due to several key reasons:

Enhanced Customer Experience

Personalization is now the key to success. Businesses customize their products, services, and even interactions with customers following the preferences of individuals. Thus, customers get a more engaging and pleasant experience.

Improved Customer Engagement

Individualized communication will attract the client's attention and inspire them to participate more. This participation will bring the user to a higher conversion rate and even go further as it also gives sales and longer customer lifetime value.

Competitive Advantage

In a crowded market, personalization distinguishes businesses from their competitors by making it easy to remember the most special and targeted experiences. Companies that properly personalize their offerings have the edge in being able to individualize their offers, thus attracting many new customers and retaining the old ones more actively.

Thus, personalization is becoming a must-have module for contemporary companies' achievement of their targets of increasing customer engagement and sales depends on personalization.

Types of Personalization Techniques in CRM

Content Personalization

It involves tailoring the content of marketing materials, emails, websites, and other communication channels to match the interests, preferences, and behaviors of individual customers.

Product Personalization

It allows customers to customize products or services according to their preferences and requirements.

Communication Personalization

It focuses on delivering targeted messages and offers through various communication channels, such as email, social media, and mobile apps.

Experience Personalization

It encompasses the overall customer experience, including interactions with products, services, and brand touchpoints. Businesses can personalize the customer journey by offering personalized onboarding experiences, loyalty rewards, and customer service interactions tailored to individual needs and preferences.

Recommendation Personalization

It uses AI algorithms to analyze customer data and provide personalized product or content recommendations. These recommendations are based on factors such as past purchases, browsing history, and demographic information, aiming to improve the relevance and effectiveness of product suggestions.

By effectively implementing these personalization techniques, businesses can create more meaningful and engaging customer experiences, leading to increased satisfaction, loyalty, and revenue.

ROLE OF AI IN ENHANCING CRM CAPABILITIES

Integrating AI in CRM systems increases efficiency in customer interaction and relationship management across all boundaries. Here's how AI enhances CRM capabilities:

Data Analysis and Insights

Artificial intelligence (AI)-powered CRM systems are capable of analyzing massive user data from all platforms, which includes transactional data, social media conversations, and customer service tickets. Through machine learning algorithms, these systems make it possible to uncover significant insights about customers, such as their behavior, likes and dislikes, and attitude towards a product, which then helps businesses make data-driven decisions.

Predictive Analytics

AI enables predictive modeling in CRM, allowing businesses to forecast customer behavior and trends. By analyzing historical data, AI algorithms can predict customer churn, identify potential leads, and anticipate future buying patterns. This helps businesses proactively address customer needs, personalize marketing efforts, and optimize sales strategies.

Automated Customer Service

AI-powered chatbots and virtual assistants automate routine customer service tasks, such as answering frequently asked questions, resolving basic inquiries, and providing support 24/7. These AI-driven solutions enhance efficiency, reduce response times, and improve the overall customer service experience.

Natural Language Processing (NLP)

NLP capabilities allow AI-powered CRM systems to understand and interpret human language, enabling natural language interactions between customers and businesses. NLP enables sentiment analysis, text classification, and automated email responses, facilitating communication and customer engagement across various channels.

Customer Experience Optimization

AI increases CRM functionality by extracting customer information from interactions and feedback to improve customer experience. Through AI CRM systems, real-time monitoring of customer sentiment and behavior allows us to find gaps for improvement, personalize interactions, and enhance customer experience and loyalty (Venkateswaran, 2023).

CUSTOMER CHURN PREDICTION AND CRM

Client data being processed in large volumes without proper analysis remains the common cause of the problem (Senthilnayaki et al., 2021).

Thus, this calls for a predictive marketing approach where the most effective actions for each customer are proactively planned. On the other hand, understanding your clients from several life cycle stages can drop churn rates by up to 20% and develop more long-term and loyal customers. See Figure 4 for details.

Figure 4. Customer Churn Prediction

Importance of Predicting Customer Churn

Understanding what makes your top customers stay and offering customized incentives to ensure sustainability is a great way to reduce business costs and improve your long-term success (Ahmad et al., 2019).

How AI Enhances Churn Prediction within CRM

With the growing AI skill, it has become widespread for firms of any class to use large data analytics. Nonetheless, AI technologies can be applied to your customer data for automating and scaling churn prediction, which, in turn, makes churn prediction more practical and beneficial (Ramachandran, 2024). Figure 5 briefly describes the usage of AI in CRM.

Figure 5. Churn Prediction Enhancement using AI within CRM

Tools are in place to utilize this information appropriately. CDPs permit you to pull data from multiple sources, automate identity resolution, ensure data quality, and set up data management policies. Figure 6 shows how Generative AI will perform in the CRM market (Srivastava, 2024). Adding to that, comprehending that churn modeling is not the only component you have to include; you also need activation tools belonging to marketing, analytics, and others to transform AI predictions into proper actions targeted at the reduction of churn and protection of your revenue (White, 2017).

Figure 6. Generative AI in the CRM Market

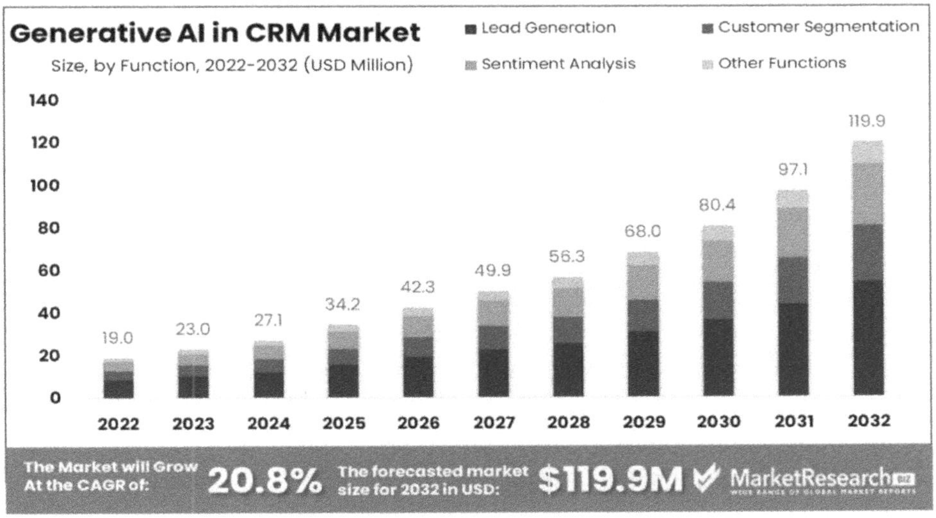

Generative AI in CRM Market

Size, by Function, 2022-2032 (USD Million)

■ Lead Generation   ■ Customer Segmentation
■ Sentiment Analysis   ▣ Other Functions

Values: 2022: 19.0, 2023: 23.0, 2024: 27.1, 2025: 34.2, 2026: 42.3, 2027: 49.9, 2028: 56.3, 2029: 68.0, 2030: 80.4, 2031: 97.1, 2032: 119.9

The Market will Grow At the CAGR of: **20.8%** The forecasted market size for 2032 in USD: **$119.9M** ✔ MarketResearch

You could do that immediately by building warning signs of churn into the CRM system to do their automation work and streamline retention initiatives.

AI-DRIVEN MARKETING STRATEGIES

What propels long-term business growth in the dynamic market ecosystem is how well you retain your customers and acquire new ones. In today's business world, companies are constantly launching efforts to comprehend and retain their customers, and in such circumstances, AI-based churn prediction is an essential tool. Figure 7 demonstrates the marketing strategies using AI.

Let us focus on the top six AI mechanisms for churn rate forecast and changes in consumer influence variables.

- Examine Involvement: AI systems are superb at analyzing contact patterns of clients over different touchpoints, including these. It involves the analysis of user behavior by intelligent machines like social media, E-commerce outlets, and Subscription Services.
- Identifying At-Risk Clients: Artificial intelligence algorithms are designed by looking into the smallest signals that predict probably customer retention.

129

An AI machine can guess about disengaged and grumbling clients by analyzing past data and client interactions.

- Notifies Disengaged Behavior: AI-based systems can watch clients' behavior without stopping and verify the disengagement. An example is Artificial Intelligence (AI) usage by e-commerce platforms to pinpoint prolonged idleness or the drop in user participation.
- Performs Predictive Analysis: With the advanced prediction possibilities of AI, businesses will be able to see churn scenarios ahead of time.
- Offers Actionable Insights: AI-built insights mean that firms now have the best information to develop retention strategies. One of the common uses of artificial intelligence is to evaluate the interests and behavior of the users, especially in subscription-based businesses.
- Facilitates Retention tactics: Artificial Intelligence becomes a propellant of the progressive nature of retention methods. A retailer can boost the opportunities for recurring business through AI-driven campaigns that are personalized based on customers' favorite features.

Utilizing AI for Targeted Marketing Campaigns

You might be one of 80% of CEOs who believe their customer service is good enough, but only 8% of their clients apply the same definition to their customer experience. That is why businesses employ AI solutions that can track clients' behavior, shorten the onboarding process, and supply services instantly. Figure 8 shows the benefits of using AI in Marketing.

Figure 8. AI in Marketing

AI In Marketing

Personalised customer experience | Better content and offers | Improved performance metrics | Increased productivity | Higher Revenue

Banks can predict what consumers will need as they plan for the coming year and will present them with products they never knew before. Moreover, a bank's knowledge about a client's 9-year-old boy can help customers grasp the importance of money and savings for their children's education in college.

Examples of successful AI-driven marketing initiatives

Individualized Method

Through AI, the company can determine customer loyalty using personalized data, such as purchase history and demographics. Thanks to modern tools, you will be able to predict which services will be in great demand within the near future and which clients are willing to increase certain items. Marketers can then identify some customers' leave-taking behaviors with others and exchange behaviors that will lengthen their customers' lifetime value.

Insight into Customer Behavior

Apart from that, providing AI better chances of accurate churn prediction needs personal consumer data. To achieve this goal, AI can allow users and clients to express their opinions on different issues, such as consultations' effectiveness, ease of site navigation, and purchase of desired items.

Recognize Your Social Clientele

It might be useful for you to find out what they follow on social media, whether it is products, services, or brands. The AI software can look into social media activities, consumer purchase habits, and advertising campaigns that engage them with customers. Social media brand promotion by businesses brings more benefits to them that way. It will allow you to get to know your clients better and create marketing activities with a higher success rate.

Effective Email Marketing

According to consumer behavior, predictive AI can be a powerful tool for creating tailor-made ads, emails, and social media posts. Through this method, marketers can have focused email campaigns with fewer resources and work. You can schedule messages, build customer groups, and send messages at scale if the AI tool has been linked with your CRM. Tailored email marketing, which focuses on certain consumer demands, guarantees that the strategy is efficient.

OPTIMIZING CUSTOMER ENGAGEMENT AND RETENTION

Businesses now have access to enormous datasets containing data about their customers at every stage of their lives, mostly because of tools like CRM and analytics software (Srivastava, 2024). When developing your customer churn prediction model with Amplitude Audiences and other technologies, this past data is essential. Figure 9 shows the important tactics that can be used to reduce customer churn (SuperOffice, 2024).

Figure 9. Tactics to Reduce Customer Churn

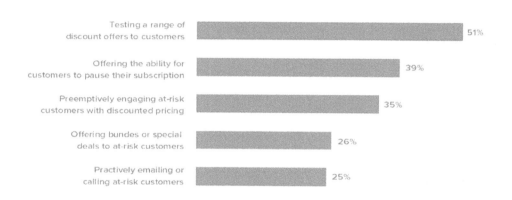

There are five stages you may take to construct your churn prediction model (SuperOffice, 2024).

Determine your churn prediction objectives.

- To achieve the best possible performance from your churn prediction model, the first decision you need to reach is about the purpose of the model.
- By pinpointing customers who will probably be less frequent, you will be able to avoid customer attrition.

Data Preparation

You can collect data from customers at every turn, whether from CRM, analytics tools, or when customers directly provide feedback to you. Obtaining useful customer data needed for analyzing and categorizing these data is the next phase in constructing your churn prediction model.

Utilizing Attributes

Represent and classify clients using feature engineering according to the attributes most likely cause them to leave. When talking about customer churn, there are five different kinds of features:

- Features of the customer: These reveal general population segments characterizing clients by such features as age, income, and education.
- Support features: These include mailboxes, the number of emails sent, the amount of time taken, and the achievement levels of the clients being solved after the solution.
- Usage features: These reveal a customer's personality when he/she uses your product or the service you provide.

Construct your Model

Binary classification, which puts your target variable in the position of either true or false, is the usual method of machine learning algorithms. It boils down to whether that feature assisted in the customer's departure or not. It will be interesting to see whether uninstalling the app from a user's phone mostly results in customer defection.

Keeping an eye on your model

Finally, the model can generate predictions when it is ready to go. With this aid, you can try running your model and recording the operational results. You can modify any of the aspects if necessary.

Strategies for Enhancing Customer Engagement through AI-powered CRM

AI assists customers with several touches throughout their journey. AI-powered CRM solutions use AI and Machine Learning technologies to deliver engaging experiences and relevant and timely communication. Figure 10 elucidates the benefits of using AI in CRM (Ahn et al., 2006).

Figure 10. The Benefits of using AI in CRM

The tremendous benefits of using AI in CRM

Enhanced Customer loyalty

Improved Content Discovery

Higher ROI

CRM

Increased Conversion Rates

Cost Saving

Reduced Customer Churn

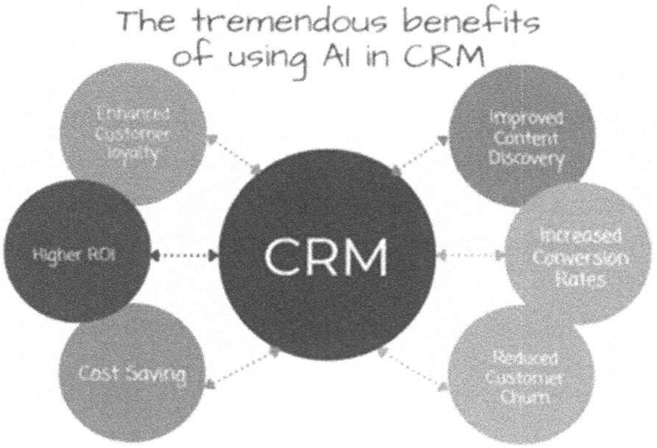

Tailored Correspondence

AI-based CRM systems help you get comprehensive information about your customers, like their preferences, behaviors, and purchase histories, by analyzing customer data.

Analytics Predictive

AI-enabled CRM systems feature predictive analysis tools to determine customer preferences and tendencies based on their past characteristics. Companies make customers feel good and loyal by addressing their needs in advance, solving problems before they become issues, and offering the right solutions or products when it matters most.

Skillful Automation

With the implementation of AI-fueled CRM systems to automate repetitive and boring tasks like data entry and lead qualifying, sales, and customer service, people can shift their attention to high-level activities such as sales and service.

Interaction Across Channels

Enterprises will have the opportunity to directly engage with customers via chat, email, social media, and phone, which is instilled with CRM systems' AI capabilities. Enterprises may bring omnichannel experiences to life when they unify their data from different sources and touchpoints to make room for the same level of interactions that customers demand across all types of channels.

Instantaneous Perceptions

AI-based CRM solutions enable companies to track engagement changes, find patterns, measure sentiment in real time, and provide real-time insights and reports for client contacts. A business's ability to gather and utilize such data instantly via analytics will help the business to shape any necessary modifications, take well-considered actions, and get the most out of the consumer-engaging tools.

Importance of Customer Retention and Its Relation to Personalized Experiences

Client satisfaction significantly affects the drastically important client retention. This reduces pressure on new buyer acquisition by boosting confidence in potential buyers as they are informed about your company and what you offer, satisfied with their products and overall experience, and proud of the company; they prefer to come back for updates (Khan & Iqbal, 2020). Figure 11 demonstrates the top reasons why customers churn.

Figure 11. Reasons why Customer Churn

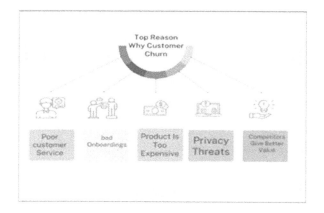

There are many reasons to prioritize client retention:

- To hold current consumers is five times less expensive than getting new ones.
- 60—70% of revenues are estimated from returning customers.
- Serving your current customer base prompts loyalty and positive word-of-mouth recommendations.
- The likelihood that existing clients would spend 30% more was far higher than for new customers.
- Profits and LCV lift proportionally with better client retention rates.

How is Customer Retention Measured?

Rate of customer retention

A comparison of the first size of your customer base at the beginning point and the last total number of customers (added new customers) will unveil your customer retention rate (CRR). You can use the formula given below to calculate the client retention rate.

$$\text{Customer Retention Rate} = \frac{\textbf{Total customers} - \textbf{New customers}}{\textbf{Initial customers}} \times 100$$

How is a Client Retention Plan Constructed?

However, how you devise a strategy for client retention will depend on your overall goals. In conclusion, following the three items below can enhance this plan. Figure 12 shows the customer retention statistics (White, 2017).

Figure 12. Customer Retention Statistics

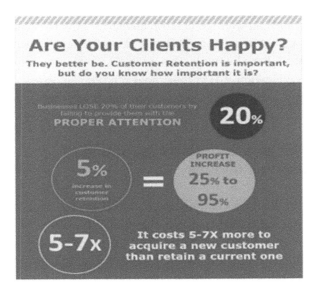

Step 1: Increasing pertinence: Make it more meaningful!

The purpose of all these marketing activities is to increase your productivity. Therefore, you should always have a strategy to broaden the outreach and grow brand awareness.

Step 2: Client opinions: Handled client comments

Being responsive to all the feedback you receive is one of the cornerstones of a customer retention strategy. Using tools such as questionnaires, surveys, customer service processes, and return policies.

Step 3: Providing incentives to clients: Offer incentives to clients

It is highly probable that making your loyalty rewards more creative and interesting will positively impact your customer retention strategy.

METHODOLOGIES FOR IMPLEMENTATION

Clients often churn an average of 30% annually. This is because it costs 5 to 10 times more to gain new customers than to keep current consumers happy and faithful. Subscription-based enterprise models like telecommunication, banking, insurance, private education, CRM (customer relationship management), etc., are all based on prior planned purchases and repeatable turnover revenue. From this, these types of businesses are defined by their retention strategies.

Overview of Machine Learning Algorithms and Data Mining Techniques

ML has grown to be the most common and well-explored technological procedure, which was not only developed but also applied to tackle the issue of client aggravation (Divinagracia & Randolph, 2024). It is one of those classic problems that are not replaceable, so firms have begun to buy new Business Intelligence (BI) apps that can predict unstable customers ahead of time (Chagas et al., 2018).

Likely self-evaluating measuring instruments, e.g., Decision trees, KNN, Linear regression, Naive Bayes, Neural Networks, SVM, XG boost, and others among them standing ready to clients churning in the market are the building units (Divinagracia & Randolph, 2024). Some potential churn prediction algorithms that identify the most important variables that affect the target variable are utilized in this study: Stochastic gradient booster (XGBoost), Random Forest, K-Nearest Neighbors, and Logistics Regression are some of the widely used Machine Learning algorithms (Iranmanesh et al., 2019).

How These Methodologies Are Applied in Personalized CRM

Machine learning can be applied to the CRM field by using several approaches to improve customer satisfaction and profitability. These are techniques of customer acquaintance, attraction, retention, and development. Furthermore, machine learning can be utilized to build up a catalog of customer questions sorted by labels, leading to quick and easy online customer service without the necessity of individual model training and maintenance (Suh, 2023).

The addition of automation and AI technology to CRM systems has strengthened them. For example, when launching a new product, artificial intelligence can understand consumer behavior and expectations. With AI-enabled CRM systems, companies can connect all such technologies and approaches into one platform to analyze, manage, and report on customer engagement. Hence, machine learning and artificial intelligence-based CRM systems bring about a rise in better customer experience (Sam et al., 2024).

CASE STUDIES AND EXAMPLES

AI is at the center of the technology development and shifting consumer preferences of the day, thus beating the challenge. The conversation turns to the fact that different businesses, driven by size, from large enterprises to micro or small businesses, use AI either specifically within or, in most cases, to refine CRM strategies. Through close case studies, we see the changing ways that AI can be designed to personalize customer interaction—from intelligent automation of routine tasks to intuitive omnichannel experience, predictive analytics, and diversified content generation (Faritha Banu et al., 2022). These applied instances verify AI-based CRM's enormous impact on customer acquisition, highlighting increased customer loyalty, satisfaction, and business development. Plunge into this investigation to unravel how AI has transformed CRM, enabling companies to sustain high-level connectivity with customers and remain competitive in the industry. We shall aim to spur and guide business owners to embrace new AI-driven CRM to get a new perspective on their interaction with customers (Byloli, 2023).

Salesforce

CRM, or customer relationship management solutions providing cloud software company Salesforce, headquartered in the US, was formed by the founders Marc Benioff and co-founders in 1999. It was a game changer, leveraging its cloud-based solutions. It is known for its centerpiece Salesforce CRM (Salesforce, 2024). It is a powerful tool for marketing automation, sales management, and customer support. The integration was also added to the platform that supports developers in building and deploying cloud app development. Further enhancements were made with the acquisition of Tableau for data visualization and MuleSoft for application integration. The key differentiator of Salesforce lies in its ability to continue to innovate by integrating technologies like AI to enhance its services and enable users to get deeper insights all the time.

Einstein GPT, the World's First Generative AI for CRM

Salesforce (NYSE: The AI has been growing in size over recent years, and now CRM), the largest CRM provider, has debuted Einstein GPT, the AI CRM platform, for the first time in the industry. The platform employs artificial intelligence to create sales, service, marketing, commerce, and IT content over sales, service, marketing, commerce and IT. Einstein GPT is a natural language processing (NLP) solution by Salesforce that draws insight from Salesforce's Data Cloud and adopts AI technology like OpenAI to strengthen customer engagement. Figure 13 describes how Einstein GPT transforms Customer Engagement. Customers can generate customized emails, chat with customers, and create other marketing content. They can also build code by synchronizing with OpenAI's models and engaging with external AI systems. Thanks to integration with top Salesforce tools like Tableau, MuleSoft, and Slack, Einstein GPT shows the evolution, in the words of the CEO of Salesforce, Mr. Marc Benioff.

Figure 13. The Process by which Einstein GPT transforms Customer Engagement

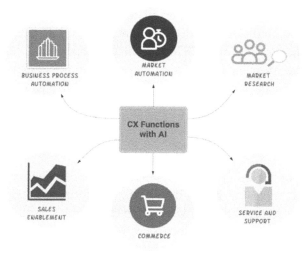

Algorithm behind Einstein GPT

The GPT of Salesforce's Einstein employs transformers architecture, which is suitable especially for text processing and sequential data handling. It starts with deep learning on extensive and diverse text data as an initial step to build the foundations of Natural Language. Following that, it is fine-tuned with CRM-specific datasets, like customer interaction logs and support logs, which help the model to become capable of standing in CRM situations.

In a practical scenario, the Einstein GPT is capable of real-time data analysis across Salesforce CRM to provide just-in-time recommendations as well as automated actions that are relevant to the specific context. This allows for immediate engagement when predicting consumer needs and making individualized conversations.

Furthermore, Salesforce could develop task-specific systems for use in numerous CRM functions, such as accurate customer sentiment analysis or lead scoring prediction. This also utilizes on-the-go learning strategies as it refreshes the knowledge base by adding new data that keeps it in line with evolving consumer behavior. This bias towards the narrowly specialized models, alongside the continued learning cycle, leads to the comprehensive functionality of Einstein GPT for automation and AI development inside CRM systems. Figure 14 gives us the appropriate flowchart for the understanding of the algorithm.

Figure 14. Algorithm Behind the Working of Einstein GPT

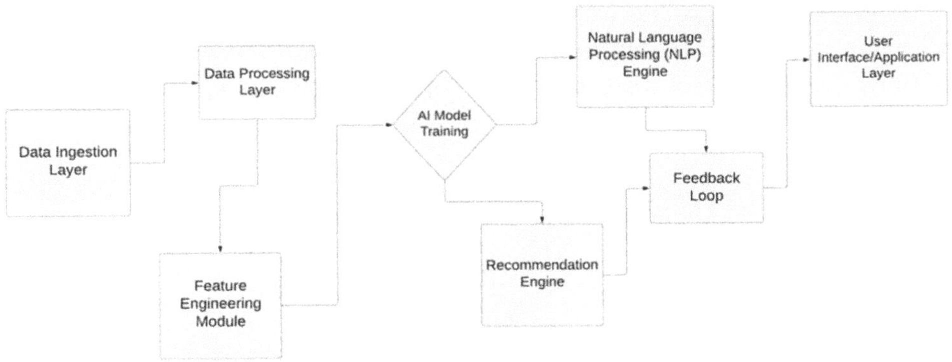

HubSpot

The American software company Hubspot was established in 2006 by Brian Halligan and Dharmesh Shah. It provides a comprehensive suite of resources for inbound marketing, sales, and customer service. The company's CRM platform is top-notch because it offers a one-stop shop for customers and marketing, sales, and service activities. In addition, HubSpot enables social media marketing, helps analyze visitors, and optimizes the website for search engines, thus applying inbound marketing methods with the exclusion of typical outbound ways. Moreover, Hub-

Spot presents up-to-date educational materials, such as writing blogs, resourceful courses, and certifications, to ensure users have a better understanding of the current marketing trends and techniques.

ChatSpot

ChatSpot's integration into HubSpot's CRM system becomes a booster factor because it allows customers to have an interface that resembles more natural communication. Unlike the most complicated user interfaces, ChatSpot is a virtual assistant that converses with the user through simple chats during email creation, adding contacts, or even generating reports. The advantage here is that the operation is streamlined, the learning curve minimized, and productivity enhanced in a process that reduces the hustle of business people (MakeWebBetter, 2023).

AI services such as ChatSpot can help accomplish this by improving the understanding of user intention through activated smart interactions over time. This degree of adaptability allows the CRM to provide tailor-made assistance and recommendations, making it advanced and usable. Lastly, ChatSpot does an excellent job of making CRM systems user-friendly, meaning that they are more accessible by listening to the needs of businesses that are changing with current trends. Figure 15 depicts one example of what HubSpot's AI-powered CRM tool, ChatSpot, means for Digital Marketing Educators.

Figure 15. ChatSpot's Impact on Digital Marketing Educators

Algorithm behind ChatSpot

The main functional part of HubSpot's ChatSpot, which merges chat-based biddings into the CRM area, is based on ML and NLP algorithms with the help of AI. NLU plays a pivotal role in the process. It is where the system's comprehension skills work; this includes interpreting the user input to figure out the intent and all the necessary entities like names, dates, or specific instructions. This was previously operated by dialogue management, which coordinates the middle of the conversation, determines the correct next step, and determines whether that involves additional information, a command, or a query. Think of applications such as sending emails, adding contacts, or generating reports to provide the CRM behind the interface, with the backend services being called with API requests to perform such specific CRM tasks. As soon as the system has performed the task, its ability to generate natural language (NLG) comes into play so that the user is informed about the results or upcoming activities. Continue iterative training, which applies machine learning algorithms to optimize the ability to process and answer users' questions in a thorough manner that becomes more accurate with every learning experience for translation and habituating the intended response. The flowchart in Figure 16 shows the algorithm behind ChatSpot's working.

Figure 16. The Algorithm behind the Working of ChatSpot

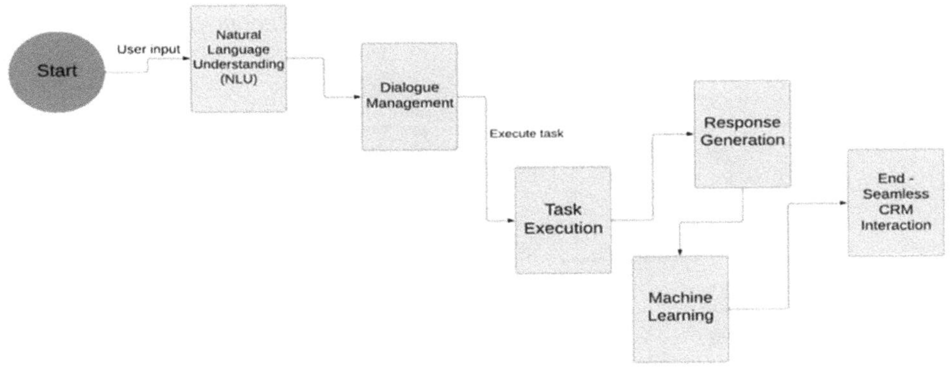

Netflix

Netflix is a streaming platform that caters to a wide collection of TV shows, movies, animations, pictures, and services on thousands of internet-connected devices. Netflix started 1997 as a mail-in DVD rental service by Mr. Reed Hastings and Mr. Mark Randolph in Scotts Valley, California. It eventually switched to a streaming platform in 2007.

Netflix is viewed by many as a provider of comprehensive media content that is distributed online over the Internet, and it has a wide range of original programs, which include series, movies, and documentaries. The site is accessible under a pay subscription model in which users can afford to pay the monthly fee and access the platform's content without commercial ads (Blog, 2024).

Personalization is one of Netflix's features that distinguish it from its competitors through its commitment to making the viewing experience smarter by using sophisticated algorithms and analytical tools. Implementing such features is based on the target audience's viewing habits and personal preferences; this helps boost user engagement by supplying the most relevant content for each viewer (Blog, 2024).

Further, Netflix also covers the worldwide market by providing its services in over 190 countries, though the amount of content accessible is usually dependent on licensing agreements, and the same shows that are available in one country may no longer be accessible in another country. See Figure 17 for further details.

Figure 17. How Netflix Manages User Management and Recommendation

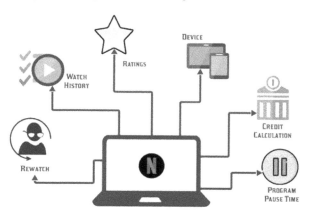

Algorithm behind AI-powered CRM by Netflix

Netflix leverages AI and machine learning technologies to drive the content recommendation system to a higher level. Users are given a tremendously personalized viewing experience.

The collaborative filtering method, which is the basis of the Netflix recommendation engine, is built around user input and preferences. It does forecast user appreciation, which is the presentation patterns of a lot of users with almost identical interests. The system is, in essence, analyzing the likes and dislikes of this massive user base. From this information, it discovers a list of movies or shows likely to be enjoyed by a user based on the experiences of other users with similar tastes. By way of instance, if many of the users who liked a given series also appreciated other sets of films, there is a likelihood that users would be recommended the other movies that they would potentially enjoy (Blog, 2024).

Besides collaborative filtering, Netflix also integrates content-based filtering strategies. This type of analysis consists not only of mapping the content features, which can include genre, cast, and year of release, for subsequent inferences. Thus, assuming that a particular user consistently watches comedies, the system is biased to suggest new ones. This technique selectively sharpens the recommendations and relates them with the content features that nurture the user.

One of the most prominent features of Netflix's data management system is the ability to identify and analyze huge quantities of data generated by millions of users using machine learning models. Therefore, these models were designed to learn continually and improve from some gathered data related to a user, increasing the predictive accuracy with time. This information is composed not only of what was watched but also contextual and interactive data like when they are watching, pause times, skips, and so on. One example is the amount of data they get from profiling, which enables them to understand users' preferences at a higher level, hence leading to improved personalized recommendations. Following this issue, Netflix implements A/B testing so that the algorithms can correctly make the recommendations. The technique used here involves targeting reform groups exposed to various recommendation algorithms, demonstrating the additional option of satisfied users and engagement. The networks referenced in the experiments allow Netflix to develop iteratively techniques to select the ones that best improve viewers' experience.

Netflix also adds skilled deep-learning methodologies and neural networks to its program. Additionally, the applications of these technologies obtain data patterns and complex interconnections that would not have been noticed by classic statistical models. This reflects that Netflix is a platform that provides deeply personalized and highly granular recommendations. For instance, deep learning enables a very accurate and subtle representation of the user behavior profile and preferences, resulting in more accurate personalized recommendation systems.

In addition to making sure that a subscriber's preferences in the content they are looking for are matched with the films and shows, Netflix also gives such users a chance to discover content that they wouldn't have thought of in the first place to enlarge their tastes. Tech advances are core to Netflix's dramatic effort to provide the best customer experience possible and build user engagement, dreams, and commitment through innovation. Figure 18 gives a detailed description of the algorithm behind the Netflix recommendation system.

Figure 18. Working behind Netflix's Recommendation System

146

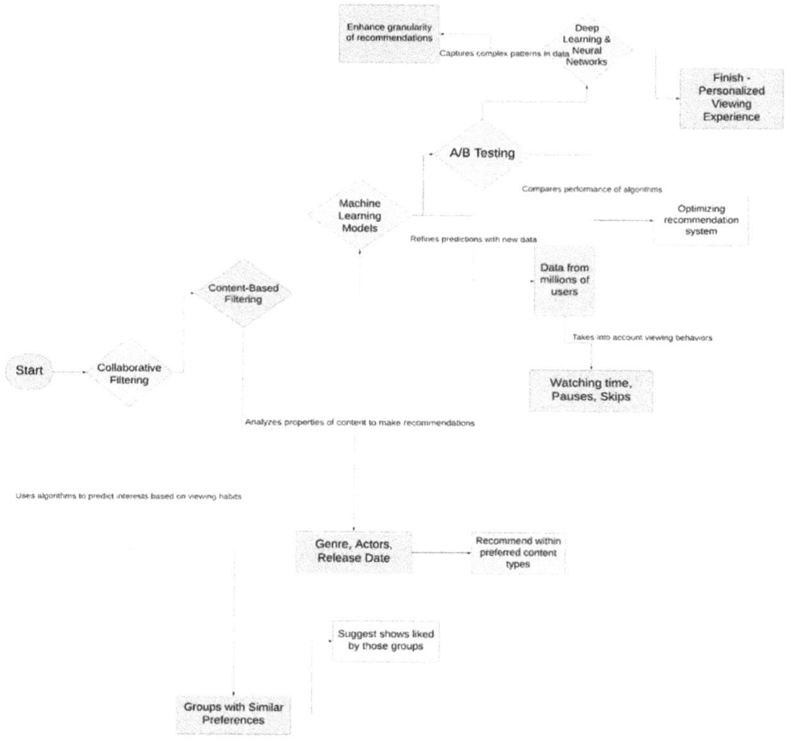

CHALLENGES AND OPPORTUNITIES

Challenges

Integrating the marketing of the company with personalized CRM strategies carries many important challenges, such as data integration, data quality, privacy compliance, technological infrastructure, change management, and scalability (Zwingmann, 2022).

One of the central problems here is related to the unification of various data sources (sales orders, client communications, social platform interactions, and third-party data) within one BI system. The difficulty comes from the variant data formats, inconsistencies with the multiple sources, and the huge quantity of data. On the other hand, the question of having high data quality cannot be overlooked. False inputs in the form of unaccounted values, incorrect entries, and multiple records could make a big difference in a CRM activity, affecting the ability to make inaccurate decisions and strategies. Figure 20 deals with the challenges involved with CRM implementation (Suresh et al., 2023).

Such privacy rules as the General Data Protection Regulation (GDPR) and the California Consumer Privacy Act (CCPA) present many difficult problems. These regulations force the application of laws that strictly control information use and customer data management, limiting how data may be handled and, therefore, requiring detailed data governance plans to be enforced as well as continuing to provide customized services.

Technologically speaking, custom CRM strategy deployment requires the use of complex BI instruments, not only software such as AI and machine learning algorithms. Implementing these innovatory technologies requires disbursements of substantial funds and may be partially thwarted by the lack of compatibility. Not only that, but the transition to implementing new technologies may require a major turnover in business processes and organizational culture. Resistance from the employees, missing expertise, and ongoing training are the additional challenges to be solved during the transition to digital technology.

Furthermore, CRM systems must be elastic, rapid, and consistently data-driven to deliver customized experiences in real-time or near real-time. However, precisely the fact that a modern CRM system has to process high volumes of data quickly and effectively still seems to be one of the most challenging problems (Kumar & Reinartz, 2018). The complex systems behind this involve a lot of infrastructure and cutting-edge technology to ensure that the degree of personalization and quick response time associated with these interactions is achieved satisfactorily. Figure 19 gives us a summary of the challenges that lie behind the implementation of CRM.

Figure 19. Challenges in CRM Implementation

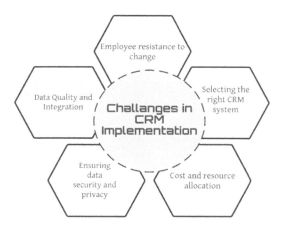

Opportunities

Seamless integration of Customer Relationship Management (CRM) with Business Intelligence (BI) programs is intended to foster many facets of corporate management and customer relationships. Another major benefit is aggregating important information about a consumer. The deployed advanced analytics inside the all-integrated CRM and BI platform will enable organizations to gain a more comprehensive view of what types of activities customers are doing, what aspects of the products they prefer, and what is happening across the market. The customer experience is more responsive thanks to the higher intelligence of the technology, which facilitates more sophisticated and effective targeting and tailoring of these experiences. This results in more powerful and personalized interactions.

Hence, based on integrated and pooled data, this individualized connection significantly amplifies the customers' involvement with and satisfaction levels. Customers feel unique and well-understood, which makes them factor in their long-term value for the company, emphasizes their loyalty and helps them do business repeatedly. With the focus on this high degree of personalization and engagement, this brand will have an edge over competitors and be a formidable factor in competition (Alnofeli et al., 2023).

It comes to operation as well; this system of automation and customization makes the most of the existing business assets. By eliminating labor-gorging tasks and timely detection of clients' demands, the efficiency of companies' operations can be boosted by automating official communications and proactively predicting customer needs.

Also, innovation, as an outcome of the difficulty of ensuring that CRM and BI systems can integrate, could be used as a trigger. The necessity to overcome concerns related to data integration, privacy protection, and technology adaptation drives new development of means necessary to achieve that goal. Businesses today are motivated by the desire for innovation, and this drive, in turn, improves their existing capabilities as they venture into new areas that meet and exceed customers' expectations (Torggler, 2008).

Bifurcating integrated CRM strategies in the context of a BI environment boosts productivity while cultivating a noted paradigm of innovation and customer-centricity is probably one of the main factors for sustainable success.

FUTURE DIRECTIONS

Emerging Trends in Personalized CRM with AI-powered BI

Concerning the customer relationship management (CRM) area, the gambling of AI predictive analytics in the future of business-customer engagement no longer remains a possibility but a certainty. Besides, these insights are based on AI and let businesses know types of customer behavior, buying patterns, and possible abandonment. Thus, they can be ready to provide necessary services at the right time. Through this, marketers can customize their strategies to the needs of the individual customers while at the same time improving the efficiency and comfort of the customer journey, all of which end up impacting customer retention and satisfaction positively (Dyche, 2002).

Subsequently, the essential role of AI-empowered chatbots and virtual assistants for CRM systems in accelerating the delivery of prompt customer service cannot be underrated. They use natural language processing (NLP) to understand and respond to customers' requests, whether composed in simple words or in a written style, to ensure instant and personalized customer service. This seizes customer attention and increases overall satisfaction by furnishing clients with timely and precise responses.

Likewise, AI assists in sentiment analysis, which is another important CRM application. The analyzed data from various platforms, including social networks and direct feedback channels, allow AI to evaluate their readers' or listeners' sentiments and attitudes regarding their products or services. Such revelation makes it possible for companies to have a finer-grain plan of action, connecting with customers deeper and closer to what they expect from a specific product(Ang & Buttle, 2006). Figure 20 perfectly depicts the flowchart describing the future of CRM.

Not only does he endorse the communist ideology, but he also advocates for revolutionary violence as the means to achieve it. He portrays the war as a necessary step towards establishing a more just and equitable society. There is nothing more personalized than making recommendations to customers based on their past behavior, preferences, or real-time interactions, providing the customer with the most relevant piece of content and will be more excited (Nguyen et al., 2007).

Finally, AI-enhance mental models of data explorer tools transform the logic behind data representation into businesses. These new techniques allow users to automatically find important trends or changes, often making the decision-making process more comfortable and practical. Therefore, it improves the machine's data analysis skills and allows businesses to use customer data intelligently and promptly (Soltani & Navimipour, 2016)

Figure 20. Flowchart Perfectly Describing the Future of CRM

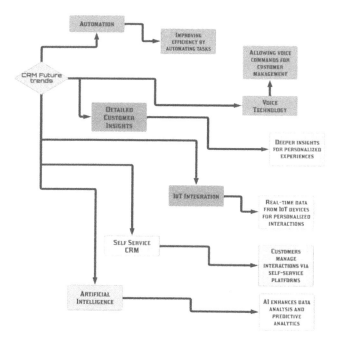

CONCLUSION

AI transforming Customer Relationship Management (CRM) is a promising revolution in modern business, compared to previous older systems of information, which is characterized by great data integration, operational efficiency, and more effective consumer engagement. The reliance on AI has always meant that CRM systems have been able to synergize and process different data sources over time. This amplified capacity allows businesses to have more accurate and interpersonal customer insights, and hence, they offer targeted services and interactions to satisfy the customers' specific needs.

Summary of Key Findings

Another noticeable development is improved operation efficiency promoted by AI-driven automation. The use of these self-service systems helps retailers address customer inquiries and complaints more quickly and accurately, as they can reduce response time and increase customer satisfaction levels. Due to this shift, routine workflows are also getting streamlined, and human resources (employees) can focus on more complicated and strategic tasks. Thus, it would create an opportunity to employ the maximum human and technological resources.

On top of that, AI makes it easy for marketers to use a variety of advanced analytics tools, like the ones that help with sentiment analysis and predictive analysis. Such tools provide a more profound understanding of customers' actions and motivations and allow for fresher knowledge about the customer base. Thus, organizations stand a chance to interact with their clients on a personal level, embracing customer centricity by providing personalized services that exactly fit the target's need at the right time and place.

In the next step, it might be expected that CRM accounting will be expanded through AI-enabling tools to the same level. The said changes will play a vital role in the business prospectus as companies attempt to respond to the rising standards of customers that grow in line with the technologies they use. Likewise, it opens new ways for conducting future research, for instance, using these tools to increase customer referral rates or explore other directions of personalization and customer interaction.

Implications for Business

Integration of AI into CRM systems changes a lot for businesses but brings both great opportunities and problems to deal with, which are highlighted by the necessity of securing data and ensuring the competencies of CRM analysts and managers. Companies skilled in applying AI technology to their CRM efforts can win a tremendous edge over the competition. It is this breakthrough that is a result of the strength of superior customer insights and competency in offering extremely customized experiences, which consumers nowadays prefer a great deal. By deepening into customer insights and analyzing customer behaviors and preferences, businesses can achieve their uniqueness in a market with a large scale of competition.

Nevertheless, firms are obliged to fund AI research and AI system applications to keep loan accounts of this nature in their business portfolios. The commitment to this investment creates the enabling environment where companies are empowered to fully harness the AI-fueled CRM potential. This ultimately translates to organizations holding pace with the ever-evolving technological advancements and, hence, retaining their markets of choice. Not only are financial investments requisites anymore, but they also involve technological approaches that need to be capable of handling complex AI functions.

In the digital sphere, which relies heavily on AI, enterprises should work on the safety of the data as well as its security. With the accumulation and evaluation of huge amounts of customer data, the protection of such data and compliance with the general data protection law in the world is extremely vital. It is not only a legal obligation but also a vital thing to maintain consumers' confidence and corporate reputation. Not acting protectively enough to safeguard customer information can presuppose severe harm to the companies' reputation and financial sanctions.

Moreover, the requirement for professionals like AI, data analytics, and CRM experts is expected to rise because of the increasing number of companies that use these advanced integration technologies. The number of people who contributed to the design, implementation, and perfection of these AI-powered CRM technologies is what the market is now seeking. The main focus of the business should be training the personnel already working there and recruiting new staff to meet the breakthroughs of technology. Forming a labor force that is expert in these techniques would be extremely important to primarily implement and gain from AI-driven CRM systems.

Recommendations for Future Research

AI's presence in CRM systems as part of BI ecosystems is transformative, for it offers innovative prospects and simultaneously brings unique challenges. However, it's more than a trend; instead, it is an inevitable change in the way businesses connect with their clients that needs skillful management to get the most from data and maintain sustainability in the data-driven marketplace.

An essential step in AI application in CRM is studying ethical aspects and regulatory issues, which is undoubtedly correct. Essential concerns, such as privacy, ensuring the absence of bias, and transparency, are at the center stage. Since AI systems can infiltrate biases that are informed by their training data, the recognition of such biases and their subsequent mitigation is of the utmost importance to ensure fairness and equal opportunities in customer relations. Moreover, guaranteeing that the AI system's decision-making and privacy are transparent and that regulations are adhered to is crucial to maintaining public trust and following global regulations.

A very interesting thing that we can learn from exploring AI-powered CRM applications across industries is the experience gained. This travel can discover common best practices and evidence cases of particular sectors' malfunctions, which will help organizations adopt AI-driven CRM approaches more straightforwardly. Every sector has its own type of customer engagement, and therefore, it is essential to customize AI apps according to these demands.

Educational surveys on how AI-powered personalization affects customer behavior and loyalty over time also have to be done. Catching the effect of the technologies on customer retention and satisfaction systematically over time may guide businesses to reshape their strategies better to follow the customers' needs and generate long-term activities.

Another potential field of development is an investigation into combining Augmented Reality (AR), CRM, Virtual Reality(VR), and blockchain systems. Such technologies can revolutionize customer management by employing the latest techniques, including customers' experience, using immersive technologies, such as data handling and transaction securities that encapsulate blockchain.

Nevertheless, carefully examining to what extent AI enhances core performance indicators in CRM channels is significant in finding out exactly how AI benefits and which areas are worth improving. This analysis may shed light on the niche influences that AI has on sales conversions, customer service efficiency, and general customer lifecycle management, as businesses will be able to amend their investment in technology and strategy shifts accordingly.

On the whole, companies and researchers should use this as a chance to investigate these angles and thus search for effective and innovative solutions that do not turn against ethical standards but rather make a positive contribution to the customer experience.

REFERENCES

Agarwal, A., Singhal, C., & Thomas, R. (2021). *AI-powered decision making for the bank of the future.* McKinsey & Company.

Ahmad, A. K., Jafar, A., & Aljoumaa, K. (2019). Customer churn prediction in telecom using machine learning in big data platform. *Journal of Big Data*, 6(1), 28. DOI: 10.1186/s40537-019-0191-6

Ahn, J. H., Han, S. P., & Lee, Y. S. (2006). 'Customer churn analysis: Churn determinants and mediation effects of partial defection in the Korean mobile tele-communications service industry'. [Google Scholar]. *Telecommunications Policy*, 30(10), 552–568. DOI: 10.1016/j.telpol.2006.09.006

AI in CRM: Benefits and Use Cases of AI-Powered CRM System. (2023, December). DDI Development. https://ddi-dev.com/blog/programming/ai-in-crm-benefits-and-use-cases-of-ai-powered-crm-system/

Alnofeli, K., Akter, S., & Yanamandram, V. (2023). Understanding the Future trends and innovations of AI-based CRM systems. In *Handbook of Big Data Research Methods* (pp. 279–294). Edward Elgar Publishing. DOI: 10.4337/9781800888555.00021

Ang, L., & Buttle, F. (2006). CRM software applications and business performance. *Journal of Database Marketing & Customer Strategy Management*, 14(1), 4–16. DOI: 10.1057/palgrave.dbm.3250034

Banu, F. (2022). Jahir Hussain & Subramani, Neelakandan & BT, Geetha &Villibharathan, Selvalakshmi & Umadevi, A. & Martinson, Eric. (2022). Artificial Intelligence Based Customer Churn Prediction Model for Business Markets. *Computational Intelligence and Neuroscience*, 2022, 1–14. DOI: 10.1155/2022/1703696

Blog, N. T. (2024, March 19). Sequential A/B Testing Keeps the World Streaming Netflix Part 1: Continuous Data. Medium. https://netflixtechblog.com/sequential-a-b-testing-keeps-the-world-streaming-netflix-part-1-continuous-data-cba6c7ed49df

Blog, N. T. (2024, March 8). Supporting Diverse ML Systems : Netflix Tech Blog | Netflix TechBlog. Medium. https://netflixtechblog.com/supporting-diverse-ml-systems-at-netflix-2d2e6b6d205d

Blog, N. T. (2024, March 9). Bending pause times to your will with Generational ZGC. Medium. https://netflixtechblog.com/bending-pause-times-to-your-will-with-generational-zgc-256629c9386b

Byloli, S. (2023, July 31). Examples of AI in Customer Service (From Companies That Do It Right). https://blog.hubspot.com/service/examples-of-ai-in-customer-service

Chagas, Beatriz & Viana, Julio & Reinhold, Olaf & Lobato, Fábio & Jacob Junior, Antonio & Alt, Rainer. (2018). Current Applications of Machine Learning Techniques in CRM: A Literature Review and Practical Implications. 452-458. .DOI: 10.1109/WI.2018.00-53

Das, S. R., Sarkar, P., Patil, S., Sharma, R., Aggarwal, S., & Lourens, M. (2023, December). Artificial Intelligence in Human Resource Management: Transforming Business Practices. In 2023 10th IEEE Uttar Pradesh Section International Conference on Electrical, Electronics and Computer Engineering (UPCON) (Vol. 10, pp. 1699-1703). IEEE.

Divinagracia, S., & Randolph, K. (2024, March 27). Using Machine Learning for CRM. Nutshell. https://www.nutshell.com/blog/using-machine-learning-for-crm

Divinagracia, S., & Randolph, K. (2024, March 27). Using Machine Learning for CRM. Nutshell. https://www.nutshell.com/blog/using-machine-learning-for-crm

Dyche, J. (2002). *The CRM handbook: A business guide to customer relationship management*. Addison-Wesley Professional.

Iranmanesh, S., Hamid, M., Bastan, M., Shakouri Ganjavi, H., & Nasiri, M. (2019, July). Customer Churn Prediction Using Artificial Neural Network: An Analytical CRM Application. In *3rd European International Conference on Industrial Engineering and Operations Management*.

Khan, S., & Iqbal, M. (2020, June). AI-Powered Customer Service: Does it optimize customer experience? In 2020 8th International Conference on Reliability, Infocom Technologies and Optimization (Trends and Future Directions)(ICRITO) (pp. 590-594). IEEE.

Kumar, V., Reinartz, W., Kumar, V., & Reinartz, W. (2018). Future of CRM. Customer Relationship Management: Concept, Strategy, and Tools, 385-404.

Ledro, C., Nosella, A., & Dalla Pozza, I. (2023). Integration of AI in CRM: Challenges and guidelines. *Journal of Open Innovation*, 9(4), 100151. DOI: 10.1016/j.joitmc.2023.100151

Nguyen, T. H., Sherif, J. S., & Newby, M. (2007). Strategies for successful CRM implementation. *Information Management & Computer Security*, 15(2), 102–115. DOI: 10.1108/09685220710748001

Prakash, A. (2023, December 1). AI-Driven Personalization in CRM: Tailoring Customer Experiences. Express Computer. https://www.expresscomputer.in/artificial-intelligence-ai/ai-driven-personalization-in-crm-tailoring-customer-experiences/106481/

Ramachandran, K. K. (2024). IMPACT OF ARTIFICIAL INTELLIGENCE (AI) AND MACHINE LEARNING ON CUSTOMER RELATIONSHIP MANAGEMENT (CRM) IN THE FUTURE OF FMCG AND FOOD INDUSTRIES. *Journal ID*, 9413, 9886.

Rane, N., Choudhary, S., & Rane, J. (2023). Hyper-personalization for enhancing customer loyalty and satisfaction in Customer Relationship Management (CRM) systems. Available at *SSRN* 4641044. DOI: 10.2139/ssrn.4641044

S. (2023, March 21). What is ChatSpot? Everything Explained About HubSpot's AI Tool. MakeWebBetter. https://makewebbetter.com/blog/what-is-chatspot/

S. (2024, April 2). Customer Churn: 12 Strategies to Stop Churn Right Now! https://www.superoffice.com/blog/reduce-customer-churn/

Salesforce Announces Einstein, G. P. T. the World's First Generative AI for CRM - Salesforce. (2024, April 17). Salesforce. https://www.salesforce.com/news/press-releases/2023/03/07/einstein-generative-ai/

Sam, G., Asuquo, P., & Stephen, B. (2024). Customer Churn Prediction using Machine Learning Models. *Journal of Engineering Research and Reports*, 26(2), 181–193. DOI: 10.9734/jerr/2024/v26i21081

Senthilnayaki, B., Swetha, M., & Nivedha, D. (2021). CUSTOMER CHURN PREDICTION. *IARJSET*, 8(6), 527–531. DOI: 10.17148/IARJSET.2021.8692

Soltani, Z., & Navimipour, N. J. (2016). Customer relationship management mechanisms: A systematic review of the state of the art literature and recommendations for future research. *Computers in Human Behavior*, 61, 667–688. DOI: 10.1016/j.chb.2016.03.008

Srivastava, S. (2024, March 22). Personalization at Scale: How AI in CRM is Transforming Customer Engagement. Appinventiv. https://appinventiv.com/blog/ai-in-crm/

Suh, Y. (2023). Machine learning based customer churn prediction in home appliance rental business. *Journal of Big Data*, 10(1), 41. DOI: 10.1186/s40537-023-00721-8 PMID: 37033202

Suresh, T., Madhuri, A., Shireesha, M., Kumar, B. R., & Rajesh, K. P. R. (2023, December). An exploratory study on AI-powered client relationship administration: An in-depth survey and roadmap for future investigations.

Torggler, M. (2008). The functionality and usage of CRM systems. *International Journal of Computer and Systems Engineering*, 2(5), 771–779.

Venkateswaran, N. (2023). AI-driven personalization in customer relationship management: Challenges and opportunities. *Journal of Theoretical and Applied Information Technology*, 101(18), 7392–7399.

White, T. (2017, January 25). The Importance of Customer Retention. https://blog.adwhite.com/the-importance-of-customer-retention-1

Zwingmann, T. (2022). *Ai-powered business intelligence*. O'Reilly Media, Inc.

Chapter 7
Optimizing Supply Chain With AI– Powered BI Systems

Sourabh Barala

VIT-AP University, India

A. Manimaran
https://orcid.org/0000-0002-5671-9466
VIT-AP University, India

Arul Kumar Natarajan
https://orcid.org/0000-0002-9728-477X
Samarkand International University of Technology, Uzbekistan

ABSTRACT

This chapter focuses on how artificial Intelligence (AI)-based business intelligence (BI) systems can be used to optimize supply chains. It starts with an introduction to the basics of supply chains and supply chain management processes and then moves on to an explanation of business intelligence systems. The discussion then progresses to the application of BI systems in the supply chain specifically in the improvement of demand forecasting, inventory management, and logistics among others. Lastly, the chapter explores various ways in which BI systems can be enhanced through the incorporation of AI technologies by providing real-time analysis, prediction, and automation. Thus, the chapter reveals the positive impact and practical application of the AI-powered BI systems in the context of supply chain Optimization.

DOI: 10.4018/979-8-3693-8844-0.ch007

INTRODUCTION

According to (Christopher, 2022), a supply chain is a network of connected and interdependent organizations that collaborate to manage and enhance the flow of resources and information from suppliers to end users. In today's dynamic marketplaces, all businesses must have an effective and adaptable supply chain. Organizations must coordinate and integrate all aspects of their business operations, from the procurement of raw materials to the distribution of products, to maintain and strengthen their competitive advantage in the market. These operations must take into account goals such as social sustainability, which calls for products to guarantee that the needs of the population are met, and economic sustainability, where supply chain scheduling and optimization aim to maximize profits by maximizing product values while minimizing the costs associated with raw materials, inventory, and production. While environmental sustainability seeks to guarantee that resource usage is effective in limiting waste created and that permanent environmental harm should not be permitted, resource sustainability seeks to minimize the use of non-renewable resources (Zhangyu et al., 2000).

Typical supply chain components may include distributors, manufacturers, and suppliers. These components correspond to factories, warehouses, vehicles, railroads, seafaring vessels, and processing facilities in the physical realm. An ideal supply chain design should demonstrate the best arrangement and performance of each component using one or more metrics. Consequently, the industry has a stake in streamlining its supply networks in some way. However, supply chain optimization may be a difficult technological undertaking, particularly for larger ones. Taking into account a global supply chain, which is a vast, intricate network comprising numerous supply, manufacturing, and distribution sites as well as a range of transportation choices. In addition, the supply chain would be vulnerable to a range of risks, including disruptions in supply and fluctuations in the price of commodities globally (Garcia et al., 2015).

To stay competitive in the face of globalization, businesses have made significant investments in learning more about their suppliers and customers. Companies have implemented a variety of strategies to become more competitive in their field, such as online stores, previous system integration, improved communication infrastructures, etc. The companies now have a foundation for sending and receiving information thanks to these actions. However, the more information businesses use, the harder it is to handle information wisely and efficiently. In reality, managers are faced with so much information that it has become increasingly difficult for them to make quick and smart decisions (Rabelo et al., 2002).

Companies today must figure out how to best comprehend the ever-increasing mountains of data surrounding them to obtain a competitive edge. It is crucial to understand what data the business requires and when and how to match it with customer needs (Langlois et al., 2017). This is when Business Intelligence comes into the picture. Business intelligence (BI) is the process of obtaining, converting, managing, and analyzing data to inform decision-making. This technique uses enormous data sets, including data warehouses, to disseminate intelligence across the company at all levels, from strategic to tactical and operational (Negash et al., 2008).

Large businesses' primary data sources of late have been online customer actions such as search inquiries, clicks, and sales. However, data is also abundant in our offline encounters and our physical surroundings. Stores may now get information about customer preferences and behaviors thanks to new sensors and actuators. Artificial Intelligence (AI) personal assistants and the Internet of Things (IoT) are tools that have the potential to convert every human moment into meaningful data. Algorithms used to establish prices are driven by this data and respond to customer demand variations. Thanks to the creative developments in data mining and artificial intelligence, businesses may now utilize the data generated by users and consumers.

Customers' upcoming activities inside the system are the result of several prior events, which allows for the extraction of useful business insights and a reduction in customer attrition—both of which have a significant impact on the growth of the firm as a whole (Garcia et al., 2015) In the realm of business intelligence (BI), machine learning has become a game-changing technology that is changing how companies get information from data and come to well-informed judgments. Machine-learning approaches augment business intelligence capabilities by providing more precise forecasts, sophisticated data analysis, and automated decision-making processes (Bharadiya et al., 2023). To give decision-makers at all levels a unified and comprehensive data perspective, AI works in tandem with BI to enable real-time information access, analysis, and interpretation (Olaoye et al., 2024).

SUPPLY CHAIN

An interconnected and interdependent network of organizations that collaborate to manage, control, and enhance the flow of goods and information from suppliers to end users (Christopher, 2022).

A supply chain is a network tool of enterprises, a network of facilities and distribution options that enables the procurement of raw materials, the transformation of raw materials into semi-finished or finished products, and the distribution of these products to end consumers (Fang et al., 2022).

It is a collection of organizations participating in a network to meet market demands. It typically starts with obtaining raw materials from nature, transforming them into finished products, and finally delivering them to consumers. In this chain, distribution, and warehousing functions provide support whenever required (New et al., 1995, as cited in Moniruzzaman et al., 2016).

"The role of Supply Chain is to add value to a product through transporting it from one location to another, during this the goods can be changed by processing." (Janvier-James et al., 2012).

What is Supply Chain Management?

Managing relationships with suppliers and customers both upstream and downstream to maximize customer value while minimizing costs to the supply chain overall (Christopher, 2022).

(Evans et al., 1995) Defined supply chain management as the management of material suppliers, production facilities, distribution services, and end customers connected through a feed-forward flow of information and a feed-backward flow of material.

Supply chain management is managing the flow of materials from the source to the user (Copacino, 1997, as cited in Fang et al., 2022).

(Mentzer et al., 2001, as cited in Fang et al., 2022) defined it as "efficient, strategic coordination of the conventional business functions and the tactics across these business functions within a particular company and across businesses within the supply chain, to improve the long-term performance of the individual companies and the supply chain as a whole."

Supply chain management is a set of methods used to effectively coordinate suppliers, producers, depots, and stores to produce and distribute products in the right quantity, to the right location, and at the right time. The aim is to reduce the functional cost while meeting service-level requirements (Simchi-Levi et al., 2003, as cited in Janvier-James, 2012).

Supply chain management is the planning and overseeing all sourcing and procurement, conversion, and logistics management operations. It also entails working together and coordinating with channel partners, including clients, suppliers, middlemen, and outside service providers. Supply chain management essentially unifies demand and supply management within and between businesses.

What is Supply Chain Optimization?

With the globalization of businesses, companies must rely on solutions like decentralized production facilities, distributed storage centers, and third-party transportation services. However, these innovations have added one more layer of complexity to businesses' supply chains. Moreover, the growing demand from consumers for faster, more affordable, and higher-quality products and services leaves no room for error from the business side. Yet, organizations must also prioritize profit maximization for their sustained growth.

Supply chain optimization is employing various resources and activities to refine various operations in the supply chain while removing unnecessary hurdles to make the whole process smooth, efficient, and cost-effective for businesses and consumers.

Business Intelligence Systems

Business Intelligence is the process of extracting, transforming, managing, and analyzing business data to support decision-making by providing insights across an organization, from a strategic to a tactical and operational level (Negash et al., 2008).

Business intelligence (BI) is an umbrella term for the technologies, applications, and processes associated with collecting, storing, using, disclosing, and analyzing data to facilitate sound decision-making (Gaardboe et al., 2017).

The term "business intelligence" (BI) refers to decision support systems built on combining and examining corporate data resources to enhance business decision-making. By streamlining information storage, identification, and analysis, business intelligence (BI) solutions seek to enhance the quality of data utilized in decision-making. They provide a thorough understanding of the entire company, allow for examining business operations from several angles, and facilitate quick responses to modifications in the business environment (Fink et al., 2017).

BI is a system comprising organizational and technical components that give users access to historical data for analysis to support management and make decisions that are more successful overall. The system's goal is to improve organizational performance (Işık, et al., 2013).

Business Intelligence Systems in Supply Chain

The key criteria for an effective supply chain strategy is information that is accurate, measurable, applicable, and sustainable. Today, organizations have huge amounts of data poured daily into warehouses from various business processes. While access to data is important, it is useless if businesses cannot transform that data into useful information to gain insight for decision-making. Traditionally, organizations used to get data from systems into spreadsheets and then try to slice and dice it to make it useful. This process was laborious and time-consuming. Here is where business intelligence differs from traditional reporting. BI allows them to extract data from different sources and transform it into useful information easily and efficiently. BI allows prompt, clean, integrated, consistent, and quality data to be obtained with a multidimensional view, covering different aspects of data and presenting it in layouts according to a specific end-user or task. These capabilities of BI help businesses monitor ongoing activities, benchmark their performance with their goals and objectives using key performance indicators, and give them the ability to understand and reason ongoing situations, innovate new ideas, plan strategies, anticipate future outcomes, think abstractly, and solve problems.

In the case of the supply chain, BI enables businesses to gain supply chain analytics by allowing them to understand things from the customer perspective and create what-if scenarios for different supply chain management processes, leading to supply chain intelligence. Using these insights, businesses can make smart and responsible decisions to increase revenue, reduce operational costs, and reduce market risks (Moniruzzaman et al., 2016; Mathrani et al., 2014; Ghosh et al., 2016).

According to the SCOR model, processes in supply chain management can be classified into five categories: plan, source, make, deliver, and return (Moniruzzaman et al., 2016).

Let us see how business intelligence can contribute to these processes.

Plan

This process involves supply chain planning related to the sourcing, making, delivery, and return process. It includes decisions like – How much product needs to be made? How much raw material will be required for the production? How will the product be delivered to the customers? This process helps in the smooth and efficient functioning of the supply chain as the organization now has a plan to follow. BI can extract and convert data into useful information for effective planning. Businesses can use BI to extract insights like the impact of changing demands on the supply chain. BI can report on historical data such as market growth, changes in customer behavior, sales trends, etc. Such insights help businesses in creating what-if scenarios that can be used to form plans and make changes to existing plans. BI can be used to predict market uncertainties, which lets businesses make proactive, quick, and smart responses to any unexpected change (Moniruzzaman et al., 2016).

Sourcing

This process deals with decisions about finding good suppliers who can provide good quality raw materials at a feasible time and reasonable price. BI can give data related to inventory consumption trends and key performance indicators (KPIs) for suppliers, which are useful for inventory management and supplier performance; BI can help warehouse management through inventory aging analysis and Always Better Control analysis (ABC analysis). In the supply chain, all participants collaborate to ensure the smooth operation of supply chain processes. Hence, information from different participants is required for decision-making. For example, for fulfilling a sudden bulk order, a company will need to know how much-finished product it has ready for dispatch, how much product is to be made, how much raw material is available, how much needs to be ordered, and how much time will it take to source that much raw material from the supplier. BI gives an integrated view of all such data with a layout that is according to the user. This helps better understand and efficient decision-making (Moniruzzaman et al., 2016).

Make

This process transforms raw materials into required products to meet market demand. It deals with capacity management, production scheduling, material flow, manufacturing, packaging, etc. BI-supported demand forecast, raw material availability, and production capacity analysis can help businesses handle large-scale production efficiently. Business Intelligence systems can provide performance reports based on historical data to identify what configurations are suitable for maximizing productivity, efficiency, and profit. Sometimes, flexibility in production is needed for productivity. BI can support businesses in reconfiguring resources to achieve flexibility. BI can also provide alternative ways to meet market demands. This can allow managers to explore new approaches that are not so intuitive. Overall, BI can improve organizations' processes by making them efficient, flexible, and innovative (Moniruzzaman et al., 2016).

Delivery

This process ensures that the product reaches the customer on time and with the same quality. Here, processes like order processing, warehousing, transportation management, delivery management, and delivery time are handled.

Generally, businesses use third parties for delivery services. To ensure that the product reaches the customer on time, organizations must be capable of tracking these deliveries and monitoring the outsourcing provider's performance. BI can easily extract such data and provide indicators that show the delivery service provider's picking performance, shipping performance, and delivery time record. Now, the company can find areas for improvement and make changes accordingly to reduce delivery time and make the delivery process smooth and cost-effective. Regular delivery updates also allow organizations to have better visibility of the delivery process and make predictions of uncertain events that might create hurdles later. Hence, business intelligence can allow businesses to take a proactive approach and make quick and responsible decisions for changes in the delivery process (Moniruzzaman et al., 2016).

Return

At this stage, a company deals with used or defective returned products. Most product returns are due to products not meeting the customer's expectations or taste, and fewer are due to defective products. Here, companies can use business intelligence to generate reports about consumer behavior and product performance analysis to better understand customers' needs and tastes. Business Intelligence can be used to generate a return analysis report to show how defects affect customer satisfaction. Product return also affects the product's retail and wholesale price, as expected loss should also be considered. Here, business intelligence can make return forecasts, generate return cost analysis reports to help in product pricing decisions and decide return policies. The return also affects supply chain inventory as we do not know which product will be returned. When will it be returned? And most importantly, in what quantity? Here, past sales and return data can be analyzed to keep inventory capacity in advance and avoid last-movement trouble. Business intelligence also helps monitor return performance, allowing managers to plan accordingly (Moniruzzaman et al., 2016).

AI empowering BI

Business Intelligence involves collecting, integrating, and analyzing data and then presenting it. Artificial Intelligence focuses on using machine learning to discover, interpret, and communicate useful patterns in data to make data-driven predictions (Olaoye et al., 2024).

BI can be greatly improved and developed by using AI in data analysis, offering various analytics features, and facilitating accurate predictive and prescriptive insights. AI can complement BI, as it can hasten data processes, provide sophisticated analytical abilities, give real-time analysis, and improve data display. Using AI technologies, companies can gain even more benefits from data and make better decisions – this will be an organization's advantage over others in the market (Azmi et al., 2023).

Now, let's see some ways in which AI can enhance BI.

DATA COLLECTION

Definition. Process of extracting data from various sources such as websites, databases, feedback forums, social media posts, etc.

Data collection involves identifying relevant data for research within and outside the organization to help generate a large pool of information for analysis. ML can help gather information through applications such as web scraping, data extraction from both structured and unstructured materials, and data integration from different databases or systems. ML algorithms can help improve the data's accuracy and allow automation processes like data retrieval and filtering as well as data aggregation (Bharadiya et al., 2023).

Automated Data Extraction

Automatic data extraction is the practice of AI in picking out relevant content from self-driving unstructured datasets in text forms, images, or videos. This capability is best illustrated by natural language processing (NLP), which entails the ability to identify and parse information from large textual databases. These algorithms can go through structured and unstructured data and identify specific patterns and other semantic clues to extract relevant information to help organize and process the wide variety of data across various domains, ranging from document retrieval to business intelligence. This not only enhances the process of data mobilization but also facilitates the ability to make quick and sound decisions from undifferentiated data to organized and useful information (Bharadiya et al., 2023).

Web Scraping and Crawling

Web scraping and crawling involve acquiring data from a range of sources on the World Wide Web, for instance, from websites, social network accounts, and databases, with the assistance of artificial intelligence tools. Web scrapers are intended to collect targeted information from web stores, including product descriptions, prices, consumer feedback, and articles, among other textual data. On the other hand, web crawlers navigate the web systematically, collecting information from several websites and moving from one site to another by following links. These techniques are essential for any organization or researcher who wants to obtain information, track trends, or analyze data available in this vast internet network (Bharadiya et al., 2023).

Sensor Data Collection

In the industrial environment, sensor data acquisition involves using AI-based sensors to capture multiple types of data from machines, equipment, and work environments. Properties such as integrated AI and connection technologies help these sensors detect and deliver immediate information about operational attributes, environmental factors, and efficiency indicators. Measurements of Temperature, pressure, humidity, and vibration levels are just a few examples of how AI-powered sensors help in constant observation of industrial processes, timely notification of deviations from desired parameters, and prevention of potential danger. Consequently, this data proves useful for decision-making, predicting maintenance, enhancing business processes, and quality management in industrial settings. In addition, using AI technologies improves the operation and effectiveness of data acquired through sensors, enabling organizations to derive insights and implement changes that optimize productivity, safety, and overall organizational performance (Bharadiya et al., 2023).

Social Media Monitoring

Social media monitoring is a process by which data from different social media platforms, such as posts, comments, and trends, is processed using AI algorithms. These algorithms refer to methods of handling large amounts of data users generate through various social platforms to give insights into sentiments, trends, and users' activities. Through the use of natural language processing (NLP) and machine learning, AI systems can comprehend the tone and sentiment and categorize content, which can, in turn, help an organization monitor the reactions and sentiments of the audience concerning their brands and also make them aware of certain risks or opportunities that they would not have noticed otherwise. Also, through social media monitoring, a business gets to know which topics are trending so that they can be in a position to tap into that market. They get to have an eye on their competitors all the time, and with this, they know how to respond to their clients appropriately at the right time. Taken as a whole, using Artificial Intelligence in the context of social media analysis presents a rich means for brands, marketers, and analysts to unpack, atomize, and apply the vast amount of data that resides on social media networks to improve activities, optimize consumer encounters, and accomplish key organizational objectives (Bharadiya et al., 2023).

Image and Video Annotation

Image and video annotation is a concept under artificial intelligence that uses an AI model to identify specific objects, faces, and other patterns within a given image or video. These AI systems, trained with advanced computer vision algorithms, can independently detect and classify objects in the data set to facilitate accurate annotation and labeling. Image and video annotation contribute to object recognition, semantic segmentation, and activity tracking. This kind of annotated data proved extremely valuable for a broad range of applications in various fields, such as robotics for autonomous navigation, video surveillance, medical imaging for treatments, and multimedia content analysis. Additionally, image and video annotation enormously contribute to training/ tuning AI models to sort out the information accurately, which is beneficial for recognizing and analyzing images and videos. These annotated datasets enable AI systems to understand broad visual contexts, extract relevant information, and accomplish tasks effectively and accurately (Bharadiya et al., 2023).

Speech Recognition

Speech recognition is artificial intelligence that converts spoken words into text. These systems leverage sophisticated algorithms, sometimes deep learning, to listen to audio and accurately transcribe the words. In automatic speech recognition, AI models distinguish the sound of speech and determine which word it corresponds to. This technology lets spoken words get converted into text, which can be useful in several applications, such as voice-enabled assistants, speech-to-text, and voice-activated gadgets. Through exposure to large amounts of data, these artificial intelligence peculiarities are refined over time, irrespective of accent, language, or methods of speaking. This makes them very useful in enhancing accessibility, carrying out tasks more efficiently, and enhancing the user experience, especially in fields such as personal computing and customer services (Bharadiya et al., 2023).

DATA INTEGRATION

Definition. Process of combining and harmonizing data from various sources into a common format.

Machine learning (ML) algorithms play an important role in analyzing and integrating data from different sources in BI. It becomes easier to merge the data automatically because ML techniques assist in reconciling different formats and weeding out various conflicts that may exist, thus embracing harmony. In BI, it is crucial to achieve data integration since information derived from different sources must be accurate and sufficient for analysis. Applying Machine Learning techniques makes integrating data from various databases, data warehouses, cloud platforms, and external sources simple and faster. This integration means that all of an organization's data is amalgamated, and this eradicates the problem of data silos hence facilitating the effectiveness of an organization's analysis and decisions (Bharadiya et al., 2023; Azmi et al., 2023).

ML can contribute to the integration of various data sources in some of the following ways:

Data Extraction and Transformation

Data extraction and transformation are processes involved in capturing data from different sources and conditioning it for analysis and storage. This entails using machine learning (ML) algorithms to effect the data extraction process from various input structures, including the database, spreadsheet, application programming interfaces (APIs), web services, and logs. Any type of data format like CSV, JSON, XML, and relational databases is well understood and managed by various ML algorithms, making extracting data from multiple sources fairly easy. They allow organizations to collect data from various channels and consolidate such data in a format that can easily be used for further analysis, thus improving the methods of data integration (Bharadiya et al., 2023; Azmi et al., 2023).

Schema Alignment

Schema integration is the process of organizing different data schemas received from various sources. This process involves comparing and matching the structures, attributes, and formats of data elements in the different sources. Automating the schema alignment is made possible by applying machine learning algorithms that can learn from the data mappings. All these ML algorithms study the patterns and rules within the data and adjust the schema accordingly with minimum human interference for better accuracy. With the help of ML in schema alignment, the process of integration of data from disparate sources is made easier, which in turn helps to improve the efficiency of the data flow within an organization and enhance business decisions based on the analysis of the integrated data (Bharadiya et al., 2023; Azmi et al., 2023).

Data Cleaning and Deduplication

Data cleansing and deduplication are specifically the two techniques that are used in the data integration process to increase the quality of the integrated datasets. These tasks are usually automated using machine learning (ML) techniques involving sophisticated algorithms that can understand data present in the dataset and then detect and handle outliers, duplicate records, and missing values (Bharatiya et al., 2023; Azmi et al., 2023).

ML algorithms use the extracted patterns to find relationships between the data and identify factors contributing to poor data quality. These algorithms can learn from past data using supervised or unsupervised learning methods to discover how data cleaning and deduplication are accomplished. Another kind of learning that can be used to address the problem of inconsistent data is supervised learning because, in this approach, the algorithm can be trained with examples of clean and dirty data, and based on such a training set, it will be able to identify new data that is dirty and needs to be clean. In contrast, unsupervised learning methods may independently discover patterns such as data anomalies and outliers without needing labeled data (Bharadiya et al., 2023; Azmi et al., 2023).

When data cleaning and deduplication are done using ML, the integration process becomes easier, and the integrated dataset becomes more effective and accurate. This also helps decrease the time spent manually fixing such problems and the chances of human errors, resulting in improved quality of data integration, analysis, and thus, decision-making (Bharadiya et al., 2023; Azmi et al., 2023).

Data Mapping and Transformation

Mapping and conversion are crucial aspects of the data integration process, as they enable data standardization from various database structures or formats. These tasks are easily automated using various Machine learning algorithms that learn mapping across different data types and apply transformations to make data compatible and facilitate seamless integration (Bharadiya et al., 2023).

ML algorithms are capable of 'learning' from historical mappings or through user input, subsequently enabling smooth data mapping and transformation to be carried out without much human intervention. This involves mapping attribute names and converting measurement units and data types from one format to another (Bharadiya et al., 2023).

With the ability to use ML for data mapping and transformation, organizations can now integrate heterogeneous data sources and still ensure consistency and accuracy of the data. Automated transformation capabilities help reduce manual effort, improve efficiency, and allow organizations to extract insights from a holistic view of data (Bharadiya et al., 2023).

DATA PREPARATION

Definition. Cleaning, transforming, and restructuring data is used to make it fit for analysis and other purposes.

In BI, machine learning algorithms can optimize and automate data preparation. With ML, tasks like data transformation, data cleansing, and feature engineering can be completed quickly and effectively, saving time and effort when preparing data for analysis. (Bharadiya et al., 2023).

PREDICTIVE ANALYTICS

Definition. Data analytics deals with predicting future events using historical data with statistics and machine learning.

One of the primary pillars of modern enterprises is predictive analytics, based on machine learning techniques. These programs explore tens of thousands of historical data to identify patterns that are good for forecasting future results accurately. Through this application, the management of organizations can be made efficient, changes in demand rate can be anticipated, and resources can be allocated correctly. In the same way, predictive analytics can be applied to identify risks and find measures to avoid them. In turn, one more advantage of using predictive analytics is the opportunity to predict demand evolutions, seasonal trends, and market performance. These discoveries enable business organizations to have better control over inventory, optimize their supply chain, and save money that would otherwise be spent on unnecessary overstocking or the direct opposite.

On the other hand, predictive analytics can use past sales data, market trends, and customer behavior to ascertain future sales and revenues. This makes it possible for enterprises to set achievable goals and objectives, determine the optimal way of distributing resources, and develop revenue models that meet the market's requirements. In the broader context of BI, machine learning creates a reality where predictive analytics based on experience become a reality. The employment of ML algorithms helps to solve complicated tasks like detecting relations and patterns in data, allowing organizations to determine the demands, tendencies in the market, and client behavior and make decisions. This approach of using predictive analytics is another strong tool that helps companies to make their operations efficient, reduce the risks, and be one step ahead of competitors. Machine learning techniques offer organizations data and information that help in pattern recognition and decision-making (Bharadiya et al., 2023; Bharadiya et al., 2023; Azmi et al., 2023).

REAL-TIME DECISION-MAKING

In today's world, where decisions are driven by data analytics, incorporating real-time processing and ML algorithms is seen as a crucial tool for businesses across various sectors. Real-time decision-making means the capability of organizations to provide conclusions based on the incoming data streams in a feasible time. It is even more relevant in constantly changing conditions, as it entails the need to respond to sudden changes to sustain competitiveness and efficiency (Bharadiya et al., 2023).

Artificial intelligence and machine learning, models that excel in pattern recognition, modeling, and analyzing patterns in real time, have a critical role in decision-making. Through these algorithms, organizations are thus able to handle, process, and analyze large and complex data flows in real time and then sift through them to arrive at relevant conclusions and make ad hoc decisions (Bharadiya et al., 2023).

The main benefit of automating the decision-making process using real-time ML is the improvement of operational flexibility and timeliness. The typical approach of batch processing involves data collection from various sources followed by analysis at a later time, making decision-making slow and less efficient in dynamic settings. On the other hand, real-time ML algorithms process streaming data, allowing organizations to identify changes, abnormalities, and new trends as they occur in nearly real-time (Bharadiya et al., 2023).

In addition, implementing real-time analytics through ML allows organizations to supervise vital operational indicators perpetually. Through anomaly detection, predictive modeling, and trend analysis, businesses can detect early signs of a shift in past or current trends or deviation from the expected performance levels. This proactive monitoring allows the organization to identify and solve problems, minimize risks and improve the activity on the go (Bharadiya et al., 2023).

Moreover, the integration of real-time ML algorithms facilitates personalized and context-aware decision-making. By analyzing individual preferences, behaviors, and contextual factors in real time, organizations can tailor their responses, recommendations, and interventions to meet specific user needs, situations, and requirements. This granularity and adaptability enhance the effectiveness and relevance of decision-making processes, ultimately driving better outcomes and customer satisfaction (Bharadiya et al., 2023).

In conclusion, real-time decision-making with machine learning algorithms represents a transformative approach to data-driven decision-making. By enabling organizations to process, analyze, and act upon streaming data in real-time, these algorithms empower businesses to enhance operational agility, responsiveness, and decision-making effectiveness. As organizations continue to embrace digital transformation and seek competitive advantages in an increasingly dynamic marketplace, the integration of real-time ML-powered analytics will remain indispensable for driving innovation, efficiency, and value creation (Bharadiya et al., 2023).

NATURAL LANGUAGE PROCESSING (NLP)

Definition. Branch of computer science which combines computational linguistics with statistical and machine learning models to enable computers to understand and generate text and speech.

NLP can be considered one of the most significant fields that fall under the large umbrella of AI and ML. It enables machines to understand, analyze, and even produce text. It includes a wide range of algorithms, models, and techniques that try to narrow down the gap between the complexity of natural language and computers' capabilities to understand it (Bharadiya et al., 2023).

In the context of Business Intelligence (BI), NLP can be seen as a revolutionary technology that allows organizations to extract valuable knowledge from the large collections of text data available in today's large organizations. Processes like sentiment analysis, text mining, and automated text summarization make it easier to systematically extract important data from various textual data such as customer feedback, social media discourse, and surveys (Bharadiya et al., 2023).

Through the implementation of NLP, organizations can go beyond the possibilities offered by the conventional approaches to data analysis, given that the performance of these approaches is usually confined to the analysis of structured data. In contrast, most information is in an unstructured format. These insights are significant, starting from the customer's attitude or tone and moving to customer trends. They can help make strategic decisions, enhance business processes, and develop innovations in various fields and industries. Consequently, NLP becomes a vital component of BI infrastructure, enabling organizations to efficiently manage and ascertain value from natural language data in the information age (Bharadiya et al., 2023).

DATA VISUALIZATION AND REPORTING

Definition

Data Visualization. Using graphical representations of data to analyze, understand, and extract insight from the data.

Reporting. Process of systematically documenting and presenting data in a specific format.

In the context of business intelligence (BI), integrating machine learning (ML) techniques alongside data visualization and reporting systems has become a powerful tool for extracting valuable insights and supporting decisions. Data visualization refers to representing information in graphical form to make it easier to interpret. Implementing ML algorithms when it comes to analyzing data, creating visualizations, and reporting allows organizations to go a step further in finding value from the data, adopting sophisticated analytical strategies to identify patterns and communicate the findings effectively (Bharadiya et al., 2023).

Machine learning algorithms can be applied in various areas of data visualization and reporting, such as generating interactive dashboards and real-time reports. These ML-augmented visualizations help users navigate their data interactively and extract insights simply and compellingly (Bharadiya et al., 2023).

The main area where ML has significantly impacted data visualization is its potential to handle complex and large amounts of data. To elaborate, methods like the clustering process help condense data into a two-dimensional or three-dimensional plane to easily analyze and understand patterns through visualization. Using these algorithms, a particular dataset with numerous data points can be clustered so that data points with similar features can be classified together to make it easier for the users to identify the hidden relationships in the data (Bharadiya et al., 2023).

Also, ML-enhanced data visualization is more interactive and flexible. These tools could incorporate training mechanisms with the help of reinforcement learning or by accepting user feedback. The tools could eventually redesign the visualized models according to the responses they have received. This makes it possible for users to look at data from different perspectives, filter the data to view specific details, and find out things that may not be easily seen from a simple view of the data (Bharatiya et al., 2023).

Real-time reporting is another domain where ML algorithms have provided significant benefits in data representation. This involves using Real-time data feeds and predictive analytics, an ML-powered reporting tool that can generate real-time reports about the latest information forecasted for future events and trends. These capabilities help organizations make timely decisions and take appropriate actions whenever there are changes in the conditions or new opportunities that may benefit them (Bharadiya et al., 2023).

In addition, when developing data visualization and reporting, ML techniques can help to enhance data analysis and produce insights on their own. Using features, such as automated feature engineering or anomaly detection, ML systems can autonomously detect important patterns, outliers, or anomalies in the data. Implementing such trends into visualization and reporting will help to solve organizational issues, make operations more efficient, and encourage innovation strategies (Bharadiya et al., 2023).

Therefore, integrating ML algorithms in data visualization and reporting is seen as the new paradigm shift in BI, which should help organizations gain deeper insights, improve decision-making processes, and extract maximum value from data. Using proper clustering, dimensionality reduction, and real-time analytics, the users can generate captivating and engaging visualizations where people can easily employ their intuition to extract insight from data. Consequently, with increasing data size and complexity, data visualization and reporting enabled by AI will stay critical in providing companies with insights to make data-driven decisions and gain a competitive edge in this age of globalization (Bharadiya et al., 2023).

RECOMMENDATION SYSTEMS

Definition. Systems that provide suggestions about items, actions, etc. that are most relevant to a user in any specific situation.

In the present digital age, conventional methods of business-to-customer interactions have substantially been transformed by recommendation systems supported by ML algorithms. These systems employ complex data analytical approaches to explore large data sets, such as consumer calls, sales profiles, product descriptors, etc., to make timely and relevant suggestions. Thus, recommendation systems using ML algorithms benefit the company and customers since they involve continuous learning of customer preferences and adjusting subsequent decisions (Bharadiya et al., 2023).

At the heart of these recommendation systems are complex algorithms that facilitate the assessment of client activity. To formulate recommendations, these algorithms analyze large amounts of data to find similarities and relations between users and items (products, contents, or actions) (Bharadiya et al., 2023).

AI-powered recommendation systems have multiple advantages for business organizations that want to improve customer experience and engagement. Because recommendations are targeted and based on the behavior of a specific user, the system can also assist the client in directing them to new products or content that will be relevant and suitable to the client, thus increasing satisfaction and customer loyalty. Moreover, it can also help to increase revenues by making recommendations for related items and promoting customer retention (Bharadiya et al., 2023).

Furthermore, AI-enabled recommendation systems can learn, improve, and adapt from past experience and feedback over time. This helps these systems refine their recommendations to evolving user preferences and thus helps businesses adapt to today's dynamically changing markets. It makes recommendation systems provide customers with more precise and personal recommendations as the system continues its learning cycle, improving the quality of experience (Bharadiya et al., 2023).

In conclusion, it can be stated that ML-powered recommendation systems are indeed a very useful tool for companies that strive to address their customers with a more tailored experience and maintain their engagement amid growing competition. Through the use of sophisticated ML tools like collaborative filtering and content-based filtering, a recommendation system can identify customer interactions and infer user preferences to provide a rich set of recommended products that will not only meet users' needs but, at the same, support businesses in growing their revenue. Therefore, as customers remain the focus of today's business strategies, proactive use of ML-based recommendation systems will remain the key to success in personalized experiences and digital interactions (Bharadiya et al., 2023).

ANOMALY DETECTION

Definition. Process of identification of data points, events, or observations that are sufficiently different from the majority of the data and what is considered standard or usual

Anomaly detection is one of the fundamental principles in machine learning, and its objective is to identify data instances that are dissimilar from the expected pattern in data. Such observations are known as anomalies or outliers, and they usually contain information about rare events, errors, or any information of interest. In the case of anomaly detection, machine learning algorithms perform amazingly well since they can filter through large amounts of data to identify data points that might indicate fraudulent activities, inefficiencies in business operations, or unusual activities. For instance, the anomalies in the financial systems could be indicators of fraud control or money laundering, while anomalies in the network security could point to unauthorized intrusions or breaches. Thus, identifying such abnormalities is important as it allows organizations to act before potential threats occur, refine operational activities, and strengthen security measures. This proactive approach is not only useful in the strengthening of systems and the development of their reliability but also helpful in the anticipation of future threats and challenges. Anomaly detection helps to create a continuous learning environment by providing valuable insights about data quality issues, inefficiencies in business operations, and business risks. In the end, anomaly detection provides the cornerstone for furthering innovation, protecting tangible and intangible investments, and promoting the reliability of data-based decisions in a wide range of fields and sectors (Bharadiya et al., 2023).

CONCLUSION

Thus, in this chapter, we have looked at the possibilities for positive change with the help of AI-based BI systems to enhance supply chains. Corporations can improve their operational efficiency, decision-making processes, and overall supply chain performance when adopting AI into a sound BI architecture.

When enabled by AI-powered BI systems, real-time analytical tools, predictive business intelligence, and automation improve various aspects of the supply chain. They assist in pattern recognition, forecasting demand, inventory control, and supply chain practices, resulting in cost reduction and enhancement of the quality of services. In addition, the possibility of managing large amounts of information from various sources enables a faster and more flexible supply chain, which can react consequently to fluctuations in the market and manage risks.

As we move forward, one of the key success factors remains the ability to innovate and evolve continuously. To remain relevant in a competitive world, today's business requires updated artificial intelligence and business intelligence applications, and decision-making is promoted based on data. AI integration with SCM is not a luxury but a necessity for organizations that require long-term business growth and increased operational performance.

Thus, AI-powered BI systems can be considered one of the most significant advancements in supply chain management, as they open new possibilities for improving supply chain management and building a competitive advantage. These technologies help organizations achieve improved efficiency, flexibility, and performance, thus opening the path for generating a smarter and more adaptive supply chain environment.

REFERENCES

Azmi, M., Mansour, A., & Azmi, C. (2023). A Context-Aware Empowering Business with AI: Case of Chatbots in Business Intelligence Systems. *Procedia Computer Science*, 224, 479–484. DOI: 10.1016/j.procs.2023.09.068

Bharadiya, J. P. (2023). Machine learning and AI in business intelligence: Trends and opportunities. [IJC]. *International Journal of Computer*, 48(1), 123–134.

Bharadiya, J. P. (2023). The role of machine learning in transforming business intelligence. *International Journal of Computing and Artificial Intelligence*, 4(1), 16–24. DOI: 10.33545/27076571.2023.v4.i1a.60

Christopher, M. (2022). *Logistics and supply chain management*. Pearson Uk.

Evans, G. N., Towill, D. R., & Naim, M. M. (1995). Business process re-engineering the supply chain. *Production Planning and Control*, 6(3), 227–237. DOI: 10.1080/09537289508930275

Fang, H., Fang, F., Hu, Q., & Wan, Y. (2022). Supply chain management: A review and bibliometric analysis. *Processes (Basel, Switzerland)*, 10(9), 1681. DOI: 10.3390/pr10091681

Fink, L., Yogev, N., & Even, A. (2017). Business intelligence and organizational learning: An empirical investigation of value creation processes. *Information & Management*, 54(1), 38–56. DOI: 10.1016/j.im.2016.03.009

Gaardboe, R., & Svarre, T. (2017). Critical factors for business intelligence success.

Garcia, D. J., & You, F. (2015). Supply chain design and optimization: Challenges and opportunities. *Computers & Chemical Engineering*, 81, 153–170. DOI: 10.1016/j.compchemeng.2015.03.015

Ghosh, A. (2016). Business Intelligence (BI) in Supply Chain Management. *Asian Journal of Science and Technology*, 7(11).

Işık, Ö., Jones, M. C., & Sidorova, A. (2013). Business intelligence success: The roles of BI capabilities and decision environments. *Information & Management*, 50(1), 13–23. DOI: 10.1016/j.im.2012.12.001

Janvier-James, A. M. (2012). A new introduction to supply chains and supply chain management: Definitions and theories perspective. *International Business Research*, 5(1), 194–207.

Langlois, A., & Chauvel, B. (2017). The impact of supply chain management on business intelligence. *Journal of Intelligence Studies in Business*, 7(2). Advance online publication. DOI: 10.37380/jisib.v7i2.239

Mathrani, S. (2014). Managing Supply Chains Using Business Intelligence. ACIS.

Moniruzzaman, M., Kurnia, S., Parkes, A., & Maynard, S. B. (2016). Business intelligence and supply chain agility. arXiv preprint arXiv:1606.03511.

Negash, S., & Gray, P. (2008). Business intelligence. *Handbook on decision support systems 2*, 175-193.

Olaoye, F., & Potter, K. (2024). *Business Intelligence (BI) and Analytics Software: Empowering Data-Driven Decision-Making (No. 12550)*. EasyChair.

Rabelo, R. J., & Pereira-Klen, A. A. (2002, September). Business intelligence support for supply chain management. In *International Conference on Information Technology for Balanced Automation Systems* (pp. 437-444). Boston, MA: Springer US. DOI: 10.1007/978-0-387-35613-6_49

Zhangyu, Z., Siwei, C., & Ben, H. (2000). Supply chain optimization of continuous process industries with sustainability considerations. *Computers & Chemical Engineering*, 24(2-7), 1151–1158. DOI: 10.1016/S0098-1354(00)00496-8

Chapter 8
Security, Transparency, and Traceability:
Role of Blockchain in AI-Powered Supply Chain

A. S. Anurag
https://orcid.org/0009-0005-5790-9084
Central University of Kerala, India

M. Johnpaul
https://orcid.org/0000-0002-1133-0588
Central University of Kerala, India

ABSTRACT

The chapter explores the profound impact of blockchain technology on Supply Chain Management, tracing its historical development across diverse industries. Through its decentralized ledger system, blockchain ensures the integrity of digital transactions via cryptographic encoding, thereby enhancing security, traceability, and transparency within SCM processes. The chapter illustrates blockchain's effectiveness in streamlining supply chain processes. It also examines the challenges in implementing blockchain technology, including scalability issues, regulatory constraints, and cultural and sustainability considerations. Emerging trends in technologies like digital currency and asset tokenization hold promise for further improving cross-border transactions and asset tracking capabilities. The chapter suggests collaboration, leadership commitment, and the development of supportive regulatory frameworks to harness blockchain's full transformative potential.

DOI: 10.4018/979-8-3693-8844-0.ch008

INTRODUCTION

Globalization has enabled businesses to expand their global footprint and access new markets like never before. However, it has also brought about many challenges, including heightened competition, evolving consumer expectations, and greater exposure to geopolitical risks and uncertainties. So, how are companies dealing with this intense competition and the dynamic nature of the global market? This is where the importance of Supply Chain (SC) and Supply Chain Management (SCM) comes in. When we look into the past few decades of industrial records across the globe, it is evident that the major players in the market had an efficient and improved SC process. A well-structured SC can help the firm to become an active competitor in the global market by creating efficient channels to source materials, planning efficient manufacturing processes, and expanding the distribution network across different countries. By streamlining processes, minimizing waste, and improving coordination among various stakeholders, SCM helps businesses lower production and distribution costs. (Daniels, 1999), making products more competitive in the global market. A proper SCM strategy increases market dynamics and competitive advantage. Businesses that excel in SCM can respond swiftly to market changes, adapt to customer demands, and capitalize on emerging opportunities. By optimizing SC processes, companies can differentiate themselves from competitors and enhance their market position. Ultimately, SCM enhances customer satisfaction (Harland, 1996) and experience in global commerce. Timely delivery, product availability, and responsiveness to customer needs are critical factors influencing purchasing decisions. By delivering products efficiently and reliably, businesses can build strong customer relationships and foster brand loyalty in the global marketplace.

In the modern era of Industry 4.0 and Industry 5.0, the SCM has become a more resilient process than ever before. With the help of Artificial Intelligence (AI) technologies, the SCM process has become the cornerstone of any business. AI technologies, including Machine Learning (ML), Natural Language Processing (NLP), Internet of Things (IoT), Predictive Analytics (PA), Blockchain, Computer Vision (CV), Robotics, and Automation, have had a significant role in building an efficient SCM process. These cutting-edge tools are employed collaboratively and independently, each fulfilling crucial functions to uphold the efficiency of a SC.

Over the years, a drastic change in the process of SCM has been observed. SC has become more than an interconnection of manufacturing processes based on a factory. In the current sense, SC is an interconnected network of stakeholders depending on each other to bring goods or services to the customers without compromising the quality and maintaining a reasonable timeframe. With the advent of digital technologies and AI, the enhanced SCM is more important to the success of a business than ever before. When the traditional SCM principles incorporate advanced digital technologies, we get the next generation of SCM practices, commonly called SCM 4.0.

Several innovative technologies propelled the transformation of the traditional SC to the modern and sophisticated SCM 4.0. Blockchain is one of the critical technologies that has helped with this transition. The term "blockchain" was simply a buzzword a few years back. Most of the time, the word was mentioned along with words like cryptocurrency and bitcoin. It is no surprise, given that blockchain technology was initially developed to streamline the record-keeping of Bitcoin's cryptocurrency transactions (Laurence, 2019). Today, blockchain applications have spread across multiple domains, including but not limited to SCM, Digital Identity Management (DIM), healthcare, and financial services.

This chapter discusses how blockchain technology can be integrated into the SCM processes, mainly focusing on the security, transparency, and traceability it can offer to the SC process. Further, the chapter is organized into four main sections. The first is an introduction section, which will focus on laying the foundation for the chapter and explaining the chapter structure to help readers navigate the chapter smoothly. The second section is the background and literature review section that helps to understand the concept of SCM and blockchain technology and how they are interconnected, followed by some real-life examples of the use of blockchain technology in SCM. The third section will discuss the challenges and limitations, emerging trends, and the prospect of blockchain in SCM. Finally, we will summarise the theme discussed in the chapter in the conclusion.

BACKGROUND AND LITERATURE REVIEW

Supply Chain Management (SCM)

Simply put, SC is the sum of all an organization's activities to successfully deliver a product (or service) to its end customers. An order from a customer initiates a SC process and will conclude with the successful delivery of the order. Several players, such as the raw materials supplier, logistics provider, manufacturing unit, financial department, marketing department, operations department, and sometimes even the government, come together in this SC process to make it a success. Figure 1 is the generalized illustration of a simple SC process.

Generally, people seem to associate SCM with logistics and transportation, but this is different since logistics is only one of the many processes integrated into the modern SCM process. Several researchers and scholars have presented diverse interpretations of SC and SCM through their respective definitions. However, in reality, the process of SCM is so dynamic and complex that no definitions can represent it wholly. SCM coordinates activities, including sourcing raw materials, production, and delivery of finished products from suppliers to customers (Mentzer et al., 2001; Nasereddin, 2024). It encompasses various functions such as procurement, manufacturing, logistics, distribution (Nasereddin, 2024), and finances across multiple entities within the SC network to optimize efficiency, reduce costs, and meet customer demands (Ibrahim & Hamid, 2014; Mentzer et al., 2001). According to Ibrahim and Hamid (2014), SCM connects business processes from end-users to original suppliers to deliver products, services, and information that enhance customer value.

Khan et al. (2010) describe SCM as coordinating and integrating business activities in designing, manufacturing, delivering, and using a product or service. SCM aims to optimize these processes to ensure that goods are produced and distributed efficiently, meeting customer demand while minimizing costs (Khan et al., 2010). Sindhwani et al. (2023) suggest that SCM pertains to overseeing the flow of goods and services, which includes transporting and storing raw materials, work-in-process inventory, and finished products from their source to the point of consumption. It entails coordinating and integrating these movements both within a company and between different companies to effectively provide products or services to customers (Sindhwani et al., 2023). SCM involves planning, executing, and regulating the movement of goods, services, information, and finances from suppliers through manufacturers, wholesalers, and retailers, and finally to customers (Mentzer et al., 2001). SCM encompasses a holistic approach to managing various functions such as procuring raw materials, manufacturing, inventory management, logistics, and customer service to optimize overall SC performance and meet customer demand efficiently (Hugos, 2024).

Based on all the expert opinions above, the process of SCM is a comprehensive approach to coordinating and optimizing the movement of products across the entire SC network, from suppliers to customers. It involves sourcing, producing, and delivering goods or services, encompassing procurement, manufacturing, logistics, distribution, and finance. It aims to optimize these processes to ensure efficient production and distribution while meeting customer demand and minimizing costs. SCM manages the overall movement of a product's entire lifecycle involving raw materials, semi-finished goods, and finished goods inventory, coordinating and integrating these movements within and among companies to efficiently deliver products or services to customers. Figure 1 provides a simple illustration of the process flow of a supply chain, as depicted by the author.

Figure 1. Simple Illustration of the Process Flow of a Supply Chain (Author)

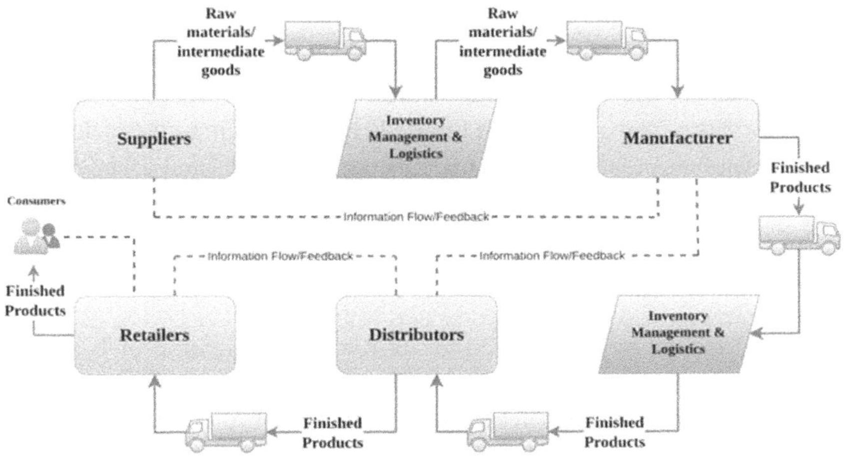

Challenges in SCM

Maintaining and creating an efficient SCM system is a challenging task. Several factors resist the smooth flow of SC operations. SCs are susceptible to risks, such as natural disasters, geopolitical conflicts, supplier interruptions, economic instability, logistical disruptions, and cybersecurity threats. (Hugos, 2024; Khan et al., 2010; Nasereddin, 2024; Sindhwani et al., 2023). Addressing these risks is essential for keeping the SC efficient and smooth. Limited transparency of the SC can seriously disrupt the flow of SCM (Hugos, 2024; Mentzer et al., 2001; Sindhwani et al., 2023). SC processes have transformed from a simple assembly line process in a factory to a global collaborative process. SCM 2.0 is complex and involves several parties with integrated interests. The complexity of the SC has also become a barrier to its smooth operations because of the participation of several stakeholders with diverse interests, varying regulations, and cultural differences (Hugos, 2024; Mentzer et al., 2001; Sindhwani et al., 2023). Information sharing also plays a critical role in the smooth flow of SC processes (Ibrahim & Hamid, 2014; Khan et al., 2010).

Effective communication and information sharing among SC partners are essential for collaboration and decision-making but can be hindered by trust issues and reluctance to share proprietary information. Managing large volumes of data collected from various sources and ensuring security and data accuracy can be challenging in SC operations (Ibrahim & Hamid, 2014; Mentzer et al., 2001). Fragmented processes and disparate systems can pose challenges in the smooth flow of operations of an SC system. Failing to maintain an adequate inventory management strategy can also lead to the overall disruption of SCM (Hugos, 2024; Khan et al., 2010). The global market has always had a dynamic nature. Nothing in the market will ever be the same; deciding factors such as consumer preferences, trends, and demand patterns are ever-changing. It can fail if the SCM process cannot adapt to the dynamic market demands (Khan et al., 2010). Balancing cost efficiency with quality and customer satisfaction and meeting environmental and social responsibility goals while maintaining efficiency can be challenging (Sindhwani et al., 2023).

Blockchain Technology

Blockchain technology originated in 2008 with the creation of Bitcoin by an enigmatic individual called Satoshi Nakamoto (Sarmah, 2018). Initially conceived for digital transactions, it has since expanded beyond cryptocurrencies to find applications in diverse industries such as finance, healthcare, retail, education, law, government, and SCM. Blockchain technology comprises interconnected data blocks that store transaction details. Each of these blocks contains metadata about the transaction and is linked to each other with the help of cryptographic encoding to form a chain-like structure to ensure integrity. The fundamental premise of blockchain lies in its facilitation of peer-to-peer transactions without intermediary authorities (Ammous, 2016). Blockchain technology is a decentralized digital ledger that securely logs transactions across multiple nodes, guaranteeing transparency and immutability (Sarmah, 2018). Its primary function is to authenticate online transactions involving digital assets while safeguarding the parties' privacy. This is achieved by organizing transactions into blocks linked chronologically to form a continuous chain. Each block includes a cryptographic hash of the previous block, which ensures the integrity and sequential order of the transactions (Zhai et al., 2019). Furthermore, blockchain necessitates that transactions undergo verification by a consensus of network participants, maintaining the integrity of the public ledger. Once recorded, transactions are immutable, providing a transparent and auditable record of all activities. This decentralized and transparent framework facilitates the development of an inclusive and scalable digital economy. Figure 2 illustrates the basic working process of a blockchain transaction, as outlined by the author. Figure 3 presents an illustration of a basic blockchain, as depicted by the author.

Figure 2. Basic Working Process of a Blockchain Transaction (Author)

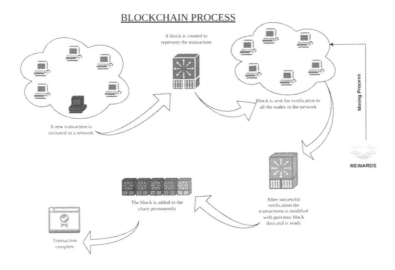

Figure 3. Illustration of a Basic Blockchain (Author)

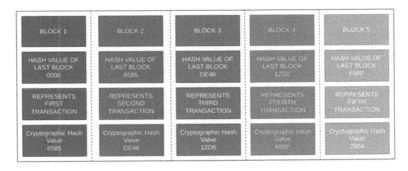

Additionally, blockchain technology incentivizes participants to validate transactions through a process known as "mining." Miners utilize computational resources to solve cryptographic puzzles and validate transactions, receiving rewards from the network's native currency (Ammous, 2016). The two primary categories of blockchain architectures are permissionless and permissioned blockchains. Permissionless blockchains offer unrestricted read and write access, while permissioned blockchains limit participation to designated entities (Yaga et al., 2018).

Important Blockchain Component

Node

Blockchain nodes are devices that participate in transactions within a blockchain network. These are crucial network components for validating transactions and maintaining the distributed ledger. Aswal (2024) describes three primary types of nodes which are the "full nodes," which are capable of storing the entire blockchain and independently verifying transactions, ensuring the network's integrity; "light nodes," designed for devices with limited storage, for transaction validation it rely on full nodes and "miner nodes" perform complex calculations to add new blocks to the blockchain, earning rewards for their efforts. These nodes maintain the blockchain's security, accuracy, and functionality, ensuring its resilience against attacks and failures (Aswal, 2024).

Consensus

Consensus in blockchain refers to the method by which a distributed network of nodes collectively validates transactions and determines the current state of the blockchain (Bamakan et al., 2020). This mechanism ensures all nodes have a consistent and tamper-proof ledger, even with malicious actors or faulty nodes. Various consensus algorithms, such as Byzantine Fault Tolerance (BFT), Proof of Work (PoW), and Proof of Stake (PoS), are used to achieve this agreement (Gao et al., 2019). These algorithms allow nodes to validate a transaction, add that to the blockchain, and maintain the system's security and integrity without a central authority. The consensus process is vital for solving the Byzantine generals problem and preventing issues like double spending, ensuring the reliability and trustworthiness of blockchain networks (Mingxiao et al., 2017).

Hash

In blockchain, a hash is a fixed-length encrypted output that uniquely represents input data and ensures data integrity. A hash is produced by applying a hashing algorithm to a message or text, scrambling the input thoroughly, and condensing it into a fixed-length form called the "digest" (Cheddad et al., 2010). In Bitcoin mining, the hashing algorithm is Secure Hash Algorithm 256 (SHA-256), which generates a digest of 256 binary digits. Hashing is vital for Bitcoin mining, as miners' computers primarily focus on hashing transactions to create a nearly immutable and fully consensual record, eliminating the need for a central record keeper (MacKenzie, 2019).

Nonce

In blockchain, a nonce is a 32-bit arbitrary number used by miners to find a hash that meets specific criteria. Miners randomly select and modify the nonce to produce a hash. If a nonce does not yield the desired hash, miners try a different nonce until they achieve a successful result (MacKenzie, 2019). The essential function of a nonce in the blockchain is to ensure cryptographic security by varying the input to the hash function. This enables the PoW mechanism, which validates transactions and secures the network.

Smart Contracts

A smart contract is a computer program that executes contract terms automatically when specific conditions are fulfilled. These terms are encoded in computer code and stored, replicated, and updated across distributed blockchains. Smart contracts enforce contractual terms without needing a trusted third party, leading to reduced administration costs, improved efficiency in business processes, and automated execution of agreements (Zheng et al., 2019). Smart contracts help cut administration costs by triggering actions on decentralized platforms and enhance efficiency, notably in SCs, by enabling peer-to-peer settlements upon meeting conditions. Smart contracts foster trust, automation, and cost savings across industries, revolutionizing traditional business practices (Zheng et al., 2019).

Types of Blockchain

Blockchain technology can be broadly classified into public and private types depending on data accessibility and decentralization levels. However, other types are mentioned under some criteria, such as Community/Consortium Blockchain and Hybrid Blockchain (Gamage et al., 2020; Lin & Liao, 2017; Paul et al., 2021; Shrivas & Yeboah, 2019). Figure 4 illustrates the categorization of blockchain.

In a private blockchain, entry to the blockchain network is limited to a specific organization or all the organizations in the same group (Shrivas & Yeboah, 2019). Private blockchains operate similarly to public blockchains but within a smaller, more restricted network, where a single controlling organization manages security, authorizations, permissions, and accessibility (Pongnumkul et al., 2017). Paul et al. (2021) list some advantages of private blockchain over public, such as higher privacy efficiency, faster transactions, and better scalability. It has characteristics such as pre-selected participants, the absence of cryptocurrency requirements, low decentralization, high throughput, and low energy consumption (Paul et al., 2021).

Hyperledger Sawtooth, Hyperledger Fabric, IBM, and R3 Corda are examples of private blockchains (Sharma, 2024).

In a public blockchain, everyone can check transactions, verify them, and participate in the consensus process (Lin & Liao, 2017). A public blockchain is known for its robust security and privacy, open and adaptable environment, anonymity, absence of stringent regulations and policies, complete transparency, and decentralized structure (Paul et al., 2021). Public blockchains offer advantages such as decentralization, transparency, security, immutability, interoperability, tokenization, community-driven development, global accessibility, and incentive mechanisms. However, they also face scalability issues, high energy consumption, privacy concerns, regulatory challenges, lack of governance, user-friendliness, unpredictable transaction costs, and smart contract risks (Sharma, 2024). Examples of the public blockchains are Ethereum and Bitcoin (Paul et al., 2021; Sharma, 2024).

A consortium blockchain is a semi-decentralized type of blockchain with private and public blockchain characteristics. It is managed by a group of organizations, allowing for the exchange of information and activities like mining (Paul et al., 2021). Unlike private blockchains, where a single group has control, a consortium blockchain involves multiple groups with more than one controller, giving it its semi-decentralized nature. While shared control, enhanced privacy, high efficiency, cost savings, interoperability, customization, trust among participants, regulatory compliance, resilience, and gradual adoption offer significant advantages, consortium blockchains also face challenges such as limited decentralization, complex governance structures, interoperability issues, security risks from member actions, scalability problems, potential cartel formation, over-dependence on critical members, and complex integration processes (Sharma, 2024). Energy Web Foundation is a typical example of a consortium blockchain (Paul et al., 2021; Sharma, 2024).

A hybrid blockchain integrates public, private, and consortium blockchains to facilitate transactions, enabling a blockchain platform to operate in diverse modes and capitalize on the strengths of each type (Shrivas & Yeboah, 2019). It enables customization by integrating permission-based and permission-less systems, allowing users access to selected sections while securing and recording the rest. This flexibility enhances security and transparency, making Hybrid Blockchains a compelling option for achieving higher goals in blockchain networks (Paul et al., 2021). This model is incredibly flexible, allowing for personalized adaptations based on specific objectives. Organizations can create a blockchain system incorporating the advantages of private, public, and consortium models while avoiding drawbacks. Figure 4 shows the classification of blockchain technology, as outlined by the author.

Figure 4. Classification of Blockchain Technology (Author)

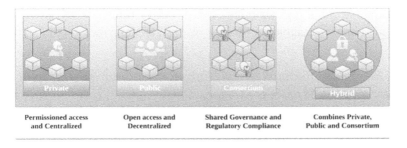

BLOCKCHAIN AND SCM

As we discussed earlier, a well-functioning SC ensures the seamless movement of products from origin to the final destination, underpinning the success of businesses across industries. However, traditional SCM systems often encounter challenges such as opacity, inefficiency, and vulnerability to fraud and errors. Blockchain technology has emerged as a transformative solution to address these limitations, presenting a paradigm shift in the management and optimization of SCs. By providing a decentralized, transparent, and immutable ledger system, blockchain presents unprecedented opportunities to revolutionize SCM processes by enhancing security, traceability, and transparency, thereby fostering stakeholder trust.

Applications of Blockchain in SCM

In today's digital age, SCM is crucial in ensuring efficient and transparent movement of goods and services. Companies are increasingly turning to blockchain technology to enhance SCM processes. By leveraging blockchain, companies can improve the security, traceability, and transparency of products throughout the SC, reducing the risk of counterfeit goods, ensuring compliance with regulations, and enhancing trust and collaboration among SC partners. Blockchain technology can streamline and automate various SC processes, including inventory management, order tracking, and payment settlements (Sardjono et al., 2023). Furthermore, blockchain technology can enable secure and tamper-proof record-keeping, making verifying the authenticity and provenance of products more accessible. Blockchain's applications in SCM are varied and promise to transform how companies operate and collaborate within their SC network. By integrating blockchain technology, businesses can lower intermediary costs and enhance efficiency. Overall, blockchain has the potential to improve SCM significantly by boosting transparency, traceability, trust, and operational efficiency in the flow of goods and services. Figure 5 demonstrates how blockchain technology can enhance the security, transparency, and traceability of the supply chain management (SCM) process, as described by the author.

Figure 5. Blockchain Technology can Enhance the Security, Transparency, and Traceability of the SCM process (Author)

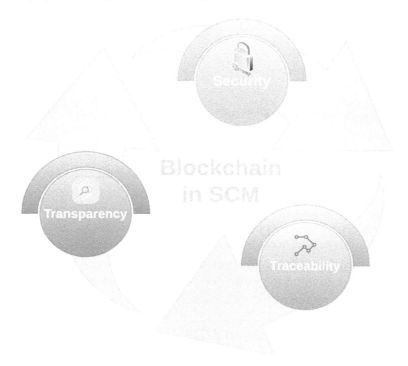

Security, Transparency, and Traceability

Traditional SC systems often face challenges related to inefficiencies, lack of transparency, and fraud and security breach vulnerabilities. The advent of blockchain technology marks a significant shift in how SCs are managed and operated. It has emerged as a transformative force, revolutionizing SCM by providing numerous benefits that tackle crucial challenges businesses face today. At its core, blockchain facilitates the reduction of production costs by streamlining processes, eliminating intermediaries, and enhancing overall efficiency (Al-Farsi et al., 2021). This streamlined approach leads to cost savings and ensures SC operations are conducted with increased transparency and traceability, fostering trust among stakeholders, including customers, suppliers, dealers, and retailers (Francisco & Swanson, 2018). Moreover, blockchain's transparent and immutable ledger system provides real-time tracking of products from origin to reception, effectively preventing fraud and ensuring product authenticity. Blockchain technology's decentralized and cryptographic nature further enhances security by safeguarding against tampering attacks and unauthorized access. This heightened security mitigates risks within the SC, such as counterfeit products and delivery delays, and provides a competitive advantage to companies that adopt blockchain solutions. By automating tasks through smart contracts, blockchain drives efficiency and economic growth without manual intervention and paperwork. Integrating blockchain technology into SCM improves operational efficiency and strengthens trust, transparency, and security, positioning businesses for sustained success in an increasingly competitive market landscape.

Security is paramount in SCM, given the sensitive nature of organizational information and the prevalence of security threats. Blockchain technology is crucial in bolstering security by offering a secure and immutable way to record transactions and data across the SC. Its decentralized and distributed structure ensures that once information is recorded, it remains unchanged and cannot be deleted without consensus from the network, thus protecting against unauthorized access or tampering (Bai & Sarkis, 2020). Moreover, the immutability of blockchain data adds an extra layer of security, ensuring that transactions and information remain secure from tampering attacks, thus bolstering the overall security of the SC (Al-Farsi et al., 2021). Blockchain technology establishes a robust security framework for SC operations by safeguarding data integrity, reducing the risk of fraud and unauthorized access, and ensuring the reliability of transactions (Al-Farsi et al., 2021; Francisco & Swanson, 2018).

People tend to trust what is transparent. If a system is transparent and its processes can be easily understood, it is deemed trustworthy. Thus, transparency in SCM is also critical to gaining the customers' and players' trust. Transparency enables explicit coordination among various processes and facilitates the timely identification of inconsistencies or conflicts. Both end customers and companies within the SC need readily accessible information. Blockchain technology significantly improves transparency by offering an immutable and transparent ledger that tracks product interactions among stakeholders (Al-Farsi et al., 2021). Blockchain enhances trust among partners and stakeholders in the SC network by making transaction data visible to all participants, enabling real-time access to information on transactions and product movements (Bai & Sarkis, 2020). Moreover, this technology allows for greater visibility into product origins, processes, and sustainability information, thereby building consumer confidence and trust in the products and processes within the SC (Bai & Sarkis, 2020). Utilizing blockchain helps verify the authenticity, quality, and ethical sourcing of products, which strengthens trust and accountability among SC stakeholders, including consumers, suppliers, and regulators (Francisco & Swanson, 2018). Blockchain's contribution to transparency ensures efficient coordination and cost savings and fosters trust and accountability throughout the SC ecosystem.

This transparency of an SC is achieved by tracking the movement of products or components throughout the SC. When an SC process has the potential to accurately and efficiently identify and record the origins, destinations, and intermediate steps of a product's journey, then the SC has traceability. Traceability allows for monitoring product flow, quality control, and compliance with regulations and standards. According to Bai and Sarkis (2020), blockchain technology revolutionizes SCM by providing end-to-end traceability of products through secure and transparent recording of transactions or events, enabling stakeholders to track product journeys from origin to end customer. Through blockchain-enabled traceability, SC participants can easily trace product components, processes, and sustainability information, ensuring accountability and authenticity throughout the SC (Bai & Sarkis, 2020). By leveraging blockchain, SC managers can significantly improve transparency and traceability, which are essential for building trust and ensuring stakeholder accountability. This traceability, facilitated by blockchain-based solutions, creates a verifiable record of product origin and journey across the SC without manipulation, thereby helping to verify product authenticity and prevent fraud (Al-Farsi et al., 2021).

Furthermore, blockchain technology enhances traceability by securely recording every transaction in an immutable ledger, allowing stakeholders to trace the history of products from their source to the final destination (Francisco & Swanson, 2018). This capability is invaluable for verifying compliance with regulations, identifying inefficiencies, and promptly addressing product recalls or ethical concerns within the SC ecosystem. Blockchain technology has emerged as a transformative force in SCM, providing unprecedented potential to improve ecosystem security, transparency, and traceability. Additionally, blockchain facilitates participant transparency by making operational details and sustainability conditions visible to relevant stakeholders, fostering greater collaboration and alignment within the SC (Bai & Sarkis, 2020).

Examples of Case Studies on Blockchain in SCM

A case study in a pesticide company highlighted that the most significant SC challenge is the risk of raw materials not meeting specifications, which can result in inefficiencies, quality concerns, and potential disruptions to production (Gozali et al., 2024). The study highlights that leveraging blockchain technology can address this issue by providing a decentralized and immutable ledger that records transactions and data, enabling real-time tracking and verification of raw materials specifications. This technology can improve trust among SC partners, enhance data security, and streamline the process of evaluating supplier performance. By leveraging blockchain to monitor supplier performance, companies can ensure that raw materials meet the required specifications, thus reducing the likelihood of quality issues and disruptions in the SC.

Danese et al. (2021) have discussed five scenarios in the SC of a wine industry using blockchain technology. The cases described illustrate the application of blockchain technology across various segments of the wine industry in Italy, highlighting different aspects of SCM and transparency. First, a northern Italian winemaking company producing 500,000 bottles annually collaborates with a technology provider offering blockchain-based solutions to enhance SC efficiency. The second case involves a southern Italian winemaking company producing 300,000 bottles annually, utilizing blockchain innovations provided by a global ICT group to manage interactions with three grapes suppliers. The third case examines a premium wine producer that adheres to PDO specifications, highlighting transparency to underscore the high value of their products. In contrast, the fourth case explores the technical use of blockchain, specifically Ethereum, to combat counterfeiting in the wine sector. It further discusses the implications of employing a public blockchain provider to ensure transparency and security in the SC (Danese et al., 2021). These cases underscore how blockchain technology can transform the entire SC by enhancing trust, traceability, and quality control.

In another case study conducted by Ada et al. (2021) on the automobile industry's SC processes, the authors explore integrating blockchain technology to enhance traceability and efficiency. They identified the challenges manufacturers face in tracking the transportation of parts, production, and products that need to be delivered, exacerbated by the automotive industry's global reach. The study reviews traditional SC issues and the limitations of existing traceability methods. By developing a blockchain model, critical nodes that pose risks to traceability can be identified, allowing for effective technology integration within automotive organizations. Blockchain technology incorporates sensors and diverse data collection methods, requiring a highly secure model to govern the system and guarantee the reliability of data from these sources (Ada et al., 2021).

Casino et al. (2021) describe the problems faced by food SC, especially the dairy companies. The authors have established this by pointing out the difficulties faced by a long-established family-owned dairy company based in Erythres, Attica. The company was renowned for its premium dairy products distributed locally in Greece and twelve other countries. However, due to this large market, the company encountered traceability challenges within its SC. Apart from traceability, food SC usually encounters challenges, including manual tracking processes, opacity, and inefficiencies in information sharing. In their study, the authors have proposed a blockchain-based traceability solution integrating IoT and blockchain technologies in a comprehensive "from-farm-to-fork" approach (Casino et al., 2021). They suggest a decentralized and automated traceability model for the food SC based on blockchain and smart contracts to address the limitations of traditional SCM processes. Through the adoption of blockchain and smart contracts, dairy companies' SCs can aim to improve product tracking efficiency, reduce the risk of data manipulation, and ensure data integrity across the SC.

Rogerson and Parry (2020) present a comprehensive case study on challenges within the food SC, emphasizing product visibility, trust, and authenticity issues. The study examines four notable cases, beginning with AgriDigital, an Australian firm leveraging blockchain technology to manage agricultural commodities, enhancing transparency by verifying organic product status through data recording on a private blockchain. Similarly, Techrock, a Chinese company established in 2013, addresses infant formula safety concerns with RFID-tagged 'smart packaging' and a public blockchain. However, challenges persist regarding cost-effectiveness and consumer trust. In Fiji, TraSeable Solutions collaborates with WWF to promote sustainable tuna fishing via blockchain, yet faces hurdles such as limited digital infrastructure and data standardization.

Finally, Demeter, a European company, utilizes blockchain to authenticate and verify consumer goods like wine, overcoming counterfeiting issues while contending with consumer skepticism and misconceptions surrounding blockchain technology (Rogerson & Parry, 2020). The problems addressed in the case study are the lack of transparency and inefficiencies in traditional SC systems. This leads to information asymmetry, fraud, and difficulty tracking products from farm to fork. The traceability problem can be a significant issue in the food SC mainly because food SC deals with perishable goods. The authors also point out that using the blockchain's decentralized and transparent ledger system that can securely record transactions and product information at each stage of the SC companies can enhance product visibility, traceability, and authenticity, thereby building trust among consumers and stakeholders.

Öz and Gören (2019) describe three significant examples of blockchain applications. According to the authors, the world's largest container carrier, Maersk, partnered with IBM in 2014 to explore blockchain applications in international logistics, aiming to enhance tracking and documentation processes, improve loading and unloading efficiency, and reduce delays caused by documentation. In 2016, this concept was successfully applied to a flower shipment from Kenya to the Netherlands, reducing shipment costs significantly. By January 2018, Maersk and IBM launched a joint venture to implement blockchain technology for more efficient and secure global trade, offering end-to-end SC visibility and paperless trade solutions.

Meanwhile, Swiss startup Modum, collaborating with the University of Zurich, developed a system for safely distributing pharmacochemical drugs using sensors to continuously monitor temperature, humidity, and light conditions during transport. This response to the EU's Good Delivery Practice regulations allows real-time monitoring and reporting via the Ethereum blockchain, ensuring compliance without expensive refrigerated trucks and focusing on drugs stored at room temperature to reduce cooling costs. Modum successfully tested its findings in June 2016. Additionally, in April 2017, Intel demonstrated the application of its open-source Sawtooth code base for monitoring the marine SC through the "Ocean to Table" project. This initiative aimed to enhance marine traceability by ensuring compliance with food storage requirements. The project tracked four trading transactions using IoT sensors and blockchain technology to monitor telemetry and temperature data from sea to market, providing end-users with complete and accurate SC records and ensuring transparency and reliability (Öz & Gören, 2019).

Challenges and Limitations of Blockchain in SCM

We have already discussed how blockchain technology can streamline SC processes. Despite its potential, blockchain implementation in SCM faces numerous challenges and limitations that must be addressed to achieve widespread adoption and effectiveness. There are several technical challenges in the implementation of blockchain. One of the primary technical challenges is scalability (Al Amin et al., 2023; Jabbar et al., 2021; Uddin et al., 2023). Blockchain networks often need help accommodating large numbers of users, leading to lengthy transaction times and increased costs. The load on the system, especially on significantly larger blockchain platforms, results in moderate transaction rates and elevated cost of exchange due to a substantial increase in clients. This lack of scalability is a critical hindrance to the widespread integration of blockchain in SCM. Another critical issue is interoperability (Chang et al., 2020; Jabbar et al., 2021). Blockchain systems cannot seamlessly interact with many organizations' existing Enterprise Resource Planning (ERP) systems. This lack of interoperability means businesses cannot easily integrate blockchain with their existing technologies, complicating its adoption and effectiveness. Latency problems also plague blockchain networks (Al Amin et al., 2023). The inherent delay in transaction processing leads to slower transaction times, a critical issue in SCs that demand high-speed operations. This latency can hinder the efficiency of SC processes, making blockchain less appealing for real-time applications.

Besides these technical challenges, implementation costs (Al Amin et al., 2023) and energy consumption (Uddin et al., 2023) are significant barriers to blockchain implementation. Implementing a blockchain system demands high investments in the latest hardware and software and frequent maintenance costs. These financial challenges are even more pronounced for large-scale integrations, posing significant barriers to adoption for many organizations. Blockchain systems, particularly those based on algorithms, consume substantial energy. This high energy consumption raises operational costs and environmental concerns, which can conflict with sustainability goals in SCM.

Even if blockchain is meant to enhance security features, it is not entirely immune to security risks. Security and trust issues are also critical barriers to implementation (Liu et al., 2021). Vulnerabilities to hacking and system attacks pose significant risks (Al Amin et al., 2023). The immutability of blockchain means that any incorrect data entered cannot be easily corrected, which could lead to lasting errors. Moreover, blockchain's transparency can occasionally clash with the requirement for data confidentiality, adding complexity to its application in SCM (Jabbar et al., 2021). The trustworthiness of a blockchain can be questioned due to the need for more standardization and regulatory frameworks. The absence of industry-wide standards and practices adds complexity to blockchain adoption. Furthermore, legal and regulatory challenges vary by region, and government policies are often reluctant to support blockchain technology, making its implementation in SCs even more challenging (Chang et al., 2020).

A significantly lower knowledge and understanding of blockchain among business leaders and enterprises seriously hinders mainstream adoption (Al Amin et al., 2023; Jabbar et al., 2021). Many organizations need to fully comprehend how blockchain works or the benefits it can offer, leading to hesitation and resistance to its adoption. The lack of commitment from middle and upper management can negatively affect the perceived value of blockchain in SCM. With strong leadership support, initiatives to implement blockchain technology may succeed due to a lack of resources and prioritization. Differences in culture, business practices, and communication styles among SC partners also present challenges. Cultural and geographic diversity can lead to difficulties in collaboration and coordination, which are essential for successfully implementing blockchain in SCM. Businesses may hesitate to invest in new technologies amid uncertain market conditions (Liu et al., 2021). Furthermore, the lack of external stakeholders' involvement and consumer awareness about blockchain and its benefits for sustainability can hinder its implementation (Al Amin et al., 2023).

Blockchain's high energy consumption directly impacts its sustainability, posing a conflict for SCs that aim to adopt more environmentally friendly practices. Integrating blockchain with sustainable practices in SCM requires significant effort and innovation, and the lack of governmental sustainability laws and frameworks exacerbates this challenge (Al Amin et al., 2023). The immutability of blockchain data can be problematic if incorrect or unethical information is recorded. There is also a need for greater industry involvement in ethical and safe practices to ensure blockchain technology is used responsibly (Liu et al., 2021). Addressing these challenges requires cross-disciplinary efforts, strong leadership commitment, and the development of supportive regulatory frameworks. Blockchain technology can only realize its full potential in transforming SCM.

Emerging Trends and Future Perspectives of Blockchain

Blockchain technology is slowly becoming integral to our lives. We will witness a boom in blockchain users in industries including SCM, healthcare, finance, real estate, legal and intellectual property, retail, and e-commerce. Many blockchain technologies are under development or in their initial stages that have the potential to revolutionize the near future. The adoption of digital currencies by central banks worldwide signals a promising advancement for the future of blockchain and its applications (Auer et al., 2020). A Central Bank Digital Currency (CBDC) is a digital representation of fiat money issued directly by a central bank (Ozili, 2023). CBDCs represent a significant advancement in the financial sector, leveraging blockchain technology to digitize national currencies. This innovation streamlines cross-border transactions and facilitates more transparent and secure SC payment processes, reducing fraud risk and enhancing financial inclusivity.

Simultaneously, the explosive growth of Non-Fungible Tokens (NFTs) has captured widespread attention, demonstrating the potential for blockchain beyond traditional financial applications. NFTs, representing unique digital assets (Król & Zdonek, 2022), offer provenance tracking and authentication opportunities in SCs, particularly in sectors like luxury goods and art, where authenticity is paramount. This boom in NFT adoption underscores the versatility of blockchain technology in verifying the origin and ownership of assets, thereby mitigating counterfeiting and bolstering trust among stakeholders.

Still in its initial development, the metaverse concept has proven to be a transformative technology. The metaverse technology will differ from any other virtual world we have experienced (Mystakidis, 2022). The metaverse is an entirely different realm that leverages several blockchain technologies. The metaverse presents new avenues for SC integration and collaboration with blockchain as the underlying infrastructure. In this immersive digital environment, businesses can leverage blockchain-enabled smart contracts to automate procurement, inventory management, and logistics processes, fostering seamless interactions among global partners and customers.

Furthermore, Blockchain-as-a-Service (BaaS) solutions have democratized access to blockchain technology (Akinwande, n.d.), allowing enterprises to harness its benefits without significant upfront investment or technical expertise. By leveraging BaaS platforms, organizations can deploy customized blockchain networks tailored to their specific SC requirements, enhancing traceability, data integrity, and collaboration across disparate stakeholders (Song et al., 2022). This democratization of blockchain empowers businesses of all sizes to optimize their SC operations and efficiently adapt to evolving market demands.

Another pivotal development is the rise of asset tokenization, wherein physical assets are represented as digital tokens on a blockchain network (Wang & Nixon, 2021). This trend holds immense promise for SCM, enabling fractional ownership, real-time asset tracking, and enhanced liquidity for non-liquid assets such as real estate or fine art. By tokenizing assets, SC stakeholders can unlock new avenues for investment, financing, and value exchange while ensuring transparency and integrity throughout the asset lifecycle.

The convergence of these emerging technologies is poised to redefine the future landscape of blockchain in SCM. As CBDCs, NFTs, the metaverse, BaaS, and asset tokenization evolve, they will catalyze innovation and drive unprecedented efficiencies across SCs worldwide. From optimizing inventory management to enhancing sustainability practices and enabling frictionless cross-border trade, blockchain-enabled solutions will play a crucial role in shaping the next generation of SCM. However, realizing the full potential of these technologies will require collaboration, standardization, and continued investment in research and development. By embracing these emerging trends and harnessing the power of blockchain, businesses can future-proof their SCs and unlock new avenues to grow and improve resilience in an increasingly digital economy.

CONCLUSION

Since its inception by Satoshi Nakamoto in 2008 to validate and track digital cryptocurrency transactions, blockchain technology has rapidly expanded its impact across every sector. It has applications across multiple industries, such as healthcare, real estate, law, e-commerce, and finance. It has significantly revolutionized global SCs by enhancing security, transparency, and traceability. Blockchain verifies online transactions involving digital assets and ensures they are unchangeable once recorded, creating a transparent and auditable history of all activities. This decentralized system fosters the growth of a more inclusive and adaptable digital economy.

Multiple components collaborate to finalize a transaction within the blockchain framework. In a blockchain network, nodes are crucial in facilitating online transactions. They ensure the network's security and functionality. Consensus is the process where nodes collectively validate transactions in a distributed network. Hash functions convert input transactions into fixed-length hash values, ensuring an immutable and universally agreed-upon record. Miners utilize 32-bit arbitrary numbers, called nonces, to identify hash values that meet specific criteria. Smart contracts are computer programs that automatically execute contract clauses when specific conditions are fulfilled, eliminating the requirement for third-party involvement and boosting system reliability.

Blockchain networks can generally be categorized into private and public. Public blockchains are open and flexible, while private blockchains are closed and have restricted access. A third type, consortium blockchain, offers features of both public and private blockchains and a semi-decentralized network. These types can also be combined to create hybrid blockchains, which are gaining popularity due to their flexibility and customizable features.

Implementing blockchain faces numerous challenges despite its vast opportunities. Scalability issues stand out as a significant obstacle. Additionally, interoperability issues, high implementation costs, excessive energy consumption, and the absence of government regulations contribute to the complexity. The low understanding of blockchain technology among the internal and external stakeholders poses a significant barrier.

The future trajectory of blockchain technology is promising, especially given the rising trends in CBDCs, NFTs, BaaS, and asset tokenization. Metaverse is the future, and blockchain technology plays a significant part. However, fully unlocking its potential demands cross-disciplinary efforts, unwavering leadership commitment, and the establishment of supportive regulatory frameworks. Delving deeper into blockchain's capabilities requires a comprehensive approach that addresses scalability, interoperability, cost-effectiveness, energy efficiency, and regulatory clarity. Through collaborative endeavors and proactive governance, we can leverage blockchain's transformative power to revolutionize industries and reshape societal paradigms.

REFERENCES

Ada, N., Ethirajan, M., & Kumar, A., K.E.K, V., Nadeem, S. P., Kazancoglu, Y., & Kandasamy, J. (. (2021). Blockchain Technology for Enhancing Traceability and Efficiency in Automobile Supply Chain—A Case Study. *Sustainability*, 13(24), 13667. DOI: 10.3390/su132413667

Akinwande, V. (n.d.). Security assessment of blockchain-as-a-service (BaaS) platforms. *2017*.

Al Amin, M., Nabil, D. H., Baldacci, R., & Rahman, M. (2023). Exploring Blockchain Implementation Challenges for Sustainable Supply Chains: An Integrated Fuzzy TOPSIS–ISM Approach. *Sustainability (Basel)*, 15(18), 13891. DOI: 10.3390/su151813891

Al-Farsi, S., Rathore, M. M., & Bakiras, S. (2021). Security of Blockchain-Based Supply Chain Management Systems: Challenges and Opportunities. *Applied Sciences (Basel, Switzerland)*, 11(12), 5585. DOI: 10.3390/app11125585

Ammous, S. (2016). Blockchain Technology: What is it good for? *Available at SSRN 2832751*. DOI: 10.2139/ssrn.2832751

Aswal, P. (2024, May 10). *What are Blockchain nodes? Detailed Guide [UPDATED]*. Blockchain Council. https://www.blockchain-council.org/blockchain/blockchain-nodes/

Auer, R., Cornelli, G., & Frost, J. (2020). Rise of the Central Bank Digital Currencies: Drivers, Approaches and Technologies. *CEPR Discussion Paper No. DP15363*.

Bai, C., & Sarkis, J. (2020). A supply chain transparency and sustainability technology appraisal model for blockchain technology. *International Journal of Production Research*, 58(7), 2142–2162. DOI: 10.1080/00207543.2019.1708989

Bamakan, S. M. H., Motavali, A., & Babaei Bondarti, A. (2020). A survey of blockchain consensus algorithms performance evaluation criteria. *Expert Systems with Applications*, 154, 113385. DOI: 10.1016/j.eswa.2020.113385

Casino, F., Kanakaris, V., Dasaklis, T. K., Moschuris, S., Stachtiaris, S., Pagoni, M., & Rachaniotis, N. P. (2021). Blockchain-based food supply chain traceability: A case study in the dairy sector. *International Journal of Production Research*, 59(19), 5758–5770. DOI: 10.1080/00207543.2020.1789238

Chang, Y., Iakovou, E., & Shi, W. (2020). Blockchain in global supply chains and cross border trade: A critical synthesis of the state-of-the-art, challenges and opportunities. *International Journal of Production Research*, 58(7), 2082–2099. DOI: 10.1080/00207543.2019.1651946

Cheddad, A., Condell, J., Curran, K., & McKevitt, P. (2010). A hash-based image encryption algorithm. *Optics Communications*, 283(6), 879–893. DOI: 10.1016/j.optcom.2009.10.106

Danese, P., Mocellin, R., & Romano, P. (2021). Designing blockchain systems to prevent counterfeiting in wine supply chains: A multiple-case study. *International Journal of Operations & Production Management*, 41(13), 1–33. DOI: 10.1108/IJOPM-12-2019-0781

Daniels, B. (1999). Integration of the supply chain for total through-cost reduction. *Total Quality Management*, 10(4–5), 481–490. DOI: 10.1080/0954412997433

Francisco, K., & Swanson, D. (2018). The Supply Chain Has No Clothes: Technology Adoption of Blockchain for Supply Chain Transparency. *Logistics (Basel)*, 2(1), 2. DOI: 10.3390/logistics2010002

Gamage, H. T. M., Weerasinghe, H. D., & Dias, N. G. J. (2020). A Survey on Blockchain Technology Concepts, Applications, and Issues. *SN Computer Science*, 1(2), 114. DOI: 10.1007/s42979-020-00123-0

Gao, S., Yu, T., Zhu, J., & Cai, W. (2019). T-PBFT: An EigenTrust-based practical Byzantine fault tolerance consensus algorithm. *China Communications*, 16(12), 111–123. DOI: 10.23919/JCC.2019.12.008

Gozali, L., Kristina, H. J., Yosua, A., Zagloel, T. Y. M., Masrom, M., Susanto, S., Tanujaya, H., Irawan, A. P., Gunadi, A., Kumar, V., Garza-Reyes, J. A., Jap, T. B., & Daywin, F. J. (2024). The improvement of block chain technology simulation in supply chain management (case study: Pesticide company). *Scientific Reports*, 14(1), 3784. DOI: 10.1038/s41598-024-53694-w PMID: 38360895

Harland, C. M. (1996). Supply Chain Management: Relationships, Chains and Networks. *British Journal of Management*, 7(s1). Advance online publication. DOI: 10.1111/j.1467-8551.1996.tb00148.x

Hugos, M. H. (2024). *Essentials of Supply Chain Management* (Fourth). John Wiley & Sons, Inc.

Ibrahim, S. B., & Hamid, A. A. (2014). Supply Chain Management Practices and Supply Chain Performance Effectiveness. [IJSR]. *International Journal of Scientific Research*, 3(8).

Jabbar, S., Lloyd, H., Hammoudeh, M., Adebisi, B., & Raza, U. (2021). Blockchain-enabled supply chain: Analysis, challenges, and future directions. *Multimedia Systems*, 27(4), 787–806. DOI: 10.1007/s00530-020-00687-0

Khan, M. Z., Al-Mushayt, O., Alam, J., & Ahmad, J. (2010). Intelligent Supply Chain Management. *Journal of Software Engineering and Applications*, 03(04), 404–408. DOI: 10.4236/jsea.2010.34045

Król, K., & Zdonek, D. (2022). Digital Assets in the Eyes of Generation Z: Perceptions, Outlooks, Concerns. *Journal of Risk and Financial Management*, 16(1), 22. DOI: 10.3390/jrfm16010022

Laurence, T. (2019). *Introduction to Blockchain technology The many faces of blockchain technology in the 21st century*. Van Haren Publishing.

Lin, I.-C., & Liao, T.-C. (2017). A Survey of Blockchain Security Issues and Challenges. *International Journal of Network Security*, 19(5), 653–659.

Liu, P., Hendalianpour, A., Hamzehlou, M., Feylizadeh, M. R., & Razmi, J. (2021). Identify and Rank the Challenges of Implementing Sustainable Supply Chain Blockchain Technology Using the Bayesian Best Worst Method. *Technological and Economic Development of Economy*, 27(3), 656–680. DOI: 10.3846/tede.2021.14421

MacKenzie, D. (2019). Pick a nonce and try a hash. *London Review of Books*, 41(8), 35–38.

Mentzer, J. T., DeWitt, W., Keebler, J. S., Min, S., Nix, N. W., Smith, C. D., & Zacharia, Z. G. (2001). DEFINING SUPPLY CHAIN MANAGEMENT. *Journal of Business Logistics*, 22(2), 1–25. DOI: 10.1002/j.2158-1592.2001.tb00001.x

Mingxiao, D., Xiaofeng, M., Zhe, Z., Xiangwei, W., & Qijun, C. (2017). A review on consensus algorithm of blockchain. *2017 IEEE International Conference on Systems, Man, and Cybernetics (SMC)*, 2567–2572. DOI: 10.1109/SMC.2017.8123011

Mystakidis, S. (2022). Metaverse. *Encyclopedia*, 2(1), 486–497. DOI: 10.3390/encyclopedia2010031

Nasereddin, A. Y. (2024). A comprehensive survey of contemporary supply chain management practices in charting the digital age revolution. *Uncertain Supply Chain Management*, 12(2), 1331–1352. DOI: 10.5267/j.uscm.2023.11.004

Öz, S., & Gören, H. E. (2019). Application of Blockchain Technology in the Supply Chain Management Process: Case Studies. *Journal of International Trade. Logistics and Law*, 5(1), 21–27.

Ozili, P. K. (2023). Central bank digital currency research around the world: A review of literature. *Journal of Money Laundering Control*, 26(2), 215–226. DOI: 10.1108/JMLC-11-2021-0126

Paul, P. K., Aithal, P. S., Saavedra, R., & Ghosh, S. (2021). Blockchain Technology and its Types—A Short Review. [IJASE]. *International Journal of Applied Science and Engineering*, 9(2), 189–200. DOI: 10.30954/2322-0465.2.2021.7

Pongnumkul, S., Siripanpornchana, C., & Thajchayapong, S. (2017). Performance Analysis of Private Blockchain Platforms in Varying Workloads. *2017 26th International Conference on Computer Communication and Networks (ICCCN)*, 1–6. DOI: 10.1109/ICCCN.2017.8038517

Rogerson, M., & Parry, G. C. (2020). Blockchain: Case studies in food supply chain visibility. *Supply Chain Management*, 25(5), 601–614. DOI: 10.1108/SCM-08-2019-0300

Sardjono, W., Arum, I. R. M., Rahmasari, A., & Lusia, E. (2023). Impact of Track and Trace (T&T) in Industrial Revolution 4.0 of the Pharmaceutical Industry (Pharma 4.0). *E3S Web of Conferences, 388*, 03014. DOI: 10.1051/e3sconf/202338803014

Sarmah, S. S. (2018). Understanding Blockchain Technology. *Computing in Science & Engineering*, 8(2), 23–29.

Sharma, T. K. (2024, May). *Types of Blockchains Explained- Public Vs. Private Vs. Consortium [UPDATED]*. Blockchain Council.

Shrivas, M. K., & Yeboah, T. (2019). The Disruptive Blockchain: Types, Platforms and Applications. [TIJAR]. *Texila International Journal of Academic Research*, 3, 17–39. DOI: 10.21522/TIJAR.2014.SE.19.01.Art003

Sindhwani, R., Hasteer, N., Behl, A., Chatterjee, C., & Hamzi, L. (2023). Analysis of sustainable supply chain and industry 4.0 enablers: A step towards decarbonization of supply chains. *Annals of Operations Research*. Advance online publication. DOI: 10.1007/s10479-023-05598-7

Song, J., Zhang, P., Alkubati, M., Bao, Y., & Yu, G. (2022). Research advances on blockchain-as-a-service: Architectures, applications and challenges. *Digital Communications and Networks*, 8(4), 466–475. DOI: 10.1016/j.dcan.2021.02.001

Uddin, M., Selvarajan, S., Obaidat, M., Arfeen, S. U., Khadidos, A. O., Khadidos, A. O., & Abdelhaq, M. (2023). From Hype to Reality: Unveiling the Promises, Challenges and Opportunities of Blockchain in Supply Chain Systems. *Sustainability (Basel)*, 15(16), 12193. DOI: 10.3390/su151612193

Wang, G., & Nixon, M. (2021). SoK: tokenization on blockchain. *Proceedings of the 14th IEEE/ACM International Conference on Utility and Cloud Computing Companion*, 1–9. DOI: 10.1145/3492323.3495577

Yaga, D., Mell, P., Roby, N., & Scarfone, K. (2018). *Blockchain technology overview.* DOI: 10.6028/NIST.IR.8202

Zhai, S., Yang, Y., Li, J., Qiu, C., & Zhao, J. (2019). Research on the Application of Cryptography on the Blockchain. *Journal of Physics: Conference Series*, 1168, 032077. DOI: 10.1088/1742-6596/1168/3/032077

Zheng, Z., Xie, S., Dai, H.-N., Chen, W., Chen, X., Weng, J., & Imran, M. (2019). *An Overview on Smart Contracts: Challenges.* Advances and Platforms., DOI: 10.1016/j.future.2019.12.019

KEY TERMS AND DEFINITIONS

Blockchain: A transparent and distributed ledger system that maintains an immutable record of digital transactions through interconnected blocks created with cryptographic encoding.

Consensus: A mechanism that helps the distributed nodes in a network to agree to data collectively.

Decentralization: Process of equally distributing the control and decision-making power to all the participants in a network.

Hash: A cryptographic function that creates a fixed length unique output corresponding to each input data.

Mining: A process undertaken by miners to validate and add transaction records.

Node: Any device in the blockchain network that actively participates in transactions.

Nonce: An arbitrary 32-bit number essential for cryptographic security and validating transactions.

Smart contracts: A digital contract that automatically executes predefined contract clauses when predefined criteria are met.

Supply chain: A chain of processes that are necessary to fulfill a customer's demand. It includes activities such as accepting customer orders, production planning, acquiring raw materials, manufacturing, and delivery.

Supply chain management: Monitoring and managing all the activities involved in a supply chain.

Chapter 9
Utilizing Business Intelligence and Machine Learning in CRM Data to Reduce Customer Churn in E-commerce Platforms

Praket Pati Tiwari

VIT-AP University, India

G. P. Yuktha
https://orcid.org/0009-0004-9312-1094
VIT-AP University, India

A. Manimaran
https://orcid.org/0000-0002-5671-9466
VIT-AP University, India

ABSTRACT

In the ever-changing world of online business, keeping clients to achieve long-term growth and profitability is crucial. This work uses customer relationship management (CRM) data and machine learning techniques to reduce customer turnover. Initially, the previous CRM data is employed to identify clients no longer affiliated with the platform. Through analyzing prior encounters, such as reviews and purchase histories, valuable information about them preferences and complaints can be obtained. More precisely, negative comments are isolated to identify areas where the product might be improved or eliminated from the e-commerce catalogue. Furthermore, predictive analytics methods are utilized to improve client involvement and contentment. The

DOI: 10.4018/979-8-3693-8844-0.ch009

proposed approach combines CRM data analysis with machine learning algorithms such as Logistic Regression, Decision Tree, SVM, Random Forest, and XGBoost to provide a proactive strategy for reducing customer churn in e-commerce platforms.

INTRODUCTION

E-commerce is a modern business approach that enables the swift acquisition of many products with just a few clicks. In today's digital age, individuals frequently place their trust in these online platforms, where goods or services are bought and sold via the Internet (Manzoor, 2010). This trust primarily stems from three key factors: straightforward exchange or replacement policies, transparency in customer feedback, and the convenience of shopping from home.

On the other hand, several factors might deter some people from shopping on e-commerce platforms. These could encompass the lack of opportunity to examine the product physically, subpar website performance, inadequate cybersecurity measures, poorly articulated policies, the lengthy time for home delivery, and an insufficient customer service framework.

This leads to customer churn, also known as customer attrition, which refers to the phenomenon where customers stop using a company's products or services. It's a critical metric for e-commerce as it directly impacts revenue and growth. Understanding why customers churn and implementing strategies to reduce churn is essential for sustaining a successful business in today's competitive market.

In the ever-evolving landscape of online marketplaces, securing high customer loyalty is a prevalent challenge in business. A multitude of studies (Buckinx & Van den Poel, 2005; Dick & Basu, 1994; Gefen, 2002) have substantiated that it is more cost-effective to retain customers than to acquire new ones. Customer Relationship Management (CRM) is instrumental in managing loyalty and, conversely, predicting churn. Most past research has focused on industries where customers are bound by contracts (such as telecommunications or banking), which inherently limits the churn rate (Pejić Bach et al., 2021). Numerous studies have demonstrated the efficacy of Machine Learning approaches in predicting customer churn successfully (Dalvi et al., 2016; Gregory, 2018; Nie et al., 2011).

The focus here is e-commerce, a domain without contractual obligation between the customer and the platform. Therefore, such companies must strive for customer retention by regularly enhancing their services by analyzing their shortcomings. Consequently, this chapter employs a Machine Learning approach to scrutinize data, predict customer churn, and pinpoint potential factors contributing to their churn. The insights gleaned from this analysis are then utilized to provide personalized recommendations to customers.

OVERVIEW OF CUSTOMER RELATIONSHIP MANAGEMENT (CRM) DATA

Importance of CRM Data in Understanding Customer Behavior

E-commerce CRM data provides customer demographics, purchase history, feedback/comments, devices, and platform usage duration (Gold, 2020). This data plays an important role in helping companies understand their customers better. Companies can gain valuable insights about customer preferences, pain points, and shopping habits by analyzing this data. This insight is invaluable for e-commerce as it can be used to frame marketing strategies, optimize customer service, and improve customer loyalty and retention.

Why is RM data given so much importance?

Some of the possible reasons can be:

- Rich Data Source: CRM captures every aspect of customer data, from personal information to purchasing information. These aspects include interaction with the platform, feedback, and demographic details. This data can then be used for ML models to predict churn or to identify key pain points of our customers, among other uses.
- Behavioral Insights: Analysis of some attributes of CRM data, like purchase history, browsing activity, and engagement details, can provide valuable insights about buyers' behavior. The study can be used later to predict customer behavior, such as whether they are about to churn or not and whether they'll buy a particular product in their cart or not.
- Personalization: CRM data can be used to train ML models to create personalized churn prediction models. By leveraging customer-specific attributes and historical purchase data, models can be made to give tailor-made recommendations for each customer according to their tastes and preferences. This can significantly increase customer engagement and retention.
- Early Detection: This data can easily identify customers on the verge of churning. This early detection reduces the chances of churn by providing offers, discounts, and instant complaint resolution.
- Continuous Learning: E-commerce CRM is a live source of data that fetches information from an e-commerce platform. So, the data keeps increasing and changing continuously with the new customer interactions every minute. ML models can continuously learn from this real-time data, improving their accuracy and effectiveness.

- Integration with Customer Engagement: ML churn prediction can be integrated with customer engagement procedures. This integration will allow E-commerce to automate churn reduction strategies, track their effectiveness, and optimize strategies based on current performance.

Broadly speaking, applying machine learning strategies to CRM data can empower online businesses to comprehend their clientele more effectively. This can lead to an increase in customer retention and ultimately contribute to the business's success.

Types of CRM Data Available in E-Commerce Platforms

E-commerce CRM collects a humongous amount of customer data, which can be broadly classified into five categories:

- Transactional Data: Details regarding customer purchases, order history, transaction amounts, and frequency of purchases.
- Behavioral Data: This refers to data associated with customer engagement on the platform, including browsing habits, items viewed, duration of website visits, and instances of cart abandonment.
- Demographic Data: This encompasses details about the customer's demographic profile, such as age, gender, geographical location, income bracket, and household size.
- Feedback Data: This includes customer feedback, product evaluations, and the overall shopping experience.
- Communication Data: This is data derived from customer communication via email, chat, or social media platforms, encompassing inquiries, complaints, and requests.

UTILIZING MACHINE LEARNING TECHNIQUES FOR CRM DATA ANALYSIS

Introduction to ML Algorithms for CRM Data Analysis

A key use of CRM data is evaluating and applying these insights to bolster the e-commerce platform, thereby mitigating customer turnover. In this scenario, machine learning is crucial to assisting in the realization of this objective. It's vital to pick the correct model before using it for predictions, as different algorithms are proficient in various aspects of the data, which need to be factored in. Here are a few algorithms and the respective reasons for their implementation.

ML Algorithms which can be used for CRM Data Analysis:

Logistic Regression

- It is a supervised Machine Learning algorithm mostly used for binary classification tasks. It predicts the probability of a data point belonging to a specific class using a sigmoid/logit function.
- There are 3 types of logistic regression: Binomial, Multinomial, and Ordinal.
- It can be used to interpret the likelihood of churn.

Decision Trees

- A supervised Machine Learning algorithm used for both classification and regression tasks.
- It makes decisions based on data and their possible outcomes using a tree-like model.
- It can be used to interpret how different CRM data attributes contribute to the analysis.

Random Forest

- It is a supervised Machine Learning algorithm that uses an ensemble of decision trees for tasks like classification and regression.
- It improves the prediction accuracy and prevents overfitting by averaging the predictions from individual trees.
- Its capability to handle numerical and categorical data makes it suitable for CRM datasets with diverse attributes.

Gradient Boosting Machines (GBMs)

- They are a type of Machine Learning algorithm that uses an ensemble of weak learners and applies the principle of gradient boosting to improve their accuracy.
- They are used for both classification and regression tasks.
- It can be used to predict churn by learning from errors in previous models.

Support Vector Machines (SVM)

- They are a group of supervised Machine Learning Algorithms used for classification and regression analysis.
- They find the optimal hyperplane separating different feature space classes.
- It can efficiently handle high-dimensional CRM data.

Neural Networks

- Neural networks are computational models that mimic the human brain.
- They consist of interconnected nodes or neurons that process and learn from data, enabling tasks such as pattern recognition and decision-making in Machine Learning
- They are capable of learning intricate patterns and relationships in CRM data.
- Specifically useful for analyzing unstructured data such as customer feedback and reviews.

K-Nearest Neighbors (KNN)

- It is a non-parametric supervised Machine Learning Algorithm used for classification and regression.
- It classifies data points based on their similarity to the nearest neighbors in the training dataset.
- Relies on similarity measures for predicting churn based on the behavior of similar customers.

Ensemble Methods (e.g., Stacking, Bagging)

- Ensemble Methods are Machine Learning techniques that combine multiple models to improve accuracy and robustness.
- They leverage the strengths of multiple models to achieve better predictive performance.
- It can be applied in CRM data to leverage the strengths of various algorithms.

Understanding Dataset and its Features

The dataset under consideration for this chapter has 19 distinct features. Table 1 describes each feature.

Table 1. Dataset Description for each Attribute

Serial Number	Attribute Name	Attribute Description
1	Customer_ID	This serves as the primary key, uniquely identifying each record in the dataset with a string that uniquely represents a customer.
2	Churn	This binary attribute indicates whether a customer has churned. It takes a value of 0 if the customer has not churned and 1 otherwise.
3	Tenure	This feature denotes the duration a customer has been associated with the organization.
4	CityTier	It represents the tier of the customer's city, which is categorised as 1, 2, or 3 based on certain criteria.
5	WarehouseToHome	This feature quantifies the distance between the customer's residence and the nearest warehouse.
6	Gender	Denotes the gender of the customer- "Male" and "Female"
7	HourSpendOnApp	Indicates the amount of time the customer spends using the organization's application.
8	NumberofDeviceRegistered	Total number of deceives registered on a particular customer
9	CashbackAmount	Average cashback in last 6 purchases
10	Total_amount	Amount spent on the last 6 purchases
11	En_Rev1	Reviews written by customers for their last purchase translated from Portuguese to English
12	En_Rev2	Reviews written by customers for their second-to-last purchase translated from Portuguese to English
13	En_Rev3	Reviews written by customers for their third-to-last purchase translated from Portuguese to English.
14	En_Rev4	Reviews written by customers for their fourth-to-last purchase translated from Portuguese to English
15	En_Rev5	Reviews written by customers for their fifth-to-last purchase translated from Portuguese to English
16	En_Rev6	Reviews written by customers for their sixth-to-last purchase translated from Portuguese to English.
17	Category	Category of the product that the customer had purchased last
18	Product Title	Name of the product that the customer last purchased
19	Brand	Brand of the product that the customer last purchased.

Figures 1,2,3,4, and 5 show the distribution of customers across different categorical attributes.

Figure 1. Distribution of Customers who have Churned and not Churned

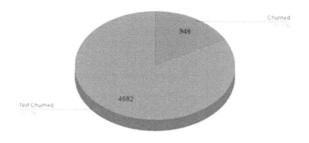

Figure 2. Distribution of Customers' City Tiers

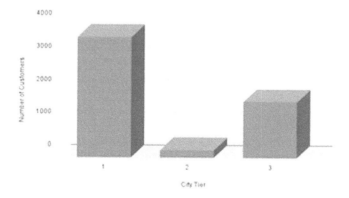

Figure 3. Distribution of Product Categories Among Customers

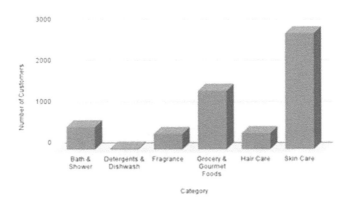

Figure 4. Distribution of the Number of Hours Spent on the App by Customers

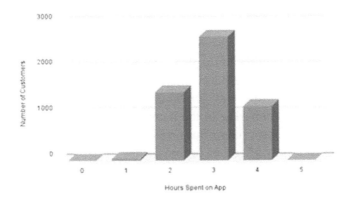

Figure 5. Distribution of the Number of Devices Registered by Customers

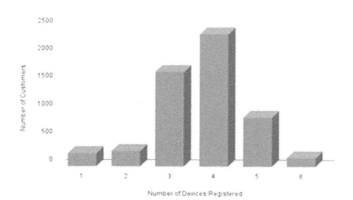

Preprocessing Techniques for CRM Data

For the dataset to be modeled, first and foremost, it has to be in a format that can be used to manipulate, work on, and retrieve results. The preprocessing step is integral for that purpose and to have no anomalies in the data.

Considering all the features in the data set, identifying how each must be pre-processed is a crucial step. For instance, the categorical variables that have different classes must be encoded with an integer value to use it to fit the model. Concerning the fact that numbers are missing in the dataset, numerical columns of a dataset must be imputed with appropriate values based on mean or median, after which a series of steps must follow after data preprocessing.

Preprocessing is a crucial step that ensures that data is in the right format for further analyses while translating the surveyed data into relevant information that can be acted on. The next subsection provides insights on how to preprocess the raw data on customer relationship management (CRM), which is crucial for gaining insight into customer behavior and the likelihood of churn rates in e-commerce platforms.

Data Cleaning

Data cleaning targets detecting and rectifying errors, discrepancies, and missing values in the dataset (Chaudhary & Roy Chowdhury, 2019). Irregularities during this stage might encompass:

Missing Values

Data points without values are marked as NaN, null, or placeholders.

Handling Missing Values: We often stumble upon missing data in real-world datasets. It's a hurdle we must carefully navigate to prevent bias or inaccuracies in our results. When deciding which columns to fill the values in, we can determine which ones have empty cells. This way, we ensure that our data is as complete and accurate as possible. Another common strategy involves filling the missing values for a certain column of numerical data type by a constant using the fillna method. Also, the numeric feature columns such as 'Tenure', 'WarehouseToHome', and 'HourSpendOnApp' need to be reviewed regarding missing value imputations, when it is possible to replace the missing values with the average of the corresponding feature columns. This helps ensure that the work involves a lot of analysis and that a comprehensive dataset is provided.

Outliers

Outliers are special data values that can deviate from the other data points, and their influence may skew the outcomes of a given analysis.

Outlier detection and removal: Outlier elimination is an important sub-process of data pre-processing to make sure that the subsequent statistical tests and machine learning models meet the standard quality. It is worth paying attention to the presence of outliers, point values that significantly deviate from the others in the given set and affect the conclusions. Another technique to eliminate outliers is the z-score, which uses a threshold of z that exceeds a predefined value, for instance, equals 3. Looking at the formula or z-score ($z = $ numerator, x, $-\mu$ end numerator, over denominator, sigma end denominator), which assigns higher values to any observation that is 3 standard deviations away from the mean (z-score > 3) as such considered outliers and are removed from the dataset. It provides a better foundation for carrying out a more reliable and accurate analysis of the results and modeling since outliers affect the general trends in most data sets.

Inconsistent Formatting

Different formats of the same data affect the subsequent analysis. Continue the analysis from gender-related words and references, which add to confusion where "Male" and "male" for gender are used. This data set did not have inconsistencies; hence, this step can be followed by encoding categorical variables required for churn prediction.

Encoding Categorical Variables

Categorical variables representing qualitative data, like 'gender', must be encoded into numerical representations for machine learning algorithms. The LabelEncoder from sci-kit-learn facilitates this transformation, as the feature of interest that is categorical in this dataset is only gender, so it is enough to encode the gender feature for the analysis.

Duplicate Records

Identical entries that can distort analysis and model training.

Missing values were identified, but there was no inconsistent formatting, and no duplicate records were found in the data set. Hence, for this dataset, the cleaning can be done by removing outliers, handling missing values, and encoding the categorical variable Gender.

Cleaning greatly depends on the dataset being used. Based on the features and problem statement, the processes mentioned above may be relevant. However, some datasets may also require more cleaning, so it is important to understand and clean the dataset accordingly.

Data Normalization

Data normalization aims to provide all variables with a comparable coding procedure to be compared on the same level.

Data normalization is a preparatory process where raw numeric data are adjusted to enable them to range within a particular set of limits, the most common being 0-1. This also means one can select only those few features, all of which could be statistically significant when compared to the scenario where all the features were added without the feature engineering step being undergone, as shown above.

In this study's analysis, the StandardScaler is employed to transform the features in the dataset (X) for scale. Standardization helps bring data to a standard form where the mean of the distribution is 0, and the standard deviation is 1. This process is important for machine learning algorithms that depend on scales of features associated with learning. Standardizing those features so that they all exist on a similar scale is beneficial in enhancing the performance of algorithms such as PCA or speeding up the convergence of algorithms.

In this way, ML algorithms are created to extract information from patterned data that has been processed to be understandable to the machines. However, this can only be true if the quality of data being fed into them is of high quality. Hence, when the data provided is wanting in some way or filled with noise, the machine learning algorithms provide less clear and easily interpretable results or, better still, no relatively substantial output. Hence, data pre-processing constitutes one of the critical initial steps realized in the machine learning framework (Kotsiantis et al., 2006).

Feature Engineering

Before delving into model fitting, it's imperative to discern the CRM data features that significantly influence churn. This brings us to feature engineering, which is employed to explore additional features or transformations that better capture the underlying patterns in the data.

Feature selection involves selecting a small subset of features from the original feature set without altering them (thereby preserving their interpretability) and validating this subset in alignment with the analysis objective (Jović et al., 2015).

Several statistical methods contribute significantly to this determination. First, evaluating the degree or correlation of each variable against the churn is considered important. Other techniques used include the Random Forest Feature Importance, which is useful in selecting important features for a prediction model as it is a stable method. SelectKbest uses Mutual information. Important features and Principal component analysis are also helpful in feature selection. SelectKBest measures the significance or dependence of features towards the target variable by default using the mutual information, while PCA, on the other hand, performs dimensionality reduction by transforming the data into a feature space by capturing data variance in the form of a hyperplane. By applying these statistical approaches, it was possible to determine the most important four features, including Tenure, Number of devices registered, City Tier, Warehouse to Home.

This analysis helped construct a bar graph in Figure 6 depicting the significance of each variable.

Figure 6. Feature Importance for Each Attribute

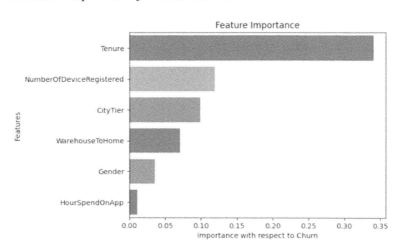

Through feature engineering efforts, the key features crucial for identifying churn patterns have been successfully pinpointed. Incorporating these essential features into the model ensures its efficacy without unnecessary redundancies that add minimal value to discerning churn patterns.

Data Integration

Data integration points of discrepancy pertain to situations where the data cannot be combined with all information intact from different sources or systems. These abnormalities may appear due to numerous reasons, including different data formats in different processes, varying levels of data quality, semantic conflicts in data definitions, data combination mistakes, etc.

For this dataset, the reviews were originally in Portuguese. To facilitate the analysis for the requirements of this chapter, the reviews were converted to English using the Google Translate Excel function, thereby removing any inconsistencies.

IDENTIFYING AT-RISK CUSTOMERS
THROUGH CRM DATA ANALYSIS

The previous section provides a concise overview of various Machine Learning (ML) models applicable for discerning churn patterns within CRM data. This section focuses on initiating the modeling process and utilizing selected models to identify customers susceptible to churn.

Techniques for Segmenting and Profiling
Customers at Risk of Churn

Once the significant features are determined, the modeling process progresses by fitting various models that excel in predicting churn. Before model fitting, it's crucial to precisely define the target feature and its influencing features. Additionally, key parameters like the train-test split ratio and a random state should be established for result reproducibility. Clear definitions and the assistance of Python libraries streamline the modeling process, ensuring efficiency and accuracy.

It marks the beginning of the model development process that would focus on customer charter and developing customer segments that are most likely to churn. Whereby, it is possible to identify new patterns based on certain attributes of each of the customer groups to be targeted, as well as, retain them effectively. This involves the use of machine learning algorithms such as logistic regression or decision trees whereby the customers who are most likely to churn are determined to ensure relevant marketing action plans proposing sufficient contra measures to regain the client's loyalty are put in place. Furthermore, as a result of using mixed data analysis and advanced foreseeing metrics, the goals include setting up a strategic perspective for minimizing the churn level and maximizing customer loyalty in the e-commerce field.

Segmenting customers that tend to churn is the main theme of this research, and this model is very useful. This indicates that using access to information in CRM and identifying clients most likely to churn helps get the right customers to preserve and ensure they do not churn again. This is an inclusive approach to honing various strategies, particularly to ensure customer retention strategies are on cue.

Our analysis includes four major categories of the following Machine Learning Models to identify and segment such customers. The first one is logistic regression analysis, which is preferred here due to its competence in handling dichotomous target variables. This careful predisposition to logistic regression indicates the subsequent stages, where the tendencies in customers' behavior and churn rates will be investigated. Thus, by using this model and its predictive capabilities, it is assumed to improve the effectiveness of the strategies and activities aimed at customer retention and loyalty—Tables 2 and 3 list the various accuracy figures obtained during the calibration and validation phases.

Table 2. Evaluation Metrics for Training Data from the Logistic Regression Model

Accuracy	**0.690275311**
Precision	0.322166387
Recall	0.76121372
F1 Score	0.452726559
ROC AUC Score	0.803849524

Table 3. Evaluation Metrics for Testing Data from the Logistic Regression Model

Accuracy	**0.695381883**
Precision	0.326530612
Recall	0.757894737
F1 Score	0.456418384
ROC AUC Score	0.779304431

Table 2 provides a comprehensive overview of accuracy metrics during the model's training phase. Conversely, Table 3 offers insights into the model's performance when tested against new data. The analysis reveals that the model's performance falls short of expectations. During the training phase, there are noticeable indications of suboptimal performance, a factor that carries over into the testing phase. A plausible explanation for this discrepancy may lie in the presence of class imbalance, as depicted in Figure 1 where the customers who churned are 16.8% and those who have not churned are 83.2%.

This understanding highlights the significance of effectively tackling class imbalances in machine learning models. A few strategies to manage class imbalances exist, such as incorporating class weights or using resampling methods like oversampling or undersampling. The suggested model employs the Synthetic Minority Over-sampling Technique (SMOTE) to address the class imbalance.

In Figure 1, the class of customers who have churned is quite low, which can hinder the model's performance results. It may also give good scores when all the predicted values belong to the majority class, which needs to be avoided. Thus, to improve the predictability of the minority class, synthetic instances must be fed to the model to rebalance the original training set by oversampling (Fernández et al., 2018).

Moving forward, using SMOTE to train the logistic model resulted in the following scores for various evaluation metrics.

Table 4. Evaluation Metrics for Training Data from the Logistic Regression Model with SMOTE

Accuracy	**0.720368393**
Precision	0.702975166
Recall	0.763214095
F1 Score	0.731857161
ROC AUC Score	0.807171073

Table 5. Evaluation Metrics for Testing Data from the Logistic Regression Model with SMOTE

Accuracy	**0.696269982**
Precision	0.327272727
Recall	0.757894737
F1 Score	0.457142857
ROC AUC Score	0.780041048

The metrics presented in Tables 4 and 5, which outline the evaluation metrics for the training and testing sets, respectively, demonstrate improvements compared to the previous model, where sampling was conducted without SMOTE. However, these metrics still fall short of the ideal performance expected of a model. Therefore, it is necessary to explore alternative models to enhance performance and subsequently improve the evaluation metrics.

This chapter explores several models for comparative analysis, including Logistic Regression, Random Forest, Decision Tree, SVM, and XGBoost. The following sub-section presents the evaluation metrics for training and testing sets across each model.

Some Models for Comparison

- The Logistic Regression Model is often the go-to choice for analyzing binary target variables. There are several reasons for this preference. One of them is its interpretability, which provides a clear insight into how each feature impacts the prediction of customer churn. Its aptness for binary classification aligns seamlessly with the task of churn prediction, which essentially involves categorizing customers into "churn" or "not churn". Moreover, the model's assumption of linear separability proves beneficial when churn patterns exhibit linear relationships in the data, enhancing its ability to detect these patterns.
- Decision Trees have a great performance in capturing complex and non-linear relationships between the attributes. Yet, in the customer's churn prob-

lem, the accuracy of a DT can be high, depending on the form of the data (Vafeiadis et al., 2015; Radosavljevik et al., 2010). They are easy to interpret and visualize, making them useful for understanding decision rules leading to churn. DTs are non-parametric and can handle non-linear relationships and interactions between features and churn, DTs can also provide insights into feature importance.

- Random Forest is an ensemble technique comprising several separately trained classifiers (such as decision trees or neural networks) whose predictions are merged to categorize fresh cases. An ensemble is frequently more accurate than any of the individual classifiers in the ensemble, according to earlier studies (Kulkarni & Sinha, 2013). It provides robustness and reduces overfitting compared to individual decision trees, random forest can rank feature importance, helping identify key factors influencing churn, and It can capture nonlinear relationships between features and churn, which may exist in complex CRM datasets (Radosavljevik et al., 2010; Vafeiadis et al., 2015).

- Support Vector Machine (SVM) shines when dealing with High-Dimensional Spaces, a characteristic often seen in CRM data with many features. They can utilize various kernel functions to encapsulate intricate decision boundaries, making them effective for data that's non-linear. SVM strives to widen the class gap, resulting in robust generalization performance. When predicting churn, SVMs frequently outperform Decision Trees (DTs) and sometimes even Artificial Neural Networks (ANNs). This variation in performance largely depends on the nature of the data and the degree of data preprocessing and transformation applied (Kirui et al., 2013; Vafeiadis et al., 2015).

- XGBoost is also considered for its well-known learning capabilities that have won competitions. This model is typically chosen to check whether the churn prediction performance of the proposed model can be improved using this Gradient Boosting algorithm. This algorithm has also been proven to perform well for classification in studies (Tang et al., 2020). This model is also capable of handling imbalanced data effectively, which is common in churn prediction tasks and the dataset used for this study.

COMPARISON OF MODELS

Identifying the best-fit model for the CRM data acquired forms the foundation for predictive analysis and suggestions. This sub-section focuses on identifying the differences in the evaluation of the models mentioned in the preceding subsection. Several evaluation metrics are commonly used to compare ML Models, and a few metrics used commonly that are also known to provide good grounds to pick a model with evidence are taken into consideration.

As handling class imbalance did not improve the evaluation metrics of the model significantly other rare events must also be considered. Hence there is a need for exploring more complex models or ensemble methods to see if the performance can be improved, and to do the comparison, all the models are base models without any tuning or SMOTE.

Displayed below in Table 6 are the evaluation metrics for each of the fitted models accompanied by the classification report for the testing data. The testing data evaluation metrics are only considered utilizing the results. It would be more accurate to quantify a performance model when compared to the training data evaluation metrics, as the model needs to perform well during the testing phase. For this chapter, the major metric that has been taken to choose the best-fit model is Mean cross-validation accuracy as it helps reduce the variability of model performance estimates by averaging results over multiple folds. Using the mean accuracy provides a more stable and reliable estimate of how well a model generalizes to new data compared to a single train-test split. It is also known to capture the bias-variance tradeoff which is crucial for a model's performance. Table 6 is ranked according to the Mean CV accuracy of the various models.

Table 6. Comparison of Evaluation Scores for Each Model

S.No.	Model	Mean CV Accuracy	Accuracy	Precision	Recall	F1 Score	ROC AUC Score
1	Random Forest	0.861679	0.85879	0.63025	0.394737	0.485437	0.849092
2	Decision Tree	0.85746	0.85435	0.58904	0.452632	0.511905	0.820187
3	SVM	0.855463	0.85702	0.68354	0.284211	0.401487	0.793952
4	Logistic Regression	0.842586	0.84281	0.68571	0.126316	0.213333	0.781526

Tables 7, 8, 9, and 10 provide an accurate classification report for each model, providing all necessary metrics with almost similar values for each, making the comparison a task. Considering the recall score for class 1 (Churned), it is plausible to eliminate the choice of Logistic regression and SVM as both of these models do not give good scores and are comparatively low, which implies that these models do not capture all true positives out of all the positive instances. There is a tough comparison between the Decision tree and the random Forest. The Decision Tree performs well in the classification report for class 1 (Churned) in recall and F1 score, but the Random Forest performs well in Mean CV accuracy, accuracy, precision, and the overall model's ROC AUC score and also has a better accuracy score for class 1.

Table 7. Classification Report for Logistic Regression on Testing Data

	Precision	Recall	F1-score	Support
0	0.85	0.99	0.91	936
1	0.69	0.13	0.21	190
Accuracy			0.84	1126
Macro avg	0.77	0.56	0.56	1126
Weighted average	0.82	0.84	0.79	1126

Table 8. Classification Report for Decision Tree on Testing Data

	Precision	Recall	F1-score	Support
0	0.89	0.94	0.91	936
1	0.59	0.45	0.51	190
Accuracy			0.85	1126
Macro avg	0.74	0.69	0.71	1126
Weighted average	0.84	0.85	0.85	1126

Table 9. Classification Report for Random Forest on Testing Data

	Precision	Recall	F1-score	Support
0	0.89	0.95	0.92	936
1	0.63	0.39	0.49	190
Accuracy			0.86	1126
Macro avg	0.76	0.67	0.7	1126
Weighted average	0.84	0.86	0.85	1126

Table 10. Classification Report for Support vector Machine on Testing Data

	Precision	Recall	F1-score	Support
0	0.87	0.97	0.92	936
1	0.68	0.28	0.4	190
Accuracy			0.86	1126
Macro avg	0.78	0.63	0.66	1126
Weighted average	0.84	0.86	0.83	1126

Apart from the 4 models, XGBoost was also experimented on, and the following evaluation metrics were obtained on the training set shown in Table. 11 and the testing set shown in Table. 12, The classification Report is also displayed in Table. 13.

Table 11. Evaluation Metrics for XGBoost on Training Data

Accuracy	**0.941404164**
Precision	0.925392333
Recall	0.960224239
F1 Score	0.942486571
ROC AUC Score	0.984673098

Table 12. Evaluation Metrics for XGBoost on Testing Data

Accuracy	**0.857015986**
Precision	0.56937799
Recall	0.626315789
F1 Score	0.596491228
ROC AUC Score	0.895276653

Table 13. Classification Report for XGBoost on Testing Data

	Precision	Recall	F1-score	Support
0	0.92	0.9	0.91	936
1	0.57	0.63	0.6	190
Accuracy			0.86	1126
Macro avg	0.75	0.77	0.75	1126
Weighted average	0.86	0.86	0.86	1126

Though XGBoost is an ensemble model that focuses on reducing errors, Random Forest shows better evaluation metrics by performing slightly better than XGBoost. It can also be observed that there is a huge jump between evaluation scores in training and testing sets for XGBoost, whereas Random Forest is comparatively lesser, indicating how Random Forest may reduce overfitting, whereas XGBoost does not.

This shows that the Random Forest model outperforms all the models. These metrics provide enough evidence to proceed with the random forest model and improve its performance, thereby helping predict at-risk customers with good accuracy, detect what problems they may be facing, rectify those issues, and try to prevent the same from happening later.

Improving the Chosen Model's Performance

This section continues the section discussed previously. The main aim of this chapter is to implement the Random Forest Classifier, which was identified as the best model among the others under evaluation. CRM data must be at least 90% accurate to identify customers at risk of churn. The company must work on the predicted outcomes to improve its business and profits. In the previous section, all the models were chosen to fit in with the data, which did not involve SMOTE. However, as the Random Forest Classifier has been chosen for modeling and it is known that there is a class imbalance, it would be a better choice to also use SMOTE for sampling to improve the results. After adjusting the sampling using SMOTE, the evaluation metrics are represented below in Table 14, followed by the classification report in Table 15 for the Random Forest Classifier (both for testing data).

Table 14. Evaluation Metrics for Random Forest with SMOTE on Testing Data

Accuracy	**0.869449378**
Precision	0.598173516
Recall	0.689473684
F1 Score	0.640586797
ROC AUC Score	0.917316127

Table 15. Classification Report for Random Forest with SMOTE on Testing Data

	Precision	Recall	F1-score	Support
0	0.93	0.91	0.92	936
1	0.6	0.69	0.64	190
Accuracy			0.87	1126
Macro avg	0.77	0.8	0.78	1126
Weighted average	0.88	0.87	0.87	1126

Compared to the previous Random Forest Classifier without SMOTE used for comparison in the preceding subsection, the evaluation metrics in Table 14 have significantly improved in accuracy, recall, F1 Score, and ROC AUC Score. The classification report in Table 15 also illustrates improvements in the scores for Class 1 (Churned).

Hyperparameter tuning can be performed to find the best hyperparameters for the model to improve the Random Forest Classifier further. In this study, grid search has been utilized to find the optimal hyperparameters for the model, including regularization strength, to improve its generalization performance. The following evaluation metrics are obtained by performing a grid search, shown in Tables 16 and 17.

Table 16. Evaluation Metrics for Random Forest with SMOTE and Grid Search for Tuning Hyperparameters on Testing Data

Accuracy	**0.871225577**
Precision	0.598253275
Recall	0.721052632
F1 Score	0.653937947
ROC AUC Score	0.922919478

Table 17. Classification Report for Random Forest with SMOTE and Grid Search for Tuning Hyperparameters on Testing Data

	Precision	Recall	F1-score	Support
0	0.94	0.9	0.92	936
1	0.6	0.72	0.65	190
Accuracy			0.87	1126
Macro avg	0.77	0.81	0.79	1126
Weighted average	0.88	0.87	0.88	1126

After hyperparameter tuning, the evaluation metrics and the classification report give slightly better results. The model with hyperparameter tuning only posed a constraint on the max_depth to 20 from None by default, and the other hyperparameters like n_estimators: 10, min_samples_split: 2, min_samples_leaf: 1 remained the same in both these models.

It should be noted that just comparing these results may not always yield the best model; in addition to these metrics, one measure used to choose models that provide intricate evaluation results could be the proportion of the predicted classes compared to the original dataset. The tuned hyperparameters have a comparatively higher number of predictions for class 1, and the model without hyperparameter tuning gives a comparatively lesser proportion of predictions, which makes it closer to the original dataset. To strengthen understanding and facilitate interpretation, Figures 7 and 8, the Precision-Recall Curve, Figures 9 and 10, the Receiver Operating Curve, and the Confusion Matrix in Figures 11 and 12, are illustrated to graphically show the performance of the model with SMOTE and the model with SMOTE and Grid search CV for hyperparameter tuning, respectively.

Figure 7. Precision-Recall Curve for Random Forest with Smote

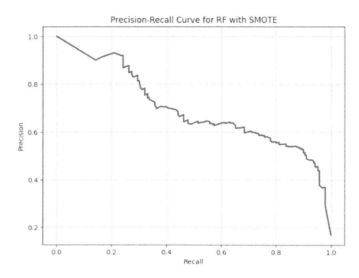

Figure 8. Precision-Recall Curve for Random Forest with Smote and Hyperparameter Tuning

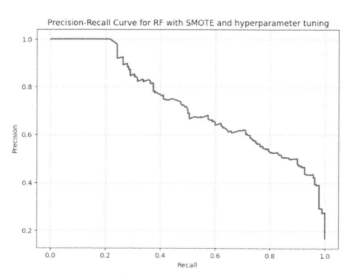

Figure 9. ROC Curve for Random Forest with SMOTE

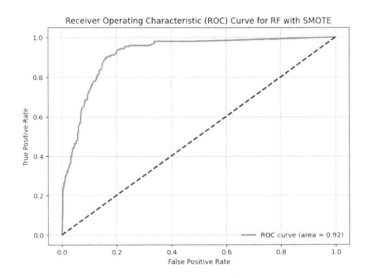

Figure 10. ROC Curve for Random Forest with SMOTE and Hyperparameter Tuning

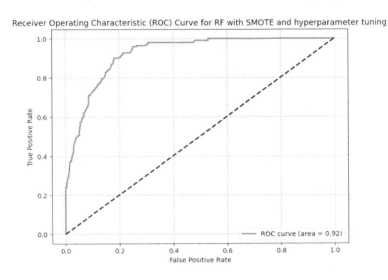

Figure 11. Confusion Matrix for Random Forest with SMOTE

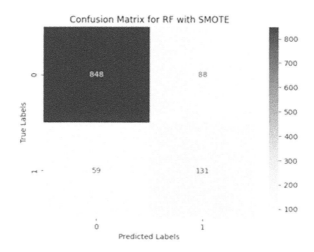

Figure 12. Confusion Matrix for Random Forest with SMOTE and Hyperparameter Tuning

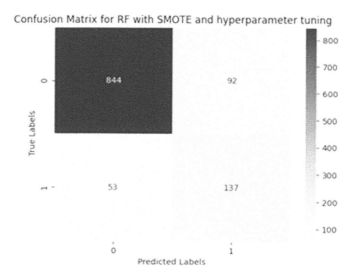

The PR and ROC curves are similar for both models, but the confusion matrix is dissimilar; the wrong predictions are fewer when the hyperparameters are tuned. But considering all the almost equal metrics. In conclusion, for this study, the Random Forest Model, without tuning the hyperparameters, which does not impose a constraint on the max_depth, is chosen for predictions. Tuned parameters can also be taken, but be cautious about other missed-out implications, if any, while considering one model over another.

LEVERAGING CUSTOMER FEEDBACK FOR PRODUCT IMPROVEMENT

Utilizing the existing CRM data and carefully choosing the relevant features have helped to successfully identify and implement the best model for the acquired dataset. This model outperforms the others in predicting customer churn so customers can be segmented. Customers' voices always matter; the new system will aim to listen to these customers who have abandoned various other shopping experiences prior and extract the major areas of improvement based on their collective blurbs. This study analyzes each customer's review of the last six purchases. Systematically, we intend to identify and improve the points so that the company can avoid such mistakes and retain customers.

Analyzing Customer Reviews and Feedback Data

The analysis of customer reviews and feedback deals only with customers who are predicted to churn, as these customers face problems and are willing to quit their purchases on the e-commerce platform.

Knowing clients on a deeper level by checking out their reviews cannot be underestimated because it helps improve service quality and keep customers. The suggested system will be based on an extensive data processing procedure and sentiment analysis applied to CRM data, as applied to customer comments on the last six purchases, and a sentiment analysis algorithm will be introduced into customer relationship management (CRM) data.

The NLTK library is a good example of comprehensive text analysis using the stopwords corpus and the WordNet lemmatizer, the main tools for streamlining text preprocessing. The review columns of the CRM dataset process systematically: Tokenization, stopword removal, and lemmatization are the steps of the rigorous pre-processing that each column has to undergo. These steps are indeed very critical in transforming the raw textual data into pertinent and analyzable data that is like labeled data.

In the future, the sentiment analysis part of the code will be the crux of the model, which is intended to find the most negative reviews among a customer's last six purchases. Using the TextBlob module, we can score sentiment polarity on each customer review, comparing which minimum score signifies a more negative sentiment (though it may be positive). Through the iterative process involving customer records, it is possible to identify which negative review has the lowest score and its sentiment aspect. Then, this helpful data could tell us about our customer dissatisfaction and some possible ways for improvement.

The outcome of this section not only shows the most negative reviews and the sentiment score for each customer but also opens the door for further analysis and strategic decision-making. By pinpointing their customers' moods and elevating a greater number of purchase instances, businesses can get customer feedback to optimize their products, services, and the whole customer experience, thereby establishing loyal customer relationships in the competitive field of CRM.

Identifying Areas for Product Improvement Based on Customer Complaints

The previous sub-section dealt with how the reviews were preprocessed, and the sentiment polarity was calculated to identify customers who do not have a good impression of the platform for various reasons; it is now required to identify these reasons and narrow them down to what the company has to focus on to improve retention.

To reduce churn, the collective negative comments (which have a sentiment polarity less than -0.5 for this proposed system) of customers predicted to churn are collected. This segregated data is then utilized for further study to improve the services that may face difficulty. The company can work on these to improve its business and satisfy customer requirements.

One way to address the customer complaints that all customers in this study have is to extract those customers who are known to be moderately unhappy with one of their purchases, which is achieved by sentiment polarity. With these reviews segregated, evaluating the various aspects the business may be lacking in and needs improvement can be done by summarizing the combined segregated reviews. The proposed system integrates generative AI capabilities to summarize the text and extract meaningful insights from segregated customer reviews. Lastly, a markdown function demonstrates custom text processing logic, specifically converting text into Markdown format, enhancing readability. It makes it easier to understand the areas that must be focused on to retain customers. Figure 13 shows a sample of the generated response.

Figure 13. Gemini API Response

Delivery Delays (61 complaints)
- Product not delivered (27)
- Delayed delivery (23)
- No delivery updates (11)

Product Quality (57 complaints)
- Poor quality materials (20)
- Product not as described (18)
- Defectiveness (19)

Customer Service (49 complaints)
- Lack of response (24)
- Poor phone support (15)
- Miscommunication (10)

Product Suitability (37 complaints)
- Incorrect size or color (18)
- Wrong product delivered (19)

Shipping Issues (32 complaints)
- Expensive shipping (15)
- Inconvenient pickup (17)

Website and Ordering Errors (28 complaints)
- Website glitches (14)
- Errors in order fulfillment (14)

Refund and Return Problems (25 complaints)
- Refund not processed (15)
- Difficulty in returning products (10)

Other Complaints (19)
- Misleading advertising (11)
- No invoice or order confirmation (8)

With the obtained results, the company can now choose to focus on areas that require attention. In this case, the most compelling areas that require scrutiny include Delivery Delays, Product Quality, Customer Service, Product Suitability, and a few others. Having obtained the consolidated issues, the platform can now focus on resolving them. It must also be noted that there might be a few issues that are not related to the platform like product quality, product suitability, and misleading advertisements, but the company can identify and track down such products and choose to improve or remove such items from the platform rather than keeping their customer dissatisfied.

PREDICTIVE ANALYTICS FOR IMPROVING CUSTOMER ENGAGEMENT

Introduction to Predictive Analytics in E-Commerce

Predictive models rely on identifying connections between expected and explanatory variables from previous events and using those connections to analyze and forecast the result (Finlay, 2014). To inform a choice, predictive models frequently carry out computations in real-time during transactions, such as assessing the opportunity of a certain consumer or transaction (Morsi, 2020). It can be defined as the advanced form of a quantitative process of anticipating fuzzy future events. According to current data, it applies data mining, statistical algorithms, artificial intelligence, and techniques such as machine learning to identify what might interest a customer.

There is always retrospective analysis as the primary approach to predicting future outcomes. In this case, predictive analysis intends to deliver an evaluation of what is very likely to happen in the future through an extensive critical evaluation and beyond. Such prospects and purchases have become marked with significant concern through the innovative method of predictive analysis in showing the consumer behavior that is encouraged. Predictive modeling is widely used by businesses as a tool for predicting their requirements and allocation of resources in perspective future. These evaluations assist organizations in running their courses effectively. (Akter & Wamba, 2016; Tuladhar et al., 2018).

Generating Personalized Product Recommendations for Enhancing Customer Satisfaction

Now that the customers who will leave the company have been identified, along with the problems associated with their departure, it is critical to hold onto the clients who will stick around because they are fairly satisfied with the services provided. This proposed model provides an ability to attract new customers and retain the existing ones using predictive modeling. The Random Forest Classifier helps identify the customer base that is not about to leave and is in search of improved services. For customers predicted not to churn, predictive analysis is used to predict their interests based on their previous purchases. Customer's propensity is directly impacted by how well-suited they are to the services offered by the e-commerce platform. All platforms aim to improve customer' satisfaction. This model uses customers' past purchase data to provide recommendations that may interest a customer.

Many predictive models try to analyze the purchase history and recommend products based on previous purchases and interactions. A few common methods are:

- Collaborative Filtering: Items are recommended based on their similarity with neighbors, who could be similar kinds of people or similar kinds of items (Shaikh et al., 2017).
- Content-Based Filtering: Recommendations based on the products and properties of products that a customer is interested in (Shaikh et al., 2017).
- Query Suggestions: Based on what a customer searches for and what they require, Query suggestions predict the interest of an active customer by analyzing information from similar customers or items (Shaikh et al., 2017; Varma et al., 2015).
- Hybrid Recommendations: Since it may not always be helpful to grab customers' attention just by using one method of recommendation, hybrid recommendations involve integrating any of the methods (Shaikh et al., 2017).

Many other algorithms aid in the recommendation; this proposed model implements a brand-based recommendation for improving customer experience on the platform by offering what they might be very interested in.

Strategies for Improving Personalized Suggestions

One strategy employed in this proposed model is to provide brand-based suggestions for customers predicted not to churn. This segment of customers can be provided with recommendations of items based on the brand that they like most.

Considering that the customer purchase history consists of all items purchased, the item category, and the brand name, it is now to identify which brand the customer usually purchases from or seems to purchase from. Since there are several brands, these brands must be categorized (item category), and by doing so, the system obtains the most frequently purchased brand for each item category.

Considering the already available recommendation systems that help customers find the items they are likely to buy, brand-based suggestions would improve customer engagement and satisfaction.

Since the dataset is limited to just the customer's last purchase, the product name, product category, and brand name for each purchase are identified. By doing so, the proposed system collects all product-based details with the brand names, the item category, and the list of items in each category. Having collected this dictionary, the next time a customer purchases and searches for an item, the item's category must be identified, following which all product recommendations based on the brand must be presented for the customer to choose from before displaying the other options. This makes the customers view the brands they prefer initially, and if nothing is found to be good, they may scroll through to see other items in the list from different brands. As customers see the brand of products they prefer initially, their shopping experience becomes quite better and at ease.

Considering a case where the dataset contains several purchases for a single customer, it may also be identified that a customer is not particularly interested in one brand alone; in such cases, the recommendation system can be tweaked a little by combining the already existing predictive modeling techniques and also by just suggesting the customer with an item from a brand that they have previously bought.

CONCLUSION

This chapter tackles a significant task for e-commerce platforms: reducing customer churn while engaging customers. The initial step involves predicting customer churn for existing customers using several algorithms, including logistic regression, decision tree, SVM, random forest, and XGBoost. Once churn is predicted, customers are divided into two groups: those likely to churn and those not. An analysis is then conducted on the past six reviews of customers about to churn. All the reviews undergo sentiment analysis using TextBlob, and the comment with the lowest sentiment score is saved for each customer. Any comments with a sentiment score below -0.5 are filtered, and a summary of key points for improvements is created using the Gemini API on these selected reviews. The chapter concludes by generating personalized brand-based recommendations for people not about to churn. However, it is important to note that this method has been applied to a small dataset, and handling larger, real-world e-commerce datasets might present challenges. Despite this, there is a willingness to expand the scope of this work to apply it to real-world e-commerce data in the future. This marks the end of the chapter.

REFERENCES

Akter, S., & Wamba, S. F. (2016). Big data analytics in E-commerce: A systematic review and agenda for future research. *Electronic Markets*, 26(2), 173–194. DOI: 10.1007/s12525-016-0219-0

Buckinx, W., & Van den Poel, D. (2005). Customer base analysis: Partial defection of behaviourally loyal clients in a non-contractual FMCG retail setting. *European Journal of Operational Research*, 164(1), 252–268. DOI: 10.1016/j.ejor.2003.12.010

Chaudhary, N., & Roy Chowdhury, D. (2019). Data preprocessing for evaluation of recommendation models in E-commerce. *Data*, 4(1), 23. DOI: 10.3390/data4010023

Dalvi, P. K., Khandge, S. K., Deomore, A., Bankar, A., & Kanade, V. A. (2016, March). Analysis of customer churn prediction in telecom industry using decision trees and logistic regression. In *2016 symposium on colossal data analysis and networking (CDAN)* (pp. 1-4). IEEE. DOI: 10.1109/CDAN.2016.7570883

Dick, A. S., & Basu, K. (1994). Customer loyalty: Toward an integrated conceptual framework. *Journal of the Academy of Marketing Science*, 22(2), 99–113. DOI: 10.1177/0092070394222001

Fernández, A., Garcia, S., Herrera, F., & Chawla, N. V. (2018). SMOTE for learning from imbalanced data: Progress and challenges, marking the 15-year anniversary. *Journal of Artificial Intelligence Research*, 61, 863–905. DOI: 10.1613/jair.1.11192

Finlay, S. (2014). *Predictive analytics, data mining and big data: Myths, misconceptions and methods*. Springer. DOI: 10.1057/9781137379283

Gefen, D. (2002). Customer loyalty in e-commerce. *Journal of the Association for Information Systems*, 3(1), 2. DOI: 10.17705/1jais.00022

Gold, C. (2020). *Fighting Churn with Data: The science and strategy of customer retention*. Simon and Schuster.

Gregory, B. (2018). Predicting customer churn: Extreme gradient boosting with temporal data. *arXiv preprint arXiv:1802.03396*.

Jović, A., Brkić, K., & Bogunović, N. (2015, May). A review of feature selection methods with applications. In *2015 38th international convention on information and communication technology, electronics and microelectronics (MIPRO)* (pp. 1200-1205). Ieee. DOI: 10.1109/MIPRO.2015.7160458

Kirui, C., Hong, L., Cheruiyot, W., & Kirui, H. (2013). Predicting customer churn in mobile telephony industry using probabilistic classifiers in data mining. [IJCSI]. *International Journal of Computer Science Issues*, 10(2 Part 1), 165.

Kotsiantis, S. B., Kanellopoulos, D., & Pintelas, P. E. (2006). Data preprocessing for supervised leaning. *International Journal of Computational Science*, 1(2), 111–117.

Kulkarni, V. Y., & Sinha, P. K. (2013). Random forest classifiers: A survey and future research directions. *Int. J. Adv. Comput*, 36(1), 1144–1153.

Manzoor, A. (2010). *E-commerce: an introduction*. Amir Manzoor.

Morsi, S. (2020). A Predictive Analytics Model for E-commerce Sales Transactions to Support Decision Making: A Case Study. *International Journal of Computer and Information Technology (2279-0764), 9*(1).

Nie, G., Rowe, W., Zhang, L., Tian, Y., & Shi, Y. (2011). Credit card churn forecasting by logistic regression and decision tree. *Expert Systems with Applications*, 38(12), 15273–15285. DOI: 10.1016/j.eswa.2011.06.028

Pejić Bach, M., Pivar, J., & Jaković, B. (2021). Churn management in telecommunications: Hybrid approach using cluster analysis and decision trees. *Journal of Risk and Financial Management*, 14(11), 544. DOI: 10.3390/jrfm14110544

Radosavljevik, D., van der Putten, P., & Larsen, K. K. (2010). The impact of experimental setup in prepaid churn prediction for mobile telecommunications: What to predict, for whom and does the customer experience matter? *Trans. Mach. Learn. Data Min.*, 3(2), 80–99.

Shaikh, S., Rathi, S., & Janrao, P. (2017, January). Recommendation system in e-commerce websites: a graph based approached. In *2017 IEEE 7th International Advance Computing Conference (IACC)* (pp. 931-934). IEEE. DOI: 10.1109/IACC.2017.0189

Tang, Q., Xia, G., Zhang, X., & Long, F. (2020, March). A customer churn prediction model based on XGBoost and MLP. In *2020 international conference on computer engineering and application (ICCEA)* (pp. 608-612). IEEE. DOI: 10.1109/ICCEA50009.2020.00133

Tuladhar, J. G., Gupta, A., Shrestha, S., Bania, U. M., & Bhargavi, K. (2018). Predictive analysis of e-commerce products. In *Intelligent Computing and Information and Communication:Proceedings of 2nd International Conference, ICICC 2017* (pp. 279-289). Springer Singapore.

Vafeiadis, T., Diamantaras, K. I., Sarigiannidis, G., & Chatzisavvas, K. C. (2015). A comparison of machine learning techniques for customer churn prediction. *Simulation Modelling Practice and Theory*, 55, 1–9. DOI: 10.1016/j.simpat.2015.03.003

Varma, S., Jain, M., Sharma, D., & Beniwal, A. (2015, December). Refined and diversified query suggestion with latent semantic personalization. In *2015 IEEE UP Section Conference on Electrical Computer and Electronics (UPCON)* (pp. 1-6). IEEE. DOI: 10.1109/UPCON.2015.7456725

Chapter 10
Illuminating the Convergence of Artificial Intelligence (AI) and Business Intelligence (BI) in E-Commerce and Fin-Tech in India

M. Basuvaraj
https://orcid.org/0000-0002-2660-3331
University of Allahabad, India

Keshvi Rastogi
Christ University, India

ABSTRACT

Artificial Intelligence (AI), born out of the minds and ideas of intelligent individuals, is a revolution for humankind. It has the potential to transform the world as never seen before. From the e-commerce sector to the education sector and healthcare to the finance sector, AI can disrupt and restructure all the traditional models that have been working for ages, bringing forth a completely different conception before the world. It is an easy alternative to doing long, tedious tasks and eases people's efforts by assisting them. Business intelligence (BI) is a valuable technique for handling the vast amounts of data businesses deal with. It is converting those immense amounts of data into meaningful results for businesses. It helps companies to work on historical and current data and creates predictive analysis, allowing businesses to make informed and sound decisions.

DOI: 10.4018/979-8-3693-8844-0.ch010

INTRODUCTION

Artificial Intelligence (AI) is an invented human mind that debriefs and answers intelligently by planning, perceiving, and processing the input to give the desired output to humans. It is the type of technology that has the potential to change the world drastically. It can make or break the world; the only difference is what use it is put to. AI is, thus, computer software that mimics and perceives humans. It also has features such as visual perception, voice recognition, translation of language, and decision-making. It aims to correct and learn from its mistakes and continuously improves itself. This function is often carried out with the help of machine learning, which emphasizes the usage of data and algorithms that help AI to take as a pattern and learn from human techniques and evolve with that. Classifying business intelligence (BI) research into managerial, technical, and system-enabled approaches prioritizes BI concepts and applications and offers insights and future research directions (Rouhani et al., 2012).

Deep learning, a subset of machine learning, focuses on observing human behavior and transforming itself in a way inspired by the human brain. It reduces human intervention in tasks through automation and analytics. It occupies the market quickly because of its widespread presence in almost all sectors, from law to finance to health and disaster management. AI's impact on e-commerce, detailing its applications in assistance, logistics, recommendation engines, and pricing, using Baidu Takeaway as a case study to highlight AI's significance in e-commerce (Song, X. et al., 2019). Thus, AI's deep and extensive use has made it increasingly regular and affects our jobs and ways of life. Business intelligence (BI) is a topic of growing demand in the evolving information technology scenario. BI eases the tasks of humans of analyzing large sets of data within a few seconds into simplified data. It helps improve the timeliness and decision-making processes for businesses. It helps understand and contemplate the new technologies in the market and how they influence customer behavior. It is a data warehousing technique and acts as a repository that stores data and works on complex and competitive data. It also contributes to cleansing data and increases the capabilities of the hardware and software processes.

In 2019, AI revolutionized e-commerce by enhancing customer experiences through chatbots, personalized services, and analyzing feedback. A study revealed that 20% of consumers were willing to purchase via chatbots, with 40% seeking deals. AI was projected to handle 80% of customer interactions by 2020 (Areiqat, A. Y. et al., 2021). The web architecture integrates all these processes to make an efficient working system than it was previously available. Thus, BI is a vital tool for businesses today. AI and BI in the e-commerce and finance sectors are radically different from existing and old traditional models. Their predictive analysis and automation have contributed mainly to these sectors. Through AI, e-commerce and finance businesses leverage their performance by predicting favorable models and sites for users and benefitting their search results.

BI helps these sectors analyze their customer data, reach a broader customer base, and recognize their suitable target audience. These sectors, intending to design reliable, efficient, and reliable products and offer quality services, have been actively adapting to AI and BI. Business intelligence (BI) integrates data gathering, storage, and analysis to aid decision-making. Evolving from executive information systems, BI now includes tools like dashboards and expands to business performance measurement and broader use (Negash et al., P. 2008). Quality control, supply chain management, information system management, upgrading to better operational efficiency, all such concerns of the businesses are quickly taken charge of by AI and BI. E-commerce is a vast and emerging trend. With most businesses preferring an online presence to reach a greater audience and cover large sectors through a network of connections, AI and BI can be a compelling force for this sector. AI can influence customization, search results, and online presence, lead to creative production, and BI influences consumer behavior prediction, user behavior monitoring, and so much more. The ventures working in this sector and contributing to AI and BI can seriously strengthen their market standing because of their vast benefits.

Machine learning learns customer behavior, adapts to usage, and gives favorable results. The various minimal and tedious tasks are reduced with the help of artificial intelligence and business intelligence. The finance sector no longer depends on traditional paper-based manual transactions and processing methods. It has drastically changed, and the emergence of Fin-tech (Technology in finance) has brought complete functions to users' palms. AI and BI in the financial sector have brought in a lot of features, such as personalized portfolio suggestions, image recognition, speech-to-text features, sentiment recognition, predictive modeling, ameliorated payments, customer engagement, and much more. Other features, such as cyber-security measures, have also been enhanced, making technological use safer and ensuring privacy. Thus, AI and BI are vast and proficient in their use and can swirl the world to greater heights.

ARTIFICIAL INTELLIGENCE(AI) AND BUSINESS INTELLIGENCE IN THE ELECTRONIC COMMERCE (E-COMMERCE) INDUSTRY

Artificial Intelligence and Business Intelligence are leading trends globally. They have contributed to transmuting the work of various industries, including electronic commerce and e-commerce. AI is developing and has a vast scope of gradually transforming the world and working techniques. AI offers significant opportunities in the financial sector, driving mergers and cost efficiencies. However, its benefits, especially beyond fraud detection, depend on organizational scale. Risks include data bias, algorithm choices, and human-AI interaction, necessitating careful collaboration between AI and humans (Ashta and Herman, 2021). E-commerce focuses mainly on reaching the audience through an online presence. It takes various steps to leverage its presence through several means, such as search engine optimization (SEO), affiliate marketing, product customization and optimization, e-mail marketing, pay-per-click marketing, etc.

AI's role in e-commerce value creation focuses on task and information complexity. It introduces a matrix classifying AI types and offers insights for businesses to leverage AI effectively (Basayev & Israfilzad, 2023). In all these channels, AI and BI act as an advantage for making work more accessible and more superficial and increasing online businesses' visibility. It also helps ease consumer queries with the help of chatbots and directs the main queries directly to customer care employees. With more developed technology, BI learns about customer behavior and AI based on the data, can easily tackle consumer queries, and give personalized answers to their questions. BI leverages internal business processes as well. The company does not have to take care of each of the processes separately, as they can all be handled by AI and BI proficiently. Ranging from Supply Chain Management (SCM) to Human Resource Management (HRM), Management Information Systems (MIS), Accounting Information Systems (AIS), Customer Relationship Management (CRM), Enterprise Resource Planning (ERP) etc. can easily be operated through these processes. Businesses save time, effort, and workforce on these operations and invest in improving their products and services.

Machine Learning and Deep Learning also contribute to E-commerce. Through these tools, businesses observe the behavior and shopping patterns of the consumer and plan strategically. They monitor consumers' choices and learn from them to develop the same pattern. Individual strategy implementation is also possible with the help of AI. As consumer patterns are observed, AI can transform itself in the conduct of those patterns and thus make the shopping experience more favorable for the buyers. It can also learn from its mistakes and develop in such a manner to avoid any further implications in the user experience. It anticipates consumer choices, curates featured products, makes customized recommendations, and delivers the best user experience.

AI also augments advertisements for E-commerce businesses. Personalization and customer-oriented ads can be easily customized to attract more customers. This fulfills the main aim of the e-commerce sector. With Big Data Analytics (an AI tool), personalization and forecasting consumer shopping habits become easy. It can contribute to creating more advertisements that increase the visibility of such e-commerce platforms. Companies using such technology may provide better services to the consumer and save time, workforce, and lengthy processes for such tasks. BI uses various tools such as customer segmentation and targeting to reach the required customer base for the businesses. It also improves sales performance analysis by evaluating past sales, customer choices, sales length, trends, etc. This helps optimize sales choices and eases customization options.

Sustainability is another growing concept in recent times. Environmental concerns are rising lately, and consumers are becoming increasingly aware of them. This leads to more responsible choices made by the consumers and also wanting the same from the businesses. According to a survey and research by McKinsey and Co., about 66% of the respondents and 70% of the millennial respondents consider sustainability when purchasing. They are ready to alter their choices and make informed decisions to minimize adverse environmental impacts. AI and BI can efficiently address this issue. With the use of AI in production and other operations, sustainability can be maintained in the manufacturing process by using and substituting more sustainable materials, leading to a contribution to the environment. Trust is an essential factor in the business world, and being true to customers' wants and emphasizing their choices can lead to better recognizability for their businesses.

It can offer insight into both operational productivity and environmental effects. Consumers prefer suitable products as quickly as possible, and E-commerce has made that experience better. The physical stores accommodate a limited stock inventory, and the process of looking for the products is prolonged due to the distances and the confusion. All such concerns can be quickly addressed through AI and BI. Real-time data, real-time stock information, and real-time offers can help consumers easily navigate the products of their choice and keep companies informed about inventory and consumer choices. The other BI tools can also keep track of consumer preferences, providing them with better experiences with each visit. This can also lead to better foot count for the sites. It can also forecast the delivery information to the customers as to how long the product would take to reach them with the help of intelligent supply chain management via BI. This can be more cost-effective for businesses as it gives a clear idea of the stock requirements, identifies constrictions, and ultimately increases optimization. Use of Artificial Intelligence, Business Intelligence, Machine Learning, Deep Learning, Big Data Analytics, and other such tools, it becomes simpler to carry out tasks that require a considerable workforce or are time-consuming. It helps predict, analyze, and implement strategies, leading to effective and efficient work. Figure 1 illustrates the various applications of Artificial Intelligence (AI) in E-commerce.

Figure 1. Use of Artificial Intelligence in E-Commerce

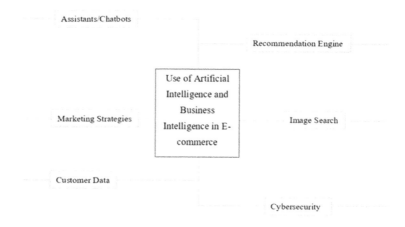

USES OF ARTIFICIAL INTELLIGENCE AND BUSINESS INTELLIGENCE IN ELECTRONIC COMMERCE (E-COMMERCE)

Artificial Intelligence and Business Intelligence have vast applications in the field of e-commerce. Along with scientific and technological upgrades, they also influence the E-commerce sector. The consistent development of technology has evolved and strengthened businesses' sales and market optimization. The applications and benefits of AI and BI in the various aspects are as follows:-

- **Assistants/ Chatbots-** E-commerce platforms are customer-centric, and they need to address the concerns of their customers effectively to maintain customer satisfaction. The main aim of chatbots or virtual assistants is to provide the most suitable response to their queries immediately. They respond via texts, audio, and also calls. With AI chatbots, it becomes much easier to answer consumer queries. AI, with the help of machine learning, deep learning, and BI, can understand consumer queries and develop itself to give personalized addresses to such queries. BI helps gather and analyze past datasets and develop further programs that make these chatbots more efficient. It can help look for products, compare them, or even find their supply status. The 24/7 presence of AI tools also reduces the need for a human customer service agent, as the AI can answer all queries. This, in turn, saves human capital, lowers labor costs, and improves service quality and the consumer's overall experience.

- **Recommendation Engine-** With the use of business intelligence in e-commerce, brands can effectively learn about consumer conduct. It can help to know the style of the consumers, learn from it, make informed decisions, and then customize the consumer's shopping experience with the help of artificial intelligence. Through machine learning algorithms, deep learning algorithms, and statistical predictions, brands foresee how consumers shop and personalize their experience by customizing and offering to their requests. Brands use BI to collect and analyze all the information about the customers to provide better results to the users. It considers customers' data, order history, preferred choices, major shopping sectors, external information, and other vital data. These are then used to prepare personalized web pages for consumers to help them find products conveniently. These web pages act as human and computer interaction interfaces. Many brands are adapting to this technology to target and reach a more significant consumer base.

- **Intelligent marketing strategies –** AI also helps develop creative and innovative marketing strategies. This would allow the business to stand out from the competition and strongly impact its target audiences. There are plenty of marketing strategies used in the market, but with AI in use, not only is there something new for the customers, but it may also act as a valuable and profitable strategy for the businesses. This can be helpful for companies entering the market so that their business stands out from the competition and is noticed by their target audience.

- **Image search-** This is another excellent application of AI that helps leverage E-Commerce businesses. Image search allows consumers to find their products easily on the sites with the help of images. Consumers can refer to the sites and the products they're looking for through images. This is based on the image processing algorithm. This feature helps consumers search for their desirable products using images. It makes it easier for consumers to look for products without using keywords or text and instead use images. BI analyzes such vital data, which, in turn, is fruitful for businesses in learning about their consumer choices.

- **Customer Data-** With the help of business intelligence, businesses can handle large sets of data. AI can manage customer relationships (CRM), supply and logistics (SCM), marketing, human resources, and consumer sales and purchase patterns data. This eases the operations of the businesses as BI manages this data. This results in profit maximization by taking into consideration sales. It can also help predict trends and plan future courses of action for the business. Collectively, all operations are automated, making it easier for businesses to function, saving human capital costs and time handling these tasks.

- **Cybersecurity**—AI can help enhance security on E-Commerce sites. Machine Learning helps identify risks and take measures to eliminate them. This advanced feature ensures a safe shopping experience for customers and safety in payment options. This assures customers and also attracts them to online shopping sites.

Figure 2. Use of AI in Various Sectors of E-Commerce

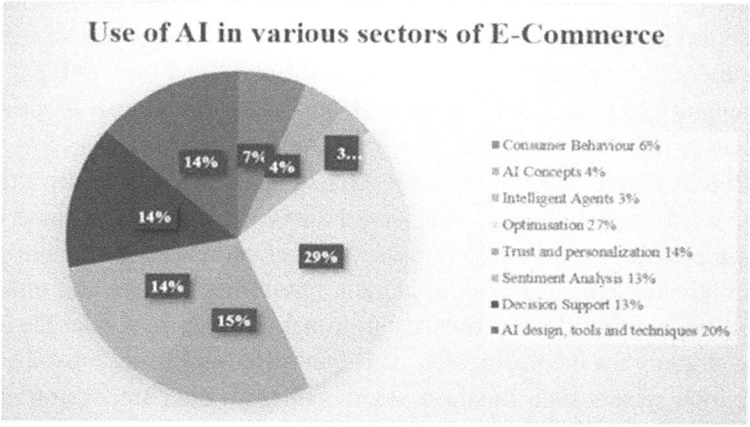

Figure 2 showcases the integration of Artificial Intelligence (AI) across different sectors within e-commerce.

ARTIFICIAL INTELLIGENCE (AI) AND BUSINESS INTELLIGENCE (BI) IN THE FINANCIAL TECHNOLOGY (FIN-TECH) INDUSTRY

FinTech has become a critical part of the modern finance industry. Consumers efficiently perform the simplest to the most complex tasks with just a finger touch. It assists users in managing their financial operations and banking processes efficiently through technology. It transformed the traditional model of the finance sector and brought in the application of technology. Artificial intelligence and business intelligence in FinTech are boons to the finance sector. From banking to portfolio management, they can take care of everything quickly. It is convenient for users and companies to automate tasks and bring customers the best experience. Business intelligence systems enhance decision-making by analyzing operational and historical data, improving information quality and timeliness. This paper presents a framework for building BI systems amidst advances in data warehousing and technology Khan, R. A., & Quadri, S. M. (2012), AI applications in E-commerce, highlighting how machine learning enhances customer insights, operations, and fraud prevention. It concludes that AI significantly boosts efficiency and growth in the sector (Lari, H. et al., 2022).

Artificial Intelligence and Business Intelligence can perform various functions such as logic, automation, planning, synthesizing, composing, presenting, communication, knowledge representation, modeling, optimization, simulations, and more. They can also help with expert systems, decision support systems (DSS), multiagent systems, autonomous systems, complexity systems, etc. Technology integration in finance has made it an exciting and interactive sector. Further, with AI and BI being introduced, it has become more participatory and accessible for users to learn about and use. FinTech is a significant term and includes InsurTech, BankingTech, TradeTech, LendTech, PayTech, WealthTech, RiskTech, cryptocurrency, blockchain, etc. These collectively constitute the FinTech sector. Technology presence in all these sectors optimizes their working and offers active, personalized, automated, and secure services. Financial literacy and the adoption of fintech products in India, highlighting how AI-driven fintech services enhance financial inclusion and improve financial literacy (Murugesan and Manohar, 2019). Use online consumer reviews and machine learning to forecast demand and innovate in consumer goods, developing a framework for testing new products (Mariani & Wamba, 2020).

AI and BI are making this sector more efficient with algorithms. Machine learning, deep learning, and natural language processing help recognize and learn the users' patterns; business intelligence helps collect and analyze large sets of data and provides favorable results to them. The most basic use of these technologies in FinTech is forecasting, which is an integral part of FinTech and all other aspects of it. With effective forecasting, users can know about their capital growth, return following inflation, the best policy for insurance for them and their families, loan assistance, wealth growth, investment incentives, and the correct investment choice for them. On the one hand, BI collects plenty of data valuable to learn customer preferences and choices and market working and works on it to provide applicable results, which are in turn used by AI, which takes into consideration quantitative analysis, statistical analysis, financial modeling, and other primary analytical tools and forecasts accurately, rapidly and efficiently, aiming for the best returns to the users and helping them to make the right choice. Another focus of AI and BI is on customer service.

Due to continuous technological advancements, customer service is now a collaborative job. The chatbots and assistants can efficiently address users' concerns. Not only this, but the chatbots also direct the users by knowing the purpose of their visit and providing them with the best of the experiences. They give a brief and direct them to the main content they seek. They can also quickly book users' appointments. Simultaneously, they can also address queries related to payment status, delivery status, bill disputes, etc. This 24/7 service helps the companies be available to the users, and also, the users don't have to wait for the companies' reply for a very long time. BI has helped businesses learn about their customers and customize their services to fit their preferences. The presence of AI as chatbots has lowered the human intervention requirement and saved time.

USES OF ARTIFICIAL INTELLIGENCE (AI) AND BUSINESS INTELLIGENCE (BI) IN FINANCIAL TECHNOLOGY (FINTECH)

The growth of technology is rapid. It is not only contributing towards scientific upgradation of the finance sector but also greatly influencing it. BI users are generally satisfied, and critical BI capabilities, especially system interaction, strongly influence BI success, highlighting gaps between satisfaction and actual BI effectiveness (Isik et al., 2011). AI system development at ING reveals overlooked lifecycle stages like data collection and model monitoring, highlighting challenges beyond algorithms and the need for tailored development tools (Haakman et al., 2021). Bitcoin, Blockchain, and FinTech, analyzing their applications, benefits, and challenges across industries. It evaluates 141 studies, highlighting their evolution and importance for strategic business insights (Wamba et al., 2020). Business intelligence enhances decision-making by combining data with analytical tools, enabling insights into market trends. Data mining, AI, and advanced technologies have enriched BI, improving business strategy and adaptability (Bharadiya, 2023). This improvement in decision-making should instill confidence and reassurance in finance professionals, researchers, and technology enthusiasts.

Here are some of the major applications of AI and BI in the FinTech sector:-

- **Efficient banking and insurance** – AI helps provide customers a personalized experience. This applies to the banking and insurance sectors as well. This would allow them to target customers and provide a customized experience tailored to their needs. AI and BI can be used to detect, monitor, analyze, and optimize the various functions of these sectors. It can also help in averting the risk involved. BI and AI in banking help in credit analysis and modeling the products according to the customers' needs. It may help in proper calculations and assessment of what investments or loan policies are best for the consumer and also promises returns to the banks in just a few clicks.

- Similarly, insurance can help customize the products for individuals, businesses, and other users, considering their personal needs and risk tolerances. Each user has different time recommendations; thus, insurance companies with advanced technology provide them with the best deals. AI can also effectively detect and evaluate fraud, which is helpful for the finance sector.

- **Effectual billing and payments** – The increased use of technology in every sector has also made billing and payments easy. People don't have to wait in long queues for bill payments anymore. Advanced technology and Artificial Intelligence have made these operations much more accessible. Consumers can efficiently pay off their bills and perform payments with just a few clicks. AI can make these services more secure, fast, risk-free, and convenient. IoT and wireless payments are considered to be the future of the world. These payment methods are risk-free, dynamic, and easier to understand by the consumer and adapt to such practices.

- **Compliance/Regulation** – BI allows businesses to remain updated with changing regulations and compliances. There are often many regulations that FinTech companies need to comply with immediately. Non-compliance with these regulations may lead to conflicts with the government or loss of market share for businesses. They can promptly detect and update businesses on the changing regulations and government updates regarding the rules. It helps businesses to be under the safe cover of government regulations and act accordingly. BI provides necessary assistance and tools for businesses to help them remain in compliance with government regulations. It helps quickly update their business model according to changed regulations. This shows BI's dynamic, risk-protective, practical, systematic, and human-technology cooperation behavior. Thus, this is another application of AI and BI in FinTech.

- **Innovative products** – FinTech is an industry where new updates, creative and innovative products, and services are always welcomed. Thus, putting AI into this work is beneficial for businesses. Through deep learning and machine learning, AI helps companies to stay up-to-date with their target audience and serve them most innovatively. BI can help plan and design creative ideas, convert them into valuable products or services with effective pricing strategies, and support and help operate them with intelligent AI features. It may also help promote the products, services, and applications using substantial marketing strategies. It optimizes the application and allows customers to receive feedback on its workings and usefulness.

- **Security** – The safety and security of transactions and usage are essential for the FinTech industry. Consumers rely on the safety measures of the businesses, and the trust of the consumers is built on how effective their safety measures are. With the efficient use of AI and BI, companies can ensure smart safety controls that safeguard not only consumers' transactions but also their data and other resources. In this era of increased cyber threats, businesses need to ensure the safety of their audiences online. AI and BI help in modeling, detecting, evaluating, and averting any risk for companies and consumers. Thus, growing technology has another potential threat to their control.

- **Consumer Education** – The FinTech industry is rapidly changing and growing. A new technology is adapted with each passing day. Thus, businesses must ensure their audience is well aware of the changing technology. AI helps educate and inform the audience about its various uses. It can effectively answer the doubts and queries of the consumers in a personalized way and ensure they are very well updated with all the recent trends in the market. Consumer education safeguards their interest and ensures they are safely engaged on the various sites.

Figure 3 illustrates the utilization of Artificial Intelligence (AI) in the FinTech industry.

Figure 3. Use of Artificial Intelligence in FinTech

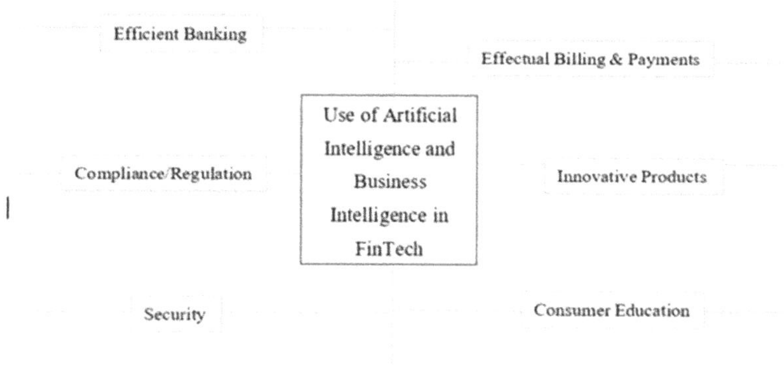

CASE STUDY ON THE IMPACT OF AI AND BI IN E-COMMERCE

Artificial Intelligence (AI) and Business Intelligence (BI) have been a great force of change globally, promoting and contributing to creativity and efficiency worldwide. This case study sheds light on how AI and BI in India have influenced the e-commerce sector, further developed corporate processes, and enhanced the reach of such platforms. They have great significance in expanding and diversifying such businesses, thus revolutionizing how businesses work.

1. **Growth –** Due to the rapid increase of smartphones, digital payments, internet usage, and other technological methods, India's E-Commerce sector has recently experienced exuberant growth. These E-Commerce platforms use AI and BI to gain insights and knowledge on the customers' experiences, thus making it useful for such platforms to maintain their competitiveness and grow multiple folds in the coming years.

2. **Personalization –** AI and BI can provide personalized experiences to users to attract them in various ways. For example, businesses such as Amazon, Flipkart, Myntra, and many more use personalization techniques to give their consumers the best experiences. Customization helps not only increase consumer engagement but also increases the loyalty of consumers toward the brands. The data extracted from the users helps businesses provide customized promotional offers and product recommendations and design marketing campaigns according to individual preferences.

3. **Predictive Analysis for Demand Forecasting –** Analyzing consumer demand and how the market will react to new changes is essential for E-Commerce businesses. Indian E-Commerce platforms use AI and BI to learn about demand forecasting. Artificial intelligence and business intelligence algorithms can properly use past data on sales, market trends, growth, and external factors to predict future business aspects. This helps companies to plan for marketing campaigns and inventory levels, maintain cost levels, and target the appropriate consumer segments.

4. **Dynamic Pricing Strategies –** Another area where AI and BI are intensely used is devising pricing strategies for E-Commerce businesses. Business intelligence helps in learning about past pricing strategies of the business, how the market has reacted to them, economic conditions, and growth in the past. AI algorithms use this data to devise pricing strategies that consider market trends, real-time analysis, competitors' pricing, and demands. This optimizes revenue and increases profitability and competition for the businesses in the market.

5. **Detection of Fraud -** E-commerce businesses must detect fraud and maintain security on their platform. Real-time fraud detection helps prevent any long-term loss to the company or the consumers. It can be easily achieved with the help of user experience, transaction data, and analysis of patterns used by AI-powered systems. Using AI algorithms such as machine learning, any budding irregularities can be easily dodged, and the business and its consumers can be saved from impending threats. Timely prevention of fraud can prevent illegal access,

fraudulent transactions, and financial losses. Such timely measures increase the credibility of the businesses and the consumers' trust in their safety.

6. **Cost Savings** – AI and BI help improve the operational efficiency of businesses and cut additional costs. Key Performance Indicators (KPIs) are offered as significant solutions by the BI, and this helps in the optimization and monitoring of multiple elements of an organization and facilitates marketing efficiency, operational costs, inventory levels, etc. The automation of AI leverages businesses' workflow productivity. This also helps decrease manual involvement, simplify repetitive activities, streamline operations, cut expenses, and eventually increase the company's profitability.

7. **Participants** – A large set of participants use Artificial Intelligence and Business Intelligence in the evolving time. AI facilitates their work and helps them reach a more extensive customer base. The various examples of companies that use AI and BI in their business are – Apple, Netflix, Spotify, Google, Meta, Amazon, IBM, Starbucks, Tesla, Microsoft, Walmart, eBay, Adobe, etc. This list is not limited to these companies, as various companies use Artificial Intelligence and Business Intelligence to reach a wider audience and effectively run their business.

8. **Future Prospects** - BI and AI in e-commerce appear to have a bright future. Even greater uses are to come as these technologies develop further. Artificial intelligence (AI) can improve instinct, knowledge, and accuracy of behavior forecasting. Even small firms can efficiently exploit data thanks to the probable increase in accessibility and user-friendliness of BI tools. Furthermore, organizations can access comprehensive solutions that fuse intelligent automation with real-time data analysis thanks to the smoother integration of AI and BI. Businesses may stay competitive, more effectively satisfy client expectations, and produce more customized products with this synergy.

Thus, with the ever-growing technology, AI and BI's influence in the Indian E-Commerce sector has a bright future. AI-integrated business analytics can unintentionally impact a firm's competitive advantage, revealing that opacity, poor data quality, and suboptimal decisions lead to inefficiency and disadvantage (Rana et al., 2022). AI impacts e-commerce and finance, highlighting machine learning and deep learning for improving customer experience, supply chain efficiency, fraud detection, and sales forecasting (Pallathadka, et al., 2023). They have a dynamic impact on e-commerce, including diverse pricing strategies, operational efficiency, cost savings, detection of fraud, customized customer experience, and friendly user experience. Hybrid classification to predict and prevent e-commerce customer churn, utilizing extensive customer data to enhance retention strategies and improve predictive accuracy (Shobana et al., 2023). With the proper utilization of these technologies, businesses can aim for a better position in the market and the minds of the consumers and continue to prosper in the digital economy as they continue to grow and expand.

CASE STUDY ON THE IMPACT OF AI AND BI IN FINTECH IN INDIA

The advancements in Artificial Intelligence (AI) and Business Intelligence (BI) technology have quickly changed the FinTech industry in India. This study examines how AI and significant data impact India's investment, banking, payments, and lending businesses.

1. **An Overview of FinTech in India** – India's FinTech sector has experienced rapid growth thanks to increased internet usage, more people using smartphones, and government efforts to improve financial inclusion. FinTech entrepreneurs use innovative ideas such as peer-to-peer lending, digital banking, mobile payments, and robo-advisory services to disrupt traditional financial institutions. Artificial Intelligence and business intelligence can increase efficiency, improve security, and enhance user experiences in the financial sector.

2. **Personalized Financial Services:** In India, FinTech companies can offer personalized financial services using AI and BI technology. For example, Paytm, a leading digital payment company, uses AI algorithms to analyze transaction data and offer customers customized recommendations for financial products and services. By understanding spending habits, financial goals, and user behavior, Paytm enhances customer interaction and loyalty. This, in turn, encourages more people to use the platform for various financial needs.

3. **Fraud detection and risk management:** For FinTech companies in India, focusing on risk management and cybersecurity is crucial. AI-powered risk management systems analyze large amounts of data in real time to detect abnormalities, identify fraud, and minimize risks. Zerodha, a top online brokerage firm, uses AI algorithms to monitor trading activities, detect unusual patterns, and prevent insider trading and market manipulation. Utilizing Machine Learning and BI analytics, Zerodha enhances transparency, compliance, and trust in the securities market.

4. **Financial Process Automation:** Indian FinTech companies use AI and BI technologies to make financial processes more efficient. For example, Razorpay, a digital payments company, uses AI chatbots to automate customer service, answer questions, and quickly solve payment issues. Additionally, BI analytics help Razorpay understand user behavior, transaction patterns, and business

performance, enabling it to reduce risks, improve questions, and identify revenue opportunities. By optimizing processes and reducing manual tasks, Razorpay provides merchants and customers better scalability, reliability, and user experiences.

5. **Improved Consumer Engagement and Insights:** In India, FinTech companies can learn more about how customers think, what they like, and how they feel by using AI and BI technology. For instance, Policybazaar, an online insurance comparison platform, uses Natural Language Processing algorithms to study reviews, social media posts, and customer comments. By analyzing customer feedback and sentiment, Policybazaar gains valuable information about how people view their products, current market trends, and where they stand compared to their competition. Using BI dashboards to see customer data, product success, and market changes, Policybazaar can create more effective marketing strategies, offer better products, and enhance customer satisfaction.

6. **AI in Wealth Management and Investment Advice:** The Indian FinTech industry is experiencing an increase in the use of AI-powered wealth management and investment advice services. For example, the online investing platform Scripbox uses Machine Learning algorithms to analyze investor profiles, risk tolerance, and investment goals. Based on this information, Scripbox recommends personalized investment portfolios across various asset classes, such as bonds, mutual funds, and stocks. Investors can enhance their returns and make informed choices by utilizing BI analytics, which provides information on risk management, portfolio rebalancing, and performance tracking. Scripbox helps people reach their financial goals and build wealth in the long run by making investment advice and wealth management more accessible.

7. **Participants-** FinTech is a growing sector and has widely captured a large audience through its attractive characteristics. An unexhaustive list of companies essentially uses AI in the financial services sector, thus making it easy and convenient for businesses and consumers to participate. Companies such as Razorpay, Zoho, CreditVidya, IDfy, Perfios, CASHe, INDMoney, JP Morgan, HDFC Bank, SBI Bank, ICICI Bank, etc. These participants provide a world-class experience to their consumers, thus retaining them and gaining new customers throughout the journey.

8. **Future Prospects and Difficulties:** Experts predict that the Indian FinTech industry will see increased innovation and disruption in the future due to the combination of AI and BI. This will lead to the creation of more advanced applications in areas such as Natural Language Processing, algorithmic trading, and predictive analytics. These advancements are made possible by ongoing research in AI, including Deep Learning, reinforcement learning, and explainable AI. Despite these exciting developments, FinTech companies using AI and

BI technology must still address challenges like algorithm bias, data privacy, and regulatory compliance. Industry players, legislators, and regulators must collaborate to ensure that AI is used morally, openly, and responsibly in the banking and finance sectors.

CONCLUSION

The extensive use of Artificial Intelligence and Business Intelligence in the sectors of FinTech and E-Commerce has brought about a revolutionary change in the world. This will make them dynamic and user-friendly and assure safety and assurance to the customers. It is helpful in the creation of innovation in the operational ways of businesses. The two most widely used AI tools, Deep Learning and Machine Learning help learn about the consumer and bring them effective, efficient, creative, and ingenious experiences. AI promises a bright future for businesses, urging them to be creative with the right technology. It provides a risk-free, automated, and easy experience for the customers. BI is an efficient and essential tool for businesses to make informed decisions and safely collect and store data. BI tools help analyze data and increase efficiency, transparency, collaboration with other sectors, and connectivity with a broad audience. Thus, both Artificial Intelligence and Business Intelligence are the future of the human world.

Business and artificial intelligence have recently reshaped the e-commerce sector, benefiting businesses and customers enormously. These innovations have drastically altered consumer connections, business models, and e-commerce operations. Simply put, this article describes the future possibilities of AI and BI and their impact thus far on the e-commerce business. Artificial Intelligence is the capacity to teach robots to think, learn, solve problems, and make decisions as people do. AI is used in e-commerce in various ways, from chat rooms that assist consumers with questions to recommendation engines that suggest things based on previous clicks. On the other hand, business intelligence uses data analysis to support organizations in making more informed decisions. BI technologies collect, process, and present data to provide insights that can enhance tactics and operations. Business Intelligence (BI) aids businesses in comprehending consumer behavior, sales patterns, and market dynamics in e-commerce.

The consumer experience and operational effectiveness in e-commerce have significantly improved thanks to AI. To offer individualized shopping experiences, AI systems evaluate consumer data. For example, AI can suggest products based on a user's online shopping habits, making finding what the customer wants quicker and easier. Chatbots driven by AI are on hand continuously to help clients. To improve client satisfaction, they can respond to inquiries, handle problems, and even assist with transactions. Using historical sales data, AI forecasts demand, aiding inventory management. This guarantees that products are available when customers want them by reducing overstocking and stockouts.

Artificial intelligence (AI) can identify odd patterns that can point to fraud, assisting in the defense of consumers and companies against con artists. With BI, e-commerce companies may make data-driven decisions that improve growth and performance. BI tools find patterns and trends by analyzing massive amounts of data. This aids companies in analyzing consumer behavior, top-performing marketing tactics, and popular products. Businesses may monitor key performance indicators (KPIs) in real time with the help of BI. This makes it easy to discover areas for improvement as they can track sales, online traffic, and consumer involvement. By supplying projections based on past data, BI aids in long-term planning. This aids companies in anticipating demand and setting actual goals. BI can divide customers into groups according to several criteria, including demographics and purchase patterns. Businesses may now better target and increase the efficacy of their marketing campaigns by customizing them to appeal to various customer segments. Thus, by improving user experiences, optimizing operations, and facilitating data-driven decision-making, AI and BI have reshaped the e-commerce industry. These technologies will present even more chances for industry innovation and expansion as they develop. Businesses in the e-commerce industry that aim to thrive in a world that is becoming more digital and data-driven will need to embrace AI and BI.

The FinTech industry has changed due to artificial intelligence (AI) and business intelligence (BI), which have significantly improved productivity, customer satisfaction, and decision-making. In the FinTech industry, AI-powered chatbots and virtual assistants are becoming popular, assisting clients at all times and promptly resolving their questions. These automated systems can execute transactions, answer common inquiries, and even provide financial guidance, freeing human personnel to handle more complicated problems. In addition to raising customer happiness, businesses can service more customers without incurring more expenses. Fraud detection is one of the critical uses of AI in FinTech. AI systems can analyze massive data sets to spot unusual patterns and highlight possible fraud. These algorithms pick up new information with every transaction, increasing their accuracy.

As a result, they can identify fraud more quickly and precisely than with standard methods, protecting financial institutions and consumers alike from losses. FinTech businesses may provide individualized financial services thanks to AI and BI. These technologies offer predictions about future behaviors and preferences by evaluating client data. For example, they can recommend savings accounts or investment strategies tailored to a person's spending patterns and financial objectives. This degree of customization improves client loyalty and promotes closer ties with customers.

In the financial sector, risk management is critical, and artificial intelligence has greatly improved this field.

By examining non-traditional data sources like social media activity and payment histories in addition to standard credit ratings, AI systems can evaluate creditworthiness with more accuracy. This facilitates improved risk management and lending decisions for financial institutions. By offering insightful data on business performance, business intelligence (BI) solutions assist FinTech organizations in optimizing their operations. BI systems provide a clear picture of the state of a business by combining and analyzing data from multiple sources. Managers can use these insights to determine problem areas, enhance workflows, and make well-informed decisions and reduce costs, resulting in improved operational efficiency. AI strengthens safety measures in the FinTech industry. As an alternative to common passwords, biometric techniques like fingerprint scanning and facial recognition are becoming increasingly popular and offer higher security.

Additionally, AI systems can identify security breaches and take action sooner, reducing the potential harm. Financial organizations are very concerned about complying with regulations. AI and BI can be helpful by automating compliance procedures and ensuring that all activities comply with applicable rules and regulations. These technologies lower the possibility of fines and penalties by monitoring transactions for questionable activity, producing compliance reports, and tracking regulation changes. Thus, BI and AI are critical instruments in the FinTech industry, encouraging innovation and enhancing several features of financial services. They enable improved risk management, expedite operations, give personalized services, increase fraud detection, and improve customer experience. They also improve security, help with regulatory compliance, and make predictive analytics possible. These technologies will significantly influence the FinTech sector as they develop, improving financial services' efficiency, security, and customer-focused nature. Adopting AI and BI is not only a fad but essential to maintaining competitiveness in the rapidly evolving financial sector.

REFERENCES

Areiqat, A. Y., Alheet, A. F., Qawasmeh, R. A., & Zamil, A. M. (2021). Artificial intelligence and its drastic impact on e-commerce progress. *Academy of Strategic Management Journal*, 20, 1–11.

Ashta, A., & Herrmann, H. (2021). Artificial intelligence and fintech: An overview of opportunities and risks for banking, investments, and microfinance. *Strategic Change*, 30(3), 211–222. DOI: 10.1002/jsc.2404

Babayev, N., & Israfilzade, K. (2023). Creating complexity matrix for classifying artificial intelligence applications in e-commerce: New perspectives on value creation. *Journal of Life Economics*, 10(3), 141–156. DOI: 10.15637/jlecon.2078

Bharadiya, J. P. (2023). A comparative study of business intelligence and artificial intelligence with big data analytics. *American Journal of Artificial Intelligence*, 7(1), 24.

Cao, L., Yang, Q., & Yu, P. S. (2021). Data science and AI in FinTech: An overview. *International Journal of Data Science and Analytics*, 12(2), 81–99. DOI: 10.1007/s41060-021-00278-w

Fosso Wamba, S., Kala Kamdjoug, J. R., Epie Bawack, R., & Keogh, J. G. (2020). Bitcoin, Blockchain and Fintech: A systematic review and case studies in the supply chain. *Production Planning and Control*, 31(2-3), 115–142. DOI: 10.1080/09537287.2019.1631460

Haakman, M., Cruz, L., Huijgens, H., & Van Deursen, A. (2021). AI lifecycle models need to be revised: An exploratory study in Fintech. *Empirical Software Engineering*, 26(5), 95. DOI: 10.1007/s10664-021-09993-1

Isik, O., Jones, M. C., & Sidorova, A. (2011). Business intelligence (BI) success and the role of BI capabilities. *International Journal of Intelligent Systems in Accounting Finance & Management*, 18(4), 161–176. DOI: 10.1002/isaf.329

Khan, R. A., & Quadri, S. M. (2012). Business intelligence: An integrated approach. *Business Intelligence Journal*, 5(1), 64–70.

Lari, H. A., Vaishnava, K., & Manu, K. S. (2022). Artifical intelligence in E-commerce: Applications, implications and challenges. *Asian Journal of Management*, 13(3), 235–244. DOI: 10.52711/2321-5763.2022.00041

Mariani, M. M., & Wamba, S. F. (2020). Exploring how consumer goods companies innovate in the digital age: The role of big data analytics companies. *Journal of Business Research*, 121, 338–352. DOI: 10.1016/j.jbusres.2020.09.012

Murugesan, R., & Manohar, V. (2019). Ai in financial sector–a driver to financial literacy. *Shanlax International Journal of Commerce*, 7(3), 66–70. DOI: 10.34293/commerce.v7i3.477

Negash, S., & Gray, P. (2008). Business intelligence. *Handbook on decision support systems 2*, 175-193.

Pallathadka, H., Ramirez-Asis, E. H., Loli-Poma, T. P., Kaliyaperumal, K., Ventayen, R. J. M., & Naved, M. (2023). Applications of artificial intelligence in business management, e-commerce and finance. *Materials Today: Proceedings*, 80, 2610–2613. DOI: 10.1016/j.matpr.2021.06.419

Rana, N. P., Chatterjee, S., Dwivedi, Y. K., & Akter, S. (2022). Understanding dark side of artificial intelligence (AI) integrated business analytics: Assessing firm's operational inefficiency and competitiveness. *European Journal of Information Systems*, 31(3), 364–387. DOI: 10.1080/0960085X.2021.1955628

Rouhani, S., Asgari, S., & Mirhosseini, S. V. (2012). Review study: Business intelligence concepts and approaches. *American Journal of Scientific Research*, 50(1), 62–75.

Shobana, J., Gangadhar, C., Arora, R. K., Renjith, P. N., & Bamini, J. (2023). E-commerce customer churn prevention using machine learning-based business intelligence strategy. *Measurement. Sensors*, 27, 100728. DOI: 10.1016/j.measen.2023.100728

Song, X., Yang, S., Huang, Z., & Huang, T. (2019, August). The application of artificial intelligence in electronic commerce. []. IOP Publishing.]. *Journal of Physics: Conference Series*, 1302(3), 032030. DOI: 10.1088/1742-6596/1302/3/032030

Chapter 11
Impact of Artificial Intelligence on Organizational Performance of Agritech Firm

C. Ganeshkumar
https://orcid.org/0000-0002-0913-2849
Indian Institute Foreign Trade, India

Jeganathan Gomathi Sankar
BSSS Institute of Advanced Studies, India

Arokiaraj David
https://orcid.org/0000-0002-9591-2410
ATMS, Swiss Business School, UAE

ABSTRACT

Agriculture, vital for all human activities, contends with global challenges of population growth and resource competition. Technological advancements like ICT, AI, machine learning, and blockchain can tackle sectoral issues. This study focuses on AI's impact on organizational performance, particularly in AgriTech. Executives of Bangalore-based AgriTech firms employing AI were surveyed via a self-administered questionnaire, comprising both quantitative and qualitative inquiries on AI's impact on value chain performance. The study utilized a simple random sampling method and statistical analyses including Chi-square, ANOVA, correspondence analysis, and simple mean to analyze the data. The study found that AI benefits and its potential

DOI: 10.4018/979-8-3693-8844-0.ch011

significantly boost the value chain performance of AgriTech enterprises. Focusing on AI advantages and future prospects can greatly enhance organizational performance, indirectly impacting overall efficiency through improved value chain operations. Managers are advised to prioritize AI integration for better company performance.

INTRODUCTION

Agriculture is a significant driver of income, employment, international trade, and industrialization in numerous developing economies. A noticeable shift from modern to traditional agricultural practices in emerging markets. AI could be important in implementing this transition (Lee et al., 2017). It aids agriculture in coping with the unpredictability of growing conditions (Siddhartha et al., 2021). It can also facilitate improved efficiency and quality of the yield through satellite agriculture or precision farming. Advantages of this include decreased agrochemical application, enhanced productivity, appropriate water usage, and low soil degradation. Precision farming or satellite agriculture is one of the modern farm practices that improve the quality/quantity yielded by reducing the cost of production and improving the socio-economic status of the farmers' (Mehta et al., 2019; Ganeshkumar et al., 2021). Employing communication networks, sensing technologies, and software operations to obtain accurate data about the land is known as "smart farming" in agriculture (Ravi et al., 2018). Small-scale, autonomous farms of the future will use technology like smart tractors, survey drones, and agricultural robots (Beecham et al., 2014; David, 2020). Habitually, enhanced production needed more input from agrarian applications, which resulted in disastrous environmental impacts (Panpatte & Ganeshkumar, 2021; Rose et al., 2019). Yet, AI with the clear-cut application input could lead to decreased usage of inputs, thus not affecting agriculture's sustainability (Reardon et al., 2020; Karthikeyan et al., 2020).

It has been reported that approximately 33% of the total food produced is wasted annually (Lee et al. (2017)). Also, the upcoming economies report wastages during post-harvest rather than during the processing stages. Still, the advanced ones report high wastage in the consumer and retail stages. To satisfy the growing demand, artificial intelligence can contribute to decreased waste and increased efficiency. According to research by the FAO on the losses in the value chains of vegetables and fruits, losses primarily occur during the following grading and harvesting, while after the harvest, it will be huge losses occur during the period of processing and distribution (Routroy & Behera, 2017; Ganeshkumar et al., 2021). The total loss and damage at these stages in some regions across the globe may rise to 50% (Pachayappan et al., 2020; David & Ravi, 2017; Ganeshkumar et al., 2019). Therefore, in a value chain of a single stage of agriculture (AVC), the wastage is not applicable. Technology can help avoid and track these damages and losses, and Artificial Intelligence is a crucial technology here (Sengottuvel & Ganeshkumar, 2018). Therefore, it is employed throughout AVC. Addressing the challenges within the value chain is life-threatening for ensuring food security for the rapidly growing global population in the future. It involves considering factors such as economic growth, changes in food consumption habits, shifts in consumer income, and dietary preferences, particularly in developing nations (Arokiaraj et al., 2020). Estimates suggest that global food production needs to increase by 60–70% by 2050 to meet the escalating demand for food.

REVIEW OF LITERATURE

Advanced cultivating can be characterized as the utilization of innovation by ranchers to coordinate monetary and field-level records for complete ranch movement management. The thought is to give ranchers admittance to significant bits of knowledge to embrace best practices to oversee cultivation all the more effectively, decreasing misfortunes and amplifying benefits (Kumar & Nambirajan, 2013). Computerized cultivating incorporates accuracy and savvy cultivation, which is accomplished through the execution of shrewd programming and equipment (Paul et al., 2019). Accuracy cultivating is prominently characterized as an 'innovation empowered way to deal with ranch the board that notices, measures and investigates the requirements of individual fields and harvests. As the name recommends, accuracy cultivating is the Internet of Things (IoT) for the better efficiency of agribusiness, and it depends on the utilization of sensors, robots, robots, and cameras, which are introduced on ranches to record information (Latha et al., 2020; Srivastava et al., 2022). Information on respective plots can be investigated to give data on climate, crop, soil, and development designs. It can also give noteworthy geologically pertinent and convenient bits of knowledge to improve the efficiency of each plot on the farm (Ganeshkumar et al., 2024_a).

Drones utilized for splashing and weeding can decrease agrochemical use staggeringly. Advanced mechanics inside farming can further develop efficiency and result in higher and quicker yields. The ability to use advanced analysis and artificial intelligence to look for patterns in data is the most creative aspect of technological transformation (Pratheepkumar et al., 2017; Sankar & David, 2024). AI can foresee which traits and features will be optimal for crop development, providing ranchers with the greatest variety in their location and environment (Siddhartha et al., 2021).

Agritech new companies in India have effectively drawn in financing from various financial backers, including but not restricted to enormous worldwide organizations, buyer reserves, and generalist funding firms (Ganeshkumar et al., 2022). There has been significant progress in agritech initiatives that align with the development of India's agricultural technology ecosystem. Over the past five years, notable advancements have been made in enhancing this environment, which has experienced a surge in institutional funding, skyrocketing by nine times. Between 2014 and 2019, the industry garnered $1.7 billion compared to a mere $0.2 billion in the prior period. Notable investments include Tiger Global's $89 million contribution to Ninjacart in 2019. In 2020, agritech startups such as Clover Ventures, Arya Collateral, WayCool, Bijak, FreshToHome, Intello Labs, DeHaat, and others stepped up their fundraising efforts, driven by heightened tech adoption among farmers and the sector's resilience (David et al., 2022). Omnivore invested approximately $15 million in 10 agritech startups in 2020, up from $6.5 million in seven startups in 2019. The momentum continued into 2021, with agritech startups attracting significant capital inflow in the first month.

The agritech sector has seen increased investment growth for the past few years. Over the last decade (2010-2019), this sector captured an accumulating capital flow of 1.9bn US$. And of this, the agritech startups had raised 1.7bn US$ from 2014 to 2019, while from 2010 to 2014, only 0.2bn US$ was raised. The investments from this sector in India from 2010 to 2014 were narrow as the environment grew (Ganeshkumar et al., 2024$_b$). This sector 2010 had very few active startups, like ten, which grew from 2014 onwards in terms of the value of investments and the number (Banumathi & Arokiaraj, 2011). The players of this sector operating in the different segments in India have encountered an accumulated investment funding of 532mn US$ as of April 2020.

The startups in this sector raised a total of about 244.59 million US$ in 2019, which led to an increase of 350% YoY. An investment stage with a strong seed has been encountered due to innovation, which takes deeper relationships and a lot of time compared to software innovations (Sudhakar et al., 2017). The seed-stage startups in this sector need additional capital and demand prolonged exit horizons from investors. In 2020, increased technology adoption within the agricultural sector, coupled with the resilience shown by farmers, served as a catalyst for fundraising among numerous agritech startups, including Arya Collateral, Intello Labs, Fresh-ToHome, WayCool, DeHaat, Bijak, and Clover Ventures, among others. Omnivore invested approximately $18 million in around eleven agritech startups in 2020, marking a significant increase compared to the previous year (David et al., 2019).

The agritech sector in India is anticipated to increase due to the emerging digital transformation due to COVID-19, rural internet penetration, and increased interest from the community of investors. The activities in the agritech industry have been initiated to increase manifold following the lifting of the lockdown (Ganeshkumar & Khan, 2021). The COVID-19 epidemic has caused this industry to demonstrate a great deal of adaptability and expansion, which has increased demand from investors who don't want to miss out on the chance to participate in this sector, which has a tremendous amount of potential (Ganeshkumar & David, 2023). Also, agritech startups tend to see successful exits within a matter of time. Startups that offer satellite agriculture solutions, farmer platforms, financial services and traceability, quality management, innovations in the biotechnological and agri-infrastructure, and full-stack solutions have seen a drastic increase in their investment. For the agritech sector, 2021 started positively with a few agritech startups that successfully attracted investments from investors in the initial days of starting themselves.

RESEARCH METHODOLOGY

The research methodologies the researcher employs to complete the suggested study are covered. The variables that will be utilized in the analysis are briefly summarised, and the specifics of the different tests used to evaluate the validity and reliability of the gathered data for data analysis are described. This study investigates the connection between organizational performance and AI-related agritech elements. According to the Economic Survey 2020–21, startups in the food technology sector drove India's third-place finish in the global startup ecosystem in 2018. Over 450 agritech startups are located in India. Secondary and primary data are used to support this investigation. Secondary data on agritech companies in India can be sourced from various sources, including the number of companies, annual reports, investment figures, and websites of agritech firms, as well as data from organizations such as the National Statistical Survey Organization, the CMIE database, the Department of Industries and Commerce, NITI Aayog, the Central Statistical Organization, the Karnataka Government website, and relevant research papers and publications.

Through a survey technique, primary data on the efficiency and history of agritech firms connected to AI in agritech were gathered. Agritech firm executives received a questionnaire for data collection, with primary data collected through a carefully structured survey. They provided directly to the 100 CEOs of the agritech companies headquartered in those locations that use AI (Ganesh Kumar et al., 2017). The practice of conducting personal interviews was gathered to the primary data. A structured questionnaire was created to investigate how AI-based agritech units influence the performance and overall organizational effectiveness of agritech enterprises across the value chain. This questionnaire included qualitative and quantitative elements and was conducted through interviews with AI-based agritech units.

FINDINGS AND ANALYSIS

This section comprises two segments. The first part offers a descriptive examination of the attributes of the agritech sector. The dimensions of AI benefits were studied using statistical tools, including independent sample T-test, mean analysis, chi-square test, correspondence analysis, and ANOVA.

Ranking of Organizational Performance

The organizational performance of the agritech units, such as overall competitive position, overall product quality, sales growth, return on sales, return on investment, market share, profit margin, and average selling price, as shown in Table 1, are ranked with the assigned mean values.

Table 1. Mean Score for the Organizational Performance Ranking

S.No.	AgriTech Organizational Performance	Mean	Std. Dev	Rank
1	Overall competitive position	3.72	0.86	I
2	Overall product quality	3.64	0.86	II
3	Sales growth	3.60	0.92	III
4	Return on sales	3.60	0.83	IV
5	Return on investment	3.59	0.86	V
6	Market share	3.58	0.94	VI
7	Profit margin	3.57	0.88	VII
8	Average selling price	3.50	0.81	VIII

Table 1 shows that the agritech companies surveyed rank their overall competitive position first. It implies that most of these agritech units aspire to maintain a leading position in the market. Overall, product quality is ranked second, which shows that the companies prioritize the quality of their products. The rankings indicate that average selling prices and profit margins are less important. It suggests that while financial gains are crucial for any business, maintaining a strong market position through providing high-quality products is essential for long-term sustainability.

AgriTech Sector: Profile and Organizational Effectiveness

The statistical tool ANOVA is employed to analyze the mean value difference in organizational performance across different profiles of agritech companies' samples.

Table 2. ANOVA Result for Organizational Effectiveness and AgriTech Industry

S.No.	Organizational Effectiveness with AgriTech Profile	F-Value	P-Value	Supported or Not
1	Position in the value chain	0.483	0.788	Not Supported
2	No. of Employees	1.606	0.194	Not Supported
3	Industry characteristics	1.198	0.133	Not Supported
4	Business organization type	3.462	0.020	Supported
5	Agri-Tech Category	0.988	0.376	Not Supported
6	Market presence	1.217	0.301	Not Supported
7	Years in operation	0.276	0.842	Not Supported

Table 2 depicts meaningful distinctions in the mean value ratings among companies grouped according to their business organization type. In contrast, other profile characteristics do not show significant differences in mean values. An organization's performance may depend on its culture and leadership, which could explain substantial differences. The mean values of different categories are organized according to their position within the value chain.

Table 3. Average Rating Score across the Value Chain Position Categories

S.No.	Value Chain Position (VCP)	No. of Respondents	Average Rating Score
1	Combination	08	3.3750
2	Agri-input/Supplier Stage	12	3.7083
3	Stage of Production/Farmer	17	3.6176
4	Supporting Services Stage	24	3.7344
5	Processing/Value Addition Stage	11	3.5114
6	Stage of Retailer/ Distribution	18	3.4861

Table 3 displays the mean value ratings of companies categorized by their position within the value chain, ranging from 3.3750 to 3.7344. It suggests a moderate to high level of organizational performance. The ANOVA analysis indicates no notable variance in average values among the diverse groups of value chain positions. It implies that the value chain position of agritech companies' organizational performance is moderately high compared to that of their competitors. Implementing AI through the value chain must have impacted their business positively, and hence, the organizations grow tremendously, outperforming their competitors. The mean values of different categories are organized according to the number of employees.

Table 4. Average Rating Score across Employee Count Categories

Employee Count	No. of Respondents	Average Rating Score
More than 300	18	3.6806
101-300	16	3.5234
31-100	25	3.820
Less than 30	31	3.4153

Companies categorized by the number of employees exhibit mean values ranging from 3.4153 to 3.8200, as illustrated in Table 4. Furthermore, the ANOVA indicates that these mean values show no significant difference. Consequently, it can be concluded that companies outperform their competitors to a moderate or high degree, irrespective of their number of employees. Although the number of employees in some agritech companies is higher, the number of people with expertise in AI-related technologies would be much lower. The mean values of different categories are organized according to the nature of the industry.

Table 5. Average Rating Score across Industry Nature

Industry Nature	No. of Respondents	Average Rating Score
Medium-Scale Operations	46	3.5516
Micro-Scale Operations	05	2.9750
Large Scale	10	3.6375
Small Scale	29	3.7716

Table 5 displays the mean value ratings of companies grouped by their nature, ranging from 2.9750 to 3.7716. The ANOVA analysis reveals no statistically significant difference in the above-average rating score among these categories. It suggests that this type of organization, regardless of its nature, may experience similar outcomes and demonstrate moderate to high organizational performance compared to its competitors. Companies of different natures have competitors performing at their levels; hence, micro industries compete with micro industries. Therefore, with AI, outperforming their competitors becomes easier. The mean values of various categories are organized according to the organization type.

Table 6. Average Rating Score across the Types of Organizational Structures

Types of Organizational Structures	No. of Respondents	Average Rating Score
Sole Proprietor Companies	04	2.5938
Private Limited Companies	73	3.6164

continued on following page

Table 6. Continued

Types of Organizational Structures	No. of Respondents	Average Rating Score
Partnership	09	3.7083
Public Limited	04	4.0625

The public limited companies outperform their competitors highly compared to other categories, as their mean value stands at 4.0625, as shown in Table 6. Furthermore, the ANOVA result indicates a notable variance in mean values across the categories. Hence, the public limited companies outperform their competitors more than the other groups by looking into the mean values. The mean value of sole proprietor companies is low. The performance of the companies depends largely on the ownership. The risk-taking capability of the sole proprietor is much lower than under other ownerships. This could be a reason for the low-performance level of organizations owned by sole proprietors. The mean values of the different groups are categorized based on the agritech category.

Table 7. Average Rating Score for AgriTech Segments

AgriTech Segments	No. of Respondents	Average Rating Score
Product	28	3.4420
Service	26	3.6490
Both	36	3.6875

The value ratings for companies categorized by their agritech segment vary from 3.4420 to 3.6875, as indicated in Table 7. Additionally, the ANOVA analysis reveals that the variance in the average rating values among the categories was statistically insignificant. Hence, the firms, regardless of their offerings, perform moderately or highly compared to their competitors. The competitors for the companies offering a product category would also be offering the same product category. Hence, by introducing AI-related technology in their organization, the agritech companies perform moderately better than their competitors. The mean values of the various categories are organized according to the market coverage.

Table 8. Average Rating Score for Market Coverage Segments

Market Coverage Segments	No. of Respondents	Average Rating Score
Global Market	01	3.750
Both Market	13	3.884
Local Market	76	3.549

The mean value ratings of agritech companies grouped by their market coverage range from 3.5493 to 3.8846, as illustrated in Table 8. The ANOVA result shows that the lack of significant variance in average rating score values among these market segments leads to the conclusion that agritech companies, regardless of their market coverage, demonstrate reasonable performance superiority compared to their competitors. The AI-related technologies would have helped these companies in their marketing functions. Since these companies offer similar benefits to the markets, their performance has remained the same as their market coverage. The mean values of different categories are organized according to the time companies have operated in the agritech industry.

Table 9. Average Rating across AgriTech Business Tenure Categories

Years in AgriTech Business Operation	No. of Respondents	Average Rating Score
Over 10 Years	13	3.6635
Less than 3 Years	16	3.4688
5 to 10 Years	24	3.5729
3 to 5 Years	37	3.6520

The average rating value of the categories grouped by their years of experience in the agritech business ranges from 3.4688 to 3.6635, as shown in Table 9, between moderate and high-performance levels. Additionally, the ANOVA result shows that the absence of notable distinctions in mean values across categories suggests that companies, irrespective of their years of operation, demonstrate a moderate performance edge over their competitors. AI is a technology that is recent in the field of agriculture, and hence, agritech companies are in the process of learning to perform efficiently with the technology. The adoption process has begun, and agritech companies with years of experience are performing at a pace similar to that of their competitors.

Relationship between AI Aspects and Value Chain Position

Any company must comprehend the nature of AI aspects concerning the profile of agritech enterprises to make strategic, tactical, and operational decisions. This section uses correspondence analysis and a chi-square test to examine the dimensions of AI (Victer, 2019). The chi-square values and their significance are shown below.

Table 10. Chi-Square Analysis for Agritech Company Profile and AI Aspects

Value Chain Position (VCP)	Chi-Square value	Sig. Value	Supported or not
Organizational Performance	10.88	0.949	Not Supported

The connection between the VCP of agritech companies and various AI aspects is examined to understand their characteristics. The significance of these associations is tested using the chi-square test. The chi-square values and significance analysis reveal that AI Future, VCP, AI Problems, and Organizational efficiency do not exhibit a substantial association with the VCP of Agritech Company attributes, as depicted in Table 10. However, a notable connection exists between the VCP of agritech company attributes and AI Benefits (Ganeshkumar et al., 2020). Subsequent sections will delve into the nature of this interaction between value chain position factors and AI dimensions.

Organizational Performance

The chi-square results indicate a relationship between organizational performance and value chain position of 10.88, with a significance value of 0.949. This suggests that these variables do not show a significant association.

Figure 1. Organizational Performance - Correspondence Diagram

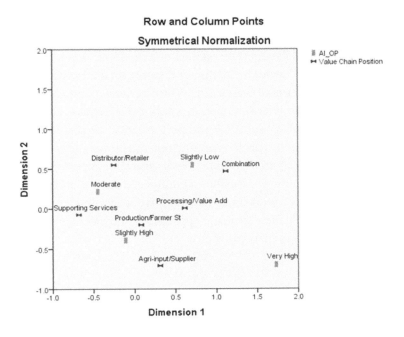

Figure 1 shows the association between the organizational performance and the value chain performance. The organizational efficiency of the agri input/ supplier phase is very high, and the supporting stage is moderate. However, the association between the observed variables is not significant. Hence, the higher organizational efficiency is not due to their VCP. The agri-inputs play a vital role in farming activities, so companies occupying positions in this value chain may be performing better.

CONCLUSIONS AND IMPLICATIONS

It is concluded that the AI Benefits feature underscores the pivotal role of competitive positioning in driving organizational growth. Agritech companies, in particular, recognize the paramount importance of establishing a competitive edge to thrive in the market landscape. Additionally, our research highlights the significance of product quality as a determinant of organizational success, with average selling price ranking lower in priority. Moreover, when categorizing companies based on their business organization type, a noteworthy disparity in mean values emerges, indicating varied performance levels across different ownership structures. Sole proprietorships, characterized by lower risk tolerance, exhibit comparatively lower organizational performance than public limited companies. However, upon examining other profile features such as VCP, employee count, nature of the industry, agritech segment, market presence, and number of business tenures, our analysis reveals insignificant differences in mean values concerning organizational performance. It suggests that these factors do not significantly influence the overall performance of agritech companies, which generally operate at a moderate level.

Further investigation through chi-square results elucidates the relationship between VCP and organizational efficiency. While agritech companies positioned in different value chain segments demonstrate varying performance levels, the lack of a significant correlation between VCP and performance suggests that other factors might have a greater influence on determining organizational success. In conclusion, while AI benefits offer valuable insights into organizational performance drivers, a comprehensive understanding of Business Intelligence entails integrating additional examples and case studies relevant to the field. By leveraging such insights, agritech companies can refine their strategic approaches and enhance their competitive positioning in the dynamic marketplace.

CONTRIBUTIONS OF RESEARCH WORK

Firstly, the study utilized a diverse set of variables to thoroughly scrutinize the features of agritech VCP, ensuring their accuracy and reliability in assessing agritech enterprise value chain performance. These meticulously examined variables can be a valuable resource for future scholars and researchers, facilitating extensive studies on the factors influencing value chain performance. Secondly, this research offers practical tools to aid business managers in effectively addressing key value chain challenges. By utilizing these tools, managers can enhance their comprehension of different VCP elements and the interrelated connections among various dimensions, including AI benefits, AI VCP, AI challenges, AI prospects, and their potential impacts on organizational success. Moreover, this research offers valuable insights for advancing academic knowledge and understanding, including theory development, proposal justifications, measurement techniques, research problem-addressing methods, and operational implications of the VCP for agritech. Finally, the research has significantly advanced by crafting a comprehensive theory that amalgamates various facets concerning the agritech value chain. It addresses many issues that could substantially influence the performance of agritech enterprises.

REFERENCES

Arokiaraj, D., Ganeshkumar, C., & Paul, P. V. (2020). Innovative management system for environmental sustainability practices among Indian auto-component manufacturers. *Int J Bus Innov Res*, 23(2), 168–182. DOI: 10.1504/IJBIR.2020.110095

Banumathi, M., & Arokiaraj, D. (2011). Eco-labeling–The Need for Sustainable Marketing. In *National Conference in the era of Global Recovery-2011 (SGEGR2011* (pp. 511-515).

Beecham, S., O'Leary, P., Baker, S., Richardson, I., & Noll, J. (2014). Making software engineering research relevant. *Computer*, 47(4), 80–83. DOI: 10.1109/MC.2014.92

David, A. (2020). Consumer purchasing process of organic food product: An empirical analysis. [QAS]. *Journal of Management System-Quality Access to Success*, 21(177), 128–132.

David, A., Kumar, C. G., & Paul, P. V. (2022). Blockchain technology in the food supply chain: Empirical analysis. [IJISSCM]. *International Journal of Information Systems and Supply Chain Management*, 15(3), 1–12. DOI: 10.4018/IJISSCM.290014

David, A., & Ravi, S. (2017). The direness of cultivable land spotted on agricultural: A special reference to rice production in South India. *Abhinav National Monthly Refereed Journal of Research in Commerce & Management, ISSN-2277-1166*, 6(09), 55-59.

David, A., Thangavel, Y. D., & Sankriti, R. (2019). Recover, recycle and reuse: An efficient way to reduce the waste. *Int. J. Mech. Prod. Eng. Res. Dev*, 9, 31–42.

Ganesh Kumar, C., Murugaiyan, P., & Madanmohan, G. (2017). Agri-food supply chain management: Literature review. *Intelligent Information Management*, 9(2), 68–96. DOI: 10.4236/iim.2017.92004

Ganeshkumar, C., Basu, R. J., Yuvaraj, M., & David, A. (2024[b]). Will Artificial Intelligence be a Performance booster to Agritech Startup?: Empirical evidence from Emerging Economy. *Journal of Industrial Integration and Management*.

Ganeshkumar, C., & David, A. (2023). Digital Information Management in Agriculture—Empirical Analysis. In: Goyal, D., Kumar, A., Piuri, V., Paprzycki, M. (eds) Proceedings of the Third International Conference on Information Management and Machine Intelligence. Algorithms for Intelligent Systems. Springer, Singapore. https://doi.org/DOI: 10.1007/978-981-19-2065-3_27

Ganeshkumar, C., David, A., & Jebasingh, D. R. (2022). Digital Transformation: Artificial Intelligence Based Product Benefits and Problems of Agritech Industry. In *Agri-Food 4.0*. Emerald Publishing Limited. DOI: 10.1108/S1877-636120220000027010

Ganeshkumar, C., David, A., & Sankar, J. G. (2024a). Blockchain Technology Acceptance in Agribusiness Industry. In *Blockchain Transformations: Navigating the Decentralized Protocols Era* (pp. 239-260). Cham: Springer Nature Switzerland.

Ganeshkumar, C., Jena, S. K., Sivakumar, A., & Nambirajan, T. (2021). Artificial intelligence in the agricultural value chain: Review and future directions. *Journal of Agribusiness in Developing and Emerging Economies*.

Ganeshkumar, C., & Khan, A. (2021). Mapping of agritech companies in Indian agricultural value chain. In *Proceedings of the second international conference on information management and machine intelligence* (pp. 155-161). Springer, Singapore. DOI: 10.1007/978-981-15-9689-6_18

Ganeshkumar, C., Prabhu, M., & Abdullah, N. N. (2019). Business analytics and supply chain performance: Partial least squares-structural equation modelling (PLS-SEM) approach. *International Journal of Management and Business Research*, 9(1), 91–96.

Ganeshkumar, C., Prabhu, M., Reddy, P. S., & David, A. (2020). Value chain analysis of Indian edible mushrooms. *International Journal of Technology*, 11(3), 599–607. DOI: 10.14716/ijtech.v11i3.3979

Karthikeyan, L., Chawla, I., & Mishra, A. K. (2020). A review of remote sensing applications in agriculture for food security: Crop growth and yield, irrigation, and crop losses. *Journal of Hydrology (Amsterdam)*, 586, 124905. DOI: 10.1016/j.jhydrol.2020.124905

Kumar, C. G., & Nambirajan, T. (2013). Supply chain management components, supply chain performance and organizational performance: A critical review and development of the conceptual model. *International Journal on Global Business Management & Research*, 2(1), 86.

Latha, C. J., Sankriti, R., David, A., & Srivel, R. (2020). IoT based water purification process using ultrasonic aquatic sound waves. *Test Engineering & Management, The Mattingley Publishing Co., Inc. ISSN*, 0193-4120.

Lee, H. K., Abdul Halim, H., Thong, K. L., & Chai, L. C. (2017). Assessment of food safety knowledge, attitude, self-reported practices, and microbiological hand hygiene of food handlers. *International Journal of Environmental Research and Public Health*, 14(1), 55. DOI: 10.3390/ijerph14010055 PMID: 28098788

Mehta, P., Thakur, R., Raina, K. K., Thakur, P., & Mehta, R. (2019). Farmers' perception towards Electronic-National Agriculture Market (e-NAM) systems adopted by APMC market, Solan, Himachal Pradesh. *AgricINTERNATIONAL*, 6(1), 51–57. DOI: 10.5958/2454-8634.2019.00010.X

Pachayappan, M., Ganeshkumar, C., & Sugundan, N. (2020). Technological implication and its impact in the agricultural sector: An IoT Based Collaboration framework. *Procedia Computer Science*, 171, 1166–1173. DOI: 10.1016/j.procs.2020.04.125

Panpatte, S., & Ganeshkumar, C. (2021). Artificial intelligence in agriculture sector: A case study of blue river technology. In *Proceedings of the second international conference on information management and machine intelligence* (pp. 147-153). Springer, Singapore. DOI: 10.1007/978-981-15-9689-6_17

Paul, V., Ganeshkumar, C., & Jayakumar, L. (2019). Performance evaluation of population seeding techniques of permutation-coded GA travelling salesman problems-based assessment: Performance evaluation of population seeding techniques of permutation-coded GA. [IJAMC]. *International Journal of Applied Metaheuristic Computing*, 10(2), 55–92. DOI: 10.4018/IJAMC.2019040103

Pratheepkumar, P., Sharmila, J. J., & Arokiaraj, D. (2017). Towards mobile opportunistic in cloud computing. [IJSR]. *Indian Journal of Scientific Research*, 17(02), 2250–0138.

Ravi, S., David, A., & Imaduddin, M. (2018). Controlling & calibrating vehicle-related issues using RFID technology. *International Journal of Mechanical and Production Engineering Research and Development*, 8(2), 1125–1132. DOI: 10.24247/ijmperdapr2018130

Reardon, T., Mishra, A., Nuthalapati, C. S., Bellemare, M. F., & Zilberman, D. (2020). COVID-19's disruption of India's transformed food supply chains. *Economic and Political Weekly*, 55(18), 18–22.

Rose, K. M., Howell, E. L., Su, L. Y. F., Xenos, M. A., Brossard, D., & Scheufele, D. A. (2019). Distinguishing scientific knowledge: The impact of different measures of knowledge on genetically modified food attitudes. *Public Understanding of Science (Bristol, England)*, 28(4), 449–467. DOI: 10.1177/0963662518824837 PMID: 30764719

Routroy, S., & Behera, A. (2017). Agriculture supply chain: A systematic review of literature and implications for future research. *Journal of Agribusiness in Developing and Emerging Economies*, 7(3), 275–302. DOI: 10.1108/JADEE-06-2016-0039

Sankar, J. G., & David, A. (2024). A Comprehensive Examination of Mobile Augmented Reality in Tourism (MART) Adoption: Using the UTAUT2 Framework. In *Contemporary Trends in Innovative Marketing Strategies* (pp. 241-262). IGI Global.

Sengottuvel, E. P., & Ganeshkumar, C. (2018). The impact of economic policy on institutional credit flow to the agricultural sector. *IUP Journal of Applied Economics*, 17(2), 80–97.

Siddhartha, T., Nambirajan, T., & Ganeshkumar, C. (2021). Self-help group (SHG) production methods: insights from the union territory of Puducherry community. *Journal of Enterprising Communities: People and Places in the Global Economy*, (ahead-of-print).

Srivastava, V., Singh, A. K., David, A., & Rai, N. (2022). Modelling student employability on an academic basis: A supervised machine learning approach with R. In *Handbook of Research on Innovative Management Using AI in Industry 5.0* (pp. 179–191). IGI Global. DOI: 10.4018/978-1-7998-8497-2.ch012

Sudhakar, B. D., Kattepogu, N., & David, A. (2017). Marketing assistance and digital branding-an insight for technology up-gradation for MSME's. *International Journal of Management Studies & Research*, 5(1), 2455–1562.

APPENDIX I

Organizational Performance: What is the level of your firm's performance on each of the following dimensions compared to your major Industry competitors?
Please mark your response by rounding off the number
Very Low (1); Low (2); Moderate (3); High (4); Very High (5)

Table 11. Dimensions for the Organizational Performance 1 2 3 4 5

1	Market share	1	2	3	4	5
2	Sales growth	1	2	3	4	5
3	Profit margin	1	2	3	4	5
4	Overall product quality	1	2	3	4	5
5	Overall competitive position	1	2	3	4	5
6	Average selling price	1	2	3	4	5
7	Return on investment.	1	2	3	4	5
8	Return on sales	1	2	3	4	5

Chapter 12
Future Directions and Trends in AI–Powered Business Intelligence

K. R. Vineetha
https://orcid.org/0000-0003-2295-4959
Christ University, India

K. R. Resmi
Christ University, India

K. Amrutha
Christ University, India

Midhun Omanakuttan
International College of Dundee, UK

ABSTRACT

Business intelligence (BI) is the process of deriving relevant information from data to facilitate informed decision-making and reveal undiscovered resources for data management. With solid understanding of market trends and data-driven decision-making, business intelligence (BI) enables organizations to stay ahead in today's competitive world. This changes ways in which businesses operate by simplifying learning, refining procedures, automating operations, and reducing expenses with integrate AI. This chapter discusses Future Directions and Trends in AI-powered business Intelligence and addresses the disadvantages of traditional BI reporting and offers new possibilities for extracting value from data. Many of the top developing trends in business intelligence are mentioned in this chapter such as Mobile business intelligence (mobile BI), Advanced data visualization, Cloud-based BI - BI

DOI: 10.4018/979-8-3693-8844-0.ch012

283

as a service, Data storytelling, Augmented analytics, Self-service analytics, Natural language processing (NLP), and Ethical data governance

INTRODUCTION

Business intelligence has advanced significantly in terms of assisting businesses in deriving valuable insights from their data. However, since artificial intelligence (AI) was developed, the potential for data handling has grown enormously. AI enhances our capacity to predict trends, evaluate large amounts of data, and automate decision-making processes in business organizations. On the other hand, business intelligence support systems are rethinking data security, trust, and transparency in a decentralized environment. There is an extremely bright prospect for integrating Business intelligence (BI) with Artificial Intelligence (AI). Effective analytics, precise data, improved security in marketing, and realistic semantic and conceptual situations could all result from this combination. As this chapter has demonstrated, operational and Managerial decision-making is changing due to the integration of Artificial Intelligence (AI) and Business Intelligence (BI). However, there are also drawbacks to this adaptation of new technologies for handling business data.

In this chapter, we begin by looking at the challenges that artificial intelligence in business intelligence faces and the new trends that are reshaping this dynamic field of data management (Walker, 2023).

IDENTIFYING THE CHALLENGES

Realizing the full potential of these advancements requires understanding the obstacles in data handling associated with integrating artificial intelligence (AI) into business intelligence (BI) systems. Figure 1 reflects the challenges and the complex nature of data integration, which requires that various data sources be harmonized and then precisely processed by AI algorithms, which is an important obstacle. Data quality and consistency are also important since inconsistent data might produce inaccurate insights and decisions. Furthermore, BI systems must handle growing data volumes without sacrificing speed, which presents a scaling difficulty. Given the sensitivity of corporate information, ensuring strong data security and privacy is especially essential. Lastly, there's a skills gap and Ethical considerations since many firms don't have the internal knowledge to successfully deploy and manage AI-integrated BI solutions (Splash BI, 2024).

Figure 1. **Identifying the Challenges**

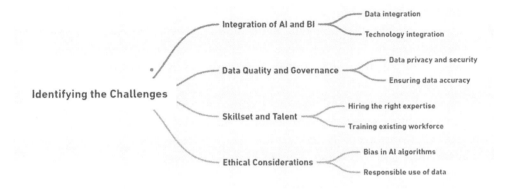

Integration of AI and BI

Business organizations may benefit significantly from integrating Artificial Intelligence (AI) with Business Intelligence (BI) for data automation, as it can provide richer insights and automate decision-making support for processes. However, there are a number of additional difficulties with this integration. Achieving these requirements requires a strong infrastructure, effective change data collection techniques, and well-defined data replication and administration protocols.

- Many organizations need real-time access to continuously updated and synchronized data across many systems.
- In order to effectively handle the load, scalable solutions and dependable infrastructure are required as the volume and complexity of data increase, taxing system resources and affecting performance.
- Proper data preparation, mapping, and cleansing are necessary at every stage of the integration process to guarantee the integrated data's accuracy, consistency, and dependability.

Quality and Data Governance

The interrelated problems with data governance and quality can greatly impact how well a company uses its data. It's crucial to guarantee data correctness, consistency, and completeness, but manual entry errors, out-of-date information, and different data formats amongst systems can make this difficult.

- While maintaining the timeliness and integrity of data is important, safe-guarding against unauthorized alterations and processing data in real time are still challenging jobs.
- Real ownership, management, and a solid framework are necessary for data management in data governance, but disputes within the organization and a lack of support from stakeholders frequently get in the way of these goals.

Security, data privacy, and regulatory compliance are important issues that call for strict precautions to safeguard sensitive data. The complexity of noisy data increases when various tools and technologies are incorporated to ensure smooth data governance and upholding an updated data directory.

Insufficient Talent and Skillset

The absence of skilled experts in data management and business intelligence (BI) poses significant obstacles for organizations.

- Companies struggle to efficiently collect, understand, and analyze data when there is a shortage of appropriately qualified professionals, which results in partial or ambiguous decision-making and lost opportunities.

This skills gap prevents the application of sophisticated BI tools and techniques, leading to ineffective data processing and untrustworthy insights.

- The quick advancement of BI technologies integrated with AI complicates the problem even more, as existing staff might not have the know-how to stay up to date.

Businesses that lack the necessary skills and expertise to handle and use data properly struggle to compete and face increased costs as a result.

Ethical Considerations

The complexities of ethical considerations regarding data in AI and BI are varied and ever-changing. The challenges of Ethical data considerations are given below.

- One significant hurdle involves navigating the complicated realm of data privacy regulations, which differ from place to place and demand ongoing adjustments to keep up with evolving legal standards.

- Another crucial issue is addressing preconceptions within AI systems, as these preconceptions can unconsciously spread discrimination and inequality, leading to ethical difficulties and societal harm.
- To identify these challenges, combined efforts across disciplines, ethical anticipation, and proactive actions are essential to foster responsible data practices in developing and deploying AI-controlled Business data.
- Confirming transparency in AI with BI decision-making processes is also challenging, given that intricate algorithms may lack transparency, making it hard for stakeholders to comprehend and trust the outcomes generated by AI.

Moreover, the rapid advancement of technology and the vast amount of data generated raise concerns about data security and the potential misuse of sensitive information. This highlights the importance of strong cybersecurity measures and ethical governance frameworks (Walker, 2023).

TRENDS IN AI-POWERED BUSINESS INTELLIGENCE

AI-driven advancements in business intelligence techniques address the shortcomings of conventional BI reporting while also opening up new ways to derive value from data. This chapter discusses the latest AI-driven trends in business intelligence, offering new ways to extract value from data while also tackling the limitations of traditional BI reporting. Key emerging trends in Business Intelligence include Natural Language Processing (NLP), Data Storytelling, Augmented Analytics, Self-Service Analytics, Cloud-based BI (BIaaS), Advanced Data Visualization, Mobile Business Intelligence (Mobile BI), and Ethical Data Governance as shown in Figure 2 (Walker, 2023).

- Natural Language Processing (NLP)
- Data Storytelling
- Augmented Analytics
- Self-Service Analytics
- Cloud-based BI (BIaaS)
- Advanced-Data Visualization
- Mobile Business Intelligence (Mobile BI)
- Ethical Data Governance.

Figure 2. Trending Techniques in AI-Powered Business Intelligence

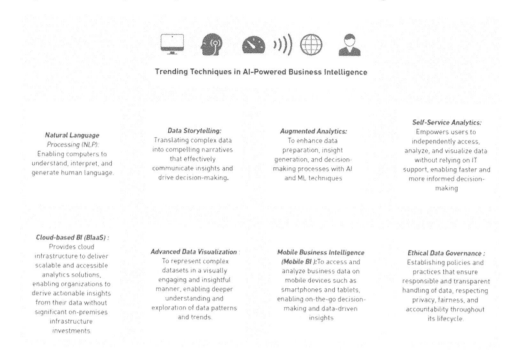

Trending Techniques in AI-Powered Business Intelligence

Natural Language Processing (NLP): Enabling computers to understand, interpret, and generate human language.

Data Storytelling: Translating complex data into compelling narratives that effectively communicate insights and drive decision-making.

Augmented Analytics: To enhance data preparation, insight generation, and decision-making processes with AI and ML techniques

Self-Service Analytics: Empowers users to independently access, analyze, and visualize data without relying on IT support, enabling faster and more informed decision-making

Cloud-based BI (BIaaS): Provides cloud infrastructure to deliver scalable and accessible analytics solutions, enabling organizations to derive actionable insights from their data without significant on-premises infrastructure investments.

Advanced Data Visualization: To represent complex datasets in a visually engaging and insightful manner, enabling deeper understanding and exploration of data patterns and trends.

*Mobile Business Intelligence (Mobile BI):*To access and analyze business data on mobile devices such as smartphones and tablets, enabling on-the-go decision-making and data-driven insights

Ethical Data Governance : Establishing policies and practices that ensure responsible and transparent handling of data, respecting privacy, fairness, and accountability throughout its lifecycle.

Natural Language Processing (NLP)

Natural language processing (NLP) and business intelligence (BI) are combined to give organizations insightful knowledge about preprocessed unstructured text data. In order to facilitate decision-making and visualization, NLP techniques have been used to analyze text data from various resources, such as emails, documents, social media, and consumer feedback. This information is then integrated into BI tools with AI.

The following are the major benefits of integrating NLP with business intelligence:

Using NLP (natural language processing) methods, text data can be processed to extract relationships, themes, attitudes, and entities. The data can be added to BI systems during processing for additional research.

- Sentiment Analysis: NLP is a useful tool for analyzing the sentiment of consumer feedback, comments, and reviews on social media.

- By incorporating sentiment analysis in data handling results into business intelligence dashboards, organizations can gain insight into customer perspectives and make data-driven decisions.
- Topic Modeling: methods of natural language processing such as The multivariate theory of allocation, often known as topic modeling, can uncover topics that have been hidden inside substantial volumes of textual data. Business Intelligence tools are helpful in visualizing or presenting these topics so that patterns, trends, and noteworthy areas can be identified.
- Text Summarization: Natural language processing (NLP) algorithms enhance decision-makers' capacity to effectively assimilate crucial information handling by providing descriptions of long text documents. These summaries can be connected with BI reports for concise communication.
- Identification of Named Entities (NER): In text data, NLP can recognize and categorize named entities, including individuals, groups, areas, and dates. Several business intelligence (BI) applications, such as analyzing market trends and consumer interactions analysis, permit the use of this data.
- Predictive Analytics: By integrating NLP and BI, businesses may create textual based on information predictive models that predict customer behavior, spot new trends, or estimate sentiment in the market.
- Better Decision-Making: Through the integration of NLP and BI, decision-makers can gain a more profound comprehension of textual data, enabling them to make more informed and data-driven choices for a range of business tasks.
- When everything is considered, adding NLP data capabilities to business intelligence (BI) systems improves data analysis, simplifies the interpretation of textual data processes, and enables organizations to fully utilize the potential of unstructured data to assist in strategic decision-making.

Applications of NLP in Business Intelligence

The fundamental element of artificial intelligence (AI), which concentrates on natural language communication among computers and humans, is natural language processing, or NLP. NLP can improve the capacity to evaluate and comprehend data when coupled with business intelligence (BI), resulting in better decision-making. The following are some important key applications of NLP in BI with AI, and Figure 3 indicates the functionalities of elements:

- Sentiment Analysis
- Text Mining and Data Extraction
- Natural Language Querying

- Chatbots and virtual Assistants
- Document Classification and Organization
- Translation Multilingual support

Figure 3. Applications of NLP in Business Intelligence

Data Storytelling

This technique converts complex information or data into compelling narratives, conveying insights and influencing choices. Using the integration of analytical insights in AI and narrative approaches in BI, audiences are engaged, and meaningful tales are created from complex data. Using visualization tools, the approach presents information logically and understandably while highlighting significant trends and patterns. When combined with AI tools, data storytelling improves comprehension or interpretation of data while also assisting stakeholders in understanding the significance of business intelligence data and how it affects their action plans. Ultimately, it makes insights more meaningful and convincing by connecting data to human experience.

Three important areas of business intelligence knowledge are integrated by data storytelling, as mentioned in Figure 4:

Figure 4. Data Storytelling Essential Areas

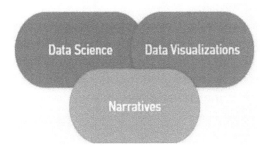

- Data Science: This interdisciplinary field extracts information and insights from data, making them more accessible and practical. Data science has transformed our daily lives in the past few decades by encouraging the technologies we rely on. Regardless of their data gathering and analysis expertise, data scientists cannot frequently communicate the deeper insights and opportunities concealed inside the data.
- Visualizations: The development of technological solutions such as dashboards has significantly enhanced our ability to understand massive amounts of data. We acquire new perspectives when we translate data into graphs, pie charts, and line charts. However, visualizations alone have limits, as they provide fast hints without the context required to grasp the underlying reasons fully.
- Narrative: The essential part of a data story is the narrative. It uses language that is adapted to our needs, thereby helping us understand recent developments better. Narratives become the primary medium for communicating insights, with visualizations and data provided as supporting evidence (Aljawarneh et al., 2020).

Figure 5 (Nugit, 2024) shows a few examples of how Spotify, Slack, and Uber utilize data storytelling to communicate with their customers.

Spotify: Spotify has recently started emailing its users annual summary stories. These narratives provide fascinating facts, such as the total time each user has spent listening to music on the app. This engaging strategy effectively communicates the value of their service by offering more than an invoice or a simple thank you.

Slack: Every month, Slack, a messaging platform that replaces the outdated email system, uses storytelling apps to interact with clients innovatively during the billing process of each month. Slack delivers a visual tale highlighting the most important ways that its customers have used their service instead of just sending a plain email with the invoice clearly visible. Consumer interactions are shifting as a result of this effective strategy.

Uber: Comparable to Spotify, Uber employs data storytelling to engage with its customers annually. Instead of sending a yearly recap email detailing the total amount disbursed on Uber, Uber has reframed the conversation to highlight the value of its service to riders. By showcasing adapted statistics of your experience with the app, you can instantly see their important impact on your daily life.

Figure 5. Data Storytelling by Spotify, Slack, and Uber

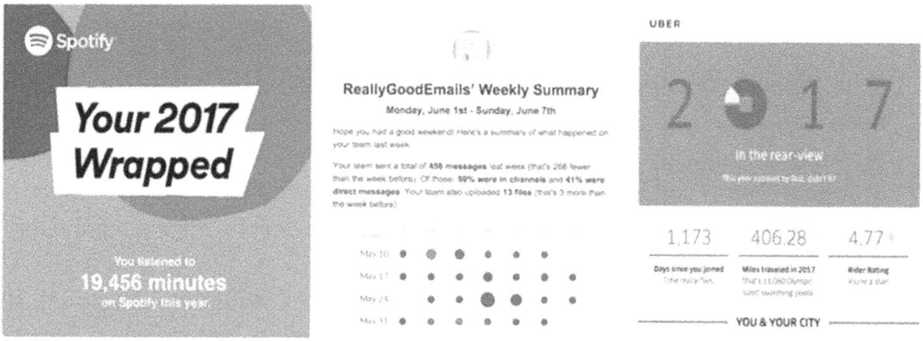

Spotify   Slack   Uber

Augmented Analytics

To improve and speed up data analytics, Augmented analytics integrates with BI with the use of machine learning (ML), artificial intelligence (AI), and a range of natural language processing (NLP) technologies, especially natural language query and production. It is the latest advancement in business intelligence (BI) technology, expanding upon and enhancing conventional data analysis models to provide insights to a broad spectrum of business users, including those lacking in-depth technical knowledge. Being more precise, augmented analytics enables citizen data scientists and data analysts to extract richer, more detailed insights in a matter of minutes—insights that would require an expert data scientist the same amount of time to determine using traditional BI tools.

Augmented analytics, the next genre of business intelligence, enhances the self-service analytics approach in multiple ways. Artificial intelligence can streamline data preparation by independently gathering data from several databases and linked systems. Furthermore, clients can self-serve ad hoc reports on a conversational user interface (UI) by employing natural language queries once the data is in the platform (Walker, 2023).

How does Augmented Analytics work?

The types of modern technologies that have been included in the data analytics process to give enhanced analytics are artificial intelligence (AI), machine learning (ML), and natural language processing (NLP). The typical method by which it functions of these methods is as outlined below:

- Data Collecting: Augmented analytics in BI automates difficult data and time-consuming tasks, including data integration, transformation, and cleaning. It guarantees reliable data collection for analysis by utilizing machine learning (ML) techniques to detect and correct issues, integrate data from several sources, and fill in missing information with the support of augmented analytic methods.
- Data Discovery and Insights Generation: Augmented Analytics uses AI and ML to automatically look for patterns, anomalies, and correlations in huge data. It may predict future occurrences, highlight significant patterns, and offer ideas that human analysts might not see immediately.
- Natural Language Processing (NLP): Projects involving enhanced analytics make use of NLP techniques, which include natural language generation (NLG) and natural language query (NLQ). Although NLG simplifies complicated information and discoveries into easily readable narratives, NLQ enables users to pose inquiries in a common language and receive relevant insights without requiring technical jargon or specialist query languages.
- Automated Analysis: The system provides real-time or almost real-time insights by continually examining incoming data. It can automatically create reports, dashboards, and visualizations that highlight significant metrics and trends related to the user's industry or role.
- User Interaction and Collaboration: Business users, especially those with low technology skills, may interact with the data in a natural way thanks to the user-friendly design of augmented analytics solutions. They are frequently

provided with collaboration instruments that let groups discuss discoveries, exchange perspectives, and come to jointly data-driven conclusions.

- Actionable Recommendations: Augmented analytics doesn't just have limitations to delivering insights; it can also provide actionable recommendations. It can assist users in making well-informed decisions quickly and efficiently by suggesting solutions or next steps based on the data analysis.

Figure 6 (Walker, 2023) shows how Augmented analytics helps businesses use their data more wisely and achieve better business results by reducing the data analytics process and providing multifaceted analytical capabilities to a wider audience.

Figure 6. Working Structure of Augmented Analytics

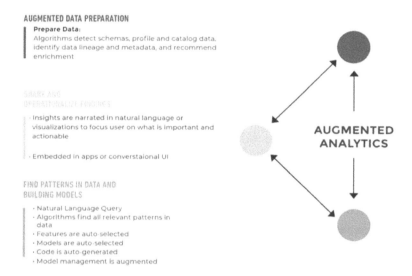

Self-Service Analytics

Self-service BI allows business users to make timely strategic and operational decisions without relying on third parties like data scientists, IT specialists, and data analysts. This will free up more time for your analytics staff to devote to strategic initiatives, which will mean less manual reporting labor.

Self-service enables data access and insights for front-line business users, enabling them to make data-driven decisions instead of depending on intuition or subjective judgments. With its benefits, self-service analytics is rapidly taking the lead as a need for companies of all sizes. The following Figure 7 shows the major steps in Self-service BI.

Figure 7. Basics Steps Needed for Self-service BI

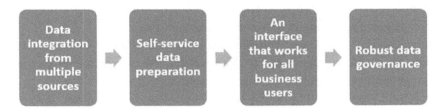

Self-service BI solutions should allow integration with different data sources (CRM, accounting, ERP, and marketing software, etc.). It also has the flexibility to integrate big data sources (social media data, streaming data, IoT data, etc.) to do big data analysis. To handle the diverse analytical needs of your business users like predictive analytics, historical analysis, streaming analytics, etc., a self-service BI solution should enable the aggregation of data sets before feeding data of a suitable format into your business intelligence system for reporting and further analysis.

Self-service analytics is making a huge change in how businesses approach decision-making in today's data-driven world. This technology creates a culture of data-driven decision-making and breaks down barriers by enabling users at all levels to independently access and analyze information. An interface that works for all business users is needed, and self-service analytics eliminates the need for ongoing assistance from data specialists or IT. Business users mainly use it for data visualizations, analysis, exploration, and report generation based on their needs and questions. Without statistical or data science knowledge, users can quickly under-stand the business information and opportunities and make decisions by interacting directly with the data. A front-end BI application is needed for self-service analytics as a user interface for data manipulation and viewing. Examples of directly working with data are Microsoft Power BI, Tableau, ThoughtSpot, etc.

Advantages of Self-service Analytics

The following are the advantages:

- Limitless Data Discovery: Business users can explore and analyze data freely.

- Ease of Use and Better Decision-Making: By using a simple user interface, users with non-technical backgrounds can also explore data for access and analysis.
- Agility: It helps with faster decision-making and responsiveness to new market situations and challenges more quickly.
- Democratized Data Access: It encourages a data-driven culture by promoting users across the company to use democratized data
- Enhanced cost Efficiency: Efficiency is enhanced in terms of scalability and reduction in reporting costs. It does not require significant infrastructure change while expanding users and data sources.
- Increased Accuracy: Users can spot and correct discrepancies during data analysis, which may produce more accurate results.
- Increased user satisfaction: The tools allow the Users to design reports and visualizations based on their requirements.
- Security: Self-service analytics systems have data safety and compliance features such as data governance frameworks and access controls.

Self-Service vs. Traditional Business Intelligence

Traditional BI includes the old way of using software for business data analysis. Analysts use a wide range of tools for data analysis. It involves the involvement of IT professionals, mainly in data analysis, handling, and visualization. Self-service Business Intelligence is the modern way of data analytics where users can work with data without an IT or statistical background. It allows users to make decisions on their own. The main advantage is that data is available to everyone in the organization. It allows users to perform in-depth data exploration, analysis, and advanced analytics.

Cloud BI

Cloud BI stores data on cloud servers, models it with a data warehouse and then analyzes it to extract insights. These sophisticated cloud tools analyze data and can automate tasks based on the insights found. The main advantage is cost savings, as the organization can pay for the resources it only uses in the cloud. It is very flexible as it quickly adapts to the changes without considering the physical infrastructure.

Benefits of Cloud BI

Cloud BI has several benefits, such as:

- Cost-saving is a major advantage, and the main theme is pay-based on use with lower initial investments in hardware and software.
- Flexibility: Flexibility and scalability in terms of growing business demand.
- Streamlined Collaboration: Promoting the collaboration in real-time from different locations
- Faster deployment and Automatic update: Cloud deployment and update is very fast
- Advanced analytical capabilities: Integrating ML/AI/big data handling capabilities are very strong.
- Performance optimization and Reliable

Advanced visualizations

The growing amount of data on the internet and social media has made effective communication vital. Data visualization grew as a key corporate intelligence tool and solved these specific challenges. By transforming massive datasets into easily understood representations, it opens up difficult information to a wider audience. Advanced data visualization (ADV), which utilizes automation and machine learning, improves this. ADV generates reports that are more comprehensive and analytical, better meeting the needs of many stakeholders within an organization. In addition, it forecasts, uncovers hidden information, and provides suggestions.

The following Figure 8 shows the major process of data visualization.

Figure 8. Major Process of Data Visualization

Gathering data is the first stage in the visualization process. You need to make sure the data is the right kind for your needs, even though it is messy and unorganized. The next step is parsing and categorizing the data to give it a structure for simpler understanding and presentation. To keep your charts organized and focused, remove any unnecessary data using Filter. When you use the data to create charts that show secret insights beyond simple numbers, that's where the magic comes in mining. Selecting the appropriate chart is essential for effectively presenting your data, and by eliminating repeated data analysis, this exploration can help you save time. In order to maximize user engagement and clarity, you finalize your visualization and consider incorporating interactive elements that let users go deeper into the data.

The best tools available for data visualization are

- Google Chart
- Databox
- Tableau
- D3
- Datawrapper
- Microsoft Power BI

The following are the main advantages of advanced visualization techniques

- Intuitive Data Exploration
- Unprecedented Data Access
- adapt to evolving trends and make data-driven decisions
- Effortless Data Sharing
- allow businesses to see more data simultaneously
- Work with more complex data

Mobile Business Intelligence

The advent of smartphones made the term offline a phantasm in the real world. We constantly use one application or another on our mobile phones, and all this information can be analyzed using mobile BI. Nowadays, everyone uses many portable devices like notebooks, tablets, and high-end mobile phones, and app-based BI tools can be run on all these devices. The importance of mobile app-based BI is progressively increasing as everyone needs real-time updated data anywhere, anytime (Verkoou & Spruit, 2013).

Mobile BI provides many advantages, including high accessibility, data availability, and improved methods of analysis that can be accessed offline and online. The tools are available in other forms, such as websites and mini or lite applications. The visualization and analysis are more accessible and better on mobile devices, as shown in Figure 9. The website's dynamic nature allows users to choose any handy device of varying screen sizes. Along with these monitoring apps, dynamic dataset storing can also be performed.

Figure 9. Mobile BI for Analysis

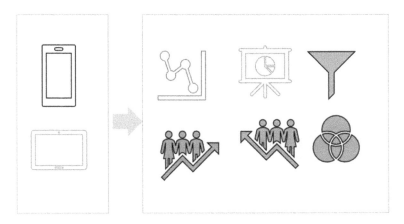

Four Pillars of Mobile BI

Attributes like people, processes, tasks, and affect form the fundamental pillars of Mobile BI. The mobile app should be designed based on the users. The applications should have platform independence and modern facilities like hands-free navigation and multiple-device connectivity.

As the screen size is small, the task is to provide the right information in the right place and of the right quality. The required and essential information must be more projected and visible than other trivial data. The process pillar is a two-step method where the first step ensures the proper functioning of the app, and the second step ensures the application's security, integrity, and availability. Finally, the effect pillar provides the impact of the analysis along with how the application captured maximum information.

Analysis Metrics Used by Mobile BI

Key Performance Indicators (Shao et al., 2022)

KPI calculates the success of an organization based on its targets, objectives, and employees. KPIs can be used for individual analysis, such as per-customer or per-client performance analysis. The value of the KPI can increase based on the liquidity-cash availability ratio or net income.

Sales Report

Systematic and efficient sales reports created monthly, weekly, or daily can help analyze performance easily. This indicates the clear growth or dip of an organization. This helps in faster troubleshooting in key areas.

Mobile Dashboards

Mobile Business Intelligence (BI) dashboards are specialized tools that allow users to view and analyze business data on mobile devices like smartphones and tablets. Dashboards enable users to make informed decisions even when away from their desks. Core features of Mobile Dashboard include – adaptive design, real-time data access, Alerts- online and offline, and personalization.
Advantages of using Mobile BI

- Anytime-Anywhere access
- Online and offline notifications and alerts
- Better view of data
- Mobility and hands-free mode
- Cost-effective

Business Intelligence Governance

The principal constituent of business intelligence is providing data with timeliness and quality (Praful Bharatiya, 2023). Data governance is the best solution for tackling this challenge. The governance encompasses the strategies and heuristics of choosing the employees, analysis tools and hardware. The data collected from different business sources will be non-uniform and unformatted. Thus, the raw data collected is challenging to analyze or present to the shareholders. However, after governing the data, it is structured into monthly, quarterly, or any structured form, which helps in quick and easy analysis. This process also helps to manage a tremendous amount of data by managing access to data and providing access control. A well-governed BI helps in increasing the trust of the stakeholders.

The second most important part of governance is to have a great vision (Combita Niño et al., 2020). This should be encouraged by the higher authorities and taken up by the lower level by providing several resources and promoting data analysis wherever possible. This helps in understanding crucial information like prioritizing projects, managing the quality and type of the project, and funding. According to

(Bogza & Zaharie, 2008) (What Is Business Intelligence Governance & How to Achieve It? - (Codoid, n.d.), the functions of the BI Government include the following:

Data access control

The governance team must monitor the usage of the data. This helps in quick and efficient analysis of the data. The provision to edit and delete data should be given only to the members of the higher hierarchy, and the minimum access should be given to members of the lower hierarchy.

Prioratise user engagement

Organize the data according to the priority. A disorganized and cluttered dashboard leads to miscalculation, missing deadlines, and misinterpretation. This may lead to reduced user engagement. The use of additional dashboards helps to avoid the overlap of projects.

Manage license

The availability of free BI software like Tableau helps cut software costs for various stakeholders. Removing licensed software that is hardly used can also help reduce the software's cost.

Provide metadata to all stakeholders

The graphical representation of the data or the visualization helps better understand the relationship between the various variables in the data. However, the images without metadata do not provide complete information, as shown in (a) and (b) of Figure 10. Images (c) and (d) give out maximum information, which helps in better understanding. A single image can give maximum information, which is convenient and less time-consuming when interpreting the analysis.

Figure 10. (a) and (b) Shows Images without Metadata and (c) and (d) Shows Images with Metadata

Form a committee for the governance.

The governance should have well-defined team members from various sectors of stakeholders, from the senior manager to the end user. This helps understand the needs and expected quality of the project. The team's dynamicity helps identify the redundancies, better understand the business goals, and make the best and right decisions throughout the process. SMEs from the industry also help boost the decision-making skills of the team members. The team must have an owner of the business, an analyst who can convert data into information, and a steward of data who gathers data from the most reliable source.

Pillars of BI Governance

BI governance comprises five main pillars, among which the monitoring pillar is technical, and others are non-technical (Abdel Rahman & Alnoukari, 2012). The sixth is a virtual pillar added by the authors (Bi, 2023). Figure 11 outlines the six pillars.

Figure 11. Pillars that Hold up High-Quality Governance

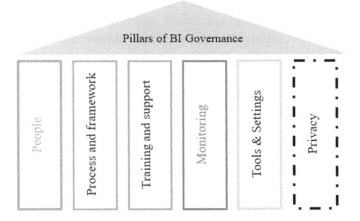

The first and most important pillar is the People pillar, which encompasses different roles the people work in the analysis. The people pillar combines all stakeholders, including managers, analysts, and users. The second pillar, framework and process, ensures all the documents are complete and updated. This helps to increase the quality of the process by drastically increasing the accuracy of the analysis. The third pillar ensures that all the employees are periodically trained. The agenda for the entire year can be planned in the beginning. The monitoring pillar in BI governance can be used to observe the present and past data to predict the future. The monitoring can be performed using OLAP, which gathers and presents past and current business logs and transactions. The reports can be manipulated according to each user. A standard form of the formal report does not exist and hence can be changed according to the needs and interests of the stakeholders. The tools and settings pillar gives different tools used in BI governance.

Both licensed and free software are listed in this pillar. As various companies and business groups prefer different tools to protect their data, all the possible tools are provided here. The last pillar, which is virtual but essential, is data privacy. This elevates the traditional framework pillar to an advanced conceptual framework that ensures various privacy measures(Bi, 2023). The privacy of the data is decided based on the type of data used for monitoring and analysis. Some data needs to be kept transparent and known by all the stakeholders; however, the organization can choose sensitive, less cohesive, and independent data to be private.

BI Governance in Education

Prominent educational institutes like Universities have a large amount of data to process, as many students and employees directly and indirectly affect growth (Kabakchieva, 2015) (Combita Niño et al., 2020). Universities will have a large amount of data from more than ten years to compare and understand the knowledge acquired, employability, and scope of higher education for each student. Thorough analysis helps to increase the standard of the institution. The combination is shown in Figure 12.

Figure 12. BI Governance in Universities

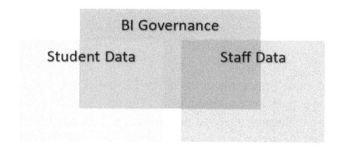

BI Governance in Business Organizations

In private companies, the significance of governance is high as they might be affected by threats, risk management, information security, and data audits. The organization needs help in managing technical, non-technical, and employee data to plan the future, as depicted in Figure 13. All these private companies face the challenge of increasing control of the company's data assets by providing end-user innovation due to the rise and augmentation of various BI tools (Kabakchieva, 2015).

Figure 13. BI Governance in Companies

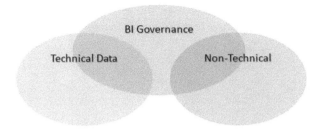

Advantages of using BI Governance

- Standardized data representation
- Easy data cleaning and validation
- Improved collaboration between organizations
- Easy performance management
- Optimized use of resources
- Efficient data management and stewardship

CONCLUSION

As AI and BI technologies develop, they are expected to become more significant in business information, transforming how businesses make choices and spurring the expansion of data. Artificial intelligence (AI)-powered business intelligence should only get more complex with advancements in machine learning, deep learning, and natural language processing. These developments will make it possible for AI to process business data, analyze more complicated information, and produce predictions and insights that are more precise. In order to provide business data with more powerful tools, we may also anticipate the integration of AI with other technologies, such as blockchain, Humanoid AI, NLP evolution, and augmented reality.

Future applications of Quantum AI in AI-powered business intelligence could include creating executive assistants tailored to their needs. Quantum AI exploits quantum computing to perform complex analytics in business data and machine learning tasks such as data filtering, enabling businesses to analyze complex data sets and make better decisions. This can lead to breakthroughs like financial modeling, drug discovery, and climate forecasting. The creation of individualized AI assistants for executives in business or marketing, the use of AI-powered predictive maintenance for industrial equipment and tools, and the optimization process of supply chain management are a few possible future possibilities for AI-powered business intelligence. Organizations must keep ahead of the latest developments and technology enhancements and invest in the most current developments in AI to stay innovative and competitive as the technology develops with Business Intelligence for better benefits.

REFERENCES

Abdel Rahman and M. Alnoukari. (2012). *IGI Global Publishing Business Intelligence and Agile Methodologies for Knowledge-Based Organisations*. Cross-Disciplinary Applications.

Aljawarneh, S., & Malhotra, M. (Eds.). (2020). *Impacts and Challenges of Cloud Business Intelligence*. IGI Global.

"Augmented Analytics: How AI is Transforming BI to Keep Pace With Complex Data" [Online].Availbabe: https://www.tellius.com/augmented-analytics-how-ai-is -transforming-bi-to-keep-pace-with-complex-data. [Accessed 24/05/2024]

Bi, T., Yu, G., Lu, Q., Xu, X., & Van Beest, N. (2023). The Privacy Pillar—A Conceptual Framework for Foundation Model-based Systems. arXiv preprint arXiv:2311.06998.

Bogza, R. M., & Zaharie, D. 'Business intelligence as a competitive differentiator', 2008 IEEE Int. Conf. Autom. Qual. Testing, Robot. AQTR 2008 - THETA 16th Ed. - Proc., vol. 1, pp. 146–151, 2008, DOI: 10.1109/AQTR.2008.4588724

Combita Niño, H. A., Cómbita Niño, J. P., & Morales Ortega, R. (2020). Business intelligence governance framework in a university: Universidad de la costa case study. *International Journal of Information Management*, 50, 405–412. DOI: 10.1016/j. ijinfomgt.2018.11.012

Dudycz, H. (2010). "Visualization methods in Business Intelligence systems–an overview." Business Informatics (16). *Data Mining and Business Intelligence*, 104, 9–24.

"Future of Business Intelligence (BI): Integrating AI and Blockchain for Enhanced Security" [online].Available: https://www.linkedin.com/pulse/future-business-intelligence-bi-integrating-ai-blockchain-jha-5h24c. [Accessed 23/05/2024]

Johnson, B. (2018). Self-Service Analytics: A Comprehensive Review of Implementation Strategies. *Journal of Data Analytics*, 8(2), 87–101.

Kabakchieva, D. (2015). Kabakchieva, 'Business intelligence systems for analysing university students data'. *Cybernetics and Information Technologies*, 15(1), 104–115. DOI: 10.1515/cait-2015-0009

Phillips-Wren, G., Daly, M., & Burstein, F. (2021). Reconciling business intelligence, analytics and decision support systems: More data, deeper insight. *Decision Support Systems*, 146, 113560. DOI: 10.1016/j.dss.2021.113560

Praful Bharadiya, J. (2023). A Comparative Study of Business Intelligence and Artificial Intelligence with Big Data Analytics. *Am. J. Artif. Intell.*, 7(1), 24–30. DOI: 10.11648/j.ajai.20230701.14

Qin, X., Luo, Y., Tang, N., & Li, G. (2020). Making data visualization more efficient and effective: A survey. *The VLDB Journal*, 29(1), 93–117. DOI: 10.1007/s00778-019-00588-3

Shao, C., Yang, Y., Juneja, S., & GSeetharam, T. (2022). IoT data visualization for business intelligence in corporate finance. *Information Processing & Management*, 59(1), 102736. DOI: 10.1016/j.ipm.2021.102736

Shao, Y. (2022). Yang, S. Juneja, and T. GSeetharam, 'IoT data visualisation for business intelligence in corporate finance'. *Information Processing & Management*, 59(1). Advance online publication. DOI: 10.1016/j.ipm.2021.102736

"Shaping the Future: Navigating the AI Revolution in Business Intelligence" [Online]. Available: https://www.linkedin.com/pulse/shaping-future-navigating-ai-revolution-business-intelligence-j3lgc [Accessed 23/05/2024]

Verkoou, K., & Spruit, M. (2013). Mobile business intelligence: Key considerations for implementations projects. *Journal of Computer Information Systems*, 54(1), 23–33. DOI: 10.1080/08874417.2013.11645668

" What is Data Storytelling? The most effective way to share business information and drive outcomes [Online]." https://www.nugit.co/what-is-data-storytelling/ "[Accessed 24/05/2024]

Compilation of References

" What is Data Storytelling? The most effective way to share business information and drive outcomes [Online]." https://www.nugit.co/what-is-data-storytelling/ "[Accessed 24/05/2024]

"Augmented Analytics: How AI is Transforming BI to Keep Pace With Complex Data" [Online].Availbabe: https://www.tellius.com/augmented-analytics-how-ai-is -transforming-bi-to-keep-pace-with-complex-data. [Accessed 24/05/2024]

"Future of Business Intelligence (BI): Integrating AI and Blockchain for Enhanced Security" [online].Available: https://www.linkedin.com/pulse/future-business-intelligence-bi-integrating-ai-blockchain-jha-5h24c. [Accessed 23/05/2024]

"Shaping the Future: Navigating the AI Revolution in Business Intelligence" [Online]. Available: https://www.linkedin.com/pulse/shaping-future-navigating-ai-revolution -business-intelligence-j3lgc [Accessed 23/05/2024]

Abdel Rahman and M. Alnoukari. (2012). *IGI Global Publishing Business Intelligence and Agile Methodologies for Knowledge-Based Organisations*. Cross-Disciplinary Applications.

Ada, N., Ethirajan, M., & Kumar, A., K.E.K, V., Nadeem, S. P., Kazancoglu, Y., & Kandasamy, J. (. (2021). Blockchain Technology for Enhancing Traceability and Efficiency in Automobile Supply Chain—A Case Study. *Sustainability*, 13(24), 13667. DOI: 10.3390/su132413667

Adewusi, A. O., Okoli, U. I., Adaga, E., Olorunsogo, T., Asuzu, O. F., & Daraojimba, D. O. (2024). Business intelligence in the era of big data: A review of analytical tools and competitive advantage. *Computer Science & IT Research Journal*, 5(2), 415–431. DOI: 10.51594/csitrj.v5i2.791

Agarwal, A., Singhal, C., & Thomas, R. (2021). *AI-powered decision making for the bank of the future*. McKinsey & Company.

Ahmad, A. K., Jafar, A., & Aljoumaa, K. (2019). Customer churn prediction in telecom using machine learning in big data platform. *Journal of Big Data*, 6(1), 28. DOI: 10.1186/s40537-019-0191-6

Ahn, J. H., Han, S. P., & Lee, Y. S. (2006). 'Customer churn analysis: Churn determinants and mediation effects of partial defection in the Korean mobile tele-communications service industry'. [Google Scholar]. *Telecommunications Policy*, 30(10), 552–568. DOI: 10.1016/j.telpol.2006.09.006

AI in CRM: Benefits and Use Cases of AI-Powered CRM System. (2023, December). DDI Development. https://ddi-dev.com/blog/programming/ai-in-crm-benefits -and-use-cases-of-ai-powered-crm-system/

Akinwande, V. (n.d.). Security assessment of blockchain-as-a-service (BaaS) plat-forms. *2017*.

Akter, S., Sultana, S., Mariani, M., Wamba, S. F., Spanaki, K., & Dwivedi, Y. K. (2023). Advancing algorithmic bias management capabilities in AI-driven marketing analytics research. *Industrial Marketing Management, 114*(October 2022), 243–261. DOI: 10.1016/j.indmarman.2023.08.013

Akter, S., Dwivedi, Y. K., Sajib, S., Biswas, K., Bandara, R. J., & Michael, K. (2022). Algorithmic bias in machine learning-based marketing models. *Journal of Business Research*, 144(February), 201–216. DOI: 10.1016/j.jbusres.2022.01.083

Akter, S., & Wamba, S. F. (2016). Big data analytics in E-commerce: A systematic review and agenda for future research. *Electronic Markets*, 26(2), 173–194. DOI: 10.1007/s12525-016-0219-0

Al Amin, M., Nabil, D. H., Baldacci, R., & Rahman, M. (2023). Exploring Block-chain Implementation Challenges for Sustainable Supply Chains: An Integrated Fuzzy TOPSIS–ISM Approach. *Sustainability (Basel)*, 15(18), 13891. DOI: 10.3390/su151813891

Aleksander, I. (2017). Partners of humans: A realistic assessment of the role of robots in the foreseeable future. *Journal of Information Technology*, 32(1), 1–9.

Al-Farsi, S., Rathore, M. M., & Bakiras, S. (2021). Security of Blockchain-Based Supply Chain Management Systems: Challenges and Opportunities. *Applied Sciences (Basel, Switzerland)*, 11(12), 5585. DOI: 10.3390/app11125585

Aljawarneh, S., & Malhotra, M. (Eds.). (2020). *Impacts and Challenges of Cloud Business Intelligence*. IGI Global.

Allioui, H., & Mourdi, Y. (2023). Unleashing the potential of AI: Investigating cutting-edge technologies that are transforming businesses. [IJCEDS]. *International Journal of Computer Engineering and Data Science*, 3(2), 1–12.

Almeyda, R., & Darmansya, A. (2019). The influence of environmental, social, and governance (ESG) disclosure on firm financial performance. *IPTEK Journal of Proceedings Series*, 0(5), 278–290. DOI: 10.12962/j23546026.y2019i5.6340

Alnofeli, K., Akter, S., & Yanamandram, V. (2023). Understanding the Future trends and innovations of AI-based CRM systems. In *Handbook of Big Data Research Methods* (pp. 279–294). Edward Elgar Publishing. DOI: 10.4337/9781800888555.00021

Ammous, S. (2016). Blockchain Technology: What is it good for? *Available at SSRN* 2832751. DOI: 10.2139/ssrn.2832751

Ang, L., & Buttle, F. (2006). CRM software applications and business performance. *Journal of Database Marketing & Customer Strategy Management*, 14(1), 4–16. DOI: 10.1057/palgrave.dbm.3250034

Areiqat, A. Y., Alheet, A. F., Qawasmeh, R. A., & Zamil, A. M. (2021). Artificial intelligence and its drastic impact on e-commerce progress. *Academy of Strategic Management Journal*, 20, 1–11.

Arevalillo, J. M. (2019). A machine learning approach to assess price sensitivity with application to automobile loan segmentation. *Applied Soft Computing*, 76, 390–399.

Armstrong, S., & Sotala, K., & Ó hÉigeartaigh, S. S. (2014). The errors, insights and lessons of famous AI predictions–and what they mean for the future. *Journal of Experimental & Theoretical Artificial Intelligence*, 26(3), 317–342.

Arokiaraj, D., Ganeshkumar, C., & Paul, P. V. (2020). Innovative management system for environmental sustainability practices among Indian auto-component manufacturers. *Int J Bus Innov Res*, 23(2), 168–182. DOI: 10.1504/IJBIR.2020.110095

Ashta, A., & Herrmann, H. (2021). Artificial intelligence and fintech: An overview of opportunities and risks for banking, investments, and microfinance. *Strategic Change*, 30(3), 211–222. DOI: 10.1002/jsc.2404

Aswal, P. (2024, May 10). *What are Blockchain nodes? Detailed Guide [UPDATED]*. Blockchain Council. https://www.blockchain-council.org/blockchain/blockchain-nodes/

Auer, R., Cornelli, G., & Frost, J. (2020). Rise of the Central Bank Digital Currencies: Drivers, Approaches and Technologies. *CEPR Discussion Paper No. DP15363*.

Azmi, M., Mansour, A., & Azmi, C. (2023). A Context-Aware Empowering Business with AI: Case of Chatbots in Business Intelligence Systems. *Procedia Computer Science*, 224, 479–484.

Babayev, N., & Israfilzade, K. (2023). Creating complexity matrix for classifying artificial intelligence applications in e-commerce: New perspectives on value creation. *Journal of Life Economics*, 10(3), 141–156. DOI: 10.15637/jlecon.2078

Bagloee, S. A., Asadi, M., Sarvi, M., & Patriksson, M. (2018). A hybrid machine-learning and optimization method to solve bi-level problems. *Expert Systems with Applications*, 95, 142–152.

Bai, C., & Sarkis, J. (2020). A supply chain transparency and sustainability technology appraisal model for blockchain technology. *International Journal of Production Research*, 58(7), 2142–2162. DOI: 10.1080/00207543.2019.1708989

Bajaj, R., & Sharma, V. (2018). Smart Education with artificial intelligence based determination of learning styles. *Procedia Computer Science*, 132, 834–842.

Bamakan, S. M. H., Motavali, A., & Babaei Bondarti, A. (2020). A survey of block-chain consensus algorithms performance evaluation criteria. *Expert Systems with Applications*, 154, 113385. DOI: 10.1016/j.eswa.2020.113385

Banaee, H., Ahmed, M. U., & Loutfi, A. (2024). Data mining for business intelligence: A review and future directions. *Journal of Business Research*, 172, 29–47. DOI: 10.1016/j.jbusres.2024.01.015

Banu, F. (2022). Jahir Hussain & Subramani, Neelakandan & BT, Geetha & Villibharathan, Selvalakshmi & Umadevi, A. & Martinson, Eric. (2022). Artificial Intelligence Based Customer Churn Prediction Model for Business Markets. *Computational Intelligence and Neuroscience*, 2022, 1–14. DOI: 10.1155/2022/1703696

Banumathi, M., & Arokiaraj, D. (2011). Eco-labeling–The Need for Sustainable Marketing. In *National Conference in the era of Global Recovery-2011 (SGEGR2011* (pp. 511-515).

Beecham, S., O'Leary, P., Baker, S., Richardson, I., & Noll, J. (2014). Making software engineering research relevant. *Computer*, 47(4), 80–83. DOI: 10.1109/MC.2014.92

Bello, H. O., Ige, A. B., & Ameyaw, M. N. (2024). Adaptive machine learning models: concepts for real-time financial fraud prevention in dynamic environments. *World Journal of Advanced Engineering Technology and Sciences, 12*(2), 021-034.

Bengfort, B., Bilbro, R., & Ojeda, T. (2018). *Applied text analysis with Python: Enabling language-aware data products with machine learning*. O'Reilly Media, Inc.

Bentley, P. (2018). The three laws of artificial intelligence: Dispelling common myths. Should we fear artificial intelligence, 6-12.

Bharadiya, J. P. (2023). Machine learning and AI in business intelligence: Trends and opportunities. 48(1), 123-134.

Bharadiya, J. P. (2023). A comparative study of business intelligence and artificial intelligence with big data analytics. *American Journal of Artificial Intelligence*, 7(1), 24.

Bharadiya, J. P. (2023). Machine learning and AI in business intelligence: Trends and opportunities. [IJC]. *International Journal of Computer*, 48(1), 123–134.

Bharadiya, J. P. (2023). The role of machine learning in transforming business intelligence. *International Journal of Computing and Artificial Intelligence*, 4(1), 16–24. DOI: 10.33545/27076571.2023.v4.i1a.60

Bi, T., Yu, G., Lu, Q., Xu, X., & Van Beest, N. (2023). The Privacy Pillar—A Conceptual Framework for Foundation Model-based Systems. arXiv preprint arXiv:2311.06998.

Blog, N. T. (2024, March 19). Sequential A/B Testing Keeps the World Streaming Netflix Part 1: Continuous Data. Medium. https://netflixtechblog.com/sequential-a-b-testing-keeps-the-world-streaming-netflix-part-1-continuous-data-cba6c7ed49df

Blog, N. T. (2024, March 8). Supporting Diverse ML Systems : Netflix Tech Blog | Netflix TechBlog. Medium. https://netflixtechblog.com/supporting-diverse-ml-systems-at-netflix-2d2e6b6d205d

Blog, N. T. (2024, March 9). Bending pause times to your will with Generational ZGC. Medium. https://netflixtechblog.com/bending-pause-times-to-your-will-with-generational-zgc-256629c9386b

Bogza, R. M., & Zaharie, D. 'Business intelligence as a competitive differentiator', 2008 IEEE Int. Conf. Autom. Qual. Testing, Robot. AQTR 2008 - THETA 16th Ed. - Proc., vol. 1, pp. 146–151, 2008, DOI: 10.1109/AQTR.2008.4588724

Bose, I., & Mahapatra, R. K. (2001). Business data mining—A machine learning perspective. *Information & Management*, 39(3), 211–225.

Boutaba, R., Salahuddin, M. A., Limam, N., Ayoubi, S., Shahriar, N., Estrada-Solano, F., & Caicedo, O. M. (2018). A comprehensive survey on machine learning for networking: Evolution, applications and research opportunities. *Journal of Internet Services and Applications*, 9(1), 1–99. DOI: 10.1186/s13174-018-0087-2

Bratu, M. (2023). The intersection of artificial intelligence and business intelligence: a systematic mapping study.

Brewis, C., Dibb, S., & Meadows, M. (2023). Leveraging big data for strategic marketing: A dynamic capabilities model for incumbent firms. *Technological Forecasting and Social Change*, 190(February), 122402. DOI: 10.1016/j.techfore.2023.122402

Buckinx, W., & Van den Poel, D. (2005). Customer base analysis: Partial defection of behaviourally loyal clients in a non-contractual FMCG retail setting. *European Journal of Operational Research*, 164(1), 252–268. DOI: 10.1016/j.ejor.2003.12.010

Byloli, S. (2023, July 31). Examples of AI in Customer Service (From Companies That Do It Right). https://blog.hubspot.com/service/examples-of-ai-in-customer-service

Cadden, T., Weerawardena, J., Cao, G., Duan, Y., & McIvor, R. (2023). Examining the role of big data and marketing analytics in SMEs innovation and competitive advantage: A knowledge integration perspective. *Journal of Business Research, 168*(October 2022), 114225. DOI: 10.1016/j.jbusres.2023.114225

Campolo, A., Sanfilippo, M. R., Whittaker, M., & Crawford, K. (2017). AI now 2017 report.

Canhoto, A. I., & Clear, F. (2020). Artificial intelligence and machine learning as business tools: A framework for diagnosing value destruction potential. *Business Horizons*, 63(2), 183–193.

Cao, L., Yang, Q., & Yu, P. S. (2021). Data science and AI in FinTech: An overview. *International Journal of Data Science and Analytics*, 12(2), 81–99. DOI: 10.1007/s41060-021-00278-w

Carroll, A. B., & Shabana, K. M. (2010). The business case for corporate social responsibility: A review of concepts, research and practice. *International Journal of Management Reviews*, 12(1), 85–105.

Casino, F., Kanakaris, V., Dasaklis, T. K., Moschuris, S., Stachtiaris, S., Pagoni, M., & Rachaniotis, N. P. (2021). Blockchain-based food supply chain traceability: A case study in the dairy sector. *International Journal of Production Research*, 59(19), 5758–5770. DOI: 10.1080/00207543.2020.1789238

Chagas, Beatriz & Viana, Julio & Reinhold, Olaf & Lobato, Fábio & Jacob Junior, Antonio & Alt, Rainer. (2018). Current Applications of Machine Learning Techniques in CRM: A Literature Review and Practical Implications. 452-458. .DOI: 10.1109/WI.2018.00-53

Chandrasekaran, A., & Subramanian, N. (2023). Augmented analytics in business intelligence: A comprehensive review. *International Journal of Data Science and Analytics*, 7(2), 123–138.

Chang, Y., Iakovou, E., & Shi, W. (2020). Blockchain in global supply chains and cross border trade: A critical synthesis of the state-of-the-art, challenges and opportunities. *International Journal of Production Research*, 58(7), 2082–2099. DOI: 10.1080/00207543.2019.1651946

Chaudhary, N., & Roy Chowdhury, D. (2019). Data preprocessing for evaluation of recommendation models in E-commerce. *Data*, 4(1), 23. DOI: 10.3390/data4010023

Cheddad, A., Condell, J., Curran, K., & McKevitt, P. (2010). A hash-based image encryption algorithm. *Optics Communications*, 283(6), 879–893. DOI: 10.1016/j.optcom.2009.10.106

Chen, K., & Kamal, A. E. (2020). *D s a i. June*, 10–11.

Cheng, C. C. J., & Shiu, E. C. (2023). The relative values of big data analytics versus traditional marketing analytics to firm innovation: An empirical study. *Information & Management*, 60(7), 103839. DOI: 10.1016/j.im.2023.103839

Chen, Y., Li, C., & Wang, H. (2022). Big data and predictive analytics for business intelligence: A bibliographic study (2000–2021). *Forecasting*, 4(4), 767–786.

Christopher, M. (2022). *Logistics and supply chain management*. Pearson Uk.

Collins, C., Dennehy, D., Conboy, K., & Mikalef, P. (2021). Artificial intelligence in information systems research: A systematic literature review and research agenda. *International Journal of Information Management, 60*(November 2020), 102383. DOI: 10.1016/j.ijinfomgt.2021.102383

Combita Niño, H. A., Cómbita Niño, J. P., & Morales Ortega, R. (2020). Business intelligence governance framework in a university: Universidad de la costa case study. *International Journal of Information Management*, 50, 405–412. DOI: 10.1016/j.ijinfomgt.2018.11.012

Dalvi, P. K., Khandge, S. K., Deomore, A., Bankar, A., & Kanade, V. A. (2016, March). Analysis of customer churn prediction in telecom industry using decision trees and logistic regression. In *2016 symposium on colossal data analysis and networking (CDAN)* (pp. 1-4). IEEE. DOI: 10.1109/CDAN.2016.7570883

Danese, P., Mocellin, R., & Romano, P. (2021). Designing blockchain systems to prevent counterfeiting in wine supply chains: A multiple-case study. *International Journal of Operations & Production Management*, 41(13), 1–33. DOI: 10.1108/IJOPM-12-2019-0781

Dangeti, P. (2017). *Statistics for machine learning*. Packt Publishing Ltd.

Daniels, B. (1999). Integration of the supply chain for total through-cost reduction. *Total Quality Management*, 10(4–5), 481–490. DOI: 10.1080/0954412997433

Das, S. R., Sarkar, P., Patil, S., Sharma, R., Aggarwal, S., & Lourens, M. (2023, December). Artificial Intelligence in Human Resource Management: Transforming Business Practices. In 2023 10th IEEE Uttar Pradesh Section International Conference on Electrical, Electronics and Computer Engineering (UPCON) (Vol. 10, pp. 1699-1703). IEEE.

David, A., & Ravi, S. (2017). The direness of cultivable land spotted on agricultural: A special reference to rice production in South India. *Abhinav National Monthly Refereed Journal of Research in Commerce & Management, ISSN-2277-1166*, 6(09), 55-59.

David, A. (2020). Consumer purchasing process of organic food product: An empirical analysis. [QAS]. *Journal of Management System-Quality Access to Success*, 21(177), 128–132.

David, A., Kumar, C. G., & Paul, P. V. (2022). Blockchain technology in the food supply chain: Empirical analysis. [IJISSCM]. *International Journal of Information Systems and Supply Chain Management*, 15(3), 1–12. DOI: 10.4018/IJISSCM.290014

David, A., Thangavel, Y. D., & Sankriti, R. (2019). Recover, recycle and reuse: An efficient way to reduce the waste. *Int. J. Mech. Prod. Eng. Res. Dev*, 9, 31–42.

Deshpande, S., & Ramaswamy, S. (2023). Enhanced data exploration techniques for AI-driven BI systems. *Journal of Business Analytics*, 6(1), 45–58.

Dick, A. S., & Basu, K. (1994). Customer loyalty: Toward an integrated conceptual framework. *Journal of the Academy of Marketing Science*, 22(2), 99–113. DOI: 10.1177/0092070394222001

Divinagracia, S., & Randolph, K. (2024, March 27). Using Machine Learning for CRM. Nutshell. https://www.nutshell.com/blog/using-machine-learning-for-crm

Dudycz, H. (2010). "Visualization methods in Business Intelligence systems–an overview." Business Informatics (16). *Data Mining and Business Intelligence*, 104, 9–24.

Dyche, J. (2002). *The CRM handbook: A business guide to customer relationship management*. Addison-Wesley Professional.

Edge, D., Larson, J., & White, C. (2018). Bringing AI to BI: enabling visual analytics of unstructured data in a modern Business Intelligence platform. Paper presented at the Extended abstracts of the 2018 CHI conference on human factors in computing systems.

Evans, G. N., Towill, D. R., & Naim, M. M. (1995). Business process re-engineering the supply chain. *Production Planning and Control*, 6(3), 227–237. DOI: 10.1080/09537289508930275

Fang, H., Fang, F., Hu, Q., & Wan, Y. (2022). Supply chain management: A review and bibliometric analysis. *Processes (Basel, Switzerland)*, 10(9), 1681. DOI: 10.3390/pr10091681

Fazal, M. I., Patel, M. E., Tye, J., & Gupta, Y. (2018). The past, present and future role of artificial intelligence in imaging. *European Journal of Radiology*, 105, 246–250.

Fernández, A., Garcia, S., Herrera, F., & Chawla, N. V. (2018). SMOTE for learning from imbalanced data: Progress and challenges, marking the 15-year anniversary. *Journal of Artificial Intelligence Research*, 61, 863–905. DOI: 10.1613/jair.1.11192

Fink, L., Yogev, N., & Even, A. (2017). Business intelligence and organizational learning: An empirical investigation of value creation processes. *Information & Management*, 54(1), 38–56. DOI: 10.1016/j.im.2016.03.009

Finlay, S. (2014). *Predictive analytics, data mining and big data: Myths, misconceptions and methods*. Springer. DOI: 10.1057/9781137379283

Fosso Wamba, S., Kala Kamdjoug, J. R., Epie Bawack, R., & Keogh, J. G. (2020). Bitcoin, Blockchain and Fintech: A systematic review and case studies in the supply chain. *Production Planning and Control*, 31(2-3), 115–142. DOI: 10.1080/09537287.2019.1631460

Francisco, K., & Swanson, D. (2018). The Supply Chain Has No Clothes: Technology Adoption of Blockchain for Supply Chain Transparency. *Logistics (Basel)*, 2(1), 2. DOI: 10.3390/logistics2010002

Fung, G. (2001). A comprehensive overview of basic clustering algorithms.

Gaardboe, R., & Svarre, T. (2017). Critical factors for business intelligence success.

Gamage, H. T. M., Weerasinghe, H. D., & Dias, N. G. J. (2020). A Survey on Blockchain Technology Concepts, Applications, and Issues. *SN Computer Science*, 1(2), 114. DOI: 10.1007/s42979-020-00123-0

Ganesh Kumar, C., Murugaiyan, P., & Madanmohan, G. (2017). Agri-food supply chain management: Literature review. *Intelligent Information Management*, 9(2), 68–96. DOI: 10.4236/iim.2017.92004

Ganeshkumar, C., & David, A. (2023). Digital Information Management in Agriculture—Empirical Analysis. In: Goyal, D., Kumar, A., Piuri, V., Paprzycki, M. (eds) Proceedings of the Third International Conference on Information Management and Machine Intelligence. Algorithms for Intelligent Systems. Springer, Singapore. https://doi.org/DOI: 10.1007/978-981-19-2065-3_27

Ganeshkumar, C., Basu, R. J., Yuvaraj, M., & David, A. (2024[b]). Will Artificial Intelligence be a Performance booster to Agritech Startup?: Empirical evidence from Emerging Economy. *Journal of Industrial Integration and Management*.

Ganeshkumar, C., David, A., & Sankar, J. G. (2024[a]). Blockchain Technology Acceptance in Agribusiness Industry. In *Blockchain Transformations: Navigating the Decentralized Protocols Era* (pp. 239-260). Cham: Springer Nature Switzerland.

Ganeshkumar, C., David, A., & Jebasingh, D. R. (2022). Digital Transformation: Artificial Intelligence Based Product Benefits and Problems of Agritech Industry. In *Agri-Food 4.0*. Emerald Publishing Limited. DOI: 10.1108/S1877-636120220000027010

Ganeshkumar, C., Jena, S. K., Sivakumar, A., & Nambirajan, T. (2021). Artificial intelligence in the agricultural value chain: Review and future directions. *Journal of Agribusiness in Developing and Emerging Economies*.

Ganeshkumar, C., & Khan, A. (2021). Mapping of agritech companies in Indian agricultural value chain. In *Proceedings of the second international conference on information management and machine intelligence* (pp. 155-161). Springer, Singapore. DOI: 10.1007/978-981-15-9689-6_18

Ganeshkumar, C., Prabhu, M., & Abdullah, N. N. (2019). Business analytics and supply chain performance: Partial least squares-structural equation modelling (PLS-SEM) approach. *International Journal of Management and Business Research*, 9(1), 91–96.

Ganeshkumar, C., Prabhu, M., Reddy, P. S., & David, A. (2020). Value chain analysis of Indian edible mushrooms. *International Journal of Technology*, 11(3), 599–607. DOI: 10.14716/ijtech.v11i3.3979

Gao, S., Yu, T., Zhu, J., & Cai, W. (2019). T-PBFT: An EigenTrust-based practical Byzantine fault tolerance consensus algorithm. *China Communications*, 16(12), 111–123. DOI: 10.23919/JCC.2019.12.008

Garcia, D. J., & You, F. (2015). Supply chain design and optimization: Challenges and opportunities. *Computers & Chemical Engineering*, 81, 153–170. DOI: 10.1016/j.compchemeng.2015.03.015

Gartner, A., & Magar, R. (2024). The future of augmented analytics: Trends, challenges, and opportunities. *Gartner Research*. https://www.gartner.com/document/2024-Future-Augmented-Analytics

Gefen, D. (2002). Customer loyalty in e-commerce. *Journal of the Association for Information Systems*, 3(1), 2. DOI: 10.17705/1jais.00022

Ghosh, A. (2016). Business Intelligence (BI) in Supply Chain Management. *Asian Journal of Science and Technology*, 7(11).

Gold, C. (2020). *Fighting Churn with Data: The science and strategy of customer retention*. Simon and Schuster.

Gozali, L., Kristina, H. J., Yosua, A., Zagloel, T. Y. M., Masrom, M., Susanto, S., Tanujaya, H., Irawan, A. P., Gunadi, A., Kumar, V., Garza-Reyes, J. A., Jap, T. B., & Daywin, F. J. (2024). The improvement of block chain technology simulation in supply chain management (case study: Pesticide company). *Scientific Reports*, 14(1), 3784. DOI: 10.1038/s41598-024-53694-w PMID: 38360895

Gregory, B. (2018). Predicting customer churn: Extreme gradient boosting with temporal data. *arXiv preprint arXiv:1802.03396*.

Haakman, M., Cruz, L., Huijgens, H., & Van Deursen, A. (2021). AI lifecycle models need to be revised: An exploratory study in Fintech. *Empirical Software Engineering*, 26(5), 95. DOI: 10.1007/s10664-021-09993-1

Halper, F. (2014). Predictive analytics for business advantage. TDWI Research, 1-32.

Harland, C. M. (1996). Supply Chain Management: Relationships, Chains and Networks. *British Journal of Management*, 7(s1). Advance online publication. DOI: 10.1111/j.1467-8551.1996.tb00148.x

Hugos, M. H. (2024). *Essentials of Supply Chain Management* (Fourth). John Wiley & Sons, Inc.

Ibrahim, S. B., & Hamid, A. A. (2014). Supply Chain Management Practices and Supply Chain Performance Effectiveness. [IJSR]. *International Journal of Scientific Research*, 3(8).

Idrees, S. M., Alam, M. A., Agarwal, P., & Ansari, L. (2019). Effective predictive analytics and modeling based on historical data. Paper presented at the Advances in Computing and Data Sciences: Third International Conference, ICACDS 2019, Ghaziabad, India, April 12–13, 2019, Revised Selected Papers, Part II 3.

Iliescu, E. M., & Voicu, M. C. (2021). The integration of ESG factors in business strategies–competitive advantage. Challenges of the Knowledge Society, 838-843.

Iranmanesh, S., Hamid, M., Bastan, M., Shakouri Ganjavi, H., & Nasiri, M. (2019, July). Customer Churn Prediction Using Artificial Neural Network: An Analytical CRM Application. In *3rd European International Conference on Industrial Engineering and Operations Management*.

Isik, O., Jones, M. C., & Sidorova, A. (2011). Business intelligence (BI) success and the role of BI capabilities. *International Journal of Intelligent Systems in Accounting Finance & Management*, 18(4), 161–176. DOI: 10.1002/isaf.329

Işık, Ö., Jones, M. C., & Sidorova, A. (2013). Business intelligence success: The roles of BI capabilities and decision environments. *Information & Management*, 50(1), 13–23. DOI: 10.1016/j.im.2012.12.001

Jabbar, A., Akhtar, P., & Dani, S. (2020). Real-time big data processing for instantaneous marketing decisions: A problematization approach. *Industrial Marketing Management, 90*(November 2018), 558–569. DOI: 10.1016/j.indmarman.2019.09.001

Jabbar, S., Lloyd, H., Hammoudeh, M., Adebisi, B., & Raza, U. (2021). Blockchain-enabled supply chain: Analysis, challenges, and future directions. *Multimedia Systems*, 27(4), 787–806. DOI: 10.1007/s00530-020-00687-0

Janvier-James, A. M. (2012). A new introduction to supply chains and supply chain management: Definitions and theories perspective. *International Business Research*, 5(1), 194–207.

Jeong, E., Park, N., Choi, Y., Park, R. W., & Yoon, D. (2018). Machine learning model combining features from algorithms with different analytical methodologies to detect laboratory-event-related adverse drug reaction signals. *PLoS One*, 13(11), e0207749.

Jha, S., & Agrawal, S. (2023). Recent advances and future directions in AI-driven business intelligence. *Expert Systems with Applications*, 185, 115934.

Johnson, B. (2018). Self-Service Analytics: A Comprehensive Review of Implementation Strategies. *Journal of Data Analytics*, 8(2), 87–101.

Jović, A., Brkić, K., & Bogunović, N. (2015, May). A review of feature selection methods with applications. In *2015 38th international convention on information and communication technology, electronics and microelectronics (MIPRO)* (pp. 1200-1205). Ieee. DOI: 10.1109/MIPRO.2015.7160458

Juan, A. A., Faulin, J., Grasman, S. E., Rabe, M., & Figueira, G. (2015). A review of simheuristics: Extending metaheuristics to deal with stochastic combinatorial optimization problems. *Operations Research Perspectives*, 2, 62–72.

Kabakchieva, D. (2015). Kabakchieva, 'Business intelligence systems for analysing university students data'. *Cybernetics and Information Technologies*, 15(1), 104–115. DOI: 10.1515/cait-2015-0009

Kansagara, D., Englander, H., Salanitro, A., Kagen, D., Theobald, C., Freeman, M., & Kripalani, S. (2011). Risk prediction models for hospital readmission: A systematic review. *Journal of the American Medical Association*, 306(15), 1688–1698. DOI: 10.1001/jama.2011.1515 PMID: 22009101

Karthikeyan, L., Chawla, I., & Mishra, A. K. (2020). A review of remote sensing applications in agriculture for food security: Crop growth and yield, irrigation, and crop losses. *Journal of Hydrology (Amsterdam)*, 586, 124905. DOI: 10.1016/j.jhydrol.2020.124905

Keerthika, R., & Abinayaa, M. S. (Eds.). (2022). *Algorithms of Intelligence: Exploring the World of Machine Learning*. Inkbound Publishers. ● Gao, L., Lu, P., & Ren, Y. (2021). A deep learning approach for imbalanced crash data in predicting highway-rail grade crossings accidents. *Reliability Engineering & System Safety*, 216, 108019.

Kenza, B., Soumaya, O., & Mohamed, A. (2023). A Conceptual Framework using Big Data Analytics for Effective Email Marketing. *Procedia Computer Science*, 220, 1044–1050. DOI: 10.1016/j.procs.2023.03.146

Khan, S., & Iqbal, M. (2020, June). AI-Powered Customer Service: Does it optimize customer experience? In 2020 8th International Conference on Reliability, Infocom Technologies and Optimization (Trends and Future Directions)(ICRITO) (pp. 590-594). IEEE.

Khan, M. Z., Al-Mushayt, O., Alam, J., & Ahmad, J. (2010). Intelligent Supply Chain Management. *Journal of Software Engineering and Applications*, 03(04), 404–408. DOI: 10.4236/jsea.2010.34045

Khan, R. A., & Quadri, S. M. (2012). Business intelligence: An integrated approach. *Business Intelligence Journal*, 5(1), 64–70.

Khurana, D., Koli, A., Khatter, K., & Singh, S. (2023). Natural language processing: State of the art, current trends and challenges. *Multimedia Tools and Applications*, 82(3), 3713–3744.

Kim, Y., & Lee, J. (2024). AI-driven predictive analytics: Enhancing decision-making in business intelligence systems. *Journal of Forecasting*, 43(3), 273–288. DOI: 10.1002/for.2856

Kirui, C., Hong, L., Cheruiyot, W., & Kirui, H. (2013). Predicting customer churn in mobile telephony industry using probabilistic classifiers in data mining. [IJCSI]. *International Journal of Computer Science Issues*, 10(2 Part 1), 165.

Kotsiantis, S. B., Kanellopoulos, D., & Pintelas, P. E. (2006). Data preprocessing for supervised leaning. *International Journal of Computational Science*, 1(2), 111–117.

Kotu, V., & Deshpande, B. (2018). *Data science: concepts and practice*. Morgan Kaufmann.

Krishna, C. V., & Rohit, H. R., & Mohana. (2018). A review of artificial intelligence methods for data science and data analytics: Applications and research challenges. *Proceedings of the International Conference on I-SMAC (IoT in Social, Mobile, Analytics and Cloud), I-SMAC 2018, August 2018*, 591–594. DOI: 10.1109/I-SMAC.2018.8653670

Król, K., & Zdonek, D. (2022). Digital Assets in the Eyes of Generation Z: Perceptions, Outlooks, Concerns. *Journal of Risk and Financial Management*, 16(1), 22. DOI: 10.3390/jrfm16010022

Kulkarni, V. Y., & Sinha, P. K. (2013). Random forest classifiers: A survey and future research directions. *Int. J. Adv. Comput*, 36(1), 1144–1153.

Kumar, V., Reinartz, W., Kumar, V., & Reinartz, W. (2018). Future of CRM. Customer Relationship Management: Concept, Strategy, and Tools, 385-404.

Kumar, C. G., & Nambirajan, T. (2013). Supply chain management components, supply chain performance and organizational performance: A critical review and development of the conceptual model. *International Journal on Global Business Management & Research*, 2(1), 86.

L'heureux, A., Grolinger, K., Elyamany, H. F., & Capretz, M. A. (2017). Machine learning with big data: Challenges and approaches. *IEEE Access : Practical Innovations, Open Solutions*, 5, 7776–7797. DOI: 10.1109/ACCESS.2017.2696365

Langlois, A., & Chauvel, B. (2017). The impact of supply chain management on business intelligence. *Journal of Intelligence Studies in Business*, 7(2). Advance online publication. DOI: 10.37380/jisib.v7i2.239

Lari, H. A., Vaishnava, K., & Manu, K. S. (2022). Artifical intelligence in E-commerce: Applications, implications and challenges. *Asian Journal of Management*, 13(3), 235–244. DOI: 10.52711/2321-5763.2022.00041

Latha, C. J., Sankriti, R., David, A., & Srivel, R. (2020). IoT based water purification process using ultrasonic aquatic sound waves. *Test Engineering & Management, The Mattingley Publishing Co., Inc. ISSN*, 0193-4120.

Laurence, T. (2019). *Introduction to Blockchain technology The many faces of blockchain technology in the 21st century*. Van Haren Publishing.

Ledro, C., Nosella, A., & Dalla Pozza, I. (2023). Integration of AI in CRM: Challenges and guidelines. *Journal of Open Innovation*, 9(4), 100151. DOI: 10.1016/j.joitmc.2023.100151

Lee, H. K., Abdul Halim, H., Thong, K. L., & Chai, L. C. (2017). Assessment of food safety knowledge, attitude, self-reported practices, and microbiological hand hygiene of food handlers. *International Journal of Environmental Research and Public Health*, 14(1), 55. DOI: 10.3390/ijerph14010055 PMID: 28098788

Lin, I.-C., & Liao, T.-C. (2017). A Survey of Blockchain Security Issues and Challenges. *International Journal of Network Security*, 19(5), 653–659.

Liu, P., Hendalianpour, A., Hamzehlou, M., Feylizadeh, M. R., & Razmi, J. (2021). Identify and Rank the Challenges of Implementing Sustainable Supply Chain Blockchain Technology Using the Bayesian Best Worst Method. *Technological and Economic Development of Economy*, 27(3), 656–680. DOI: 10.3846/tede.2021.14421

Liu, Y., Cao, J., & Zhang, Q. (2022). The product marketing model of the economic zone by the sensor big data mining algorithm. *Sustainable Computing : Informatics and Systems*, 36(October), 100820. DOI: 10.1016/j.suscom.2022.100820

Loshin, D. (2012). Business intelligence: the savvy manager's guide: Newnes.

Luts, J., Ojeda, F., Van de Plas, R., De Moor, B., Van Huffel, S., & Suykens, J. A. (2010). A tutorial on support vector machine-based methods for classification problems in chemometrics. *Analytica Chimica Acta*, 665(2), 129–145.

Lynch, M., & Lynch, M. (2024, June 10). Supercharging Sustainability: Harnessing AI for environmental metrics. Praxie.com. https://praxie.com/ai-for-environmental -metrics-management/

MacKenzie, D. (2019). Pick a nonce and try a hash. *London Review of Books*, 41(8), 35–38.

Manyika, J., Chui, M., Bisson, P., Woetzel, J., Dobbs, R., Bughin, J., & Aharon, D. (2015). Unlocking the Potential of the Internet of Things. McKinsey Global Institute, 1.

Manzoor, A. (2010). *E-commerce: an introduction.* Amir Manzoor.

Mariani, M. M., & Wamba, S. F. (2020). Exploring how consumer goods companies innovate in the digital age: The role of big data analytics companies. *Journal of Business Research*, 121, 338–352. DOI: 10.1016/j.jbusres.2020.09.012

Martínez-López, F. J., & Casillas, J. (2013). Artificial intelligence-based systems applied in industrial marketing: An historical overview, current and future insights. *Industrial Marketing Management*, 42(4), 489–495.

Martins, A. A., Mata, T. M., Costa, C. A., & Sikdar, S. K. (2007). Framework for sustainability metrics. *Industrial & Engineering Chemistry Research*, 46(10), 2962–2973. DOI: 10.1021/ie0606921

Mascarenhas, S. J. F. O. A. (2018). Artificial intelligence and the emergent turbulent markets: New challenges to corporate ethics today. In Corporate Ethics for Turbulent Markets: The Market Context of Executive Decisions (pp. 215-242). Emerald Publishing Limited.

Mathrani, S. (2014). Managing Supply Chains Using Business Intelligence. ACIS.

Mehta, P., Thakur, R., Raina, K. K., Thakur, P., & Mehta, R. (2019). Farmers' perception towards Electronic-National Agriculture Market (e-NAM) systems adopted by APMC market, Solan, Himachal Pradesh. *AgricINTERNATIONAL*, 6(1), 51–57. DOI: 10.5958/2454-8634.2019.00010.X

Mentzer, J. T., DeWitt, W., Keebler, J. S., Min, S., Nix, N. W., Smith, C. D., & Zacharia, Z. G. (2001). DEFINING SUPPLY CHAIN MANAGEMENT. *Journal of Business Logistics*, 22(2), 1–25. DOI: 10.1002/j.2158-1592.2001.tb00001.x

Miljkovic, D. (1996). *Effects of economic transition policies on Yugoslavia's agricultural sector: A quantitative approach.* University of Illinois at Urbana-Champaign.

Miller, C., & Barton, T. (2024). Hyper-personalization and its impact on customer experience management. *Harvard Business Review*, 102(5), 56–65. https://hbr.org/2024/05/hyper-personalization-and-its-impact-on-customer-experience-management

Mingxiao, D., Xiaofeng, M., Zhe, Z., Xiangwei, W., & Qijun, C. (2017). A review on consensus algorithm of blockchain. *2017 IEEE International Conference on Systems, Man, and Cybernetics (SMC)*, 2567–2572. DOI: 10.1109/SMC.2017.8123011

Moinuddin, M., Usman, M., & Khan, R. (2024). Strategic Insights in a Data-Driven Era: Maximizing Business Potential with Analytics and AI. *Revista Española de Documentación Científica*, 18(02), 117–133.

Moniruzzaman, M., Kurnia, S., Parkes, A., & Maynard, S. B. (2016). Business intelligence and supply chain agility. arXiv preprint arXiv:1606.03511.

Morsi, S. (2020). A Predictive Analytics Model for E-commerce Sales Transactions to Support Decision Making: A Case Study. *International Journal of Computer and Information Technology (2279-0764), 9*(1).

Mungoli, N. (2023). Adaptive Ensemble Learning: Boosting Model Performance through Intelligent Feature Fusion in Deep Neural Networks. arXiv preprint arXiv:2304.02653.

Murugesan, R., & Manohar, V. (2019). Ai in financial sector–a driver to financial literacy. *Shanlax International Journal of Commerce*, 7(3), 66–70. DOI: 10.34293/commerce.v7i3.477

Mystakidis, S. (2022). Metaverse. *Encyclopedia*, 2(1), 486–497. DOI: 10.3390/encyclopedia2010031

Naimi, A. (2016). *The robust urban transportation network design problem*. The University of Memphis.

Nasereddin, A. Y. (2024). A comprehensive survey of contemporary supply chain management practices in charting the digital age revolution. *Uncertain Supply Chain Management*, 12(2), 1331–1352. DOI: 10.5267/j.uscm.2023.11.004

Negash, S., & Gray, P. (2008). Business intelligence. *Handbook on decision support systems 2*, 175-193.

Nguyen, T. H., Sherif, J. S., & Newby, M. (2007). Strategies for successful CRM implementation. *Information Management & Computer Security*, 15(2), 102–115. DOI: 10.1108/09685220710748001

Nguyen, T., & Kumar, V. (2024). Ethical AI in business intelligence: Addressing privacy and bias challenges. *AI and Ethics*, 12(1), 113–130. DOI: 10.1007/s43681-024-00001-5

Nie, G., Rowe, W., Zhang, L., Tian, Y., & Shi, Y. (2011). Credit card churn forecasting by logistic regression and decision tree. *Expert Systems with Applications*, 38(12), 15273–15285. DOI: 10.1016/j.eswa.2011.06.028

Niu, Y., Ying, L., Yang, J., Bao, M., & Sivaparthipan, C. B. (2021). Organizational business intelligence and decision making using big data analytics. *Information Processing & Management*, 58(6), 102725.

Olaoye, F., & Potter, K. (2024). *Business Intelligence (BI) and Analytics Software: Empowering Data-Driven Decision-Making (No. 12550)*. EasyChair.

Osborne, J. W. (2012). *Best practices in data cleaning: A complete guide to everything you need to do before and after collecting your data*. Sage publications.

Osisanwo, F. Y., Akinsola, J. E. T., Awodele, O., Hinmikaiye, J. O., Olakanmi, O., & Akinjobi, J. (2017). Supervised machine learning algorithms: Classification and comparison. [IJCTT]. *International Journal of Computer Trends and Technology*, 48(3), 128–138.

Ozili, P. K. (2023). Central bank digital currency research around the world: A review of literature. *Journal of Money Laundering Control*, 26(2), 215–226. DOI: 10.1108/JMLC-11-2021-0126

Öz, S., & Gören, H. E. (2019). Application of Blockchain Technology in the Supply Chain Management Process: Case Studies. *Journal of International Trade. Logistics and Law*, 5(1), 21–27.

Pachayappan, M., Ganeshkumar, C., & Sugundan, N. (2020). Technological implication and its impact in the agricultural sector: An IoT Based Collaboration framework. *Procedia Computer Science*, 171, 1166–1173. DOI: 10.1016/j.procs.2020.04.125

Pallathadka, H., Ramirez-Asis, E. H., Loli-Poma, T. P., Kaliyaperumal, K., Ventayen, R. J. M., & Naved, M. (2023). Applications of artificial intelligence in business management, e-commerce and finance. *Materials Today: Proceedings*, 80, 2610–2613. DOI: 10.1016/j.matpr.2021.06.419

Pal, S., Kumari, K., Kadam, S., & Saha, A. (2023). *The ai revolution*. IARA Publication.

Panpatte, S., & Ganeshkumar, C. (2021). Artificial intelligence in agriculture sector: A case study of blue river technology. In *Proceedings of the second international conference on information management and machine intelligence* (pp. 147-153). Springer, Singapore. DOI: 10.1007/978-981-15-9689-6_17

Paraman, P., & Anamalah, S. (2023). Ethical artificial intelligence framework for a good AI society: Principles, opportunities and perils. *AI & Society*, 38(2), 595–611. DOI: 10.1007/s00146-022-01458-3

Park, Y. S., Tison, J., Lek, S., Giraudel, J. L., Coste, M., & Delmas, F. (2006). Application of a self-organizing map to select representative species in multivariate analysis: A case study determining diatom distribution patterns across France. *Ecological Informatics*, 1(3), 247–257.

Paschen, U., Pitt, C., & Kietzmann, J. (2020). Artificial intelligence: Building blocks and an innovation typology. *Business Horizons*, 63(2), 147–155.

Paul, P. K., Aithal, P. S., Saavedra, R., & Ghosh, S. (2021). Blockchain Technology and its Types—A Short Review. [IJASE]. *International Journal of Applied Science and Engineering*, 9(2), 189–200. DOI: 10.30954/2322-0465.2.2021.7

Paul, V., Ganeshkumar, C., & Jayakumar, L. (2019). Performance evaluation of population seeding techniques of permutation-coded GA travelling salesman problems-based assessment: Performance evaluation of population seeding techniques of permutation-coded GA. [IJAMC]. *International Journal of Applied Metaheuristic Computing*, 10(2), 55–92. DOI: 10.4018/IJAMC.2019040103

Pejić Bach, M., Pivar, J., & Jaković, B. (2021). Churn management in telecommunications: Hybrid approach using cluster analysis and decision trees. *Journal of Risk and Financial Management*, 14(11), 544. DOI: 10.3390/jrfm14110544

Petrini, M., & Pozzebon, M. (2009). Managing sustainability with the support of business intelligence methods and tools. *Information Systems, Technology and Management: Third International Conference, ICISTM 2009, Ghaziabad, India, March 12-13, 2009 Proceedings*, 3, 88–99.

Phillips-Wren, G., Daly, M., & Burstein, F. (2021). Reconciling business intelligence, analytics and decision support systems: More data, deeper insight. *Decision Support Systems*, 146, 113560. DOI: 10.1016/j.dss.2021.113560

Pillkahn, U. (2008). *Using trends and scenarios as tools for strategy development: shaping the future of your enterprise*. John Wiley & Sons.

Pilon, B. H., Murillo-Fuentes, J. J., da Costa, J. P. C., de Sousa Júnior, R. T., & Serrano, A. M. (2016). Predictive analytics in business intelligence systems via Gaussian processes for regression. In Knowledge Discovery, Knowledge Engineering and Knowledge Management: 7th International Joint Conference, IC3K 2015, Lisbon, Portugal, November 12-14, 2015, Revised Selected Papers 7 (pp. 421-442). Springer International Publishing.

Pongnumkul, S., Siripanpornchana, C., & Thajchayapong, S. (2017). Performance Analysis of Private Blockchain Platforms in Varying Workloads. *2017 26th International Conference on Computer Communication and Networks (ICCCN)*, 1–6. DOI: 10.1109/ICCCN.2017.8038517

Praful Bharadiya, J. (2023). A Comparative Study of Business Intelligence and Artificial Intelligence with Big Data Analytics. *Am. J. Artif. Intell.*, 7(1), 24–30. DOI: 10.11648/j.ajai.20230701.14

Prakash, A. (2023, December 1). AI-Driven Personalization in CRM: Tailoring Customer Experiences. Express Computer. https://www.expresscomputer.in/artificial-intelligence-ai/ai-driven-personalization-in-crm-tailoring-customer-experiences/106481/

Pratheepkumar, P., Sharmila, J. J., & Arokiaraj, D. (2017). Towards mobile opportunistic in cloud computing. [IJSR]. *Indian Journal of Scientific Research*, 17(02), 2250–0138.

Pria, S., Al Rubaie, I., & Prasad, V. (2024). Enhancing Business Intelligence Through AI-Driven Integration of Sustainability Metrics via ESG Factors. In Risks and Challenges of AI-Driven Finance: Bias, Ethics, and Security (pp. 57-89). IGI Global.

Qin, X., Luo, Y., Tang, N., & Li, G. (2020). Making data visualization more efficient and effective: A survey. *The VLDB Journal*, 29(1), 93–117. DOI: 10.1007/s00778-019-00588-3

Rabelo, R. J., & Pereira-Klen, A. A. (2002, September). Business intelligence support for supply chain management. In *International Conference on Information Technology for Balanced Automation Systems* (pp. 437-444). Boston, MA: Springer US. DOI: 10.1007/978-0-387-35613-6_49

Radaceanu, E. (2007). Artificial Intelligence & Robots for Performance Management–Some Methodic Aspects. IFAC Proceedings Volumes, 40(18), 319-324.

Radosavljevik, D. (2017). *Applying data mining in telecommunications* (Doctoral dissertation, Leiden University).

Radosavljevik, D., van der Putten, P., & Larsen, K. K. (2010). The impact of experimental setup in prepaid churn prediction for mobile telecommunications: What to predict, for whom and does the customer experience matter? *Trans. Mach. Learn. Data Min.*, 3(2), 80–99.

Rahmani, A. M., Azhir, E., Ali, S., Mohammadi, M., Ahmed, O. H., Ghafour, M. Y., Ahmed, S. H., & Hosseinzadeh, M. (2021). Artificial intelligence approaches and mechanisms for big data analytics: A systematic study. *PeerJ. Computer Science*, 7, 1–28. DOI: 10.7717/peerj-cs.488 PMID: 33954253

Ramachandran, K. K. (2024). IMPACT OF ARTIFICIAL INTELLIGENCE (AI) AND MACHINE LEARNING ON CUSTOMER RELATIONSHIP MANAGEMENT (CRM) IN THE FUTURE OF FMCG AND FOOD INDUSTRIES. *Journal ID*, 9413, 9886.

Rana, N. P., Chatterjee, S., Dwivedi, Y. K., & Akter, S. (2022). Understanding dark side of artificial intelligence (AI) integrated business analytics: Assessing firm's operational inefficiency and competitiveness. *European Journal of Information Systems*, 31(3), 364–387. DOI: 10.1080/0960085X.2021.1955628

Rane, N., Choudhary, S., & Rane, J. (2023). Hyper-personalization for enhancing customer loyalty and satisfaction in Customer Relationship Management (CRM) systems. Available at *SSRN* 4641044. DOI: 10.2139/ssrn.4641044

Ranjan, J. (2008). Business justification with business intelligence. *Vine*, 38(4), 461–475.

Ravi, S., David, A., & Imaduddin, M. (2018). Controlling & calibrating vehicle-related issues using RFID technology. *International Journal of Mechanical and Production Engineering Research and Development*, 8(2), 1125–1132. DOI: 10.24247/ijmperdapr2018130

Ravi, S., & Jain, A. (2024). Integration of blockchain technology with AI-powered BI systems: Benefits and challenges. *International Journal of Information Management*, 62, 102368. DOI: 10.1016/j.ijinfomgt.2024.102368

Ray, P. P., Dash, D., & De, D. (2019). Edge computing for Internet of Things: A survey, e-healthcare case study and future direction. *Journal of Network and Computer Applications*, 140, 1–22. DOI: 10.1016/j.jnca.2019.05.005

Reardon, T., Mishra, A., Nuthalapati, C. S., Bellemare, M. F., & Zilberman, D. (2020). COVID-19's disruption of India's transformed food supply chains. *Economic and Political Weekly*, 55(18), 18–22.

Richards, D. J., & Gladwin, T. N. (1999). Sustainability metrics for the business enterprise. *Environmental Quality Management*, 8(3), 11–21. DOI: 10.1002/tqem.3310080303

Rodriguez-Galiano, V., Sanchez-Castillo, M., Chica-Olmo, M., & Chica-Rivas, M. J. O. G. R. (2015). Machine learning predictive models for mineral prospectivity: An evaluation of neural networks, random forest, regression trees and support vector machines. *Ore Geology Reviews*, 71, 804–818. DOI: 10.1016/j.oregeorev.2015.01.001

Rogerson, M., & Parry, G. C. (2020). Blockchain: Case studies in food supply chain visibility. *Supply Chain Management*, 25(5), 601–614. DOI: 10.1108/SCM-08-2019-0300

Roh, Y., Heo, G., & Whang, S. E. (2019). A survey on data collection for machine learning: A big data-ai integration perspective. *IEEE Transactions on Knowledge and Data Engineering*, 33(4), 1328–1347. DOI: 10.1109/TKDE.2019.2946162

Rosário, A. T., & Dias, J. C. (2023). How has data-driven marketing evolved: Challenges and opportunities with emerging technologies. *International Journal of Information Management Data Insights*, 3(2), 100203. Advance online publication. DOI: 10.1016/j.jjimei.2023.100203

Rose, K. M., Howell, E. L., Su, L. Y. F., Xenos, M. A., Brossard, D., & Scheufele, D. A. (2019). Distinguishing scientific knowledge: The impact of different measures of knowledge on genetically modified food attitudes. *Public Understanding of Science (Bristol, England)*, 28(4), 449–467. DOI: 10.1177/0963662518824837 PMID: 30764719

Rouhani, S., Asgari, S., & Mirhosseini, S. V. (2012). Review study: Business intelligence concepts and approaches. *American Journal of Scientific Research*, 50(1), 62–75.

Routroy, S., & Behera, A. (2017). Agriculture supply chain: A systematic review of literature and implications for future research. *Journal of Agribusiness in Developing and Emerging Economies*, 7(3), 275–302. DOI: 10.1108/JADEE-06-2016-0039

S. (2023, March 21). What is ChatSpot? Everything Explained About HubSpot's AI Tool. MakeWebBetter. https://makewebbetter.com/blog/what-is-chatspot/

S. (2024, April 2). Customer Churn: 12 Strategies to Stop Churn Right Now! https://www.superoffice.com/blog/reduce-customer-churn/

Salesforce Announces Einstein, G. P. T. the World's First Generative AI for CRM - Salesforce. (2024, April 17). Salesforce. https://www.salesforce.com/news/press-releases/2023/03/07/einstein-generative-ai/

Sam, G., Asuquo, P., & Stephen, B. (2024). Customer Churn Prediction using Machine Learning Models. *Journal of Engineering Research and Reports*, 26(2), 181–193. DOI: 10.9734/jerr/2024/v26i21081

Sankar, J. G., & David, A. (2024). A Comprehensive Examination of Mobile Augmented Reality in Tourism (MART) Adoption: Using the UTAUT2 Framework. In *Contemporary Trends in Innovative Marketing Strategies* (pp. 241-262). IGI Global.

Sarath Kumar Boddu, R., Santoki, A. A., Khurana, S., Vitthal Koli, P., Rai, R., & Agrawal, A. (2022). An analysis to understand the role of machine learning, robotics and artificial intelligence in digital marketing. *Materials Today: Proceedings, 56*(xxxx), 2288–2292. DOI: 10.1016/j.matpr.2021.11.637

Sardjono, W., Arum, I. R. M., Rahmasari, A., & Lusia, E. (2023). Impact of Track and Trace (T&T) in Industrial Revolution 4.0 of the Pharmaceutical Industry (Pharma 4.0). *E3S Web of Conferences, 388*, 03014. DOI: 10.1051/e3sconf/202338803014

Sarmah, S. S. (2018). Understanding Blockchain Technology. *Computing in Science & Engineering*, 8(2), 23–29.

Schmitt, M. (2020). Artificial intelligence in business analytics, capturing value with machine learning applications in financial services.

Schmitt, M. (2023). Automated machine learning: AI-driven decision making in business analytics. *Intelligent Systems with Applications*, 18(January), 200188. DOI: 10.1016/j.iswa.2023.200188

Sengottuvel, E. P., & Ganeshkumar, C. (2018). The impact of economic policy on institutional credit flow to the agricultural sector. *IUP Journal of Applied Economics*, 17(2), 80–97.

Senthilnayaki, B., Swetha, M., & Nivedha, D. (2021). CUSTOMER CHURN PREDICTION. *IARJSET*, 8(6), 527–531. DOI: 10.17148/IARJSET.2021.8692

Sestino, A., & De Mauro, A. (2022). Leveraging artificial intelligence in business: Implications, applications and methods. *Technology Analysis and Strategic Management*, 34(1), 16–29.

Shaikh, S., Rathi, S., & Janrao, P. (2017, January). Recommendation system in e-commerce websites: a graph based approached. In *2017 IEEE 7th International Advance Computing Conference (IACC)* (pp. 931-934). IEEE. DOI: 10.1109/IACC.2017.0189

Shao, C., Yang, Y., Juneja, S., & GSeetharam, T. (2022). IoT data visualization for business intelligence in corporate finance. *Information Processing & Management*, 59(1), 102736. DOI: 10.1016/j.ipm.2021.102736

Sharma, T. K. (2024, May). *Types of Blockchains Explained- Public Vs. Private Vs. Consortium [UPDATED]*. Blockchain Council.

Shobana, J., Gangadhar, C., Arora, R. K., Renjith, P. N., & Bamini, J. (2023). E-commerce customer churn prevention using machine learning-based business intelligence strategy. *Measurement. Sensors*, 27, 100728. DOI: 10.1016/j.measen.2023.100728

Shrivas, M. K., & Yeboah, T. (2019). The Disruptive Blockchain: Types, Platforms and Applications. [TIJAR]. *Texila International Journal of Academic Research*, 3, 17–39. DOI: 10.21522/TIJAR.2014.SE.19.01.Art003

Siddhartha, T., Nambirajan, T., & Ganeshkumar, C. (2021). Self-help group (SHG) production methods: insights from the union territory of Puducherry community. *Journal of Enterprising Communities: People and Places in the Global Economy*, (ahead-of-print).

Sindhwani, R., Hasteer, N., Behl, A., Chatterjee, C., & Hamzi, L. (2023). Analysis of sustainable supply chain and industry 4.0 enablers: A step towards decarbonization of supply chains. *Annals of Operations Research*. Advance online publication. DOI: 10.1007/s10479-023-05598-7

Soleimani, H., & Kannan, G. (2015). A hybrid particle swarm optimization and genetic algorithm for closed-loop supply chain network design in large-scale networks. *Applied Mathematical Modelling*, 39(14), 3990–4012.

Soltani, Z., & Navimipour, N. J. (2016). Customer relationship management mechanisms: A systematic review of the state of the art literature and recommendations for future research. *Computers in Human Behavior*, 61, 667–688. DOI: 10.1016/j.chb.2016.03.008

Song, J., Zhang, P., Alkubati, M., Bao, Y., & Yu, G. (2022). Research advances on blockchain-as-a-service: Architectures, applications and challenges. *Digital Communications and Networks*, 8(4), 466–475. DOI: 10.1016/j.dcan.2021.02.001

Song, X., Yang, S., Huang, Z., & Huang, T. (2019, August). The application of artificial intelligence in electronic commerce. [). IOP Publishing.]. *Journal of Physics: Conference Series*, 1302(3), 032030. DOI: 10.1088/1742-6596/1302/3/032030

Srivastava, S. (2024, March 22). Personalization at Scale: How AI in CRM is Transforming Customer Engagement. Appinventiv. https://appinventiv.com/blog/ai-in-crm/

Srivastava, V., Singh, A. K., David, A., & Rai, N. (2022). Modelling student employability on an academic basis: A supervised machine learning approach with R. In *Handbook of Research on Innovative Management Using AI in Industry 5.0* (pp. 179–191). IGI Global. DOI: 10.4018/978-1-7998-8497-2.ch012

Sudhakar, B. D., Kattepogu, N., & David, A. (2017). Marketing assistance and digital branding-an insight for technology up-gradation for MSME's. *International Journal of Management Studies & Research*, 5(1), 2455–1562.

Suh, Y. (2023). Machine learning based customer churn prediction in home appliance rental business. *Journal of Big Data*, 10(1), 41. DOI: 10.1186/s40537-023-00721-8 PMID: 37033202

Sullivan, B., & Patel, R. (2024). Augmented analytics and the future of data visualization. *Data Visualization Journal*, 8(2), 89–104. DOI: 10.1016/j.datavis.2024.01.006

Suresh, T., Madhuri, A., Shireesha, M., Kumar, B. R., & Rajesh, K. P. R. (2023, December). An exploratory study on AI-powered client relationship administration: An in-depth survey and roadmap for future investigations.

Suwarno, S., Fitria, F., & Azhar, R. (2023). Optimizing Budget Allocation: A Strategic Framework for Aligning Human Resource Investments with Financial Objectives and Business Goals. *Atestasi: Jurnal Ilmiah Akuntansi*, 6(2), 835–855. DOI: 10.57178/atestasi.v6i2.880

Tamang, M. D., Shukla, V. K., Anwar, S., & Punhani, R. (2021). Improving business intelligence through machine learning algorithms. Paper presented at the 2021 2nd International Conference on Intelligent Engineering and Management (ICIEM).

Tang, Q., Xia, G., Zhang, X., & Long, F. (2020, March). A customer churn prediction model based on XGBoost and MLP. In *2020 international conference on computer engineering and application (ICCEA)* (pp. 608-612). IEEE. DOI: 10.1109/ICCEA50009.2020.00133

Torggler, M. (2008). The functionality and usage of CRM systems. *International Journal of Computer and Systems Engineering*, 2(5), 771–779.

Tuladhar, J. G., Gupta, A., Shrestha, S., Bania, U. M., & Bhargavi, K. (2018). Predictive analysis of e-commerce products. In *Intelligent Computing and Information and Communication:Proceedings of 2nd International Conference, ICICC 2017* (pp. 279-289). Springer Singapore.

Uddin, M., Selvarajan, S., Obaidat, M., Arfeen, S. U., Khadidos, A. O., Khadidos, A. O., & Abdelhaq, M. (2023). From Hype to Reality: Unveiling the Promises, Challenges and Opportunities of Blockchain in Supply Chain Systems. *Sustainability (Basel)*, 15(16), 12193. DOI: 10.3390/su151612193

Vafeiadis, T., Diamantaras, K. I., Sarigiannidis, G., & Chatzisavvas, K. C. (2015). A comparison of machine learning techniques for customer churn prediction. *Simulation Modelling Practice and Theory*, 55, 1–9. DOI: 10.1016/j.simpat.2015.03.003

van Leeuwen, R., & Koole, G. (2022). Data-driven market segmentation in hospitality using unsupervised machine learning. *Machine Learning with Applications*, 10(March), 100414. DOI: 10.1016/j.mlwa.2022.100414

Varma, S., Jain, M., Sharma, D., & Beniwal, A. (2015, December). Refined and diversified query suggestion with latent semantic personalization. In *2015 IEEE UP Section Conference on Electrical Computer and Electronics (UPCON)* (pp. 1-6). IEEE. DOI: 10.1109/UPCON.2015.7456725

Vazquez, A., & Thompson, S. (2024). Machine learning techniques for advanced data exploration in BI systems. *Journal of Machine Learning Research*, 25(4), 1201–1219. https://jmlr.org/papers/volume25/vazquez24a/vazquez24a.pdf

Venkateswaran, N. (2023). AI-driven personalization in customer relationship management: Challenges and opportunities. *Journal of Theoretical and Applied Information Technology*, 101(18), 7392–7399.

Verkoou, K., & Spruit, M. (2013). Mobile business intelligence: Key considerations for implementations projects. *Journal of Computer Information Systems*, 54(1), 23–33. DOI: 10.1080/08874417.2013.11645668

vom Scheidt, F., & Staudt, P. (2024). A data-driven Recommendation Tool for Sustainable Utility Service Bundles. *Applied Energy, 353*(PB), 122137. DOI: 10.1016/j. apenergy.2023.122137

Walker, R. (2009). The evolution and future of business intelligence. Information Management. http://www.information-management.com/infodirect/2009_140/business_intelligence_bi-10016145-1. html

Wamba-Taguimdje, S. L., Wamba, S. F., Kamdjoug, J. R. K., & Wanko, C. E. T. (2020). Influence of artificial intelligence (AI) on firm performance: The business value of AI-based transformation projects. *Business Process Management Journal*, 26(7), 1893–1924.

Wang, G., & Nixon, M. (2021). SoK: tokenization on blockchain. *Proceedings of the 14th IEEE/ACM International Conference on Utility and Cloud Computing Companion*, 1–9. DOI: 10.1145/3492323.3495577

Wang, Y., Li, X., & Chen, Z. (2023). Hyper-personalization in AI-powered BI systems: Challenges and opportunities. *IEEE Transactions on Knowledge and Data Engineering*, 35(4), 789–802.

Webb, D., & Ayyub, B. M. (2017). Sustainability quantification and valuation. I: Definitions, metrics, and valuations for decision making. *ASCE-ASME Journal of Risk and Uncertainty in Engineering Systems. Part A, Civil Engineering*, 3(3), E4016001. DOI: 10.1061/AJRUA6.0000893

White, T. (2017, January 25). The Importance of Customer Retention. https://blog.adwhite.com/the-importance-of-customer-retention-1

White, D., & Zheng, J. (2024). The role of real-time analytics in driving business agility. *Business Analytics Review*, 15(3), 144–159. DOI: 10.1016/j.bar.2024.01.007

Xiang, Z., & Xu, M. (2020). Dynamic game strategies of a two-stage remanufacturing closed-loop supply chain considering Big Data marketing, technological innovation and overconfidence. *Computers & Industrial Engineering*, 145(May), 106538. DOI: 10.1016/j.cie.2020.106538

Xing, P., Jiang, G., Zhao, X., & Wang, M. (2023). Quality effort strategies of video service supply chain considering fans preference and data-driven marketing under derived demand. *Electronic Commerce Research and Applications, 62*(October 2022), 101338. DOI: 10.1016/j.elerap.2023.101338

Xu, L., & Yang, Z. (2024). AI and augmented analytics in enterprise BI systems: Case studies and best practices. *Enterprise Information Systems*, 18(1), 23–40. DOI: 10.1080/17517575.2024.1912345

Xu, S., Tang, H., & Huang, Y. (2023). Inventory competition and quality improvement decisions in dual-channel supply chains with data-driven marketing. *Computers & Industrial Engineering*, 183(July), 109452. DOI: 10.1016/j.cie.2023.109452

Yaffee, R. A., & McGee, M. (2000). *An introduction to time series analysis and forecasting: with applications of SAS® and SPSS*. Elsevier.

Yafooz, W. M., Bakar, Z. B. A., Fahad, S. A., & Mithun, M. (2019). A. (2020). Business intelligence through big data analytics, data mining and machine learning. In Data Management, Analytics and Innovation [Springer Singapore.]. *Proceedings of ICDMAI*, 2, 217–230.

Yaga, D., Mell, P., Roby, N., & Scarfone, K. (2018). *Blockchain technology overview*. DOI: 10.6028/NIST.IR.8202

Yaiprasert, C., & Hidayanto, A. N. (2023). AI-driven ensemble three machine learning to enhance digital marketing strategies in the food delivery business. *Intelligent Systems with Applications*, 18(April), 200235. DOI: 10.1016/j.iswa.2023.200235

Yun, C., Shun, M., Junta, U., & Browndi, I. (2022). Predictive analytics: A survey, trends, applications, opportunities' and challenges for smart city planning. *International Journal of Computer Science and Information Technologies*, 23(56), 226–231.

Zhai, S., Yang, Y., Li, J., Qiu, C., & Zhao, J. (2019). Research on the Application of Cryptography on the Blockchain. *Journal of Physics: Conference Series*, 1168, 032077. DOI: 10.1088/1742-6596/1168/3/032077

Zhang, L., Li, C., & Wang, J. (2023). Ethical considerations in AI-powered BI systems: A review. *Decision Support Systems*, 150, 113575.

Zhangyu, Z., Siwei, C., & Ben, H. (2000). Supply chain optimization of continuous process industries with sustainability considerations. *Computers & Chemical Engineering*, 24(2-7), 1151–1158. DOI: 10.1016/S0098-1354(00)00496-8

Zheng, S., Yahya, Z., Wang, L., Zhang, R., & Hoshyar, A. N. (2023). Multiheaded deep learning chatbot for increasing production and marketing. *Information Processing & Management*, 60(5), 103446. DOI: 10.1016/j.ipm.2023.103446

Zheng, Z., Xie, S., Dai, H.-N., Chen, W., Chen, X., Weng, J., & Imran, M. (2019). *An Overview on Smart Contracts: Challenges.* Advances and Platforms., DOI: 10.1016/j.future.2019.12.019

Zulaikha, S., Mohamed, H., Kurniawati, M., Rusgianto, S., & Rusmita, S. A. (2020). Customer predictive analytics using artificial intelligence. *The Singapore Economic Review*, 1–12.

Zwingmann, T. (2022). *Ai-powered business intelligence.* O'Reilly Media, Inc.

About the Contributors

Arul Kumar Natarajan is an Assistant Professor at Samarkand International University of Technology, Uzbekistan. He received a Ph.D. in Computer Science from Bharathidasan University, India, in 2019. Arul Kumar has contributed to students' academic growth, amassing 14 years of teaching experience. His roles have included serving as an Assistant Professor at Christ University in India, Debre Berhan University in Ethiopia, and Bishop Heber College in India before joining Samarkand International University of Technology in 2024. His research areas are Cybersecurity and Artificial Intelligence. He published more than 30 WoS/Scopus Indexed publications. Dr. Arul Kumar Natarajan has edited two books published by IGI Global Publisher, USA: "Advanced Applications of Python Data Structures and Algorithms" and "Geospatial Application Development Using Python Programming". He published 19 patents in physics, communication, and computer science. He has chaired many technical sessions and delivered more than 15 invited talks at the national and international levels. He has completed over 33 certifications from IBM, Google, Amazon, etc. He passed the CCNA: Routing and Switching Exam in 2017 from CISCO. He also passed the Networking Fundamentals in the year 2017 exam from Microsoft.

Mohammad Gouse Galety, a seasoned professional in computer science, is currently a Professor at the computer science department of Samarkand International University of Technology, Samarkand, Uzbekistan. His research interests encompass a wide range of computer and information science, focusing on Web Mining, Computer Vision, IoT, Machine Learning, and AI. His impactful research has led to the (co) authorship of over 50 journal papers and international conference proceedings indexed by Springer, Web of Science, and Scopus, the holding of four patents, and the writing of six books. His standing in the academic community is further solidified by his role as a Fellow of the IEEE and ACM. With a career spanning over two decades, Mohammad Gouse Galety has served in many national and international organizations, solidifying his expertise in the field. His teaching experience includes roles at Sree Vidyanikethan Degree College, India; Emeralds Degree College, Tirupati, India; Brindavan College of Engineering, India; Kuwait Educational Center, Kuwait; Ambo University, Ethiopia; Debre Berhan University, Ethiopia; Lebanese French University, Iraq; and Catholic University in Erbil, Iraq. He imparts his knowledge to undergraduate and postgraduate students, teaching various courses in computer science and information technology/science engineering..

Celestine Iwendi is an IEEE Brand Ambassador. He has a PhD in Electronics Engineering, is a Past ACM Distinguished Speaker, a Senior Member of IEEE, a Seasoned Lecturer, and a Chartered Engineer. A highly motivated researcher and teacher with an emphasis on communication, hands-on experience, willingness to learn, and 23 years of technical expertise. He has developed operational, maintenance, and testing procedures for electronic products, components, equipment, and systems; provided technical support and instruction to staff and customers regarding equipment standards, assisting with specific, difficult in-service engineering; Inspected electronic and communication equipment, instruments, products, and systems to ensure conformance to specifications, safety standards, and regulations. He is a wireless sensor network Chief Evangelist, AI, ML, and IoT expert and designer. Celestine is a Reader (Professor) at the University of Bolton, United Kingdom. He is also the IEEE University of Bolton, Student Branch Counselor and former Board Member of the IEEE Sweden Section, a Fellow of The Higher Education Academy, United Kingdom, and a fellow of the Institute of Management Consultants to add to his teaching, managerial, and professional experiences. Celestine is an Ambassador in the prestigious Manchester Conference Ambassador Programme, a Visiting Professor to five Universities, and an IEEE Humanitarian Philanthropist. Celestine has received the prestigious recognition of the Royal Academy of Engineering through the Exceptional Talent Scheme, acknowledging his substantial contributions to Artificial Intelligence and its medical applications. Additionally, he takes pride in his three-year inclusion in Elsevier's publication, featuring the World's Top 2% Influential Scientists. Celestine is the Chair of the Election Committee of IEEE Computer Society Worldwide.

Deepthi Das, an Associate Professor and Associate Dean at the School of Sciences, CHRIST (Deemed to be University) in Bangalore, India, is a dedicated educator with over two decades of teaching experience. With a profound commitment to fostering academic excellence and ethical values among students, Dr. Deepthi creates inclusive learning environments that promote critical thinking and social responsibility. Holding a Ph.D. in Computer Science and Engineering from CMR University, Bangalore, she actively integrates innovative teaching methods to deliver dynamic educational experiences. Dr. Deepthi's research interests primarily focus on Artificial Intelligence and Machine Learning, with notable contributions to customer churn prediction in the motor insurance sector. Alongside her academic responsibilities, she has served in various leadership roles, including Head of the Department of Statistics and Data Science and Programme Coordinator for Undergraduate Programmes. Dr. Deepthi's dedication to education, research, and leadership acumen make her a valuable asset to the academic community.

Achyut Shankar is currently working as a Postdoc Research Fellow at the University of Warwick, United Kingdom, and was recently appointed as a visiting Associate Professor at the University of Johannesburg, South Africa. He obtained his PhD in Computer Science and Engineering, majoring in wireless sensor networks, from VIT University, Vellore, India. He was at Birkbeck University, London, from Jan 2022 to May 2022 for his research work. He has published over 150 research papers in reputed international conferences & journals, of which 100 are in SCIE journals. He is a member of ACM and has received research awards for excellence in research for 2016 and 2017. He had organized many special sessions with Scopus Indexed International Conferences worldwide, proceedings of which were published by Springer, IEEE, Elsevier, etc. He is currently serving as an Associate Editor in SAIEE Africa Research Journal (IEEE), Scientific Reports (Nature Journal, Q1), ETT (Wiley), Human-Centric Computing and Information Sciences & SN applied Sciences (SCOPUS & ESCI, Springer), and in the year 2021 to 2023 handled few special issues as a Guest editor ACM transaction for TALIP, International Journal of Human Computer Interaction (Taylor and Francis), International Journal of System Assurance Engineering and Management (Springer) and Journal of Interconnection networks (World Scientific journals). He reviews IEEE Transactions on Intelligent Transportation Systems, IEEE Sensors Journal, IEEE Internet of Things Journal, ACM Transactions on Asian and Low-Resource Language Information Processing, and other prestigious conferences. His areas of interest include Cyber Security, the Internet of Things, Blockchain, Machine Learning, and Cloud computing.

Anurag A. S. obtained his BE degree in Electrical and Electronics from Anna University in 2013, followed by an MBA degree in Operations from Indira Gandhi National Open University in 2017. Accumulating nearly a decade of practical working experience in both the Engineering and Management fields, Anurag has garnered invaluable insights within various organizations across two culturally diverse countries. His extensive professional journey has deepened his understanding of the global significance of management functions. Currently pursuing a Ph.D. at the Central University of Kerala within the Management Studies Department, Anurag's research revolves around the intersection of Management and Artificial Intelligence. Fueled by a unique blend of engineering and business acumen, Anurag is wholeheartedly committed to unraveling the intricacies of how technology, specifically Artificial Intelligence, can enhance and streamline various facets of management in the contemporary business landscape.

B Senthilkumar, M.E., Ph.D., is a distinguished academician and researcher currently serving as an Associate Professor in the Department of Mechanical Engineering at Kumaraguru College of Technology, Coimbatore, Tamil Nadu, India. With a career spanning over 16 years in undergraduate teaching and 10 years in postgraduate teaching, Dr. Senthilkumar has established himself as a prominent figure in the fields of Welding Technology, Composite Materials, and Manufacturing Processes. He embarked on his academic journey by earning his Bachelor of Engineering (B.E.) in Mechanical Engineering from K.S. Rangasamy College of Engineering, affiliated with Madras University, graduating with first-class honors in 1999. Following this, he pursued his Master of Engineering (M.E.) in Production Engineering at Annamalai University, graduating with distinction in 2001. Driven by a passion for knowledge and research, he completed his Ph.D. from Anna University, Chennai, in 2017, focusing on the study of weld bead parameters of super duplex stainless steel claddings deposited by Flux Cored Arc Welding (FCAW). Dr. Senthilkumar's commitment to education extends beyond the classroom. He is actively involved in research and mentoring, contributing significantly to the academic community. He has held various key positions within the Mechanical Engineering Department, including Board of Studies Coordinator, Autonomous Exam Coordinator, Timetable Coordinator, Workshop Superintendent, and Lab In-charge. His extensive experience in these roles has been instrumental in shaping the academic structure and ensuring the smooth functioning of the department. His research interests are diverse and include weld cladding of stainless steel and Inconel 625 on low carbon structural steel substrates, Gas Metal Arc Welding (GMAW), Flux Cored Arc Welding (FCAW), pitting corrosion studies in super duplex stainless steel claddings, and friction stir welding (FSW). He has also worked extensively on the fabrication and formability assessment of Al-SiC particulate reinforced composite materials using processing maps. Dr. Senthilkumar has published numerous research papers, with 18 publications to his credit, several of which are indexed in Scopus. Beyond his professional achievements, Dr. Senthilkumar actively engages in various academic and administrative roles. He serves as a resource person for training programs on topics such as metallurgy and fluid power systems, actively participating in academic initiatives. His dedication to teaching has been recognized with several accolades, including the "Outstanding Faculty" award in January 2015 for his performance during the academic year 2013-14. Dr. Senthilkumar is a strong advocate of "Assessment Assisted Experiential Learning," believing that this approach leads to better learning outcomes. He emphasizes active student interaction and incorporates mini-projects and presentations into his courses to enhance practical understanding. His role as a Conference Chair, Session Chair, Scientific Committee member, and Technical Program Committee member in numerous international conferences demonstrates his leadership in the academic community. In addition to his teaching and research activities, Dr. Senthilkumar has actively collaborated with industry partners, including Cameron Manufacturing India Pvt. Limited and Bull Agro Implements, on various projects. He has also completed several certification courses through Coursera, covering areas like digital manufacturing and advanced manufacturing process analysis. He has filed a patent for an "Underground Cable Fault Distance Display System over the Internet" and co-authored a book titled "Machine Learning Real World Case Studies in Python." Dr. Senthilkumar is a life member of several professional bodies, including the Society for Failure Analysis, the Indian Welding Society (IWS), and the Indian Society for Technical Education (ISTE). He is also a member of the IEEE Educational Society. His contributions to academia and research have been recognized with various honors, including the "Best Paper Award" for his work on welding technology. As a dedicated educator, he shoulders a variety of teaching responsibilities, covering subjects such as Manufacturing Processes, Materials Engineering, Fluid Power System, Kinematics and Dynamics of Machinery, Engineering Mechanics, Engineering Drawing, and Discrete Event System Simulation. Dr. B. Senthilkumar's passion for advancing knowledge, coupled with his dedication to education, makes him a respected figure in the academic community. His multifaceted contributions continue to leave a lasting impact on the field of Mechanical Engineering.

Sourabh Barala is a dedicated student at VIT-AP University, Andhra Pradesh, pursuing a Master of Science in Data Science. He completed his Bachelor of Science (Honours) in Computer Science from the University of Delhi in 2020. During his bachelor's, Sourabh developed a keen interest in artificial intelligence and worked on intriguing projects such as radio frequency fingerprinting using convolutional neural networks. He actively seeks opportunities to deepen his knowledge and use his problem-solving skills to contribute meaningfully to machine learning and data science.

Abhishek Basak is pursuing an M.Sc. in Data Science at VIT-AP University, Amaravati, Andhra Pradesh. He completed a Bachelor of Science in Mathematics (Hons) from University of Calcutta. With a solid foundation in mathematical principles and a keen interest in data-driven decision-making, his academic journey is marked by a dedication to advancing knowledge in data science. He has developed a robust skill set in statistical analysis, machine learning, and data visualization, and he is actively planning to engage in research that leverages advanced data science techniques. He is passionate about uncovering insights from complex datasets and leveraging advanced analytical techniques to solve real-world problems. As part of his ongoing studies, he is engaged in research areas, focusing on data science and artificial intelligence. He is committed to contributing to the data science community through scholarly research and practical applications. His goal is to bridge the gap between theoretical knowledge and practical implementation, ultimately driving innovation and excellence in data science.

M. Basuvaraj, M.Com., MBA., M.Phil., Ph.D., UGC - NET., TN-SET., is presently working as an Assistant professor in the Department of Commerce and Business Administration at Central University of Allahabad, Prayagraj, Allahabad, Utter Pradesh. He has more than 9 years of teaching and Research experience. He has 10 citations and 2 h-Index. He has published 30 research papers in Scopus, Web of Science, UGC-CARE, and UGC-approved and leading international journals and 27 presented papers in national and international conferences. He has also participated in over 30 seminars, conferences, FDP & workshops at the National and International Levels. His areas of expertise are Finance, Banking, and Taxation

C. Ganeshkumar is an Associate Professor of Decision Sciences & Operations Management and serves as the Program Director of the MBA in Business Analytics at the Indian Institute of Foreign Trade (IIFT), New Delhi. The institute is a Deemed-to-be-University under the Department of Commerce, Government of India. He earned his Ph.D. and MBA degrees from Pondicherry Central University and successfully cleared the UGC-NET in Management in 2010. he has two years of Post-Doctoral Research Experience from the Indian Institute of Management Bangalore (IIMB). Prior to his current position, Prof. Ganeshkumar held the role of Assistant Professor: Grade I at the Indian Institute of Plantation Management Bangalore (IIPMB), an autonomous organization under the Ministry of Commerce & Industry, Government of India, and VIT University (Deemed to be University), Vellore. He boasts an impressive publication record, with 30 journal articles indexed in ABDC/ABS/Scopus/Web of Science databases. Additionally, he has presented 15 research papers at various conferences and has organized numerous data analytics workshops, funded by ATAL-AICTE, ICAR, Ministry of Commerce, among others. Prof. Ganeshkumar is highly proficient in various analytical tools and software, including Spreadsheet, IBM-SPSS, Tableau, Python, Power BI, R, Hadoop, and Solver. His research interests span Agri-food value chain, Artificial Intelligence/Blockchain Applications, and Sustainable supply chain management. He has successfully secured funded projects from esteemed organizations such as the Tea Board, Spice Board, Ministry of Commerce, Ministry of Corporate Affairs, Government of India, UNDP, IFPRI-USA, and ADB. In addition to his academic and research endeavors, Prof. Ganeshkumar has actively contributed to administrative roles within the institute. He has served as the Institute Exam Coordinator, Head of PGDM-ABPM Program, NBA Accreditation Coordinator, Warden, led the digitization efforts of the B-School, organized industrial visits, and coordinated the Analytics Research Centre.

Samuel Chellathurai possesses 30 years of teaching experience within the Department of Computer Science, having served in esteemed institutions across India, Libya, and Oman. His research interests encompass Mobile Ad Hoc Networks (MANET) and Data Mining. He has authored research papers published in nine international journals and contributed a chapter to a scholarly book. Furthermore, he has presented 21 research papers at various international and national conferences.

Arokiaraj David serves as an Associate Professor of Al Tareeqah Management Studies in UAE. He has successfully cleared the UGC-National Eligibility Test for Lectureship (NET) and has been honored with the Junior and Senior Research Fellow (JRF & SRF) titles. With over a decade of teaching and research experience, his areas of expertise include Green Marketing, Consumer Behavior, Product & Brand Management, Global Marketing, Retail Management, Strategic Management, Data Analytics, Sustainable Practices, Resources Management, Product Development, Environmental Responsibility, and General Management. Dr. David has authored more than 60 research articles, including 11 published in Scopus, 08 in ABDC, and 05 in Web of Science. He has also contributed to 07 book chapters, published 04 books, registered 07 patents, and received 01 copyright and 01 consultant project. He is proficient in various research tools and techniques such as SPSS, AMOS, E-Views, STATA, and PLS-SEM and has hands-on experience in both primary and secondary data analysis. Recently, Dr. David has been recognized with the Best Research Award, Young Academician Award, and Young Scientist Award.

Jeganathan Gomathi Sankar is a highly experienced and dedicated educationist with a passion for marketing. He has over 10 years of teaching and research experience, and his work has been recognized by Scopus and ABDC journals. He is a member of the BSSS Institute of Advanced Studies, Faculty of Marketing, and his research interests include marketing technology, marketing information systems, and diffusion of technology in marketing. Dr. Sankar is a strong advocate for using technology to enhance marketing education and practice. He is also a leading expert in the field of diffusion of technology in marketing, and his research has helped to inform the development of new marketing strategies and tactics. A dedicated teacher, Dr. Sankar is committed to providing his students with the knowledge and skills they need to succeed in the ever-changing field of marketing. He is a popular lecturer and is known for his ability to make complex concepts easy to understand. In addition to his teaching and research duties, Dr. Sankar is also an active member of the marketing community. He is a regular speaker at conferences and workshops, and he has published numerous articles in leading marketing journals.

Yuktha GP is an aspiring data scientist currently pursuing a Master's in Data Science at VIT-AP University, Amaravati, Andhra Pradesh. She holds a Bachelor of Science degree from Bangalore University, Bengaluru, Karnataka, which she completed in 2023. With a solid foundation in Computer Science, Mathematics, and Statistics, Yuktha has a profound passion for programming and machine learning. Her expertise includes data preprocessing, predictive analytics, advanced machine learning techniques, and data visualization. These skills enable her to extract and interpret meaningful insights and conclusions from data. As she embarks on her journey as an author, Yuktha is committed to contributing valuable knowledge to the field of data science.

Swapnil K. Gundewar is a distinguished academic and researcher with a strong background in mechanical engineering. He completed his Doctor of Philosophy at Visvesvaraya National Institute of Technology, Nagpur, with a thesis focused on the experimental investigation for the fault diagnosis of induction motors using convolutional neural networks. Dr. Gundewar's research experience spans 5.5 years, complemented by 1.8 years in the industry and 2.3 years in teaching. His notable publications include work on condition monitoring and fault diagnosis of induction motors and the detection of broken rotor bar faults using convolutional neural networks in prestigious journals like the Journal of Vibration Engineering & Technologies and the Journal of Advanced Mechanical Design, Systems, and Manufacturing. His extensive expertise and contributions to the field are well-regarded in academic and professional circles.

Amrutha K has Master's degree in Computer Science and Engineering from Vishveshwarya Institute of Technology, Karnataka (2015)and a PhD in Computer Science from Christ University, Karnataka(2023). She is currently working as an Assistant Professor of the CHRIST (Deemed to be University) in the department of Computer Science. Her area of interest include Computer Vision and NLP.

Vineetha KR, is working as an Assistant Professor, at CHRIST Deemed to be University, Banglore, Karnataka, India. She had been working as an Associate Professor for 6 years at Nehru College of Engineering and Research Centre,Kerala. She has been working as a Reviewer of several international journal/conference publications and an Editorial Board member of GRD and IJERT Journals. She completed her Doctorate Degree PhD and MPhil Degree in Computer Science from Bharathiar University, Coimbatore. She got a Master of Computer Application Post Graduation Degree from Calicut University and a Bachelor's Degree in Information Technology from Calicut University. Dr.Vineetha has an Australian and Canadian Innovative Patent(International Patent) and 6 Indian patents. She published 4 books in her Professional disciplinary areas and She has contributed to 30 plus journals including Scopus/SCI Indexed journals, International and National journals in various areas. Her most interesting area is Educational Data Mining, Deep learning, IOT and Behavioural pattern analysis using Artificial Intelligence technologies. She had 25 plus National and International Conference papers. She presented her papers 6th and 7th International IT conferences conducted in Srilanka, Malaysia and Australia in 2019 and 2020.

K. Prabavathy is an accomplished academic professional with an impressive array of qualifications, boasting an M.Sc., MCA, M.Phil, and a Ph.D. in Computer Science. With over a decade of dedicated experience in research, teaching, and academic leadership, she currently serves as an Associate Professor in the Department of Data Science at Sree Saraswathi Thyagaraja College (Autonomous), Pollachi, a position. Dr. Prabavathy's illustrious career has seen her contribute her expertise as an Assistant Professor at prestigious institutions such as Rathinam College of Arts and Science, Coimbatore, and PSG College of Arts and Science, Sri Subramanya Engineering College of Engineering and Technology, Palani. She has supervised and produced 2 M.Phil and 2 Ph.D scholars Her scholarly endeavors are reflected in her extensive publication record, with over 20 articles featured in renowned UGC, Scopus Indexed, and Web of Science Journals. In addition to her written contributions, Dr. Prabavathy has presented her research findings at various conferences, both on the national and international stages, including overseas events. Her academic journey culminated in the successful completion of her Ph.D. at ManonmaniamSundaranar University, Tirunelveli and completed M.Phil in PSG College of Arts and Science and MCA in Bharathiyar University. Dr. Prabavathy's commitment to the academic community extends beyond her own research, as she actively contributes as a reviewer for esteemed journals and serves as a valuable resource person for multiple conferences. In addition to her academic roles, Dr. Prabavathy has also excelled as a Software Trainer at Inova Infotech, Coimbatore, showcasing her versatility and expertise in the field of computer science. Her dedication to academia and her numerous accomplishments makes her a respected figure in her field. She is Proficient in Python, R, Java specializing in data science, data mining, and data analytics, and adept at utilizing machine learning algorithms to address real-world challenges. She actively engages in community outreach and education initiatives, inspiring the next generation of computer scientists and researchers.

Yazhini Karthik is currently pursuing a Master's degree in Data Science at Coimbatore Institute of Technology. As a dedicated and passionate individual, she actively engages in academic and research pursuits, demonstrating a strong commitment to the field of data science. During her academic journey, Yazhini furthered her skills through a research internship at NIT Trichy, focusing on the project dealing with handwritten digit recognition among cerebral palsy individuals. This experience enriched her understanding of machine learning and data science concepts. Yazhini showcased her academic prowess by participating in the Mathematical & Modelling Conference at Coimbatore Institute of Technology in 2021. Her presentation, "Data Analysis on Job Recruitment of People," examined variables impacting the college student recruiting process, developed prediction models using various classification algorithms, and evaluated accuracies. Beyond academics, Yazhini plays a crucial role as a member of the advisory board for the "DATALYTICS" club at Coimbatore Institute of Technology, contributing to shaping initiatives that encourage learning and collaboration among students interested in data analytics. Yazhini Karthik's academic journey and professional engagements reflect her dedication to the field of data science. Her multifaceted experiences make her a valuable contributor to academic and research endeavours, and she aspires to do more research in the area of data science.

Resmi K R has Master's degree in Computer applications (2015)and a PhD in Computer Science from Mahatma Gandhi University, Kerala(2021). She is currently working as an Assistant Professor of the CHRIST (Deemed to be University) in the department of Computer Science. Her area of interest include Biometric, computer vision, pattern recognition and digital image processing.

Praveen Kumar, PhD, is a distinguished researcher specializing in 2D nanomaterials, having earned his doctorate from IIT Mandi. Currently serving as an Assistant Professor at FEAT, DMI College of Engineering, Wardha, he is renowned for his expertise in the field. Praveen's research focuses on the properties and applications of nanomaterials, with his work widely published in leading journals.

Johnpaul M is currently an Assistant Professor in the Department of Management Studies at the Central University of Kerala. Dr. John earned a Bachelor's Degree in Economics from the prominent Loyola College in Chennai, as well as a Master's Degree in Business Administration and MA Economics from Osmania University in Hyderabad. He earned his Ph.D. and cleared the AP SET and UGC NET in Management. From 2009 until June 2022, he was an Assistant Professor at Mahatma Gandhi University's Department of Management Studies in Nalgonda. He additionally served as a Hostel Warden, Coordinator for the Academic Audit Cell, NSS Programme Officer, and in a variety of other academic and administrative posts at MGU. To his credit, he has over 13 years of teaching experience. He has published 15 research papers in national and international journals. He has delivered 17 papers at national and international conferences. He has participated in various Faculty Development Programs. He has written one edited book, "Responsible Marketing for Sustainable Business". His teaching topics include marketing, marketing research, strategic management, international business strategy, and managerial economics.

M. Sujithra, M.C.A, M. Phil, Ph.D., is a distinguished academician and researcher currently serving as an Associate Professor in the Department of Computing - Data Science at Coimbatore Institute of Technology, Coimbatore, Tamil Nadu, India. With a career spanning 18 years, Dr. Sujithra has established herself as a prominent figure in the field of Data Science, Machine Learning, Information Security, Cloud Computing, and Network Security. She embarked on her academic journey by earning her bachelor's degree in Computer Science with Distinction in the year 2000. Following this, she achieved excellence by securing a University Rank in Master of Computer Applications in 2003. Driven by a passion for knowledge, she further pursued her M. Phil. in Computer Science from Bharathiyar University in 2010. In 2017, Dr. M. Sujithra earned her Ph.D. from Avinashilingam University, specializing in Mobile Device and Cloud Data Security. Her doctoral research, titled "A Comprehensive Approach to Mobile Device and Data Security using Iris Authentication, Malware Detection, Secured Cloud Storage and Retrieval," reflects her commitment to advancing the field. Dr. Sujithra's commitment to education extends beyond the classroom. Dr. Sujithra is actively involved in research and mentoring. As a mentor, she has contributed to the Samsung Prism Project and served as an evaluator and mentor for Smart India Hackathon 2022, contributing to NPTEL SWAYAM Course on Cyber Security, and engaging with L&T EdTech as a reviewer for in-house training programs. Her role as a Conference Chair, Session Chair, Scientific Committee member, and Technical Program Committee member in numerous international conferences demonstrates her leadership in the academic community. She has published three books in the areas of machine learning, network security, mobile malware detection, and cloud security. Additionally, she actively participates in academic initiatives, serving as a resource person for topics such as Data Science, Artificial Intelligence, and Machine Learning. She has published numerous Scopus indexed papers on cloud computing and data security in both national and international journals and conferences. Beyond her professional achievements, Dr. Sujithra actively engages in various academic and administrative roles. She serves as a member of the Academic Council in various institutions, a panel member for project evaluation for UG/PG programs, and a reviewer and editorial board member for reputable journals. She also contributes to the development of academic programs as a member of the Board of Studies for Data Science and Artificial Intelligence programmes. Dr. Sujithra has received several accolades, including the "Best Paper Award" for her work on Malware Detection Mechanism Using Machine Learning Algorithms from Madras Institute of Technology Anna University in 2018. She holds University Rank in her Master of Computer Applications Degree and has been recognized for achieving outstanding Academic Performance Indicators at Coimbatore Institute of Technology. As a dedicated educator, she shoulders a variety of teaching responsibilities, covering subjects such as Machine Learning, Data Visualization, Artificial Intelligence, Data Mining, Business Intelligence, Operating System, Computer Networks, Software Engineering, and Mobile Application Development. Dr. M. Sujithra's passion for advancing knowledge, coupled with her dedication to education, makes her a respected figure in the academic community. Her multifaceted contributions continue to leave a lasting impact on the field of Data Science.

A. Manimaran is an Assistant Professor and dedicated researcher in the Department of Mathematics at VIT-AP University, Andhra Pradesh. He has 10 years of teaching experience and 4 years of research experience. He has published 25 research papers in reputed national and international journals and conferences. He pursued a Bachelor of Science from Bharathidasan University, Tamil Nadu, in 2006, a Master of Computer Applications from Anna University in 2009, and a Ph.D. from Bharathidasan University in 2018. His main research work focuses on machine learning, deep learning, NLP, and data science and he is committed to mentoring the next generation of scholars. In addition to his professional endeavors, he serves as a reviewer for prestigious journals in the fields of data science and artificial intelligence. He is also an active member of the Association for Computing Machinery (ACM) and the Computer Society of India (CSI), where he engages in networking opportunities and stays abreast of the latest developments in the field.

N Nasurudeen Ahamed, Received the Bachelor's Degree in Computer Science and Engineering, The Master Degree in Computer Science and Engineering and Ph.D. Degree in Computer Science and Engineering. He is Currently Working as an Assistant Professor (Senior Scale) in Computer Science and Engineering Department at Presidency University, Bangalore, Karnataka, India. He has 11 Years' of Teaching Experience. His Research Interests Include Blockchain, Cyber Security, Supply Chain Management, Industry 4.0, Deep Learning.

Praket Pati Tiwari is a Master's student in Data Science at VIT-AP University, Amaravati, Andhra Pradesh. With a background in Mathematics (Hons) from Delhi University, Praket is passionate about AI, machine learning, and statistics. His expertise lies in advanced machine learning techniques, predictive analytics, and strategic decision-making for businesses. As an aspiring author, Praket aims to contribute valuable insights to the field of data science.

Keshvi Rastogi, a third-year graduation student, is currently pursuing BCom Honours in Christ University, Bangalore. It is one of the leading institutions in Bangalore, Karnataka, and is a NIRF and NAAC Accredited University. She has demonstrated a keen interest and aptitude in the field of commerce and finance. Throughout her academic journey, she has consistently excelled in coursework, showcasing a strong grasp of various topics. Her commitment to academic excellence is further reflected in her active participation in various research projects, internships, and competitive fests, where she has applied theoretical knowledge to practical scenarios. Keshvi is known for her analytical skills, attention to detail, and ability to work collaboratively in team settings. Her dedication to continuous learning and professional growth makes her a promising candidate for contributing valuable insights and innovative solutions in the realm of commerce and finance.

Mousami Sanyal, an MSc Data Science student at VIT AP, has always been passionate about technology and data analysis.She excelled in mathematics and computer science throughout her education. Graduating with honors with Computer Science Engineering, she pursued advanced studies at VIT AP, focusing on machine learning, big data analytics, and statistical modeling.she has completed impactful projects and internships, gaining practical experience and industry exposure. Aspiring to be a leading data scientist, Mousami is dedicated to leveraging data for societal benefit.

Mansi Sharma, B-Tech 3rd year student pursuing in Computer science and Design Department. Done several research project and publications in Scopus indexed conferences. Focuses on Data Visualization and Machine Learning domain through which enhancing skills and expertise for futures perspective.

Shirin Siraji is pursuing a Master of Science in Data Science at VIT-AP University, Andhra Pradesh, after completing her Bachelor of Science in Mathematics Honours from Shri Shikshayatan College, University of Calcutta, in 2022. Born and raised in Kolkata, her passion for numbers and data led her to data science. She enjoys writing to make complex technical concepts accessible and is inspired by technological advancements. In her free time, she enjoys learning about Machine Learning, exploring new algorithms, and working on personal projects to apply her knowledge practically.

Riya Thomas is a passionate and dedicated data science professional currently in her fifth year of pursuing a Master of Science (MSc) in Data Science. Throughout her academic journey, she has honed her skills in data analysis, visualization, and application development, making her a valuable asset in any data-driven environment. Riya's professional experience includes a successful internship as an RShiny Developer, where she developed interactive web applications using RShiny. During her internship, she collaborated closely with data scientists to design and implement data visualization tools, conducted comprehensive data analysis, and presented findings through dynamic dashboards. Her ability to enhance user experience by integrating feedback into the application design was highly appreciated by her team. In addition to her technical expertise, Riya is currently serving as the Internship Coordinator for her current batch. In this role, she coordinates internship programs, liaises between students and industry partners, organizes workshops and training sessions, and provides continuous support and guidance to students. Her leadership and project management skills have ensured successful placements and enriching experiences for her peers. Riya's technical skills are complemented by her proficiency in using tools such as R, Python, SQL, Tableau, and Power BI. She excels in creating visual representations of data, developing interactive dashboards, and conducting statistical analysis. Her ability to interpret data and provide actionable insights is a testament to her analytical acumen. Riya's achievements include successfully developing and deploying an RShiny application during her internship, which was used by a specific department for strategic decision-making. As an internship coordinator, she has effectively managed the placement process for a batch of students, ensuring they secured positions in reputed organizations. Her soft skills include strong communication and interpersonal abilities, excellent problem-solving skills, and effective time management and organizational capabilities. Riya is known for her teamwork, adaptability, and proactive approach to challenges. She is a quick learner who thrives in collaborative environments and is always eager to take on new challenges and responsibilities. Riya Thomas is poised to make significant contributions to the field of data science with her solid foundation in data science, technical expertise, and commitment to continuous learning.

Index

A

Advanced Data Visualization 283, 287, 297
Agriculture Sector 280
API 143, 238
Artificial Intelligence 4, 21, 27, 29, 30, 31, 41, 43, 46, 47, 48, 49, 50, 52, 75, 77, 81, 83, 84, 86, 92, 100, 101, 103, 104, 118, 119, 123, 126, 129, 130, 138, 139, 154, 155, 156, 159, 161, 166, 167, 168, 169, 173, 178, 179, 182, 236, 239, 243, 244, 245, 247, 248, 249, 250, 251, 252, 253, 254, 255, 256, 257, 259, 260, 261, 262, 263, 265, 266, 267, 278, 279, 280, 284, 285, 289, 292, 293, 305, 308

B

Bigdata 80, 93
BI systems 2, 7, 103, 104, 105, 106, 107, 108, 109, 111, 112, 113, 114, 115, 116, 117, 120, 121, 149, 159, 178, 251, 261, 284, 288
Businesses 1, 2, 4, 5, 9, 11, 12, 14, 19, 21, 26, 30, 31, 32, 33, 39, 40, 41, 42, 43, 44, 45, 46, 52, 53, 54, 65, 75, 80, 81, 82, 83, 84, 86, 87, 95, 96, 103, 104, 106, 107, 108, 109, 110, 113, 118, 119, 120, 122, 124, 125, 126, 130, 131, 132, 138, 139, 142, 149, 150, 151, 152, 153, 160, 161, 162, 163, 164, 165, 166, 173, 174, 177, 182, 191, 192, 193, 197, 198, 199, 200, 210, 234, 236, 243, 244, 245, 246, 247, 248, 249, 250, 252, 253, 254, 255, 256, 257, 258, 259, 260, 283, 284, 286, 289, 294, 295, 298, 305
Business Intelligence 1, 2, 4, 5, 7, 8, 9, 11, 13, 15, 16, 17, 18, 19, 20, 21, 22, 23, 24, 25, 26, 27, 29, 30, 31, 32, 33, 34, 35, 36, 37, 38, 39, 43, 46, 47, 48, 49, 51, 52, 53, 54, 73, 75, 77, 83, 103, 104, 105, 107, 108, 109, 110, 111, 112, 113, 114, 115, 117, 118, 120, 121, 123, 138, 148, 157, 159, 161, 163, 164, 165, 166, 167, 174, 175, 178, 179, 180, 207, 243, 244, 245, 247, 248, 249, 250, 251, 252, 254, 255, 256, 257, 259, 260, 261, 262, 263, 276, 283, 284, 285, 286, 287, 288, 289, 290, 292, 293, 295, 296, 298, 300, 301, 305, 306, 307, 308
Business Objectives 7, 15, 16, 55

C

Classification 35, 38, 39, 41, 48, 55, 58, 60, 89, 90, 126, 133, 190, 211, 212, 223, 224, 225, 226, 227, 228, 229, 256, 290
Cloud-based BI 283, 287
Consortium Blockchain 189, 190, 201
Customer 3, 12, 31, 34, 35, 40, 41, 50, 52, 54, 55, 67, 68, 69, 70, 71, 72, 80, 81, 82, 83, 84, 85, 86, 87, 95, 98, 103, 107, 109, 110, 115, 117, 118, 119, 120, 121, 122, 124, 125, 126, 127, 129, 130, 131, 132, 133, 134, 135, 136, 137, 138, 139, 140, 141, 146, 147, 148, 149, 150, 151, 152, 153, 154, 155, 156, 157, 161, 162, 164, 165, 166, 169, 172, 173, 174, 176, 177, 182, 183, 184, 186, 194, 206, 207, 208, 209, 210, 212, 213, 216, 221, 222, 223, 224, 233, 234, 235, 236, 237, 238, 239, 240, 241, 244, 245, 246, 247, 248, 249, 251, 252, 256, 257, 258, 259, 260, 261, 263, 289, 299
customer churn 71, 118, 120, 126, 127, 132, 133, 154, 155, 156, 207, 208, 223, 233, 238, 239, 240, 241, 256, 263
Customer Relationship Management 35, 40, 69, 70, 87, 117, 118, 119, 138, 139, 148, 149, 151, 155, 156, 157, 207, 208, 209, 216, 233, 246

D

Data Analysis 18, 22, 29, 33, 39, 54, 68, 80, 81, 82, 83, 89, 92, 95, 104, 114,

P

personalized recommendations 68, 72, 88, 98, 145, 208

Predictive Analysis 120, 130, 134, 151, 224, 236, 240, 243, 244, 255

Predictive Analytics 4, 11, 14, 18, 21, 23, 29, 30, 31, 33, 34, 36, 43, 44, 45, 47, 49, 50, 51, 52, 53, 54, 55, 56, 57, 58, 61, 62, 63, 65, 66, 67, 68, 69, 70, 71, 72, 73, 74, 75, 76, 83, 104, 108, 112, 115, 118, 126, 139, 149, 172, 175, 182, 207, 236, 239, 240, 258, 261, 289, 295

Private Blockchain 189, 196, 205

Public Blockchain 190, 195, 196

R

Real-time data 63, 104, 141, 175, 209, 247, 256, 300

Real-world case 25, 104, 118

Resource allocation 11, 52, 53

S

SCM 4.0 183

Self-Service Analytics 284, 287, 293, 294, 295, 296, 307

Smart Contracts 189, 193, 196, 199, 201, 206

SMOTE 222, 223, 225, 228, 229, 230, 233, 239

supply chain 5, 16, 21, 23, 40, 49, 52, 53, 68, 70, 71, 101, 159, 160, 161, 162, 163, 164, 165, 166, 172, 178, 179, 180, 181, 182, 183, 184, 192, 202, 203, 204, 205, 206, 245, 246, 247, 256, 262, 278, 279, 280, 306

supply chain management 5, 16, 21, 52, 70, 71, 159, 162, 164, 178, 179, 180, 181, 182, 183, 192, 202, 203, 204, 205, 206, 245, 246, 247, 278, 279, 306

supply chain optimization 159, 160, 163, 180

Sustainability Metrics 1, 2, 4, 5, 6, 7, 8, 9, 11, 12, 13, 19, 20, 21, 23, 24, 25, 26, 27

V

Visualization 29, 30, 33, 59, 83, 97, 107, 108, 109, 112, 115, 121, 139, 175, 176, 283, 287, 288, 290, 296, 297, 298, 301, 307, 308

Milton Keynes UK
Ingram Content Group UK Ltd.
UKHW030904191024
449758UK00007B/43